MULTI-LEVEL PRODUCTION/INVENTORY CONTROL SYSTEMS: THEORY AND PRACTICE

STUDIES IN THE MANAGEMENT SCIENCES

Editor in Chief

ROBERT E. MACHOL

Volume 16

NORTH-HOLLAND PUBLISHING COMPANY – AMSTERDAM · NEW YORK · OXFORD

MULTI-LEVEL PRODUCTION/ INVENTORY CONTROL SYSTEMS: THEORY AND PRACTICE

Edited by

LEROY B. SCHWARZ

NORTH-HOLLAND PUBLISHING COMPANY — AMSTERDAM · NEW YORK · OXFORD

This North-Holland/TIMS series is a continuation of the Professional Series in the Management Sciences, edited by Robert E. Machol.

ISBN: 0 444 86096 7

Published by:

NORTH-HOLLAND PUBLISHING COMPANY
AMSTERDAM, NEW YORK, OXFORD

Sole distributors for the U.S.A. and Canada:

ELSEVIER NORTH-HOLLAND, INC.
52 VANDERBILT AVENUE
NEW YORK, NY 10017

Printed in The Netherlands

TABLE OF CONTENTS

ACKNOWLEDGMENTS

This volume is the result of the dedication and hard work of many people and many organizations. It is impossible to name all but those few whose contribution was in some way special. Thanks to Warren H. Hausman and Robert E. Machol for their encouragement. Thanks to the Faculty and Deans of the Krannert Graduate School of Management, Purdue University, for their encouragement and financial support. Very special thanks to the authors and referees; without their dedication to the advancement of our field this volume would not exist. My gratitude to Sandra Skiles and Judy McKinley for their secretarial and administrative support. My lasting indebtedness to my mentor, Gary D. Eppen, for initiating my interest in this very interesting and challenging area. Finally, my sincere thanks to my loving wife, Rona, whose confidence and warm encouragement maintained me through the long editorial process.

LBS

REFEREES

Every author and editor knows the vital role that referees play in the process of bringing new ideas into the literature. Every paper in this volume has benefited from the careful reading, critical appraisal, and wise counsel of two or more referees who gave freely of their time in order to advance the frontiers of knowledge. It is not possible to cite each referee's individual contribution to each of the papers in this volume, but, on behalf of the field of multi-level production/inventory control, I would like to recognize the following scholars and practitioners for their contribution to the refereeing of the papers in this volume:

Ralph D.Badinelli
Krannert Graduate School of Management
Purdue University

Zeev Barzily
School of Engineering and Applied Science
The George Washington University

Suresh Chand
Krannert Graduate School of Management
Purdue University

Morris Cohen
The Wharton School
University of Pennsylvania

David A. Collier
Graduate School of Business Administration
Duke University

W. Steven Demmy
Wright State University

Bryan L. Deuermeyer
Department of Industrial Engineering
Texas A & M University

Gary D. Eppen
Graduate School of Business
University of Chicago

Richard V. Evans
Department of Business Administration
University of Illinois

Murray A. Geisler
Logistics Management Institute

Stephen C. Graves
Sloan School of Management
Massachusetts Institute of Technology

Donald Gross
School of Engineering and Applied Science
The George Washington University

Warren H. Hausman
Department of Industrial Engineering and
    Engineering Management
Stanford University

Edward J. Ignall
School of Engineering and Applied Science
Columbia University

Robert E. Johnson
Faculty of Management
The Ohio State University

Alan J. Kaplan
U.S. Army Inventory Research Office

Uday S. Karmarkar
Graduate School of Management
University of Rochester

Karl Kruse
U.S. Army Inventory Research Office

Marc Lambrecht
Department of Economics
Catholic University of Leuven

ix

Timothy J. Lowe
Krannert Graduate School of Management
Purdue University

William L. Maxwell
School of Operations Research and
    Industrial Engineering
Cornell University

Bruce McLaren
Department of Finance and Management
Indiana State University

Harlan C. Meal
Sloan School of Management
Massachusetts Institute of Technology

Jeffrey G. Miller
Graduate School of Business Administration
Harvard University

Thomas Morton
Graduate School of Industrial Adminis-
    tration
Carnegie-Mellon University

John A. Muckstadt
School of Operations Research and
    Industrial Engineering
Cornell University

Steven Nahmias
Department of Quantitative Methods
University of Santa Clara

E.F. Peter Newson
School of Business Administration
The University of Western Ontario

Gregory P. Prastacos
The Wharton School
University of Pennsylvania

Victor J. Presutti
Air Force Logistics Command
U.S. Air Force

Larry Ritzman
Faculty of Management Science
The Ohio State University

Gary M. Roodman
School of Management
SUNY – Binghamton

Barbara A. Rosenbaum
Distribution Systems Development
Eastman Kodak Company

Bernard Rosenman
U.S. Army Inventory Research Office

Gene Sand
Eastman Kodak Company

Linus Schrage
Graduate School of Business
University of Chicago

Craig C. Sherbrooke
Mathtech

Howard Singer
Bell Laboratories

Boghos D. Sivazlian
Department of Industrial and Systems
    Engineering
University of Florida

Andrew Szendrovitz
Faculty of Business
McMaster University

Harvey M. Wagner
School of Business Administration
University of North Carolina

George O. Wesolowsky
Faculty of Business
McMaster University

Gordon P. Wright
Krannert Graduate School of Management
Purdue University

Chu-Tao Wu
School of Business Administration
The University of Wisconsin – Milwaukee

Shelemyahu Zacks
Department of Statistics
Virginia Polytechnic Institute

TIMS Studies in the Management Sciences 16 (1981) 1—9
© North-Holland Publishing Company

INTRODUCTION

Leroy B. Schwarz

Practitioners of the art of management science have observed: (1) there is nothing more practical than a good theory; [1] and (2) that challenging problems yield rich theory. If these observations are true then few — if any — areas of management decision-making offer more potential for rich theory than problems involving the design and/or operation of a multi-level production/inventory system. Furthermore, few areas of management endeavor offer larger pay-offs for the application of good theory.

In order to understand this potential, consider the following facts: approximately one-third of the current assets of the average US business is devoted to inventory. This is about 90% of the same firm's working capital. In absolute terms the 1976 book value of US manufacturing and trade inventories was $ 276 billion, approximately 17% of the United States' gross national product. And this statistic does not include the enormous inventories held by local, state, and the federal government, including the United States' armed services. Most of this inventory is managed (or mismanaged) within a multi-level production/inventory system.

In general terms, multi-level (or multi-echelon [2] production/inventory systems are concerned with production and/or inventory problems involving two or more interrelated activities. An *activity* is defined generally to be an entity that produces, services, or holds an inventory of the good in question. For example, in a distribution network typical activities would be retailers, regional warehouses, district warehouses, and, perhaps, a national warehouse. Activities can also be production sites, work-in-process inventory sites, repair facilities, and even the vehicles and/or containers used for transport between other activities. In general the analyst determines both the number and type of activities under consideration by the nature of the specific problem at hand, the detail of the desired analysis, the span and level of management control involved, and other factors. Multi-level production/inventory systems can be modeled as directed networks wherein nodes represent activities and links represent the flow of goods. Three types of networks have been singled out for special attention: the *assembly system,* in which each node has at most one successor node; the *arborescent system,* in which each node has at most one

---

[1] Cynics dispute the pre-eminence of good theory, placing it third behind a "big" hammer and a "bigger" hammer, respectively.

[2] In this volume, the terms "multi-level" and "multi-echelon" will be used as synonyms.

predecessor; and the *serial system,* in which each node has at most one successor and at most one predecessor.

The roots for much of the early theory of multi-level systems are, of course, models of single-activity systems. Surveys of such work are provided by Vienott [236], Iglehart [103], and Aggarwal [3] who also survey some early multi-level work. The body of published work on multi-level systems dates from the late 1950s and is due to Allen [5], Evans [67], Simpson [219], Hannsman [96], and others. The subsequent 20 years has shown sustained development (see [93]), with significant contributions by Clark and Scarf [39], Scarf *et al.* [200], Sherbrooke [210], and Zangwill [254]. See Clark [34] for an excellent survey of multi-level production/inventory control. Progress, though sustained, has been slow. The reasons lie in the challenging nature of the problems themselves.

Why are multi-level problems so challenging?

As befitting their name, there are several ways in which multi-level problems are unusually challenging ones for theoreticians and managers alike. Here is a partial list:

The demand process. However well behaved the demand process at the outlet activities of a multi-level system, that process *in combination* with the production/inventory policy at those activities determine the demand process at their predecessors' activities, which in combination with the predecessor activities' own production/inventory policy determine the demand process at their predecessors, and so on through the system. As a consequence, well-behaved demand distributions (e.g., identical Poisson unit demand distributions) in relatively simple multi-level systems (e.g., 1-warehouse N-identical retailers) using relatively straightforward operating policies (e.g., stationary (Q, r) policies) yield demand processes at upper level activities which are analytically quite difficult to model (e.g., the warehouse demand process is a superposition, or overlay, of N identical Erlang processes). For example, see the papers by Ehrhardt *et al.* and Deuermeyer and Schwarz in this volume.

Simultaneous optimization. Given the above, system optimality is only rarely achieved by the sequential process of determining the optimal policy at the outlet activities and then, given that, determining the optimal policies for its predecessors, etc. Such a rarity is Clark and Scarf [39]. However, in general, all policy variables must be simultaneously optimized.

Treatment of shortages. Shortages result whenever demand on an activity exceeds supply. In a single-activity production/inventory system the consequences of a shortage (e.g., backorders, lost sales, or some combination thereof) depend only on the status of the activity in question and other variables outside the model (e.g., the outside demand). In a multi-level system the consequences of a shortage at a given activity depend on the status of the *system*. For example, in a warehouse/retailer distribution system the consequences of a shortage at the warehouse may be a transshipment from another retailer, a shortage at the retailer, or nothing at all, depending on the status of inventory at all the other retailers. Or, in a Material Requirements Planning environment the probability of being able to produce 50 units of a finished product corresponds to the joint probability of having sufficient inventory of *all* its components.

Computing requirements. The complex nature of multi-level problems requires orders of magnitude more in computing resources than single-level systems. This is true whether these computations are used to solve multi-level multi-variable dynamic programs, or to evaluate the consequences of a limited set of alternative system policies, or even to implement a rather straightforward heuristic (e.g., Material Requirements Planning).

Organizational implementation issues. By definition, implementation of a new procedure for managing a single activity involves a single manager or, at most, a single organization. However, implementation of new procedures for managing a multi-level system involves the coordinated effort of two or more different activities whose local interests may hinder successful implementation.

There are, of course, other factors. For example there is the inherent complexity of scheduling problems [188], which are usually a *subset* of multi-level production/ inventory problems. There is also the incentive structure in which scholars and practitioners exchange ideas. For example, consider the manager who has developed an effective procedure for operating a given multi-level system: should the manager "tell the world" and perhaps lose a competitive edge? Will the company's lawyers *allow* a public exchange of ideas? Perhaps the manager in question has made a similar attempt in the past only to be condescendingly informed that what has been developed is an "unproven heuristic". Or consider the young scholar contemplating a dissertation topic or an idea for a journal article. The tradeoffs here are clear: attempt solution to a "hard" problem or add a bell or a whistle to an existing model. The penalty for failing to solve the "hard" problem is high; the probability of failure is also high. The bell or whistle alternative has a lower payoff but a much higher probability for success.

Given all of this, it is remarkable, perhaps, that much progress in modeling or managing multi-level production/inventory control systems has been made. However, progress has been made and it will go on. It will go on because eager scholars and concerned managers see the challenge of these problems and, against all odds and some reason, are motivated to solve them.

The papers in this volume

This volume presents a sample of the broad spectrum of contemporary research and applications in multi-level production/inventory control. The topics covered include: the design of a multi-level system; e.g., number of activities and their configuration in the corresponding network (the first and second papers); a review and extension of existing theory on lot sizing in assembly system (papers 3 and 4); interesting application papers on the coordination of machine loading in manufacturing systems and the coordination of production and shipping schedules in a requirements planning system (papers 5 and 6); highlights of basic research into the demand process at the warehouse in warehouse—retailer systems operating with (s, S) or (Q, r) policies, examination and test of approximations to this process, and exploratory research into incorrect assumptions and/or the non-stationarity of this process (papers 7—11); a comprehensive review of reparable inventory control theory (paper 12); an examination of applications of multi-level inventory theory in the US Air Force (paper 13); a description of the progress and set-backs sometimes encountered in moving a multi-level model from theory to practice (paper 14); an introduction to the application of convex analysis to the analysis of multi-level models (paper 15); and an introduction and some preliminary analysis in the important area of multi-level control of perishable goods (paper 16).

System design

The design of a multi-level production/inventory system, the determination of the number of activities, their size, and network configuration, is in many ways the most important and difficult challenge that the theoretician or manager may confront. Until recently, there has been relatively little published work [177], [178], [63] on this topic.

In the first paper in this volume Gross, Pinkus, and Soland describe a framework for determining the design of a multi-product, multi-level inventory system. In this framework the optimal (or near-optimal) cost of managing each separate product is determined for each network alternative; then, the globally optimal network structure is determined using a unique fixed charge location-allocation model. This framework is illustrated using Clark's dynamic programming method [32] to assess optimal or near-optimal product costs for each alternative network structure and a 0—1 optimization model to determine the globally optimal structure given product-structure costs. Examples and computational experience with the model are reported in some detail.

In the second paper, Eppen and Schrage analyze a depot—warehouse system with independent, normally-distributed, stationary warehouse demand; identical proportional costs of holding and backordering; and no transshipment. Under the "allocation" assumption the paper derives approximately optimal costs of a base stock policy (no fixed order cost) at the depot when the depot holds no stock, and compares this cost to two alternative policies: a centralized policy in which the warehouses are deleted, and a decentralized policy in which the depot is deleted from the network. The paper also determines the approximately optimal policy and cost for the depot operating with fixed order costs. There are some interesting parallels here with single activity (Q, r) systems.

Coordinated systems

Policies for managing multi-level production/inventory systems may be classified as coordinated/requirements planning type systems (e.g., Material Requirements Planning) or uncoordinated/demand—replenishment systems (e.g., (Q, r) systems). In the former, the so-called "dependent" nature of a given activity's demand process upon its successor activities' production/inventory policy is explicitly considered; in the latter this dependent demand is ignored and compensated for in various ways (e.g., safety stock). Although it is obvious that, other things being equal, coordinated policies should yield lower system costs or higher system profits and reliability than uncoordinated policies — all other things are seldom equal. In particular, coordinated policies generally require much more communication, cooperation, computation, and forecasting than uncoordinated policies. Until the costs of these "unequal" things can be reduced or eliminated — if ever — it seems likely that both types of policies will continue to be recommended and used. Four papers in this volume consider coordinated systems.

Lambrecht, Vander Eecken, and Vanderveken consider the lot-size problem for serial production/inventory systems operating with deterministic, dynamic, periodic demand. They review the characteristics of the optimal policy for the uncapacitated [255] and capacitated [77] versions of this problem, present two algorithms for optimization in the capacitated problem, and examine the performance of several heuristics for both problems. They conclude that the costs of the heuristically based policies differ only slightly from the costs of the optimal policies and are far more efficient computationally.

Graves examines a similar model (deterministic, nonstationary, periodic demand) for uncapacitated *assembly* systems. His paper presents a "multi-pass" heuristic, quite different from the conventional "single-pass" heuristics (e.g., part-period balancing, POQ, level-by-level Wagner—Whitin). He tests this heuristic against two single-pass heuristics and solutions from an optimum-finding algorithm. Graves reports that the multi-pass heuristic found optimal solutions in 90% of the cases tested versus 60% and 5% for two alternative single-pass heuristics. Computation times are approximately double those of the single-pass heuristics, but only a small fraction of the time taken by the optimum-finding procedure. Extensions to capacitated assembly systems are discussed.

In their paper Caie and Maxwell describe a machine load planning system installed at General Motors Corporation to determine economic run quantities for each manufacturing stage of a multi-stage production process. Inputs to the system are part demand, part bills-of-material, part "bills-of-tool", available resources, available storage capacity, and major and minor set-up costs and times. The system can be used for short-range scheduling decisions (e.g., in one application the system is used to load approximately 1500 dies on 300 presses) and for long-range management decisions with respect to manpower planning, capacity planning, and warehouse design. Implementation of the system (e.g., input data, reports, and uses) is discussed. Future developments are briefly described.

Management of a multi-level production/inventory system often involves the coordination of production decisions and transportation decisions. In their paper, Maxwell and Muckstadt describe a multi-facility system operated by a large automobile manufacturer. The system consists of a component plant with several production lines used to produce components for automobiles, and a set of destination plants at which different automobiles are assembled. The schedule for automobile assembly is given for each week of a 12-week planning horizon. The problem is to determine shift production by product and to schedule full rail car shipment of containers to destination assembly plants in order to meet assembly schedules. The real problem examined involved 100 products, 10 production lines, 11 shifts/week, 40 assembly plants, 18 containers per rail car, and the capacity to ship 20 rail cars per shift. The problem is modeled using a multi-level aggregation/disaggregation scheme.

Arborescent systems

The next five papers in this volume focus on two-level arborescent distribution systems (e.g., one-warehouse N-retailer systems) with particular attention given to the analysis and approximation of the demand processes.

Ehrhardt, Wagner, and Schultz's paper considers inventory replenishment rules for a wholesale facility whose sole demand consists of replenishment orders from retail facilities which follow (s, S) policies. Such wholesale facilities typically face highly erratic autocorrelated demand. The important issues in the analysis of stocking policies for such wholesalers are: (1) the consequences of ignoring these demand characteristics versus incorporating them, and (2) the related question of how these characteristics can be cost-effectively incorporated. The paper explores warehouse policies of a stationary (s, S) form, and, using simulation, finds "best" (s, S) policies. These policies are compared with two easily computed heuristics, one which assumes independent identically distributed demand, and the other, based on the Power Approximation of Ehrhardt [57], which models the autocorrelated demand process from knowledge of its mean and variances. Characteristics of the resulting policies and costs are compared in a wide variety of system environments.

Deuermeyer and Schwarz analyze a similar system — a one-warehouse N-retailer system operating under a continuous review demand replenishment, (Q, r), policy. The paper develops and tests an analytical model for estimating sytem service level (e.g., backorders and fill rate) as a function of system parameters: warehouse and retailer lot sizes, reorder points, warehouse and retailer lead times, and retailer demand parameters. Such a model is potentially important because: (1) it provides a framework for understanding system service level as a function of policy parameters, and (2) it provides a vehicle for system optimization. A portion of their model involves the approximation of the warehouse demand process using well-known results from renewal theory.

Rosenbaum describes the application of a heuristic model developed to aid Eastman Kodak management in determining safety stock placement in a two-level finished goods distribution system. This distribution system consists of a central distribution center (DC) and up to seven regional distribution centers (RDCs), depending on the given product. Within Kodak's existing management system safety stock quantities are based on fill rates individually set at each stocking location, the DC and the RDCs. The model described was developed to determine that combination of individual fill rates which minimizes system-wide safety stock while guaranteeing a pre-specified level of system performance. The paper also describes field test of the model, including training of the inventory planners, selection of the products, implementation and monitoring, and analysis of the results.

One element of the Kodak model involves analysis and approximation of the demand process at the DC. Sand, in her paper, describes the construction and test of two approximate models for forecasting DC demand during the DC inventory review time plus lead time and tests these models on a sample of Kodak's black and white paper products.

In most published models for managing single-level production/inventory systems and almost all published models for managing multi-level production/inventory systems, it is assumed either that outside demand is deterministic or that it is described by a known probability distribution with known parameters. In the area of multi-level systems the work of Zacks is a notable exception. Here, Zacks describes some exploratory research on the robustness of Bayes adaptive control in a two-activity serial distribution system. In this system monthly customer demand is assumed to occur on activity E according to a Poisson distribution. At the beginning of each month, activity E places an order on activity D. This order may be negative, indicating returns, or positive; however, negative orders may not exceed E's on-hand inventory and positive orders may not exceed D's on-hand inventory. There are fixed lead times between D and E and between an outside supplier and D. System costs are linear in procurement, holding, and shortage (no backordering). In previous work [248], Zacks determined Bayes adaptive policies for both stages under the assumption of stationary Poisson demand with unknown (gamma distributed) mean. In this work the robustness of these policies is tested relative to erroneous assumptions concerning: (1) the initial control parameters, (2) the stationarity of the mean of the Poisson demand process, and (3) the nature of the demand distribution.

Reparable inventory

One extremely active and important area of multi-level production/inventory control deals with items whose nature and costs make them far more economical to repair than discard. Such items or their spare parts can account for a significant share of an organization's inventory investment. For example, it has been estimated that well over half of the US Air Force's inventory investment is in such recoverable items. In his paper, Steven Nahmias reviews published mathematical models for determining policies for reparable-item inventory systems. Nahmias' paper analyzes several well-known models (e.g., METRIC) and several lesser known but important models (e.g., periodic review models), concentrating on the analytical approach used in each case.

Military applications

Given their enormous investment in both reparable and consumable inventory, the US military has been a long-time sponsor of new theory and a long-time innovator of new applications in the area of multi-level production/inventory control. Demmy and Presutti briefly describe the US Air Force's management system for reparables ($ 10 billion investment) and consumables ($ 2 billion investment) and review those elements of multi-echelon theory which have proven particularly useful in their management. Several models are reviewed, including METRIC, MOD-METRIC, the LMI Procurement, and Procurement-Repair models. Applications of these models to problems involving initial provisioning, replenishment spares, budgeting, and distribution are discussed.

In his paper, Clark, one of the early innovators in the theory of multi-level systems, shares his extensive personal experiences with the process of bringing theory into practice. He highlights these experiences by describing the events leading to the initial formulation and development of a model for Navy logistics support, chronicling the subsequent models' development and evaluation, successes, and setbacks. The story features bureaucratic barriers, shifting, sometimes conflicting criteria, and the ever-present specter of "infant mortality". This informative paper provides considerable insight into the gap between theory and practice.

New approaches, new problems

The concluding papers in this volume represent some of the work on new approaches and new problems in the area of multi-level production/inventory control. Karmarkar points out that several multi-location inventory models have a common mathematical structure which may be exploited by convex analysis [189] to determine the form of their corresponding optimal policies. Using the classic "Newsboy" model to motivate the approach, Karmarkar illustrates the use of convex analysis in constructing optimal or heuristic policies for a variety of problems whose analysis is otherwise complex or cumbersome. It is hoped that future development and application of this technique will not only provide new solutions to old problems, but "first" solutions to old and new problems as well.

In the final paper, Cohen, Pierskalla, and Yen consider a model for a multi-echelon distribution system for products which are age-differentiated (e.g., food, blood, photographic film, etc.). The general problem examined here is a single-product system consisting of a central depot and several satellite warehouses operating in an environment of stochastic demand. The paper examines the interaction between optimal order policies and age allocation policies for the case of stationary critical number order policies and either fixed or random (proportional to demand) age allocation policies. A general condition for convexity of expected costs is developed for the random allocation rule. Closed-form results for the optimal warehouse order policy are derived for each allocation rule under the assumption that the depot stocking level is either fixed or determined independently of warehouse stocking levels.

TIMS Studies in the Management Sciences 16 (1981) 11–49
© North-Holland Publishing Company

DESIGNING A MULTI-PRODUCT, MULTI-ECHELON INVENTORY SYSTEM

Donald GROSS, Richard M. SOLAND
The George Washington University

and

Charles E. PINKUS
California State Polytechnic University, Pomona

Large-scale inventory distribution systems typically require a hierarchy of retail stores and warehouses to satisfy the demands of their customers. This paper presents a 0–1 optimization model for finding the best design of such systems. To use this model it is necessary to know the optimal inventory policies for a set of multi-echelon systems. Therefore, part of this paper is devoted to describing how a dynamic programming approach, first suggested by Clark, can be used to obtain these policies. The paper presents examples of the use of this approach and also illustrates the use of the optimization model to find the design of an inventory distribution system. We also present a reformulation of the optimization model as a 0–1 linear programming model, incorporate capacity constraints at the retail stores and warehouses, and illustrate the use of the new model.

1. Introduction

Distribution systems are often composed of a hierarchy of warehouses that stock goods for distribution to other warehouses and to retail stores where demand for these goods originates. A multi-facility distribution system such as this is generally called a multi-echelon inventory system. Of course, such systems are not limited to warehouses and retail stores. For example, the factory which produces the goods could be part of the system. The factory's inventories would include raw materials and work-in-process at various stages of completion. Another example would be a reparable item system where there are depot and field repair stations. Other factors that can make a distribution system more complex are transshipments, that is, the redistribution of stock between warehouses on the same level, repair facilities at some or all distribution points (combination of reparable and consumable products), and exogenous demand at any facility in the system, to mention only a few.

Once the number of installations and their locations have been fixed, the problem is to find the best inventory policy for each product at each installation. Much is known about his problem, but there are also many unanswered questions.

The problem addressed in this paper pushes the decision process back one step by assuming that neither the number of installations nor their locations have been fixed for a multi-product distribution system.

In section 2 we present a mathematical model for finding the number of echelons, number of installations, and where products should be stocked for a multi-product, multi-echelon inventory system. This model relies heavily on the ability to determine inventory policies for a given multi-echelon system. A method for finding these policies via dynamic programming is presented in section 3. Section 4 generalizes the model presented in section 2 to include capacity constraints, and presents a 0—1 linear programming formulation of this generalized model. In section 5 we present some computational experience obtained in solving the two design models given in this paper and indicate areas of future research. This introductory section concludes with an illustration of the design problem and a discussion of the premises on which it is based.

1.1. The design problem

Fig. 1 shows a three-installation arborescent-configuration system. Installation B (warehouse) obtains goods from a source (factory) and feeds the two lower level installations, A_1 and A_2 (retail stores), where exogenous demands, D_1 and D_2, occur.

Fig. 2 gives two alternative designs for this system. In fig. 2(a) installation B has been removed from the system and A_1, A_2 are supplied directly from the source of production. Fig. 2(b) shows another alternative design for the basic three-installation arborescent system. A_2 has been removed and its demand goes directly to B. Since the exogenous demand is still physically located near where A_2 had been

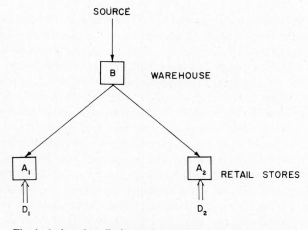

Fig. 1. A three-installation, arborescent-configuration system.

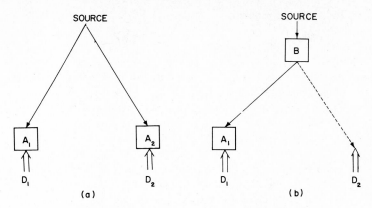

Fig. 2. Alternative designs for the system of fig. 1.

located, the dashed line indicates that individual shipments are made one at a time to the customers represented by D_2. This can be thought of as mail-order business.

The phrase *echelon structures* will be used in referring to the alternative designs for a multi-echelon distribution system. The *basic echelon structure* will be thought of as the one containing the maximum number of levels and installations under consideration. For example, if fig. 1 represents a basic echelon structure then the system has a maximum of $2^3 = 8$ possible alternative echelon structures. [1] In general, if a basic echelon structure is composed of p installations, then the number of alternative echelon structures is 2^p.

The multi-product, multi-echelon inventory system design problem discussed in this paper is based upon two premises. First, there is no reason to assume that the minimum cost design of the system will be one in which all products use the same echelon structure. That is, given the set of echelon structures under consideration, if we were to find the best inventory policy independently for each product stocked under each echelon structure, it would very likely be found that different echelon structures were best for different products. Second, minimization of *total* system cost will usually be accomplished only if some products do *not* use the echelon structure that would be "best" for them if each product were considered independently. This is because different products stored at the same installation will share the fixed cost of that installation.

The next section presents a mathematical model for solving the design problem described in this section.

---

[1] This number would increase if we considered more situations than an installation simply being in the system or not in the system. For example, a third possibility is to have an installation carry a lifetime supply of a product.

2. Analysis of the design problem

In this section a mathematical model for determining the best design for a multi-product, multi-echelon distribution system is presented. The purpose of this model is to find the best echelon structure for each product, *bearing in mind that the products are not independent when it comes to sharing installations.* A super-position of these echelon structures then results in the best system design.

2.1. Measure of effectiveness

We first consider what is meant by "best". The measure of effectiveness to be used will be one that minimizes some measure of *total* system cost, for example total expected cost per year or total discounted cost for the lifetime of the system. The system cost will include all the out-of-pocket operating expenses of the system, capital expenditures for building the system, and those intangible factors to which a cost can be assigned. The penalty cost for loss of goodwill as a result of back-ordering (not meeting demand when it occurs) is an example of such an intangible cost.

For a given product and a given echelon structure, we separate these system costs into two categories. The first includes all the costs associated with the inventory policy. We call these the *inventory costs*; they include the costs of procurement, carrying inventory, filling orders, and stockouts. The second category includes all the costs associated with operating the installations of an echelon structure regardless of the number of products using the installations. We call these *facility costs;* they include the capital expenditure for building the installations, along with a number of fixed costs associated with operating the installations, for example, administrative expenses, the expense of renting facilities (if they are not built), and certain other fixed operating expenses for a given product that do not depend on the inventory policies used at the various installations. The facility costs are all fixed costs that are normally considered sunk costs because the echelon structure has been set.

2.2. Mathematical model of the design problem

Let

a_{ij} = the inventory cost of product j using echelon structure i,

b_k = the facility cost of installation k, and

b_{ik} = the facility cost of installation k when echelon structure i is used,

where

$$b_{ik} = \begin{cases} b_k, \text{ if installation } k \text{ is included in echelon structure } i , \\ 0, \text{ otherwise } . \end{cases}$$

The costs a_{ij} and b_{ik} are arrayed in the matrix $[a_{ij} : b_{ik}]$ of fig. 3. If the facility

| | PRODUCTS (*j*) | | | | INSTALLATIONS (*k*) | | | |

ECHELON STRUCTURES (i)

PRODUCTS (*j*)　　　　　　　　INSTALLATIONS (*k*)

	1	2	...	*n*		1	2	...	*p*
1	a_{11}	a_{12}	...	a_{1n}		b_{11}	b_{12}	...	b_{1p}
2	a_{21}	a_{22}	...	a_{2n}		b_{21}	b_{22}	...	b_{2p}
⋮	⋮					⋮			
m	a_{m1}	a_{m2}	...	a_{mn}		b_{m1}	b_{m2}	...	b_{mp}

Fig. 3. Array of inventory costs and facility costs.

costs b_{ik} were all zero, all products could be treated independently and the solution to this problem would be obvious. We would select the minimum element in each column of matrix $[a_{ij}]$, that is, the minimum inventory cost of each product. The echelon structure *i* associated with this minimum cost for product *j* would be the echelon structure used by product *j*. Unfortunately, the b_{ik} are not all zero.

The design problem is similar to the assignment problem of linear programming in that it is desired to assign products to echelon structures so that minimum cost over the a_{ij} is achieved. Unlike the assignment problem, however, multi-assignments in any row are permitted and the assignment of products to echelon structures can create additional costs (facility cost), depending upon which installations are required in the echelon structures chosen. A further complication occurs because each facility cost, b_k, is a fixed cost, regardless of the number of products using installation *k*.

We now define decision variables and give a mathematical formulation for the design problem.

Let x_{ij} = 1 if product *j* uses echelon structure *i*,
　　　　= 0 otherwise.
Then the problem is to find a matrix $X = [x_{ij}]$ which minimizes

$$F(X) = \sum_{i=1}^{m}\sum_{j=1}^{n} a_{ij}x_{ij} + \sum_{k=1}^{p} u\left[\sum_{i=1}^{m}\left(b_{ik}\sum_{j=1}^{n}x_{ij}\right)\right]b_k \tag{1}$$

subject to

$$\sum_{i=1}^{m} x_{ij} = 1, \qquad j = 1, 2, ..., n, \tag{2}$$

$$x_{ij} = 0 \text{ or } 1, \qquad \text{for all } i \text{ and } j, \tag{3}$$

where

$$u(y) = 0 \text{ if } y \leq 0,$$
$$= 1 \text{ if } y > 0.$$

Thus the problem of designing a multi-product, multi-echelon distribution system has been formulated as a 0−1 nonlinear optimization problem. The objective is to find a matrix X^* which minimizes $F(\cdot)$. This nonlinear optimization problem can be reformulated as a linear one (see section 4), and the resulting model resembles that of the classical fixed-charge uncapacitated facility location problem; see e.g., Erlenkotter [66]. It differs in a very important way, however, in that the relation between products and facilities is not a direct one; assignment of product j to echelon structure i requires the system to include *all* facilities used in echelon structure i, not just a facility indexed by i. This difference will be discussed further in section 4.

We have solved the above mathematical model using a branch-and-bound algorithm (see Pinkus, Gross and Soland [178]). However, one of the weaknesses of this model is that it assumes that there is no limit to the storage space available at a given installation. One purpose of this paper is to overcome this weakness by incorporating capacity constraints. Before doing that, however, we describe one way of finding the inventory costs, a_{ij}.

3. Multi-echelon inventory model

This section is concerned with obtaining the value of a_{ij}, the inventory cost of product j, using echelon structure i. [2]

3.1. Clark's approach

A modification of Clark's approach [32] will be used to determine the values of a_{ij} for the design model of this paper. It should be noted that any method for determining multi-echelon inventory policies could be used to find the values of a_{ij}. The selection of a method is, of course, dependent upon the characteristics of the inventory situation for which a multi-echelon system is being designed. Clark's approach has been selected because: (1) the determination of the a_{ij} is an immediate by-product of the calculation of the optimal inventory policies; (2) the dynamic programming calculations are straightforward; and (3) the model is rich enough to include many multi-echelon inventory situations.

3.2. Review of classicial inventory models

Before describing Clark's method for finding optimal inventory policies for a single product stored in a multi-echelon system, we review the classical dynamic, periodic review, stochastic demand with backordering inventory model for a single

---

[2] To avoid confusion in this section, the notation a_{ij} will be used rather than the phrase inventory cost, where the particular echelon structure i or the particular product j is immaterial. The methods for obtaining a_{ij} will be applicable for all i and for all j.

item at a single installation. This model forms the basis for the Clark multi-echelon model.

3.2.1. Classical inventory problem

A purchasing decision is to be made at the beginning of each of a number of regularly spaced periods of time, for example at the beginning of each week. This decision will be based on the level of inventory at the time, ordering, holding, and backorder penalty costs during the period, and the effect the decision will have on future periods.

Let

z = purchase quantity, $z \geqslant 0$,

$c(z)$ = cost of purchasing z units,

λ = number of time periods lag between an order and its delivery, the possible values for λ being $0, 1, 2, ...,$

$\phi(t)$ = probability density function of demand during a period, where demand is a continuous random variable and is independent from period to period,

u = inventory on hand at the end of a period, where $-\infty < u < \infty$ (a negative value indicates that demand occurred during the period that could not be filled),

$h(u)$ = holding cost charged on inventory on hand at the end of a period,

$p(u)$ = shortage cost charged for failure to meet demand during a period,

x_n = inventory on hand at the beginning of the nth period, before an order is received, that is, the inventory on hand at the end of the previous period,

y_n = inventory on hand at the beginning of the nth period, immediately after an order is received, and

$L(y_n)$ = expected holding and shortage cost during the nth period (hereafter referred to as the period cost)

$$
= \begin{cases} \int_0^{y_n} h(y_n - t)\,\phi(t)\,dt + \int_{y_n}^{\infty} p(t - y_n)\,\phi(t)\,dt\,, & y_n \geqslant 0 \\ \\ \int_0^{\infty} p(t - y_n)\,\phi(t)\,dt\,, & y_n < 0\,. \end{cases} \qquad n = 1, 2, ...
$$

If a delivery is to be received during a given period as a result of an order placed λ periods before, then it is assumed this order arrives at the beginning of the period and before the purchase decision for the period is made. Furthermore, it is assumed the supplier carries an infinite supply of the item, that is, the supplier never backorders the installation. The dynamic programming formulation of this problem is now given. In this formulation it is assumed that $\lambda = 0$, that is, delivery is instantaneous, and that excess demand is backordered.

Let

$C_n(x_n, y_n)$ = total expected discounted inventory cost for a problem lasting n periods, when inventory on hand at the beginning of period n prior to ordering is x_n and immediately after ordering is y_n, $n = 1, 2, ...,$ and

α = discount factor.

The periods are numbered backwards in time; thus, period number one is the last period of the problem. It is assumed that units on hand at the end of the last period have no salvage value.

Suppose we are at the beginning of the nth period of the problem, that is, there are n periods of business remaining for the installation, and x_n is the inventory on hand before an ordering decision is made. The optimal policy for the nth period is the policy which minimizes $C_n(x_n, y_n)$. The well-known dynamic programming recursive relation for this problem is

$$\hat{C}_n(x_n) = \min_{y_n \geqslant x_n} \left\{ c(y_n - x_n) + L(y_n) + \alpha \int_0^\infty \hat{C}_{n-1}(y_n - t)\, \phi(t)\, dt \right\}$$

$$n = 1, 2, ... \tag{4}$$

where $\hat{C}_n(x_n)$ equals minimum total expected discounted cost for a problem lasting n periods, $n = 1, 2, ...$. In this equation $\hat{C}_n(x_n)$ has been broken down into three components: the purchasing cost for the nth period; the period cost for the nth period; and the total expected discounted cost for $n - 1$ periods of operation, assuming an optimal inventory policy is followed during the last $n - 1$ periods. This recursive relation is used to find the optimal value of y_n, which we call S_n. Clearly, the desired inventory level at the beginning of the nth period, S_n, has an effect on all future levels S_i, $i = 1, 2, ..., n - 1$.

Two well-known results for this model are now given.

3.2.2. No fixed cost of ordering

Assume the purchasing cost is linear with no fixed cost of ordering. Then

$$c(z) = c \cdot z, \qquad z > 0.$$

Assume $L(y_n)$ is convex. Then it has been shown by Karlin [109] that the optimal policy for an n-period problem can be characterized by a sequence of critical numbers $S_1, S_2, ..., S_n$. The policy for the kth period is

if $x_k \leqslant S_k$, order $S_k - x_k$,

if $x_k > S_k$, order nothing.

3.2.3. Positive fixed cost of ordering

Assume the purchasing cost is linear with a fixed cost of ordering equal to K.

Fig. 4. A multi-echelon system with N installations in a series configuration.

Then

$$c(z) = c \cdot z + K , \qquad z > 0 ,$$
$$= 0 , \qquad\qquad z = 0 .$$

Assume $L(y_k)$ is convex. Scarf [199] has shown that the optimal policy for the kth period is defined by a pair of critical numbers, (S_k, s_k). The policy for the kth period is

if $x_k \leqslant s_k$, order $S_k - x_k$,

if $x_k > s_k$, order nothing .

3.3. Finding a_{ij} for series structures

Suppose there are N installations, where installation N supplies stock to installation $N - 1$, $N - 1$ supplies stock to $N - 2$, ..., installation 2 supplies stock to installation 1. This series configuration is pictured in fig. 4. The highest installation in the series, N, receives its stock from the source of production. [3] The notation and assumptions given at the beginning of this section still generally apply and are not repeated here, with the following exceptions: Let

---

[3] The source of production could be included in the series as the highest installation. Then, its source of stock would be the supplier of raw material.

x_n^i = inventory on hand at echelon i at the beginning of the nth period before an order is received,

y_n^i = inventory on hand at echelon i at the beginning of the nth period, immediately after an order is received,

$L_i(y_n^i)$ = period cost of echelon i, and

$c_i(z)$ = ordering cost function for echelon i, $z \geq 0$.

It is important to note the following distinction between an installation and an echelon. The stock at installation i refers only to the stock physically at that location. But when we refer to the stock at echelon i, we mean the *sum* of all the stocks at installations i, $i - 1$, ..., 2, 1 plus all the stock in transit between installations i, $i - 1$, ..., 2, 1.

The formulation of the Clark model follows. It is assumed that:

(1) Demand, exogenous to the system, occurs at installation 1 only.
(2) The purchasing cost between installations is linear without a fixed cost of ordering. This cost can be thought of as the cost to transport a unit from one installation to the next installation in the system. The only exception to this assumption is at the highest installation, where a fixed cost of ordering is allowed.
(3) Demand in excess of supply at any installation is backlogged.
(4) The functions $L_i(y_n^i)$ are convex, $i = 1, 2, ..., N$.
(5) Delivery at each installation is instantaneous. [4]
(6) The functions $c(z)$, $h(u)$, $p(u)$ and $\phi(t)$ are stationary. [4]

The model is described for the special case $N = 2$. Let

$\hat{C}_n(x_n^1, x_n^2)$ = minimum total expected discounted cost of the system at the beginning of period n before an order is placed, $n = 1, 2, ...$.

Following the approach for the single-installation model, we get the recursive relation

$$\hat{C}_n(x_n^1, x_n^2) = \min_{\substack{x_n^1 \leq y_n^1 \leq y_n^2 \\ y_n^2 \geq x_n^2}} \left\{ c_1(y_n^1 - x_n^1) + c_2(y_n^2 - x_n^2) + L_1(y_n^1) + L_2(y_n^2) \right.$$

$$\left. + \alpha \int_0^\infty \hat{C}_{n-1}(y_n^1 - t, y_n^2 - t)\, \phi(t)\, dt \right\}, \qquad n = 1, 2, ...$$

The problem with this approach is that in the general case $\hat{C}_n$ is a function of N variables. Therefore, the recursive calculations of dynamic programming would be prohibitively long, even for a high-speed computer, if the function $\hat{C}_n$ is left in this form. Clark and Scarf [39] have overcome this difficulty. They proved that the

---

[4] These assumptions can be relaxed. Non-zero leadtimes can be accommodated, with some added complexity (see Karlin and Scarf [11]). In addition, the dynamic programming formulation can easily handle non-stationary functions.

function $\hat{C}_n(x_n^1, x_n^2, ..., x_n^N)$ can be decomposed into N functions, each of a single variable, that is,

$$\hat{C}_n(x_n^1, x_n^2, ..., x_n^N) = \hat{D}_n^1(x_n^1) + \hat{D}_n^2(x_n^2) + ... + \hat{D}_n^N(x_n^N) .$$

This permits the computation of the optimal inventory level at each echelon separately using the same method that is used for the classical single-installation model. What is involved is described by returning to the special case, $N = 2$:

$$\hat{C}_n(x_n^1, x_n^2) = \hat{D}_n^1(x_n^1) + \hat{D}_n^2(x_n^2) , \qquad n = 1, 2, ...$$

Begin by considering the lower echelon and assume there is no limitation on the stock available to it from the higher echelon:

$$\hat{D}_n^1(x_n^1) = \min_{y_n^1 \geqslant x_n^1} \left\{ c_1(y_n^1 - x_n^1) + L_1(y_n^1) + \alpha \int_0^\infty \hat{D}_{n-1}^1(y_n^1 - t) \, \phi(t) \, dt \right\} ,$$

$$n = 1, 2, ... \tag{5}$$

It has been assumed that $L_1(y_n^1)$ is convex and the purchasing (transportation) cost is linear without a fixed cost of ordering, that is, $c_1(y_n^1 - x_n^1) = c_1 \cdot (y_n^1 - x_n^1)$. Therefore, recursive relation (5) is identical to equation (4), and the optimal policy for this echelon is described by the sequence of critical numbers $S_1^1, S_2^1, ..., S_n^1$, where S_i^1 is the optimal level of inventory for echelon 1 in the ith period. This conclusion has assumed that installation 2 can satisfy the demand of installation 1. This will not always be the case. However, Clark and Scarf show that installation 2 should satisfy as much of the demand from installation 1 as is possible and backlog the rest. [5]

The fact that installation 2 might not be able to satisfy the demand of installation 1 suggests that in solving for the optimal policy of echelon 2, a shortage penalty, in addition to the penalty included in L_2, be incurred by installation 2 when it must backlog the demand that installation 1 places on it. This penalty is simply the additional expected cost suffered at installation 1 because installation 2 could not satisfy its demand. This penalty is determined as follows.

Consider the kth period at echelon 1. Suppose $x_k^1 < S_k^1$. Then echelon 1 will order $S_k^1 - x_k^1$ stock from echelon 2, and the total cost for k periods at echelon 1

---

[5] It is assumed that installation 2 will deliver at most one shipment each period to installation 1 and that this shipment goes out in the "split second" after installation 2 has made its reorder decision but before its stock is replenished. This sequence of decisions is necessary in order to force this example, with $\lambda = 0$, to behave like a real problem with $\lambda > 0$.

will be

$$\hat{D}_k^1(x_k^1) = c_1 \cdot (S_k^1 - x_k^1) + L_1(S_k^1) + \alpha \int_0^\infty \hat{D}_{k-1}^1(S_k^1 - t)\,\phi(t)\,dt\,.$$

If the stock level at echelon 2 is such that $x_k^2 < (S_k^1 - x_k^1)$, that is, installation 2 cannot satisfy all the demand from installation 1, then echelon 1 will have x_k^2 stock on hand after ordering, rather than S_k^1 stock. This means that the order received by installation 1 is $x_k^2 - x_k^1$. In other words, all the available stock at installation 2 was shipped to installation 1. Under this situation, the total cost for k periods at echelon 1 will be

$$\bar{D}_k^1(x_k^1, x_k^2) = c_1 \cdot (x_k^2 - x_k^1) + L_1(x_k^2) + \alpha \int_0^\infty \hat{D}_{k-1}^1(x_k^2 - t)\,\phi(t)\,dt\,.$$

Let $\Delta_n^i(\cdot)$ = the additional shortage penalty at echelon i for not being able to meet demand at echelon $i-1$ during the nth period, $i = 2, 3, ..., N$, $n = 1, 2, ...$

The penalty $\Delta_k^2(\cdot)$ is

$$\bar{D}_k^1(x_k^1, x_k^2) - \hat{D}_k^1(x_k^1)$$

$$= c_1 \cdot (x_k^2 - x_k^1) - c_1 \cdot (S_k^1 - x_k^1) + L_1(x_k^2) - L_1(S_k^1)$$

$$+ \alpha \int_0^\infty [\hat{D}_{k-1}^1(x_k^2 - t) - \hat{D}_{k-1}^1(S_k^1 - t)]\,\phi(t)\,dt$$

$$= c_1 \cdot (x_k^2 - S_k^1) + L(x_k^2) - L(S_k^1)$$

$$+ \alpha \int_0^\infty [\hat{D}_{k-1}^1(x_k^2 - t) - \hat{D}_{k-1}^1(S_k^1 - t)]\,\phi(t)\,dt$$

$$= \Delta_k^2(x_k^2)\,.$$

A more complete statement of the function Δ_n^2 is

$$\Delta_n^2(x_n^2) = c_1 \cdot (x_n^2 - S_n^1) + L_1(x_n^2) - L_1(S_n^1) + \alpha \int_0^\infty [\hat{D}_{n-1}^1(x_n^2 - t)$$

$$- \hat{D}_{n-1}^1(S_n^1 - t)]\,\phi(t)\,dt\,, \qquad \text{for } x_n^2 \leqslant S_n^1\,, \qquad n = 1, 2, ...$$

$$= 0\,, \qquad \text{for } x_n^2 > S_n^1\,, \qquad n = 1, 2, ...$$

The fact that Δ_n^2 is a function of x_n^2 alone is very significant. It means that the

recursive relation for the total cost of n periods of operation at echelon 2 is a function of the single variable x_n^2. Thus, a dynamic programming solution is feasible.
The optimal policy at echelon 2 is now described.

$$\hat{D}_n^2(x_n^2) = \min_{y_n^2 \geqslant x_n^2} \left\{ c_2(y_n^2 - x_n^2) + L_2(y_n^2) + \Delta_n^2(x_n^2) \right.$$

$$\left. + \alpha \int_0^\infty \hat{D}_{n-1}^2(y_n^2 - t)\, \phi(t)\, dt \right\}, \qquad n = 1, 2, \dots . \tag{6}$$

It has been assumed that $L_2(y_n^2)$ is convex and the purchasing cost is linear with a fixed cost of ordering, that is, $c_2(y_n^2 - x_n^2) = c_2 \cdot (y_n^2 - x_n^2) + K$. Since Δ_n^2 is the sum of convex functions, it is a convex function. Therefore, the solution of (6) follows the solution given for the classical model with a fixed cost of ordering, and the optimal policy for the nth period at echelon 2 is described by the pair of critical numbers (S_n^2, s_n^2), where the superscript indicates the echelon.

The procedure described here for two echelons can be used for any number of echelons in series. Clark and Scarf show that the policies obtained in this way are optimal policies, and their proof allows for $\lambda > 0$.

A summary of the important ideas behind the Clark approach follows:

(1) The decision variable is the stock level of an echelon, not the stock level of an installation.
(2) An N installation problem in N decision variables becomes N separate problems, each in one decision variable. Each separate problem is a special case of the classical single-installation stochastic demand inventory problem and can be solved by dynamic programming.
(3) The cost function for each echelon i (except the first) includes the additional shortage penalty Δ_n^i for not being able to supply the complete order of echelon $i - 1$ in the nth period. This covers the additional expected cost resulting from echelon $i - 1$ not being able to achieve its optimal level of stock for the period. The penalty Δ_n^i is obtained from the solution of echelon $i - 1$.

We now present an example of a two-installation problem. The optimal policies are calculated for two periods.

3.4. Two-installation, series-configuration example

Let u_i = inventory on hand in echelon i at the end of a period,
$h_i^*(u_i)$ = holding cost at installation i,
$h_i(u_i)$ = holding cost at echelon i,
$p_i^*(u_i)$ = shortage cost at installation i, and
$p_i(u_i)$ = shortage cost at echelon i.

Suppose $h_1^*(u_1) = 2.2u_1$,

$\qquad h_2^*(u_2) = 2.0u_2$,

$\qquad p_1^*(u_1) = 72u_1$,

$\qquad p_2^*(u_2) = 5u_2$,

$\qquad c_1(z) \quad = 5z$,

$\qquad c_2(z) \quad = 50z + 30$,

$\qquad \alpha \qquad = 1$,

where all costs are in dollars.

Since this model determines optimal echelon policies, the period cost L_i, $i = 1, 2$, must be based upon echelon costs, not installation costs. The holding and shortage costs at echelon 2 are merely these respective costs at installation 2. Thus,

$$h_2(u_2) = h_2^*(u_2) = 2u_2 \,,$$

$$p_2(u_2) = p_2^*(u_2) = 5u_2 \,.$$

To find the holding cost at echelon 1, it is noted that any units on hand at echelon 1 at the end of a period have already been charged $ 2 holding cost because they were counted in the stock of echelon 2 that was on hand at the end of the same period. The same reasoning applies to the penalty cost at echelon 1. Thus,

$$h_1(u_1) = h_1^*(u_1) - h_2^*(u_1) = 2.2u_1 - 2.0u_1 = 0.2u_1 \,,$$

$$p_1(u_1) = p_1^*(u_1) - p_2^*(u_1) = 72u_1 - 5u_1 = 67u_1 \,.$$

If there were N installations arranged in series, the holding and shortage costs at echelon N would be obtained the same way as for echelon 2 in this example, and the costs for echelons $N - 1, N - 2, ..., 1$ would be obtained using the cost-added concept that was used for echelon 1 in this example. Note that the cost-added concept implies that $h_{n-1}^* \geq h_n^*$ and $p_{n-1}^* \geq p_n^*$ for $n = 2, 3, ..., N$.

Suppose the demand $\phi(t)$ for this example follows a Poisson distribution, and the mean demand is one unit per period. The period cost is found by evaluating the following expression:

$$L_i(y_n^i) = \sum_{t=0}^{y_n^i} h_i \cdot (y_n^i - t) \, \phi(t) + \sum_{t=y_n^i+1}^{\infty} p_i \cdot (t - y_n^i) \, \phi(t) \,,$$

$$\text{for } y_n^i \geq 0 \,, \qquad i = 1, 2, \qquad n = 1, 2, ...$$

$$= \sum_{t=0}^{\infty} p_i \cdot (t - y_n^i) \, \phi(t) \,,$$

$$\text{for } y_n^i < 0 \,, \qquad i = 1, 2 \,, \qquad n = 1, 2, ... \,.$$

Note that the functions $L_i(y_n^i)$, $i = 1, 2$, satisfy the assumptions of convexity because the holding and shortage cost functions are convex.

We now evaluate the recursive relations $\hat{D}_n^1$ and $\hat{D}_n^2$ for $n = 1$ and $n = 2$, from which the optimal policies will be obtained. The results appear in tables 1 and 2, which are read from right to left. This follows the way dynamic programming is used to find the optimal policy of the last period (period 1) and then moves backwards in time, calculating successively the optimal policies for periods 2, 3, ..., n. Wherever possible the notation defined earlier is used to head the columns of these tables. Each table is split into two parts, the lower, representing echelon 1, and the upper, representing echelon 2.

Table 1 shows the various possible costs for period 1 at different stock levels. The actual interpretation of stock level [columns (1) and (8)], that is, whether it is stock on hand before or after receiving an order, depends on the cost column under consideration. Columns (2) and (9) show zero cost because this is the last period of operation and there are no future costs. Successive differences of the entries in column (4) are shown in column (5). These are used to locate the critical number S_1^1. It can be shown (see Karlin [109]) that for the classical single-installation model without a fixed cost of ordering, the critical number S_n satisfies $W_n^1(S_n) = -c$, where

$$W_n(S_n) \equiv L(S_n) + \alpha \int_0^\infty \hat{C}_{n-1}(S_n - t)\,\phi(t)$$

Since we have shifted to discrete valued functions, the method of finite differences must be used to find S_n^1. It can be shown that the critical number S_n^1 satisfies the relation

$$W_n^1(S_n^1) - W_n^1(S_n^1 - 1) \leqslant -c_1 \leqslant W_n(S_n^1 + 1) - W_n^1(S_n^1) . \tag{7}$$

Successive differences are shown in column (5) until the inequality (7) is satisfied. In the case of echelon 1 during period 1,

$$-5.19 \leqslant -c_1 = -5 \leqslant -1.08 ,$$

thus $S_1^1 = 3$.

Column (6) of table 1 shows the total expected cost after ordering, for various stock levels before ordering. Since it is optimal to have a stock level of three units at the beginning of period 1, if $x_1^1 < 3$, we purchase $3 - x_1^1$ units and add the cost of this purchase, $5 \cdot (3 - x_1^1)$, to $\hat{D}_1^1(3)$. Column (7) shows the cost of not being able to bring the stock level up to S_1^1. This cost, Δ_1^2, is equal to column (4) minus column (6) and is the penalty charged to echelon 2 as a result of installation 2 back-ordering installation 1.

The echelon 2 section of table 1 shows the costs involved in obtaining the critical numbers (S_1^2, s_1^2). Much of this section is similar to the echelon 1 section. Only the differences are commented upon. Column (10) is equal to column (7). In column (12) the function W_1^2 includes the additional cost Δ_1^2. Column (13) shows that $S_1^2 = 0$. Column (14) is obtained by assuming an order is always placed to bring the stock level up to zero if $x_1^2 < 0$. In comparing columns (14) and (12), note that

Table 1

Period 1 solution of two-installation, series-configuration example

Stock level (8)	$\alpha \sum_{t=0}^{\infty} \hat{D}_0^2(y_1^2 - t)\,\phi(t)$ (9)	$\Delta_1^2(x_1^2)$ (10)	$L_2(y_1^2)$ (11)	$W_1^2(\cdot)$ total expected cost before ordering (12)	$W_1^2(x_1^2) - W_1^2(x_1^2 - 1)$ (13)	$\hat{D}_1^2$ assuming always order when $x_1^2 < S_1^2$ (14)	$\hat{D}_1^2(x_1^2)$ (15)
7	0.00	0.00	12.00	12.00	2.00	12.00	12.00
6	0.00	0.00	10.00	10.00	2.00	10.00	10.00
5	0.00	0.00	8.00	8.00	1.97	8.00	8.00
4	0.00	0.00	6.03	6.03	1.87	6.03	6.03
3	0.00	0.00	4.16	4.16	1.25	4.16	4.16
2	0.00	0.19	2.72	2.91	−12.41	2.91	2.91
1	0.00	12.75	2.57	15.32	−39.70 ↑	15.32	15.32
0	0.00	50.02	5.00	55.02	−67.00 ↓	55.02	55.02
−1	0.00	112.02	10.00	122.02		135.02	122.02
−2	0.00	174.02	15.00	189.02		185.02	185.02
−3	0.00	236.02	20.00	256.02		235.02	235.02
−4	0.00	298.02	25.00	323.02		285.02	285.02

Echelon 2

Stock level (1)	$\alpha \displaystyle\sum_{t=0}^{\infty} \hat{D}_0^1(v_1^1 - t)\,\phi(t)$ (2)	$L_1(v_1^1)$ (3)	$W_1^1(\cdot)$ total expected cost before ordering (4)	$W_1^1(x_1^1) - W_1^1(x_1^1 - 1)$ (5)	$\hat{D}_1^1(x_1^1)$ (6)	$\Delta_1^2(x_1^2)$ (7)
7	0.00	1.20	1.20	0.20	1.20	0.00
6	0.00	1.00	1.00	0.16	1.00	0.00
5	0.00	0.84	0.84	-0.04	0.84	0.00
4	0.00	0.88	0.88	-1.08	0.88	0.00
3	0.00	1.96	1.96	-5.19	1.96	0.00
2	0.00	7.15	7.15	↑	6.96	0.19
1	0.00	24.70	24.70		11.96	12.75
0	0.00	66.98	66.98		16.96	50.02
-1	0.00	133.98	133.98		21.96	112.02
-2	0.00	200.98	200.98		26.96	174.02
-3	0.00	267.98	267.98		31.96	236.02
-4	0.00	334.98	334.98		36.96	298.02

Echelon 1

it is not always wise to order when $x_1^2 < 0$. When $x_1^2 = -1$, the total cost after ordering is \$ 135.02, while if we had not ordered, the total cost would have been \$ 122.02. The stock level, s_1^2, at which the costs in column (14) are less than or equal to the costs in column (12), is the level at which ordering should begin. In this case, $s_1^2 = -2$. Column (15) shows the total expected cost after ordering, for various stock levels before ordering. The entries of column (15) are the minimum of the entries in columns (12) and (14).

Table 2 shows the determination of the critical numbers for period 2. Columns (6) and (15) of table 1 have been brought back one period in time to become columns (2) and (9), respectively, of table 2. The calculations in table 2 are obtained as described for table 1.

The critical numbers for the last two periods of this problem are

$$S_1^1 = 3 \qquad (S_1^2, s_1^2) = (0, -2),$$

$$S_2^1 = 3 \qquad (S_2^2, s_2^2) = (2, 0).$$

If we are interested in using this two-installation, series-configuration example in the design of a multi-echelon system, which would be in business for only two periods, and if there are zero units on hand at each installation at the beginning of period 2 before an order is placed, then a_{ij} for this echelon structure is

$$\hat{D}_2^1(0) + \hat{D}_2^2(0) = \$ 23.92 + \$ 165.95 = \$ 189.87.$$

The calculation of the critical numbers for this example was carried out for 20 periods. The critical numbers for the 20th period are

$$S_{20}^1 = 5. \qquad (S_{20}^2, s_{20}^2) = (7, 1).$$

The total expected discounted (inventory) cost of this echelon structure for this product, that is, a_{ij}, when it is assumed zero units are on hand at each installation before an order is placed at the beginning of the 20th period, is

$$\hat{D}_{20}^1(0) + \hat{D}_{20}^2(0) = \$ 1438.17.$$

The series configuration of installations does not represent a very realistic multi-echelon system. If Clark's approach is to be used to obtain the a_{ij} for the design model, it will have to be applied to the more realistic arborescent configuration of installations. The next section shows how this approach is used to find the critical numbers and the a_{ij} for installations arranged in arborescence, and extends the method to allow for exogenous demand at any installation.

Table 2

Period 2 solution of two-installation, series-configuration example

Stock level	$\alpha \sum\limits_{t=0}^{8} \hat{D}_1^2(v_2^2 - t)\,\phi(t)$	$\Delta_2^2(x_2^2)$	$L_2(v_2^2)$	$W_2^2(\cdot)$ total expected cost before ordering	$\hat{W}_2^2(x_2^2) - \hat{W}_2^2(x_2^2 - 1)$	$\hat{D}_2^2$ assuming always order when $x_2^2 < S_2^2$	$\hat{D}_2^2(x_2^2)$
(8)	(9)	(10)	(11)	(12)	(13)	(14)	(15)
7	10.02	0.00	12.00	22.02	3.91	22.02	22.02
6	8.11	0.00	10.00	18.11	3.53	18.11	18.11
5	6.58	0.00	8.00	14.58	2.00	14.58	14.58
4	6.55	0.00	6.03	12.58	−2.95	12.58	12.58
3	11.37	0.00	4.16	15.53	−20.42	15.53	15.53
2	28.04	5.19	2.72	35.95	−53.70 ↑	35.95	35.95
1	64.34	22.74	2.57	89.65	↓	115.95	89.65
0	119.20	65.02	5.00	189.22		165.95	165.95
−1	180.24	132.02	10.00	322.26		215.95	215.95
−2	235.02	199.02	15.00	449.04		265.95	265.95
−3	285.02	266.02	20.00	571.04		315.95	315.95
−4	335.02	333.02	25.00	693.04		365.95	365.95

Echelon 2

30 D. Gross et al., Designing an inventory system

Stock level (1)	$\alpha \sum_{t=0}^{\infty} \hat{D}_1^1(y_2^1 - t)\,\phi(t)$ (2)	$L_1(y_2^1)$ (3)	$W_2^1(\cdot)$ total expected cost before ordering (4)	$W_2^1(x_2^1) - W_2^1(x_2^1 - 1)$ (5)	$\hat{D}_2^1(x_2^1)$ (6)	$\Delta_2^2(x_2^2)$ (7)
7	1.08	1.20	2.28	0.19	2.28	0.00
6	1.11	1.00	2.11	-0.40	2.11	0.00
5	1.67	0.84	2.51	-1.77	2.51	0.00
4	3.40	0.88	4.28	-4.64	4.28	0.00
3	6.96	1.96	8.92	-10.19	8.92	0.00
2	11.96	7.15	19.11	$\uparrow$	13.92	5.19
1	16.96	24.70	41.66		18.92	22.74
0	21.96	66.98	88.94		23.92	65.02
-1	26.96	133.98	160.94		28.92	132.02
-2	31.96	200.98	232.94		33.92	199.02
-3	36.96	267.98	304.94		38.92	266.02
-4	41.96	334.98	376.94		43.92	333.02

Echelon 1

3.5. Finding a_{ij} for arborescent structures

Fig. 5 shows the simplest multi-echelon, arborescent-configuration system, where the two installations at the lowest level of the system, A_1 and A_2, are fed by installation B. The situation illustrated in fig. 5 will be used to describe how Clark's approach is applied to arborescent configurations.

The assumptions in the previous section for the series-configuration system apply here with the following exception. Demand, exogenous to the system, occurs at all the installations at the lowest level of the system, not at only one installation. The notation defined in the previous section will be used in this section. A more cumbersome method of labeling the installations is employed so that the level as well as the installation is easy to identify.

Using Clark's approach to calculate the inventory policies for the kth period for each echelon of the system, we would proceed as follows:

(1) Assume installations A_1 and A_2 are independent. Determine the inventory policy for A_1 by applying the same method that was used for echelon 1 in the series example, that is, assume stock is available at B to satisfy the order from A_1. Also, calculate Δ_k^{B,A_1}, the additional cost that would be experienced by installation A_1 if installation B cannot satisfy the demand at A_1 during the kth period.

(2) Repeat step (1) for installation A_2, that is, calculate its inventory policy assuming B can satisfy the demand of A_2. Calculate Δ_k^{B,A_2}.

(3) Construct the additional shortage penalty Δ_k^B from the marginal per unit costs associated with Δ_k^{B,A_1} and Δ_k^{B,A_2}. The penalty Δ_k^B is an additional period cost for echelon B during the kth period, in the same manner that the penalty Δ_k^2 was applied to echelon 2 of the example in the previous section.

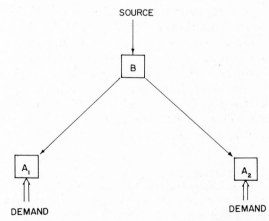

Fig. 5. Three-installation, arborescent-configuration system.

(4) Determine the inventory policy for echelon B. Since a fixed cost of ordering is allowed at installation B, the highest installation in this sytem, the method for determining the two critical numbers (S_k^B, s_k^B) follows the method used for echelon 2 of the series-configuration example.

In short, the method outlined above says to calculate the inventory policies for each echelon separately by the methods used for the classical single-installation situation. This procedure can be extended easily to apply to a situation where B feeds more than two installations or to a system containing more than two levels.

Recall that $\hat{C}_n(x_n^{A1}, x_n^{A2}, x_n^B)$ is the minimum total expected discounted cost for the entire system of this example at the beginning of period n before an order is placed. If the inventory policies calculated by this method are to minimize the total expected discounted cost of the system, it is necessary that

$$\hat{C}_n(x_n^{A1}, x_n^{A2}, x_n^B) = \hat{D}_n^{A1}(x_n^{A1}) + \hat{D}_n^{A2}(x_n^{A2}) + \hat{D}_n^B(x_n^B) . \tag{8}$$

Unfortunately, it has been shown by Clark and Scarf [39] that decomposition (8) does not always hold for the arborescent configuration of installations. They give an argument for such a decomposition by assuming that the stock levels at the lowest installations, in this case A_1 and A_2, are not out of balance. By this they mean that for a given period the ratios of stock on hand after ordering to expected demand are approximately the same for A_1 and A_2 (hence *in balance*). In practical situations they feel that the stock levels at the lowest installations are rarely out of balance, and therefore they conclude that Clark's approach gives excellent approximations, if not optimal solutions, for the best inventory policies of an arborescent configuration. [6]

If the holding, shortage, and transportation costs per unit at each of the lowest level installations are of the same order of magnitude, then it is felt that the stock levels at the lowest installations generally will be in balance. Experience with Clark's approach for obtaining inventory policies of installations arranged in an arborescent configuration indicates that his method is probably quite good. [7]

An assumption was made which should not be overlooked. It was assumed in step (1) that installations A_1 and A_2 were independent. This means that transshipments between A_1 and A_2 are not allowed. Thus, an installation will be allowed to receive stock only from its designated supplier at a level higher in the system.

Clark's approach is now used to obtain the inventory policies for a three-installation, arborescent-configuration problem.

---

[6] The notations $\hat{C}$ and $\hat{D}$ will continue to be used in the remainder of this section, even though it cannot be proven that these are the minimum costs.

[7] Clark [38] used this approach to obtain the inventory policies that were used in the simulation of a large arborescent-configuration system. In personal conversations with him he indicated that the policies produced for this simulation were excellent.

3.6. Three-installation, arborescent-configuration example

Suppose

$$h^*_{A_1}(u_{A_1}) = 2.2u_{A_1} \, ,$$

$$h^*_{A_2}(u_{A_2}) = 2.1u_{A_2} \, ,$$

$$h^*_B(u_B) \quad = 2.0u_B \, ,$$

$$p^*_{A_1}(u_{A_1}) = 72u_{A_1} \, ,$$

$$p^*_{A_2}(u_{A_2}) = 69u_{A_2} \, ,$$

$$p^*_B(u_B) \quad = 5.0u_B \, ,$$

$$c_{A_1}(z) \quad = 5z \, ,$$

$$c_{A_2}(z) \quad = 3z \, ,$$

$$c_B(z) \quad = 50z + 30 \, ,$$

$$\alpha \quad = 1 \, .$$

Using the cost-added concept described in the series-configuration example, the echelon holding and shortage costs are

$$h_{A_1}(u_{A_1}) = 0.2u_{A_1} \, ,$$

$$h_{A_2}(u_{A_2}) = 0.1u_{A_2} \, ,$$

$$h_B(u_B) \quad = 2.0u_B \, ,$$

$$p_{A_1}(u_{A_1}) = 67u_{A_1} \, ,$$

$$p_{A_2}(u_{A_2}) = 64u_{A_2} \, ,$$

$$p_B(u_B) \quad = 5u_B \, .$$

Suppose the demands at installations A_1 and A_2 each follow a Poisson distribution, with mean demand one unit per period. The demand experienced by echelon B is the convolution of the demands experienced by the two installations fed by B. Therefore, the demand at echelon B follows a Poisson distribution, with a mean demand of two units per period.

The calculations for the inventory policies at each echelon for period 1 are now described. We follow the four-step procedure given above.

(1) The costs and demand distribution for echelon A_1 are identical to those given for echelon 1 of the series-configuration example. Therefore, the echelon 1 sec-

D. Gross et al., Designing an inventory system

Table 3

Period 1 solution for echelon A_2 in the arborescent-configuration example

Δ_1^{B,A_2} (7)	$\hat{D}_1^{A_2}(x_1^{A_2})$ (6)	$W_1^{A_2}(x_1^{A_2}) - W_1^{A_2}(x_1^{A_2} - 1)$ (5)	$W_1^{A_2}(\cdot)$ total expected cost before ordering (4)	$L_{A_2}(y_1^{A_2})$ (3)	$\alpha \sum\limits_{t=0}^{\infty} \hat{D}_0^{A_2}(y_1^{A_2} - t)\, \phi_{A_2}(t)$ (2)	Stock level (1)
0.00	0.60	0.10	0.60	0.60	0.00	7
0.00	0.50	0.06	0.50	0.50	0.00	6
0.00	0.44	−0.13	0.44	0.44	0.00	5
0.00	0.57	−1.12	0.57	0.57	0.00	4
0.00	1.69	−5.04	1.69	1.69	0.00	3
2.04	4.69	↑	6.73	6.73	0.00	2
15.87	7.69		23.56	23.56	0.00	1
53.29	10.69		63.98	63.98	0.00	0
114.29	13.69		127.98	127.98	0.00	−1
175.29	16.69		191.98	191.98	0.00	−2
236.29	19.69		255.98	255.98	0.00	−3
297.29	22.69		319.98	319.98	0.00	−4

tion of table 1, columns (1)–(7), gives the calculations for period 1 of echelon A_1 in this example and $S_1^{A_1} = 3$. Column (7) of table 1 is Δ_1^{B,A_1}.

(2) Table 3 gives the calculations for period 1 of echelon A_2. The arrow indicates the location of the critical number and $S_1^{A_2} = 3$.

(3) We now show how Δ_1^{B,A_1} and Δ_1^{B,A_2} are used to construct Δ_1^B. If installation B cannot satisfy the demand from A_1 and A_2, it has a choice of backordering A_1, A_2, or both A_1 and A_2. It desires a plan for backordering that will penalize it the least. For example, if B is short one unit in the first period, it is clear by examining column (7) in table 1 and column (7) in table 3 that it is cheaper to backorder A_1 one unit, where the penalty is \$ 0.19, than to backorder A_2 one unit, where the penalty is \$ 2.04. Similarly, if B were short three units in period 1, it has the following four alternatives:

(a) backorder A_1 three units at a cost of \$ 50.02;
(b) backorder A_1 two units and A_2 one unit at a cost of \$ 12.75 + \$ 2.04 = \$ 14.79;
(c) backorder A_1 one unit and A_2 two units at a cost of \$ 0.19 + \$ 15.87 = \$ 16.06, or
(d) backorder A_2 three units at a cost of \$ 53.29.

Thus, B would choose alternative (b) in order to minimize the cost of not being able to bring the lower installations up to their desired stock levels. It is assumed that installation B will use the minimum cost backordering alternative, and furthermore, that B generally has a choice regarding how much it will backorder each lower level installation. To determine the penalty Δ_1^B for all possible backordering situations, we first calculate the marginal per unit costs associated with

Table 4
Determination of Δ_1^B from Δ_1^{B,A_1} and Δ_1^{B,A_2} for three-installation, arborescent-configuration example

Stock level	Δ_1^{B,A_1}	Marginal Δ_1^{B,A_1}	Δ_1^{B,A_2}	Marginal Δ_1^{B,A_2}	Ranked marginal Δ_1^{B,A_1} and Δ_1^{B,A_2}	Δ_1^B
7	0.00	0.00	0.00	0.00	0.00	0.00
6	0.00	0.00	0.00	0.00	0.00	0.00
5	0.00	0.00	·0.00	0.00	0.19	0.19
4	0.00	0.00	0.00	0.00	2.04	2.23
3	0.00	0.00	0.00	0.00	12.56	14.79
2	0.19	0.19	2.04	2.04	13.83	28.62
1	12.75	12.56	15.87	13.83	37.28	65.90
0	50.02	37.28	53.29	37.42	37.42	103.32
−1	112.02	62.00	114.29	61.00	61.00	164.32
−2	174.02	62.00	175.29	61.00	61.00	225.32
−3	236.02	62.00	236.29	61.00	61.00	286.32
−4	298.02	62.00	297.29	61.00	61.00	347.32

Δ_1^{B,A_1} and Δ_1^{B,A_2}, called marginal Δ_1^{B,A_1} and marginal Δ_1^{B,A_2} in table 4. These give the additional cost for backordering one more unit at A_1 and A_2, respectively. The marginal penalties are then ranked in value, starting with the smallest. The ranked penalties are then successively added to form Δ_1^B. This procedure guarantees that the least cost combination in backordering the lower-level installation is used. These calculations are shown in table 4. The positive ranked marginal Δ_1^{B,A_1} and Δ_1^{B,A_2} start at stock level 5 because if echelon B has less than six units, then either A_1 or A_2 are below their desired level of three units each.

(4) Using the $\Delta_1^B(\cdot)$ from table 4, the inventory policy for echelon B at the beginning of period 1 can be determined. The calculations are shown in table 5 and follow the calculations for echelon 2 of the series-configuration example, given in table 1. The critical numbers as indicated by the arrows are $(S_1^B, s_1^B) = (0, -2)$.

If interest were only in one period of operation for this three-installation arborescent-configuration example, and if the on-hand inventory at each installation at the beginning of period 1 before ordering were zero units, then the total expected discounted cost of the system would be

$$\hat{D}_1^{A_1}(0) + \hat{D}_1^{A_2}(0) + \hat{D}_1^B(0) = \$\ 16.96 + \$\ 10.69 + \$\ 113.32 = \$\ 140.97\ .$$

This would be the inventory cost a_{ij} for the design model. The calculations given here for one period were carried out for 20 periods. The critical numbers for the 20th period, that is, with 20 periods of business remaining, are

$$S_{20}^{A_1} = 5\ , \qquad S_{20}^{A_2} = 5\ , \qquad (S_{20}^B, s_{20}^B) = (11, 3)\ .$$

The total expected discounted cost for 20 periods is $\$\ 2681.29$, and this would represent the inventory cost, a_{ij}, in the design model if we were designing a system to last for 20 time periods.

3.7. Shadow installations

The method just described for obtaining near optimal inventory policies for N installations having an arborescent configuration will be satisfactory for many of the echelon structures to be considered by the design model. But there is one situation which cannot be handled directly by Clark's approach for arborescent configurations. This is the situation in which one or more of the lowest level installations, where exogenous demand exists, is *not* included in the echelon structure. This would be the situation if one or both of installations A_1 or A_2 were removed from the system of fig. 5. For example, fig. 6 shows this system with installation A_2 removed. Although installation A_2 is not physically included in the echelon

Table 5

Period 1 solution for echelon B in the arborescent-configuration example

$\hat{D}_1^B(x_1^B)$ (8)	$\hat{D}_1^B$ assuming always order when $x_1^B < S_1^B$ (7)	$W_1^B(x_1^B) - W_1^B(x_1^B - 1)$ (6)	$W_1^B(\cdot)$ total expected cost before ordering (5)	$L_B(v_1^B)$ (4)	Δ_1^B (3)	$\alpha \sum\limits_{t=0}^{\infty} \hat{D}_0^B(v_1^B - t)\, \phi_B(t)$ (2)	Stock level (1)
10.00	10.00		10.00	10.00	0.00	0.00	7
8.04	8.04	1.96	8.04	8.04	0.00	0.00	6
6.35	6.35	1.69	6.35	6.15	0.19	0.00	5
6.76	6.76	−0.41	6.76	4.35	2.23	0.00	4
18.32	18.32	−11.56	18.32	3.53	14.79	0.00	3
32.41	32.41	−14.09	32.41	3.79	28.62	0.00	2
71.85	71.85	−39.44	71.85	5.95	65.90	0.00	1
113.32	113.32 ↑	−41.47	113.32	10.00	103.32	0.00	0
179.32	193.32	−66.00	179.32	15.00	164.32	0.00	−1
243.32	243.32 ↓		245.32	20.00	225.32	0.00	−2
293.32	293.32		311.32	25.00	286.32	0.00	−3
343.32	343.32		377.32	30.00	347.32	0.00	−4

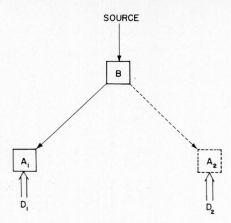

Fig. 6. Arborescent configuration with a shadow installation.

structure of fig. 6, it is represented on the diagram by dashed lines because demand still exists where this installation would be located if it were included in the structure. We call installation A_2 a shadow installation. Any time an echelon structure does not include one of the lowest level installations, that installation is called a shadow installation.

In the echelon structure of fig. 6, demand D_2 must be satisfied by installation B on an individual basis, that is, it is a "mail-order" demand. [8] Suppose we desire to determine the inventory policies for echelons A_1 and B, taking into account that mail-order demand D_2 exists at the location where installation A_2 would be placed if it were included in the system. To do this, we need a method which includes the transportation cost from installation B to the customers represented by D_2, and a penalty cost at B for not satisfying the demand at D_2. There is no need for a holding cost at A_2 since this installation is not in the system. Let

$\overline{p}_i^*$ = the shortage cost per unit for customers at the shadow installation i, and
$\overline{c}_i$ = the transportation cost per unit in getting an item to the customers of shadow installation i from their supplier.

The echelon structure of fig. 6 is used to describe the method for obtaining the inventory policies and a_{ij} for a multi-echelon configuration with a shadow installation. The procedure for the kth period is

---

[8] We use the phrase "mail-order" in referring to these individual demands, but the manner in which they are processed is completely arbitrary, as long as they are processed on an individual basis. Therefore, if the product is of great enough importance to the customer, he will probably telephone the demand to installation B and request an air express delivery.

(1) Assume demand D_2 can only be satisfied by installation B, that is, it cannot be satisfied by installation A_1. Determine the inventory policy for A_1 and Δ_k^{B,A_1} using Clark's approach for arborescent configurations.

(2) No calculations are required for echelon A_2, since installation A_2 does not exist.

(3) To construct Δ_k^B, it is necessary to consider a penalty at echelon B for not being able to satisfy the demand D_2, as well as the demand from A_1. Thus, we need something similar to the marginal per unit cost of Δ_k^{B,A_2}. Whenever a customer from demand D_2 is backordered by installation B, he incurs a cost of $\overline{p}_{A_2}^*$. But part of this cost has already been applied by p_B^*; therefore, using the cost-added concept, we let $\overline{p}_{A_2}$ equal the cost per unit added by penalty $\overline{p}_{A_2}^*$. Then, marginal $\Delta_k^{B,A_2} = \overline{p}_{A_2}$.

(4) The inventory policy for echelon B is determined in the same way that it was found in the arborescent configuration, with the following exception. The period cost, $L_B(\cdot)$, must include the additional cost of meeting the expected demand of D_2, λ_2, or in this case

$$L_B(y_k^B) = \overline{c}_{A_2}\lambda_2 + \sum_{t=0}^{y_k^B} h_B(y_k^B - t)\,\phi_B(t)$$

$$+ \sum_{t=y_k^B+1}^{\infty} p_B(t - y_k^B)\,\phi_B(t), \qquad y_k^B \geqslant 0, \qquad k = 1, 2, \ldots$$

$$= \overline{c}_{A_2}\lambda_2 + \sum_{t=0}^{\infty} p_B(t - y_k^B)\,\phi_B(t), \qquad y_k^B < 0, \qquad k = 1, 2, \ldots .$$

4. The design problem with storage space constraints

In this section we generalize the design problem formulated in section 2 to allow for storage space constraints at the various facilities. The resulting model yields a 0–1 *linear* programming problem, which includes the previously discussed design problem without capacity constraints as a special case.

Formulation of the design problem with capacity constraints requires notation in addition to that given in section 2, and, for convenience, we give here all notation used in the model. The echelon structures are indexed by i, $i = 1, \ldots, m$; the products are indexed by j, $j = 1, \ldots, n$; the installations are indexed by k, $k = 1, \ldots, p$. Let

a_{ij} = the inventory cost of product j using echelon structure i,

b_k = the facility cost of installation k,

r_k = the storage space available at installation k, and

d_{ijk} = the storage space required at installation k for product j when product j uses echelon structure i.

The d_{ijk} values could be measured on the basis of either the *maximum* space required (over time) or the *average* space required (over time). The former seems more appropriate for this type of design problem, and the r_k values must then be determined accordingly. Note that the d_{ijk}, $k = 1, ..., p$, values are obtained as outputs of the multi-echelon inventory problem solved in calculating a_{ij}. Thus $d_{ijk} = 0$ for all $j = 1, ..., n$ if echelon structure i does *not* use installation k.

The decision variables are:

$x_{ij} = 1$ if product j uses echelon structure i ,

$= 0$ otherwise ,

$y_k = 1$ if installation k is used ,

$= 0$ otherwise .

The problem, henceforth called problem (P), is then to find x_{ij} and y_k values that

$$\text{minimize} \quad \sum_{i=1}^{m}\sum_{j=1}^{n} a_{ij}x_{ij} + \sum_{k=1}^{p} b_k y_k \tag{9}$$

subject to

$$\sum_{i=1}^{m} x_{ij} = 1 , \qquad j = 1, ..., n , \tag{10}$$

$$\sum_{i=1}^{m}\sum_{j=1}^{n} d_{ijk}x_{ij} - r_k y_k \leqslant 0 , \qquad k = 1, ..., p , \tag{11}$$

$$x_{ij}, y_k = 0 \text{ or } 1 , \qquad \text{for all } i, j, k . \tag{12}$$

Comparison of this formulation with that of section 2 shows that the objective functions (1) and (9) are equivalent and constraints (2) and (10) are the same. The constraints (11) serve to impose the storage space limitations at the same time that they force the use of an installation if any echelon structure using it is chosen. If $y_k = 0$ and $d_{ijk} > 0$, then x_{ij} must be 0 in order to satisfy (11). Note that the previous formulation without storage space constraints can be easily obtained as a special case of problem (P) by letting d_{ijk} equal 1 if echelon structure i uses installation k (and 0 otherwise) and setting all r_k equal to n.

Problem (P) bears a resemblance to the well-known fixed-charge location-allocation problem (or capacitated facility location problem) — see, e.g., Geoffrion [85] or Ross and Soland [195]. There are very significant differences between the two, however, and to point this out we first give a statement of the location-allocation problem, henceforth called problem (L−A), in a form resembling problem (P). Problem (L−A) is to find x_{kj} and y_k values that

minimize

$$\sum_{k=1}^{p} \sum_{j=1}^{n} a_{kj} x_{kj} + \sum_{k=1}^{p} b_k y_k \tag{13}$$

subject to

$$\sum_{k=1}^{m} x_{kj} = 1, \qquad j = 1, ..., n, \tag{14}$$

$$\sum_{j=1}^{n} d_j x_{kj} - r_k y_k \leqslant 0, \qquad k = 1, ..., p, \tag{15}$$

$$x_{kj} \geqslant 0, \qquad y_k = 0 \text{ or } 1, \qquad \text{for all } j, k. \tag{16}$$

Here x_{kj} is interpreted as the fraction of customer j's demand that is supplied by a facility at location k. In problem (L−A) there is a direct connection between the assignments made and the facilities required and each assignment affects only one facility; i.e., the assignment $x_{kj} > 0$ has a bearing on only *one* of the constraints (15) and therefore on only one variable y_k. In contrast, in problem (P) the connection between the assignments made and the facilities required is indirect, and each assignment may affect several facilities; i.e., the assignment $x_{ij} = 1$ bears on *all* of the constraints (11) for which $d_{ijk} > 0$. Now consider the relative difficulty of the two problems. While problem (L−A) is not easy to solve, branch and bound approaches have been successful in dealing with it because once values are specified for the y_k the x_{kj} are found by solving a transportation problem. Problem (L−A) becomes more difficult if the constraints $x_{kj} \geqslant 0$ in (16) are replaced by $x_{kj} = 0$ or 1 in order to preclude supply of customer j's demand by more than one facility. With this change, problem (L−A) may be treated as a generalized assignment problem (GAP), an integer programming problem for which a relatively efficient branch and bound algorithm exists (see Ross and Soland [195] for details). Problem (P) is more difficult than this variation of problem (L−A) because of the indirect connections between assignments and facilities mentioned above. Note that even after values have been specified for all the y_k, problem (P) remains a difficult 0−1 linear programming problem because of the interaction of the constraints (11).

The design problem with storage space constraints has been formulated in this section as a 0−1 LP problem. In the next section we illustrate its use for designing a multi-product, multi-echelon inventory distribution system.

5. Illustration of models

This section presents illustrative computational results using the three models given in this paper — the dynamic programming model to find optimal inventory policies for a multi-echelon distribution system, the design model without storage space constraints, and the design model with storage space constraints. The section concludes with a discussion of some problems yet to be resolved.

5.1. Illustration

In this illustration five alternative echelon structures, which include up to three echelons and eight facilities, are being considered for the design of a four-product, multi-echelon inventory distribution system. The five echelon structures are shown in fig. 7. Echelon structure 1 is the full system, that is, it consists of the maximum number of facilities under consideration (a central warehouse, two regional ware-

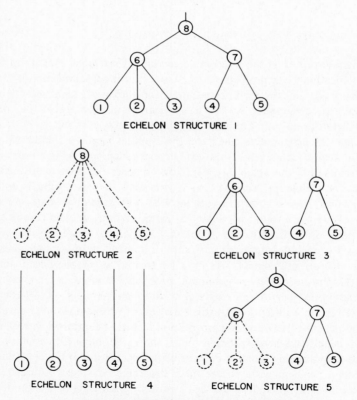

Fig. 7. The five echelon structures used in the illustration.

houses, and five retail stores) arranged in three echelons. Although eight facilities generate $2^8 = 256$ possible echelon structures, only the four additional echelon structures shown are being considered for this system. Echelon structure 2 is a one-echelon system with mail order delivery from the central warehouse to customers located where the retail stores would be if they were in the system. Echelon structure 3 is a two-echelon system without a central warehouse. In this case the two regional warehouses are supplied directly by the sources of production. Echelon structure 4 is a single-echelon system where the retail stores are supplied with products directly from the sources of production, while echelon structure 5 is similar to echelon structure 1, with the exception that customers at retail stores 1, 2, and 3 are supplied by mail order from regional warehouse 6.

The dynamic programming approach, described in section 3, was used to find the multi-echelon inventory policies and the resulting a_{ij}'s for the four products of this example. Table 6 summarizes the input data needed to obtain these policies. It is assumed that the stock levels of this inventory system are reviewed quarterly and the demand for each product has a Poisson distribution, with the mean demand per quarter assumed to be the same at each retail store. If echelon structure 1 is used to stock a product, it is generally assumed that the cost to transport the product from the central warehouse (facility 8) to one of the retail stores is 6% of the procurement cost, that is, the cost to get the product to facility 8. [9] Referred to in table 6 as "normal" transportation cost, this cost is divided evenly between the cost to move the product between facility 8 and one of the regional warehouses (facility 6 or 7) and the cost to move the product between the regional warehouse and one of the retail stores.

In the case of echelon structures with shadow installations, the transportation costs to satisfy mail-order demands will generally increase significantly. Table 6 shows these costs as a percentage of the normal transportation costs described above. Also shown are the changes in transportation cost when either the central warehouse or regional warehouses are not used to stock a given product. For products 1 and 2 we assume under such a two-echelon system that there would be no change from the normal transportation cost, whereas with products 3 and 4 it is assumed that the transportation costs double (200% of normal cost) under these circumstances. Tables 6 also gives the holding and stockout penalty costs used in this illustration. The holding costs per quarter range from 2% to 8% of the total cost to get the product to the facility where this holding cost is incurred. The shortage costs at the retail stores (or shadow installations) vary from 110% to 190% of the cost to get a product to these stores. At facilities other than the retail stores, a shortage cost equal to 10% of the facility's holding cost is applied to cover the nuisance created by backordering.

---

[9] In two cases, for products 2 and 4 transported to retail stores 4 and 5, this cost is assumed to be 3% of the procurement cost.

Table 6

Input data needed to find multi-echelon inventory policies for four-product example

Product	Mean demand at each retail store (units per quarter)	Costs per unit						
		Procurement cost ($)	Normal transportation cost to retail stores 1–3 (% of procurement cost)	Normal transportation cost to retail stores 4 and 5 (% of procurement cost)	Mail order transportation cost (% of normal transportation cost)	Transportation cost without central or regional warehouses (% of normal transportation cost)	Holding cost (% of procurement plus transportation costs)	Stockout penalty cost at retail stores (% of procurement plus transportation costs)
1	0.2	7000	6	6	1500	100	5	150
2	0.2	9000	6	3	1500	100	2	110
3	0.2	5000	6	6	500	200	8	190
4	1.3	700	6	3	1500	200	8	190

Finally, the following data or characteristics were assumed to be common to all the products:

(1) the life of the system is 20 quarters (five years), that is, each product is stocked for 20 quarters,
(2) there is no inventory on hand at the beginning of the first period of operation,
(3) the interest rate is $1\frac{1}{2}\%$ per quarter, resulting in a discount factor of 0.985, and
(4) the fixed cost of ordering is $ 100.

Table 7 gives the dynamic programming results. The a_{ij} represent the total expected discounted cost for stocking product j under echelon structure i for 20 quarters, and the inventory policies shown are for the 20th quarter. The computer program written to generate these results also gives the order policies at each facility for each of the 20 periods. It is interesting to note that steady-state policies were generally reached quickly. With the exception of three of the 20 results, the policy shown for the 20th quarter was reached by the fifth quarter, and sometimes sooner.

Two types of inventory policies, S and (S, s), are shown in table 7. At the highest level facility in a system (the facility that orders the product from the source of production) it is assumed that a fixed cost of ordering is incurred, hence (S, s) type policies result. Since there is no fixed cost of ordering at other facilities, S type policies are found. The time to calculate these critical numbers and to find the inventory costs, a_{ij}, averaged 30 seconds per product for a given echelon structure on an IBM 360/50 computer.

The major computational limitation to the efficiency of this dynamic programming procedure for finding inventory policies is the magnitude of the demand. Products with large demands could be handled by scaling, that is, considering units in sizes of tens or hundreds. The number of periods can be readily extended, although under stationary conditions this would not be necessary since policies seem to stabilize quickly.

Next we determine the best design for this four-product system, using the model given in section 2, that is, we assume there are no constraints on the amount of space available at each of the facilities where products might be stored. The inventory costs, a_{ij}, given in table 7, and the facility costs, b_{ik}, for this problem are arrayed by echelon structure i in fig. 8. The facility costs are consistent with values found in previous research (see Pinkus [176]) and take into account the fact that the fixed cost of operating a warehouse, in proportion to the value of goods that might be stocked there, is less than the fixed cost of operating a retail store, due to economies of scale and lower property values.

The solution to this problem is to stock all four products under echelon structure 5, which means that each product will be stocked at retail stores 4 and 5 and at warehouses 6, 7, and 8. The total (5-year) expected discounted cost of this solution is $ 766,000. It is interesting to note that of the four products, only products 1 and

Table 7

Inventory policies and resulting a_{ij} for four-product example

Echelon structure (i)	Product (j)	a_{ij}	Total expected discounted inventory cost (a_{ij}) for 20 quarters (\$ × 1000)	S or (S, s) inventory policy at facility k							
				1	2	3	4	5	6	7	8
1	1	a_{11}	195	2	2	2	2	2	6	4	(5, 4)
2	1	a_{21}	235	—	—	—	—	—	—	—	(1, 0)
3	1	a_{31}	196	2	2	2	2	2	(3, 2)	(2, 1)	—
4	1	a_{41}	199	(1, 0)	(1, 0)	(1, 0)	(1, 0)	(1, 0)	—	—	—
5	1	a_{51}	191	—	—	—	2	3	6	4	(3, 2)
1	2	a_{12}	219	3	3	3	3	3	6	6	(5, 4)
2	2	a_{22}	272	—	—	—	—	—	—	—	(1, 0)
3	2	a_{32}	221	3	3	3	3	3	(3, 2)	(2, 1)	—
4	2	a_{42}	224	(1, 0)	(1, 0)	(1, 0)	(1, 0)	(1, 0)	—	—	—
5	2	a_{52}	229	—	—	—	3	3	1	6	(3, 2)
1	3	a_{13}	155	2	2	2	2	2	6	4	(5, 4)
2	3	a_{23}	143	—	—	—	—	—	—	—	(1, 0)
3	3	a_{33}	160	2	2	2	2	2	(3, 2)	(2, 1)	—
4	3	a_{43}	167	(1, 0)	(1, 0)	(1, 0)	(1, 0)	(1, 0)	—	—	—
5	3	a_{53}	128	—	—	—	2	2	1	4	(3, 2)
1	4	a_{14}	104	6	6	6	6	6	15	12	(20, 14)
2	4	a_{24}	139	—	—	—	—	—	—	—	(6, 5)
3	4	a_{34}	107	6	6	6	6	6	(12, 8)	(8, 5)	—
4	4	a_{44}	112	(4, 2)	(4, 2)	(4, 2)	(4, 2)	(4, 2)	—	—	—
5	4	a_{54}	112	—	—	—	6	6	4	12	(10, 9)

| | | PRODUCT (j) | | | | | | FACILITY (k) | | | | |
	1	2	3	4		1	2	3	4	5	6	7	8
ECHELON STRUCTURE (i) 1	195	219	155	104		14	14	14	14	14	28	19	31
2	235	272	143	139		0	0	0	0	0	0	0	31
3	196	221	160	107		14	14	14	14	14	28	19	0
4	199	224	167	112		14	14	14	14	14	0	0	0
5	191	229	128	112		0	0	0	14	14	28	19	31

Fig. 8. Array of inventory costs and facility costs for four-product example.

3 use the echelon structure that minimizes their inventory cost. If products 2 and 4 were to use echelon structure 1, which minimizes their inventory cost, the fixed cost of the system would increase because products 2 and 4 would now be stocked at retail stores 1–3, as well as at facilities 4–8. Under this solution the savings in inventory cost do not compensate for the increased facility cost, and the total cost of the system is $ 790,000.

The solution to this problem was obtained in 11 seconds on an IBM 370/148 using the branch-and-bound algorithm described in Pinkus, Gross and Soland [178]. Although initially written to handle 10 echelon structures, 30 products, and 30 facilities, the computer program for this algorithm can easily be expanded to handle larger values of m, n, and p.

Finally, we have solved the same problem with storage space constraints using the model presented in section 4. The storage space available at each facility, r_k, is given in table 8, and the amount of storage space required for each product is given in table 9. To find d_{ijk}, we multiply the per unit storage space required to stock product j (see table 9) by the maximum number of units (S) that will be stocked at facility k when echelon structure i is used (see table 7). For example, $d_{1,1,1}$ is 800

Table 8
Storage space available at each facility

Facility (k)	r_k (ft^2)
1	3,500
2	3,500
3	3,500
4	2,000
5	2,000
6	7,000
7	5,000
8	8,000

Table 9
Storage space required by each product

Product (j)	Storage space required per unit (ft^2)
1	400
2	300
3	500
4	300

(that is, 400×2), $d_{2,2,6}$ is 900 (that is, 300×3), and $d_{5,4,8}$ is 3,000 (that is, 300×10).

The solution to the problem with space constraints is to stock products 1, 2, and 4 under echelon structure 4, and product 3 under echelon structure 2, that is, products 1, 2, and 4 are stocked only at the retail stores, which are supplied directly by the sources of production, and product 3 is stocked only at the central warehouse (facility 8), from which customers receive product 3 by mail order. The total (5-year) expected discounted cost for this solution is $ 779,000. In this case, none of the products are stocked under the echelon structure that minimizes the inventory cost for a given product. This solution was obtained in 145 seconds using a 0—1 linear programming computer code run on a Hewlett-Packard HP3000 computer.

5.2. Discussion

We conclude this paper with a discussion of some problems yet to be resolved.

The design model with storage space constraints, problem (P), has $mn + p$ 0—1 variables and $n + p$ constraints, so the problem dimensions may be fairly high for problems of practical size. For example, with $m = n = 30$ and $p = 20$, problem (P) has 920 variables and 50 constraints. The 0—1 LP computer code used to solve the design problem with storage space constraints in the previous section can handle only 40 variables and 20 constraints. This fact, together with the special structure of problem (P), suggests that a specialized algorithm for its solution would be much more efficient for practical problems than the general integer linear programming algorithm that was used to get the results in section 5.1. Such a special algorithm is presently being developed and tested.

There is another aspect of this work that needs to be examined. It can be shown that the model with space constraints, problem (P), might not obtain the best solution to this design problem. This is because we have restricted ourselves to using the optimal inventory policy and resulting a_{ij} for a given product stocked under a given echelon structure. With the introduction of space constraints, a situation can occur where by making a reduction in the optimal value of S for a given product, we might be able to satisfy a space constraint that would not otherwise be satisfied. Such a reduction in S would yield a sub-optimal (greater) value for a_{ij}, but this increased inventory cost could be compensated for by the reduction in facility cost resulting from enabling the product to be squeezed into a set of facilities used by other products. We plan to investigate several heuristic solution methods in order to allow the possibility of using sub-optimal inventory policies to reduce the total cost of the system.

Acknowledgments

The authors wish to thank Krishan L. Chhabra for assistance in obtaining some of the results given in section 5. The authors also wish to express their appreciation to the Office of Naval Research for their support of this work under Contract N00014-75-C-0729, Project NR 347 020.

TIMS Studies in the Management Sciences 16 (1981) 51–67

CENTRALIZED ORDERING POLICIES IN A MULTI-WAREHOUSE SYSTEM WITH LEAD TIMES AND RANDOM DEMAND

Gary EPPEN and Linus SCHRAGE

University of Chicago

This paper models a depot—warehouse system with independent normally distributed stationary demand (known parameters) at the warehouses, identical proportional costs of holding and backordering at the warehouses, and no transshipment. The operating policy is periodic review and the depot does not hold inventory. Under an assumption that the incoming order is large enough so that an equal probability of stockout can be achieved at each warehouse, the paper derives approximately optimal policies and costs of: (1) a base stock policy at the depot, assuming no fixed order costs, and (2) an (m, y) policy at the depot, assuming fixed order costs at the depot. An (m, y) policy is one in which every m periods the system inventory position is raised to a base stock of y.

1. Introduction

In certain industries, particularly steel, important considerations are the long lead times and the highly random demand at the "retail" end of the system. We consider a distribution system consisting of a supplier, a depot, and N warehouses, with material flowing from supplier, to depot, to warehouse, in order to satisfy random demand at the warehouses.

The parameters and variables of the system are:

N = number of warehouses,

e_{ij} = demand at warehouse i in period j, an independent normally distributed random variable assumed stationary over time,

μ_i = mean demand per period at warehouse i, i.e., the expected value of e_{ij},

σ_i = standard deviation in demand per period at i,

L = lead time (a constant) from the supplier to the depot,

l = lead time (a constant) from the depot to any warehouse,

h = holding cost per unit per period; this is assumed the same for all warehouses plus the depot,

p = penalty cost per unit of demand backlogged per period at any warehouse,

K = fixed cost of making a shipment from the supplier to the depot, and

I_{it} = inventory on hand plus that already allocated to warehouse i at the beginning of period t.

We shall also assume that unsatisfied demand is backlogged and the material is non-perishable.

We will restrict our attention to the case in which the depot does not hold any inventory. There are two physical interpretations of this assumption. The obvious one is

(a) Goods are physically shipped from the supplier to the depot, where supplier orders are "broken" into smaller lots and shipped to the warehouses, possibly after having been delayed at the depot for a while.

The other interpretation is

(b) Goods are physically shipped directly from the supplier to warehouses. The depot is only an order-coordinating center.

In interpretation (b), the lead time L is the production lead time at the supplier, while the lead time l is the transportation lead time from the supplier to the warehouse.

There are two justifications for inserting this type of depot between the supplier and the warehouses:

(1) exploit quantity discounts available from the supplier as a result of combining orders from several warehouses, and
(2) exploit the "portfolio efficiencies" or "statistical economies of scale" which are possible by carrying, at least in part, a single-system inventory rather than N individual inventories.

These factors suggest that the depots may be especially useful in an industry like steel where the production lead times are large compared to the delivery times and quantity discounts are an important consideration. Of course, a depot that could hold inventory might also be useful in such circumstances. However, a depotless firm can typically adjust its operation relatively easily to a depot that does not hold inventory. In contrast, there may well be major capital needs as well as a significant lead time required to produce the physical plant and the operating system required for an inventory control system based on a central warehouse that can hold inventory. Further, it is not at all clear that a depot system that holds inventory is more economical than one that does not. Thus, for our purposes, a depot that cannot hold inventory seemed to be an appropriate object for investigation.

The models we will consider fall within the class of multi-echelon, multi-period inventory models in which demand at each location is a sequence of independent, identically-distributed random variables. There is a vast literature that is related to this class of problems. Summaries of many of the results and extensive bibliographies are available in the summary articles by Veinott [236], Aggarwal [3], and Clark [34]. More specifically, our models might be described as allocation models, that is, models in which, in addition to the ordering decision, there is an opportunity to allocate (operate on in a more general sense) the inventory on hand. There is also a fairly large literature in this area. In three early papers, [5], [6], and [7], Allen considers a one-period model in which inventory is reallocated among N locations in order to minimize transportation and penalty costs. Gross [87] presents a two-location, one-period model in which each location can order from a warehouse or transship from one location to the other. Some consideration is given to the N-location and multi-period problems. Das [50] also develops a one-period transshipment model. In his model the reallocation occurs during the period and is not part of the ordering decision. Simpson [217] considers a problem with repairable items and derives results that are much like those found by Eppen and Fama [64] for the three asset cash balance problems. Karmarkar and Patel use nonlinear programming to investigate a one-period N-location distribution problem. This type of approach is exploited by Karmarkar sometimes in concert with a co-author in several related papers − [1], [2], [115], [114], and [112]. On pages 331−352 of this volume Karmarkar investigates the relationship among many of these models. Other related works include the multi-product models of Ignall and Veinott [106] and Veinott [235], as well as the capital allocation model of Iglehart and Lalchandani [105]. Finally, some of the literature dealing with perishable items is related, especially the papers by Yen [245] and Prastacos [180].

This paper will consider two models. In one, the depot will order items from the supplier and allocate them to the warehouse each period. In the other, the depot does its ordering and allocation every m periods. This difference in operating policy is motivated by the absence or presence of a fixed ordering cost at the depot. In both models, the depot uses a base stock policy, that is, every m periods the depot orders enough items to bring the inventory on hand, plus on order, up to a predetermined level. An approximately optimal operating policy and its associated expected cost are considered for each of these models in sections 3 and 4, respectively. The results are approximate because certain assumptions are made in order to obtain results that are relatively simple and have some potential for influencing actual practice. The most important assumption is referred to as the Allocation Assumption and it is considered in some detail in section 2.

2. The Allocation Assumption

The Allocation Assumption implies that each time an allocation is made, the depot receives enough material from the supplier to be able to allocate the material to each warehouse so that an equal fractile point is achieved on an appropriately chosen demand distribution. This distribution is the $l + m − 1$ fold convolution of the single-period demand at each location. In other words, we assume:

Allocation Assumption: In each allocation period, t, the depot receives sufficient goods from the supplier so that each warehouse can be allocated goods in sufficient quantity to ensure that the probability of stockout in period $t + l + m - 1$ is the same at all warehouses.

Consider the order-every-period-model ($m = 1$). At the beginning of period t, the depot will order $\Sigma_{i=1}^{N} e_{i,t-1}$ items. This order arrives at the depot after the lead time L, and is allocated to the warehouses. The allocation is intended to return the warehouses to an equal fractile position. Suppose the warehouses were in an equal fractile position at the beginning of period $t + L - 1$. At warehouse i, the condition is disturbed by the occurrence of the demand $e_{i,t+L-1}$. The question is, then, whether $\Sigma_{i=1}^{N} e_{i,t-1}$ is sufficient to repair the damage done by the $e_{i,t+L-1}$ for $i = 1, 2, ...,$ N, that is, to return the system to an equal fractile position. Note that $e_{i,t-1}$ and $e_{i,t+L-1}$ are independent observations from the same distribution.

Lemma 1.   If the system was in an equal fractile position at the beginning of a period, it can be returned to an equal fractile position if

$$\sum_{i=1}^{N} e_{i,t+1} \geqslant \max_{j=1,...,N} \left\{ \sum_{i \neq j} e_{i,t+L-1} + e_{j,t+L-1}\left(1 - \frac{\Sigma \sigma_i}{\sigma_j}\right) \right\}. \tag{1}$$

Proof.   At the beginning of period $t + L - 1$, the inventory on hand, plus on order, is equal to the same fractile point of the $l + m - 1$ convolution of the demand distribution at each location. Because e_{ij} is $N(\mu_i, \sigma_i)$, it follows that

$$I_{i,t+L-1} = l\mu_i + k_1 \sqrt{(l)}\,\sigma_i, \qquad i = 1, ..., N. \tag{2}$$

The demand $e_{i,t+L-1}$ then occurs. The order placed at time t which equals $\Sigma_{i=1}^{N}$ $e_{i,t-1}$ arrives and we allocate a_i units to location i. Thus,

$$I_{i,t+L} = l\mu_i + k_1 \sqrt{(l)}\,\sigma_i - e_{i,t+L-1} + a_i. \tag{3}$$

An equal fractile position can be achieved if one can find a set of a_i's such that

$$\sum_{i=1}^{N} a_i = \sum_{i=1}^{N} e_{i,t-1} \quad \text{and} \quad a_i \geqslant 0, \qquad i = 1, ..., N,$$

and

$$I_{i,t+L} = l\mu_i + k_2 \sqrt{(l)}\,\sigma_i, \qquad i + 1, ..., N.$$

Thus,

$$a_i = (k_2 - k_1)\sqrt{(l)}\,\sigma_i + e_{i,t+L-1} \tag{4}$$

and

$$\sum_{i=1}^{N} a_i = \sum_{i=1}^{N} e_{i,t-1} = (k_2 - k_1)\sqrt{(l)}\sum_{i=1}^{N} \sigma_i + \sum_{i=1}^{N} e_{i,t+L-1} . \qquad (5)$$

Solving for $(k_2 - k_1)$ and substituting yields

$$a_i = \frac{\left(\sum_{i=1}^{N} e_{i,t-1} - \sum_{i=1}^{N} e_{i,t+L-1}\right)}{\sqrt{(l)}\sum_{i=1}^{N} \sigma_i} \sqrt{(l)}\sigma_i + e_{i,t+L-1} . \qquad (6)$$

Note that

$$a_j \geq 0$$

if

$$\sum_{i=1}^{N} e_{i,t-1} \geq \sum_{i=1}^{N} e_{i,t+L-1} - \frac{\sum_{i=1}^{N} \sigma_i}{\sigma_i} e_{i,t+L-1} . \qquad (7)$$

All $a_j \geq 0$, if

$$\sum_{i=1}^{N} e_{i,t-1} \geq \max_{\substack{j=1,\ldots,N}} \left\{ \sum_{\substack{i=1 \\ i \neq j}}^{N} e_{i,t+L-1} + e_{j,t+L-1}\left(1 - \frac{\sum_{i=1}^{N} \sigma_i}{\sigma_j}\right)\right\} \quad \text{QED} . \qquad (8)$$

Lemma 1 can be used to approximate the probability that the Allocation Assumption is satisfied in a given period. The word approximate is used advisedly for two reasons: (i) in an ongoing system, one cannot be sure that an equal fractile state existed in the previous period, and (ii) we can only offer an approximation for the required probability.

Note that

$$\text{prob} \left[\left\{ \sum_{i=1}^{N} e_{i,t-1} - \sum_{\substack{i=1 \\ i \neq j}}^{N} e_{i,t+L-1} - e_{j,t+L-1}\left(1 - \frac{\sum_{i=1}^{N} \sigma_i}{\sigma_j}\right)\right\} \geq 0 \right] \quad \text{for } j = 1, \ldots, N$$

$$\geq 1 - \sum_{j=1}^{N} \text{prob}\left[\left\{ \sum_{i=1}^{N} e_{i,t-1} - \sum_{\substack{i=1 \\ i \neq j}}^{N} e_{i,t+L-1}\right.\right.$$

$$\left.\left. - e_{j,t+L-1}\left(1 - \frac{\sum_{i=1}^{N} \sigma_i}{\sigma_j}\right)\right\} < 0 \right] \qquad (9)$$

This is Bonferroni's inequality; see Miller [149].

If all warehouses are the same, that is $\mu_i = \mu$, $\sigma_i = \sigma$, then

$$\sum_{i=1}^{N} e_{i,t-1} - \sum_{\substack{i=1 \\ i \neq j}}^{N} e_{i,t+L-1} - e_{j,t+L-1}\left(1 - \frac{\sum \sigma_i}{\sigma_j}\right) \tag{10}$$

is normally distributed with expectation $N\mu$ and standard deviation $N\sigma$. In this case, the Bonferroni inequality allows us to conclude:

$$P\{\text{equal fractile allocation}\} \geqslant 1 - N\Phi(-\mu/\sigma).$$

Table 1 contains the evaluation of this lower bound for various combinations of the parameters.

A simulation study was used to investigate the goodness of the previous approximations as an estimate of the probability of achieving an equal fractile allocation. For each combination of parameters $(N, \mu/\sigma)$, a sample of 10,000 periods was used. The results are presented in table 2.

The data in tables 1 and 2 reveal that the approximation is quite good. They also show that if μ/σ is large, then the Allocation Assumption is satisfied with high probability. Using an exponential distribution substantially increased the probabilities for corresponding sets of parameters.

All of the results concerning the Allocation Assumption have been derived for the order-every-period model ($m = 1$). However, with an appropriate change in the values of μ and σ the same results hold for any m. If we think of each ordering

Table 1

N	μ/σ				
	0.50	1.00	1.50	2.00	2.50
2	0.38	0.68	0.87	0.95	0.99
3	0.07	0.52	0.80	0.93	0.98
4	0	0.37	0.73	0.91	0.98
5	0	0.21	0.67	0.89	0.97
6	0	0.05	0.60	0.86	0.96
7	0	0	0.53	0.84	0.96
8	0	0	0.47	0.82	0.95

Table 2

N	0.500	1.000	1.500	2.000	2.500	Exponential demand $\mu/\sigma = 1$
2	0.326	0.663	0.858	0.952	0.988	0.704
3	0.201	0.547	0.798	0.930	0.981	0.635
4	0.114	0.431	0.733	0.901	0.973	0.594
5	0.076	0.365	0.686	0.883	0.965	0.588
6	0.046	0.299	0.632	0.864	0.961	0.565
7	0.028	0.245	0.591	0.841	0.955	0.560
8	0.016	0.204	0.543	0.820	0.946	0.552

interval as a period, exactly the same analysis goes through. Obviously, the parameters of demand in the ordering interval are $m\mu$, $\sqrt{(m)}\ \sigma$. Thus, the ratio of mean demand to the standard deviation increases proportionally to the square root of m.

We know m increases as K, the fixed cost of making a shipment from the supplier to the depot, increases. We conclude that when K is large, the probability that the Allocation Assumption will hold is also large.

3. The order-every-period model

The first model considered is appropriate when the fixed cost K is small relative to the holding cost h. In this case, we assume the depot and each warehouse place an order each period.

We assume that the following sequence of events occurs each period at the depot and warehouses:

(1) The state of the system is observed and any orders are placed.
(2) Any orders scheduled to arrive this period arrive. The depot allocates stock to warehouses as dictated by the policy used.
(3) Demand occurs.
(4) Holding and penalty costs are incurred.

Any unsatisfied demand is backlogged.

We start by assuming that the depot follows a policy of ordering an amount from the supplier at the beginning of each period so as to bring the total system stock (on hand and on order) up to a number y. There are two questions: (a) what should be the value of y?; and (b) how should stock be allocated to warehouses as it becomes available for distribution at the depot?

Suppose that at the beginning of period 1 an order is placed that brings the total system stock up to y. Define:

$$V = \sum_{t=1}^{L} \sum_{j=1}^{N} e_{jt} \, ,$$

$$W_i = \sum_{t=L+1}^{L+l} e_{it} \, .$$

Thus, V is the total system demand during the first L periods and W_i is the total demand at warehouse i during periods $L + 1$ through $L + l$.

At the beginning of period $L + 1$ there are $y - V$ units in the system. If the e_{it} are Normal distributed and independent, and x_i is the amount allocated to warehouse i, then the stock on hand at i at the end of period $L + l$ has expectation $x_i - (l + 1) \mu_i$ and standard deviation $\sigma_i \sqrt{(l + 1)}$. Note that x_i includes those items that were already at i, plus the new items that were assigned to i.

The Allocation Assumption implies that the $y - V$ units in the system can be allocated, so an equal fractile allocation is achieved. Equal fractile allocation and Normal demands imply that the allocation in period $L + 1$ should be such that there exists a scalar ν such that

$$\sum_{i=1}^{N} x_i = \sum_{i} [(l + 1) \mu_i + \nu \sigma_i \sqrt{(l + 1)}] = y - V \, . \tag{11}$$

Solving for ν and substituting yields

$$x_j = (l + 1) \mu_j + \left(y - V - \sum_{k=1}^{N} (l + 1) \mu_k \right) \sigma_j \Big/ \sum_{i=1}^{N} \sigma_i \, . \tag{12}$$

Thus, if the system stock is brought up to y and equal fractile allocation is used, the (random) stock level, S_j, at the end of period $L + l$ at warehouse j will be

$$S_j = (l + 1) \mu_j + \left(y - V - \sum_{k=1}^{N} (l + 1) \mu_k \right) \sigma_j \Big/ \sum_{i=1}^{N} \sigma_i - W_j \, . \tag{13}$$

Thus, under this policy the expected one-period cost at warehouse j is

$$\int_{0}^{\infty} hx \, \mathrm{d}F_{S_j}(x) - \int_{-\infty}^{0} px \, \mathrm{d}F_{S_j}(x) \, . \tag{14}$$

When $S_j = s - \xi_j$, where s is a constant, the expression can be written

$$\int_{0}^{s} h(s - x) \, \mathrm{d}G(x) + \int_{s}^{\infty} p(x - s) \, \mathrm{d}G(x) \, , \tag{15}$$

where $G_j(\cdot)$ is the c.d.f. of ξ_j.

Note that

$$S_j = (l+1)\,\mu_j + \left(y - \sum_{k=1}^{N} (l+1)\,\mu_k\right) \sigma_j \bigg/ \sum_{k=1}^{N} \sigma_k$$

$$- \left(W_j + \left[\sigma_j \bigg/ \sum_{k=1}^{N} \sigma_k\right] V\right). \tag{16}$$

Thus, by letting

$$s = (l+1)\,\mu_j + \left(y - \sum_{k=1}^{N} (l+1)\,\mu_k\right) \sigma_j \bigg/ \sum_{k=1}^{N} \sigma_k \tag{17}$$

and

$$\xi_j = W_j + \left[\sigma_j \bigg/ \sum_{k=1}^{N} \sigma_k\right] V, \tag{18}$$

we see that expression (15) represents the expected one-period cost at warehouse j. The usual Newsboy arguments indicate that the optimal value for s is provided by the expression

$$G_j(s) = \frac{p}{p+h}. \tag{19}$$

When demand at warehouse j has a Normal distribution with parameters (μ_j, σ_j) we note that ξ_j is also Normal with parameters $\hat{\mu}_j, \hat{\sigma}_j$. The parameters are

$$\hat{\mu}_j = (l+1)\,\mu_j + \left[\sigma_j \bigg/ \sum_{k=1}^{N} \sigma_k\right] L \sum_{k=1}^{N} \mu_k \tag{20}$$

and

$$\hat{\sigma}_j = \left[\left(\sigma_j \bigg/ \sum_{k=1}^{N} \sigma_k\right)^2 L \sum_{k=1}^{N} \sigma_k^2 + (l+1)\,\sigma_j^2\right]^{1/2}. \tag{21}$$

Thus,

$$G_j(s) = \Phi(z),$$

where $\Phi(\cdot)$ is the c.d.f. of the standard normal distribution and

$$z = \frac{\left(\sigma_j \bigg/ \sum\limits_{k=1}^{N} \sigma_k\right)\left[y - (L+l+1) \sum\limits_{k=1}^{N} \mu_k\right]}{\sigma_j \left[\dfrac{L \sum\limits_{k=1}^{N} \sigma_k^2}{\left(\sum\limits_{k=1}^{N} \sigma_k\right)^2} + (l+1)\right]^{1/2}} \tag{22}$$

or

$$z = \frac{y - (L + l + 1) \sum_{k=1}^{N} \mu_k}{\left[L \sum_{k=1}^{N} \sigma_k^2 + (l + 1) \left(\sum_{k=1}^{N} \sigma_k \right)^2 \right]^{1/2}} .$$ (23)

Clearly z is independent of j. Thus, the optimal value of y is the same for all warehouses j and is determined by the relationship

$$\Phi(z) = p/p + h .$$

It is interesting to compare this result to the standard Newsboy problem. In the Newsboy problem

$$z = \frac{y - \mu}{\sigma} ,$$

where μ and σ are the mean and standard deviation, respectively, of demand during the period.

In the depot–warehouse system, the holding and penalty costs are assessed at the warehouses $L + l + 1$ periods after the order is placed. The total system demand over these $L + l + 1$ periods is a normal random variable with mean

$$(L + l + 1) \sum_{i=1}^{N} \mu_i$$

and standard deviation

$$\left[(L + l + 1) \sum_{i=1}^{N} \sigma_i^2 \right]^{1/2} .$$

Thus, if all of this demand occurred at one location (centralized demand), the appropriate value of z would be

$$z = \frac{y - (L + l + 1) \cdot \sum_{i=1}^{N} \mu_i}{\left[(L + l + 1) \sum_{i=1}^{N} \sigma_i^2 \right]^{1/2}} .$$

On the other hand, if each warehouse ordered separately (decentralized demand)

and y_i was the order-up-to value for warehouse i, then

$$z = \frac{y_i - (L + l + 1)\,\mu_i}{(L + l + 1)^{1/2}\,\sigma_i}.$$

Now compare the total system inventory on hand, plus on order, immediately after an order is placed in each of the three systems:

Depot

$$y = (L + l + 1) \sum_{k=1}^{N} \mu_k + z \left[L \sum_{k=1}^{N} \sigma_k^2 + (l + 1)\left(\sum_{k=1}^{N} \sigma_k \right)^2 \right]^{1/2},$$

Centralized

$$y = (L + l + 1) \sum_{k=1}^{N} \mu_k + z \left[(L + l + 1) \sum_{k=1}^{N} \sigma_k^2 \right]^{1/2},$$

Decentralized

$$y = \sum_{i=1}^{N} y_i = (L + l + 1) \sum_{k=1}^{N} \mu_k + z \left[(L + l + 1)^{1/2} \sum_{k=1}^{N} \sigma_k \right].$$

The total inventory on hand, plus on order, is greater for the decentralized system than the centralized system. The depot system lies between the two. In the depot system, the multiplier for z appears to consist of an L period centralized system and an $(l + 1)$ period decentralized system.

Using the approach presented in [63], the expected total cost per period for the system is

$$hl \sum_{j=1}^{N} \mu_j + h \sum_{j=1}^{N} \hat{\sigma}_j z + (p + h) \sum_{j=1}^{N} \hat{\sigma}_j R(z),$$

where $R(\cdot)$ is the unit normal right-tail linear loss function, i.e.,

$$R(z) = \int_{z}^{\infty} (x - z) \frac{1}{\sqrt{(2\pi)}} e^{-x^2/2} \, dx.$$

The first term is the cost of holding the inventory in transit from the depot to the warehouses. Note that this quantity does not depend on y or on the allocation decision. Because of the base stock policy, the depot will order the quantity demanded in the previous period, regardless of the value for y.

If all warehouses have the same standard deviation, σ, then

$$\hat\sigma_j = \sigma \sqrt{\frac{L}{N} + l + 1} \, .$$

Then the expected total cost per period can be written:

$$hl \sum_{j=1}^{N} \mu_j + N\sigma \sqrt{\frac{L}{N} + l + 1} \ (hz + (h + p) R(z)) \, .$$

Obviously, the cost associated with the inventory in transit increases linearly with the total mean demand and, thus, linearly with the number of warehouses if the warehouses are identical.

4. Ordering policies under fixed-order setup cost

When a setup cost is incurred at the depot for placing an order it no longer need be optimal to order every period. We will assume that the depot places an order every m periods so as to bring the system stock up to a number y. Upon receipt of goods, the depot distributes the goods to the warehouses. We will be interested in determining optimum values for m and y, and an allocation policy.

Note that the (m, y) policy under consideration may be non-optimal. Unfortunately, the optimal policy may be a function of the vector of inventories on hand and on order for each warehouse. We do not know the form of the optimal policy. The (m, y) policy is easy to implement. Further, the derivation of this policy provides insight into reorder point, reorder quantity policies.

When a delivery arrives at the depot, the question of how much to allocate to each warehouse arises. Suppose a delivery arrives at the depot in period 1 and is allocated so as to bring warehouse i's pipeline stock up to y_i. The holding and penalty cost in periods $l + 1, ..., l + m$ are affected by this allocation.

Define

$$F_{it}(x) = \text{prob}\left\{\sum_{j=1}^{t} e_{ij} \leqslant x\right\} . \tag{24}$$

The marginal expected value of an additional unit to warehouse i is

$$\sum_{t=l+1}^{l+m} \{hF_{it}(y_i) - p[1 - F_{it}(y_i)]\}$$

$$= \sum_{t=l+1}^{l+m} \{(h + p) F_{it}(y_i)\} - mp . \tag{25}$$

With equal costs over all warehouses, an optimal allocation has

$$\sum_{t=l+1}^{l+m} F_{it}(y_i) = \sum_{t=l+1}^{l+m} F_{jt}(y_j) \qquad \text{for all } i \text{ and } j \text{ .} \tag{26}$$

Because

$$\sum_{t=l+1}^{l+m} F_{it}(y_i)$$

is a monotone nondecreasing function of y_i for each warehouse, it is conceptually easy to calculate the y_i's necessary to achieve an optimal allocation. In addition, the Allocation Assumption guarantees that the incoming order will be large enough to achieve this goal.

It is, however, difficult to proceed analytically from this point. It is also useful to consider an allocation system that would be easy to implement. We, thus, again turn our attention to an allocation of the form

$$y_i = (l + m)\,\mu_i + v\sigma_i \text{ .}$$

Such an allocation is optimal if $\mu_i/\sigma_i = \alpha$ (a constant independent of i). This follows from the fact that in this case

$$F_{it}(y_i) = \Phi\!\left(\frac{l + m - t}{\sqrt{t}}\,\alpha + \frac{v}{\sqrt{t}}\right). \tag{27}$$

Now for each t, the function $F_{it}(y_i)$ does not depend on i, the warehouse. It is only a function of v. Thus, by choosing v, the condition specified in equation (26) is satisfied.

The allocation $y_i = (l + m)\,\mu_i + v\sigma_i$ yields a good approximation to optimality if μ_i/σ_i is reasonably large (say ≥ 2). Note that

$$F_{it}(y_i) = \Phi\!\left(\frac{l + m - t}{\sqrt{t}}\left(\frac{\mu_i}{\sigma_i}\right) + \frac{v}{\sqrt{t}}\right). \tag{28}$$

Setting $t = (l + m)$ yields $\Phi(v/\sqrt{t})$, which is the probability of satisfying demand in the last period before the next order arrives. One would hope to be able to choose v large enough to make this probability large, perhaps 0.90 or above. For $t < l + m$ the value of the argument of the function increases; thus, $F_{it}(y_i) \cong 1.0$ for $t < l + m$. Further in this extreme tail of the distribution, even relatively large differences in the value of the arguments among different warehouses would yield small differences in the value of the function. Thus, an allocation of the form $y_i = (l + m)\,\mu_i + v\sigma_i$ yields approximate equality in (26).

With an allocation of this form, the stock level at warehouse j just before the next delivery is made at j is

$$(l + m) \mu_j + \frac{\sigma_j}{\displaystyle\sum_{k=1}^{N} \sigma_k} \left(y - V - \sum_{i=1}^{N} (l + m) \mu_i \right) - W_j , \tag{29}$$

where

$$V = \sum_{t=1}^{L} \sum_{j=1}^{N} e_{jt} \quad \text{and} \quad W_j = \sum_{t=L+1}^{L+l+m} e_{jt} .$$

Since demands at each warehouse are independent and identically distributed over time and demands are uncorrelated across warehouses, it follows that

$$E(V) = L \sum_{j=1}^{N} \mu_j ,$$

$$E(W_j) = (l + m) \mu_j ,$$

$$\sigma_V^2 = L \sum_{j=1}^{N} \sigma_j^2 ,$$

$$\sigma_{W_j}^2 = (l + m) \sigma_j^2 .$$

Now define

$$\hat{\mu}_j = \frac{\sigma_j}{\displaystyle\sum_{k=1}^{N} \sigma_k} (L + l + m) \sum_{i=1}^{N} \mu_i . \tag{30}$$

The ending stock at j has mean

$$\frac{\sigma_j}{\displaystyle\sum_{i=1}^{N} \sigma_i} y - \hat{\mu}_j$$

and standard deviation

$$\hat{\sigma}_j = \sqrt{\left[\left(\sigma_j \bigg/ \sum_{i=1}^{N} \sigma_i \right)^2 L \sum_{k=1}^{N} \sigma_k^2 + (l + m) \sigma_j^2 \right]} .$$

Using the approximation that shortages occur only in the last period before a warehouse delivery, the expected cost per cycle of m periods at warehouse j can be written

$$mh\left\{\sigma_j y \Big/ \sum_{i=1}^{N} \sigma_i - \hat{\mu}_j \right\} + hm(m-1)\,\mu_j/2$$

$$+ (h+p)\,\hat{\sigma}_j R\left(\left[\sigma_j y \Big/ \sum_{i=1}^{N} \sigma_i - \hat{\mu}_j\right]\Big/\hat{\sigma}_j\right),\tag{31}$$

where, as before, $R(z)$ is the unit Normal right-tail linear loss function.

Note again that $(\sigma_j y\, \Sigma_{i=1}^{N}\, \sigma_i - \hat{\mu}_j)/\hat{\sigma}_j$ can be rewritten as

$$z = \frac{\left[y - (L+l+m)\displaystyle\sum_{i=1}^{N}\mu_i\right]\Big/\displaystyle\sum_{i=1}^{N}\sigma_i}{\sqrt{\left(\dfrac{L\displaystyle\sum_{k=1}^{N}\sigma_k^2}{\left(\displaystyle\sum_{k=1}^{N}\sigma_k\right)^2}+l+m\right)}},\tag{32}$$

which is independent of j.

Summing over j, the cost for a cycle of length m is

$$mh\left\{y - (L+l+m)\sum_{i=1}^{N}\mu_i\right\} + hm(m-1)\sum_{i=1}^{N}\mu_i/2$$

$$+ (h+p)\sum_{j=1}^{N}\hat{\sigma}_j R(z) + K.\tag{33}$$

Holding m fixed and taking the first derivative of this expression with respect to y yields the marginal cost of increasing y by one unit. Because $R'(z) = -[1 - \Phi(z)]$ the expression for the marginal cost is

$$mh - (h+p)[1 - \Phi(z)].$$

Setting this equal to zero and solving, we get the following Newsboy-like formula for determining y:

$$\Phi(z) = \frac{p - (m-1)h}{p+h}.$$

The total expected system cost per period can be rewritten as

$$hl \sum_{j=1}^{N} \mu_j + \left[mh \sum_{j=1}^{N} \hat{o}_j z + hm(m-1) \sum_{j=1}^{N} \mu_j/2 \right.$$

$$\left. + (h+p) \sum_{j=1}^{N} \hat{o}_j R(z) + K \right] / m . \tag{34}$$

In our experience, it has been easy to find the optimal value of m and y by using a computer and simply searching over m.

If we denote the optimal z and m by z^* and m^*, then we have approximately that

$$m^* \cong \sqrt{\left(2\left[K + (h+p) \sum_j \hat{o}_j R(z^*) \right] \middle/ h \sum_j \mu_j \right)} . \tag{35}$$

Including the cost of inventory in transit from depot to warehouse, the expected cost per period of the optimal policy is approximately

$$hl \sum_{j=1}^{N} \mu_j + \sqrt{\left(2h \sum_{j=1}^{N} \mu_j \left[K + (h+p) \sum_j \hat{o}_j R(z^*) \right] \right)}$$

$$+ h\left[\sum_{j=1}^{N} (\hat{o}_j z - \mu_j/2) \right] . \tag{36}$$

By substituting the expression for m^* into the numerator of the expression for z, the optimal value for system order-up-to quantity y is found to be approximately

$$y = \sqrt{\left(2\left[K + (h+p) \sum_{j=1}^{N} \hat{o}_j R(z^*) \right] \sum_{j=1}^{N} \mu_i/h \right)} + (L+l) \sum_{j=1}^{N} \mu_j$$

$$+ z^* \sum_{j=1}^{N} \sigma_j \sqrt{\left[\frac{L \sum_{k=1}^{N} \sigma_k^2}{\left(\sum_{k=1}^{N} \sigma_k \right)^2} + l + m^* \right]} . \tag{37}$$

The sum of the last two terms can be thought of as a system reorder point. The last term can be thought of as a system safety stock, while the first term can be thought of as an expected order quantity.

5. Comments

In the systems we have studied, a common order has been placed for all warehouses. Such systems take advantage of quantity discounts offered by the supplier and reduce the system inventory because of a portfolio effect over the lead time from the supplier. One might refer to this as the joint ordering effect.

A second possible advantage, which one might call the depot effect, remains to be studied. To exploit this advantage, the depot would hold inventory and allocate it to the warehouses between the times at which orders arrive at the depot. (Recall that the current system is a pass-through system in which orders that arrive from the supplier are immediately allocated to the warehouses.) The advantage of depoting is that final allocation decisions would not have to be made until more information was available and, thus, one should be able to reduce the probability of stockouts in future periods. The disadvantage is that orders held at the depot are not available to satisfy demands in the current period, and thus the probability of stockouts in the current period is increased. An examination of this problem is underway.

Acknowledgements

The presentation has benefited from discussions with Chuck Schmidt. David Baier of Joseph T. Ryerson and Sons, Inc. introduced us to the problem.

TIMS Studies in the Management Sciences 16 (1981) 69–94
© North-Holland Publishing Company

REVIEW OF OPTIMAL AND HEURISTIC METHODS FOR A CLASS OF FACILITIES IN SERIES DYNAMIC LOT-SIZE PROBLEMS

Marc R. LAMBRECHT, Jacques VANDER EECKEN and
Hugo VANDERVEKEN

Katholieke Universiteit Leuven

This paper focuses on optimal and heuristic procedures for both uncapacitated and capacitated facilities in series dynamic lot-size problems. Several heuristics are evaluated, and on the basis of large sets of simulation experiments it can be concluded that these heuristics differ only marginally from the optimal solutions and are far more efficient as far as computational effort is concerned.

1. Introduction

There has been a widespread interest in the deterministic dynamic production and inventory models since the publication of the classic paper of Wagner and Whitin [243]. Their model deals with the search for optimal production (ordering) and inventory schedules for a single-stage, single-product system given a fluctuating deterministic demand pattern over a finite horizon. Presumed computational difficulties with Wagner and Whitin's algorithm have led to the development of a number of heuristic approaches such as Part-Period Balancing [52], Least Unit Cost [52], the Silver and Meal Heuristic [216], Order Moment Heuristic [146], etc.

In recent years various papers have appeared on dynamic production—inventory planning in multi-echelon or multi-stage systems. In a multi-echelon system, the manufacture of a final product requires several different production processes. Each process is assumed to take place in a given facility. Of the vast number of possible configurations a few have been singled out for special attention.

The simplest multi-echelon configuration is a serial one [255], where each facility except the first and the last has exactly one predecessor and one successor. More complex systems involve an assembly structure [48] where each intermediate facility has exactly one successor but possibly several predecessors, and the arborescent structure [108], where each intermediate facility has exactly one predecessor but possibly several successors.

The work reported here deals with facilities in series models, both with and without capacity constraints on the last facility. Serial systems are frequently found in processing industries; e.g., the steel industry and the chemical industry. Exogenous requirements (demand) for a single product occur periodically. No backlogging is permitted and so requirements must be met as they occur. It is assumed that one unit of production at any facility requires as input one unit of production from the preceding facility, and production is instantaneous. The objective is to find a production—inventory plan for each facility minimizing the total production and inventory holding cost. When capacity constraints are introduced, they need not be equal in every period. In many practical situations, limitations may be imposed on the amount produced at the last facility because of the highly time-consuming finishing operations. The varying capacity structure may be related to conditions such as the number of shifts scheduled during a production period or the number of hours worked per shift. These limitations are imposed by the aggregate plans and schedules for the use of the various sources of capacity.

In sections 2 and 3 the model formulation, characterization of optimal production—inventory plans, and optimal solution algorithms will be summarized for the uncapacitated and capacitated models, respectively. In section 4 a multi-level and several level-by-level heuristics for the uncapacitated problem are compared to the existing optimal models. Multi-level heuristics assign production quantities to all facilities on a period-by-period basis. The level-by-level methods, on the other hand, assign production lots over the complete planning horizon to a specific facility and use the resulting program as demand vector for the preceding facility. Section 5 compares for the capacitated problem the solutions obtained using several multi-level heuristic procedures with the optimal ones.

2. Uncapacitated facilities in series dynamic lot-size model: optimal methods

2.1. Model formulation and network representation

Let r_i, $r_i \geqslant 0$ be the market demands for the finished product in period i, $i = 1, ..., n$. Define $x_{j,i}$ as the production of facility j, $j = 1, ..., m$ in period i. Let $I_{j,i}$ be the inventory stored at facility j at the end of period i. Let $P_{j,i}(x)$ be the cost of producing x units and $H_{j,i}(I)$ be the cost of holding I units in stock. $P_{j,i}(x)$ and $H_{j,i}(I)$ are both concave functions.

The appropriate programming problem is as follows:

minimize

$$\sum_{j=1}^{m} \sum_{i=1}^{n} \{P_{j,i}(x_{j,i}) + H_{j,i}(I_{j,i})\} , \tag{1}$$

subject to

$$I_{j,i-1} + x_{j,i} - I_{j,i} - x_{j+1,i} = 0 , \qquad \begin{array}{l} j = 1, ..., m - 1 , \\ i = 1, ..., n , \end{array} \tag{2}$$

$$I_{m,i-1} + x_{m,i} - I_{m,i} = r_i , \qquad i = 1, ..., n , \tag{3}$$

$$I_{j,i} \geqslant 0 , \qquad x_{j,i} \geqslant 0 , \qquad \forall (i, j) , \tag{4}$$

$$I_{j,0} = I_{j,n} = 0 , \qquad \forall j . \tag{5}$$

Zangwill [255] has cleverly represented the constraints as flow constraints in a single-source network (see fig. 1). Equations (2) and (3) demonstrate nodal conservation of flow in the network. The determination of the optimal production–inventory schedule is then equivalent to finding the corresponding network optimal flow.

2.2. Characterization of an optimal production–inventory plan

Constraints (2)–(5) define a closed bounded convex set, and since the objective function is concave it is clear that it will attain its minimum at an extreme point of the convex set of feasible solutions to the problem. Given that in a basic feasible solution the vectors representing the coefficients of the basic variables are linearly independent, and that a basic feasible solution cannot be written as a convex combination of two non-basic feasible solutions, Lambrecht [131] shows that an optimal production–inventory schedule has the property that for each facility, if there is production in period i, then the incoming inventory must be zero; and conversely, if the incoming inventory in period i is positive, then the production must

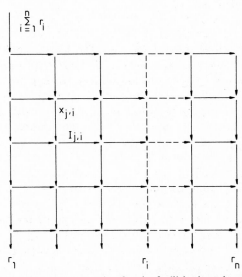

Fig. 1. Network representation for the facilities in series model.

be zero, i.e.

$$x_{j,i} \cdot I_{j,i-1} = 0 , \qquad \forall (i, j) . \tag{6}$$

Zangwill [255] obtained the same result, observing that the optimal solution to the equivalent network problem must be an extreme flow and using the property that an extreme flow cannot contain positive loops.

As a consequence of (6), one can easily show that for each facility either the production in period i or the inventory carried over into period i must satisfy demand over an integral number of periods.

Assuming the following cost assumptions:

$$P_{j,i}(x) \geqslant P_{j,i+1}(x) , \qquad \begin{array}{l} j = 1, ..., m , \\ i = 1, ..., n - 1 , \end{array} \tag{7}$$

$$H_{j,i}(I) \leqslant H_{j+1,i}(I) , \qquad \begin{array}{l} j = 1, ..., m - 1 , \\ i = 1, ..., n , \end{array} \tag{8}$$

i.e., that production costs are non-increasing over time, whereas the inventory holding costs are non-decreasing over the production facilities, Love [139] proves the following property of an optimal production—inventory schedule. If in a given period i production starts at facility j, then all its successors must also produce in period i; that is, given $x_{j,i} > 0$ then $x_{l,i} > 0, j + 1 \leqslant l \leqslant m$. Such production schedules are called "nested".

2.3. Optimal solution algorithms

Zangwill [255] developed a dynamic programming algorithm which efficiently exploits property (6) of an optimal solution. The special cost structure which validates the nested schedule property allowed Love [139] to formulate an algorithm which permits a drastic reduction in the number of computations required to find the optimal production—inventory schedule. The models proposed by Crowston and Wagner [48] for the assembly structure can also be used to solve the facilities in series problem. Their first model is based on dynamic programming where, through efficient sequencing, computational savings can be obtained compared to complete enumeration. Their second model is a branch-and-bound approach, where the subproblems are solved by dynamic programming. Graves [86], on the other hand, proposes an iterative procedure to solve multi-stage lot-sizing problems.

The algorithms of Zangwill, Love, and Crowston and Wagner were programmed in FORTRAN IV. The execution times (all computational results contained in this paper were obtained using an IBM 370/158 model 3, OS/VS2, computer system) increase linearly with the number of facilities and exponentially with the number of periods included in the planning horizon. Figs. 2a and 2b are based on the average execution times obtained through the experimental analysis described in section

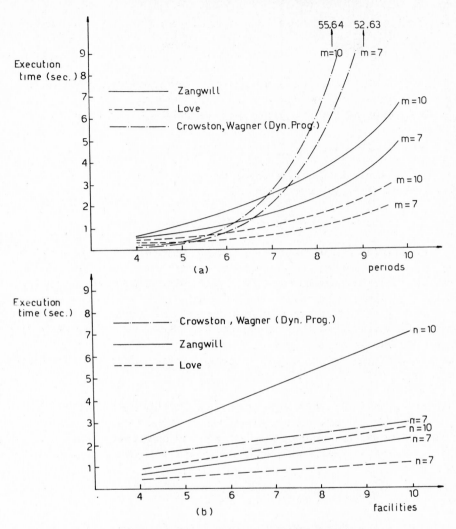

Fig. 2. CPU times for computing optimal solutions using the algorithms of Zangwill, Love, and Crowston and Wagner (dynamic programming).

4.3. Note that no results are reported for the branch-and-bound algorithm of Crowston and Wagner, the reason being that for the branch-and-bound approach, execution times are highly dependent on the problem data. To illustrate this point: for a 10 period, 4 facility problem the execution times ranged from 0.5 to 84 sec.

3. Facilities in series capacity constrained dynamic lot-size model: optimal methods

3.1. Model formulation and network representation

Let $c_{m,i}$, $i = 1, ..., n$ be the capacities imposed on the production at the last facility. The appropriate programming problem is then given by the objective function (1) and the constraint set (2)–(5), augmented by the capacity constraint

$$x_{m,i} \leqslant c_{m,i}, \qquad i = 1, ..., n . \tag{9}$$

The network of fig. 1 remains unchanged, except that the arcs representing production at the last facility are now capacitated.

3.2. Characterization of an optimal production–inventory plan

Constraints (2)–(5) and (9) define a closed and bounded convex set; hence the concave objective function (1) attains its minimum at an extreme point of the convex set, or in network terminology, the optimal solution must be an extreme flow. The characterization of extreme flows in capacitated networks is more complex than in uncapacitated ones. A feasible flow is extremal if and only if each of its positive loops contains at least one saturated arc. Based on this observation, the following theorems give the characteristics of an optimal production program. The first theorem holds for the last facility m, and the second theorem holds for all other stages [132].

Theorem 1. The production sequence of the last facility must satisfy the Florian and Klein [77] property: between each pair of regeneration points defined as periods where ending inventory is zero, there is at most one partial production period, defined as a period with production level greater than zero but less than capacity.

Theorem 2. For $i = 1, ..., n$ and $j = 1, ..., m - 1$: $x_{j,i} \cdot I_{j,i-1} = 0$.

As a consequence of the first theorem it is now possible to have two positive inputs into nodes (m, i), $i = 1, ..., n$. A procedure to find all production–inventory plans satisfying this theorem is given in [77] for the case of equal capacities and in [133] for the case of varying capacities. Moreover, the two theorems state that each production plan for the last facility can be seen as a demand vector for the corresponding facilities in series problem with $m - 1$ facilities. This can be summarized in the following collorary.

Collorary 1. The input into a node (j, i), $j = 1, ..., m - 1$ and $i = 1, ..., n$ must satisfy production requirements over an integral number of periods, where these production requirements are defined to be the production levels of some production plan for facility m, satisfying theorem 1.

The next theorem holds assuming that the cost functions are of the following type: the production cost function is of the fixed charge type, i.e. $P_{j,i}(x_{j,i}) = S_j \cdot \delta(x_{j,i}) + v_{j,i} \cdot x_{j,i}$, $\delta(x_{j,i}) = 1$ if $x_{j,i} > 0$ and $\delta(x_{j,i}) = 0$ if $x_{j,i} = 0$, with S_j as the setup cost and $v_{j,i}$ as the unit variable production costs, and the inventory holding cost function $H_{j,i}(I_{j,i}) = h_j \cdot I_{j,i}$ is a linear function of the amount of inventory.

More specifically we assume that

$$H_{j,i}(I) \leqslant H_{j+1,i}(I) , \qquad \begin{array}{l} j = 1, ..., m-1 , \\ i = 1, ..., n , \end{array} \tag{10}$$

and

$$v_{j,i} \geqslant v_{j,i+1} , \qquad \begin{array}{l} j = 1, ..., m , \\ i = 1, ..., n-1 . \end{array} \tag{11}$$

Note that (10) and (11) satisfy the Love conditions (7) and (8) and, as a consequence, optimal production—inventory plans must be nested [139].

Theorem 3. Given the cost assumptions (10) and (11), the production schedules for the last facility must have the following property: if at the last facility there is positive inventory carried over from a previous period, then production is either at capacity or zero; on the other hand, if there is positive production at a level less than capacity, then incoming inventory must be zero.

As a consequence of this theorem we will not forgo optimality by examining only those last facility production sequences for which the following property holds: if a pair of regeneration points (k, l) contains a partial production period, then it must be period $k + 1$.

Note that there may be more than one such sequence for each pair of regeneration points when periods of zero production are possible. The proof of this theorem is given in appendix I.

3.3. Optimal solution algorithms

Lambrecht and Vander Eecken developed two algorithms: one involving decomposition, the other consisting of a computationally more efficient one-stage procedure. We will limit ourselves to a brief discussion of both methods and refer to [132] for a detailed description of these algorithms.

3.3.1. Solution by means of a series of Zangwill models
Suppose there are q possible production—inventory plans for the last facility

satisfying theorem 1. One could then solve q uncapacitated Zangwill problems with $m - 1$ facilities (the last facility being omitted), where the demand vector for each of these problems is given by one of the feasible production sequences. Let the minimum cost solution of each of these subproblems be denoted by $K(s_k)$, $k = 1, ..., q$, where s_k denotes an admissible production program for the last facility. Let $C(s_k)$, $k = 1, ..., q$ denote the cost of producing and holding inventory at facility m in accordance with the production sequence s_k. The minimum cost solution for the facilities in series dynamic lot-size problem with capacity constraints on the last facility is then given by

$$\min_{k=1,...,q} \{C(s_k) + K(s_k)\} .$$

(12)

This approach has the following drawback: observe that the last facility production plans are composed of periods with production being either at capacity, or at zero, or at an intermediate level. Hence, the sum of different production requirements over a given number of periods could result in the same total input into some nodes (j, i). These inputs must then repeatedly be evaluated in the course of solving the corresponding uncapacitated Zangwill problems, resulting in duplication of computations. To illustrate this, consider the following example.

Example 1.   Demand: $r_1 = 10$, $r_2 = 20$ and $r_3 = 30$; 3 facilities; capacity constraints on the last facility: $x_{3,1} \leqslant 15, x_{3,2} \leqslant 40$ and $x_{3,3} \leqslant 15$.
   The production plans satisfying theorem 1 are

$$s_1 = 15, 30, 15 ,$$

$$s_2 = 10, 35, 15 ,$$

$$s_3 = 10, 40, 10 ,$$

$$s_4 = 15, 40, \ \ 5 .$$

Consider an input of 50 units into node $(2, 2)$. This amount can satisfy production requirements for both periods 2 and 3 according to the production plans s_2 and s_3. Hence the reduced uncapacitated Zangwill problems with s_2 and s_3 as demand vectors will evaluate the same input of 50 units into node $(2, 2)$.
   Observe also that if theorem 3 applies, then plans s_1, s_3 and s_4 can be eliminated without forgoing optimality.

3.3.2. A one-stage algorithm
   The basic idea is that input combinations which are the same for a subset, denoted s^*, of admissible last facility production schedules, denoted by the set R, will be evaluated only once.
   The proposed one-stage algorithm is an extension of the model of Zangwill

[255] in the sense that it works simultaneously with different demand vectors. This multi-dimensionality results in the following extension of his notation. Zangwill denotes, by $S_{j,i}(\alpha, \beta)$, the input of $\Sigma_{l=\alpha}^{\beta} r_l$ units into node (j, i) and, by $C_{j,i}(\alpha, \beta)$, the minimum cost of shipping these units from node (j, i) to destinations (m, α), $(m, \alpha + 1)$, ..., (m, β). We let $S_{j,i}^{s*}(\alpha, \beta)$ denote the input of the amount $\Sigma_{l=\alpha}^{\beta} x_{m,l}^s$, $s \in s^*$, into node (j, i) and $C_{j,i}^{s*}(\alpha, \beta)$ denote the minimum cost of shipping these units from node (j, i) to destinations $(m, \alpha), (m, \alpha + 1), ..., (m, \beta)$. Note that the amount $\Sigma_{l=\alpha}^{\beta} x_{m,l}^s$, $s \in s^*$ is the same for all the production plans $s^*, s^* \in R$, where R is the set of the last facility plans satisfying theorem 1. With this extended notation a recursion formula is constructed similar to the one given by Zangwill [255].

To test the efficiency of the two algorithms a number of test problems (with $n \leqslant 5$ and $m \leqslant 7$) were solved. The execution times for the one-stage algorithm are from 25 to 50% lower than those required by the decomposition approach. Fig. 3 illustrates these results for a number of 3 and 4 period problems.

4. Facilities in series uncapacitated dynamic lot-size model: heuristic methods

One multi-level and several level-by-level heuristic procedures will be discussed and their performance examined. A multi-level heuristic assigns production quantities to all facilities on a period-by-period basis. Level-by-level heuristics, on the

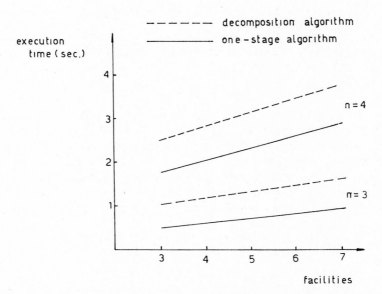

Fig. 3. CPU times for computing optimal solutions using a series of Zangwill models and the one-stage algorithm.

other hand, assign over the complete planning horizon production quantities to a specific facility, and use the resulting production program as a demand vector for the
preceding facility.

The following cost assumptions are made:

(1) The production cost function $P_{j,i}(x)$ is of the fixed charge type. It is the same
for all periods but may differ from facility to facility. Note that since the unit
production cost is constant, it has no influence on the optimal plan

$$P_{j,i}(x_{j,i}) = S_j \cdot \delta(x_{j,i}) + v_j \cdot x_{j,i}, \qquad \forall (i, j), \tag{13}$$

where S_j and v_j denote the set-up cost and the variable production cost for
facility j, and

$$\delta(x_{j,i}) = 1 \qquad \text{if } x_{j,i} > 0,$$
$$= 0 \qquad \text{if } x_{j,i} = 0.$$

(2) The inventory holding cost function $H_{j,i}(I)$ is linear and constant over time. It
may differ from facility to facility but must be non-decreasing throughout the
production process

$$H_{j,i}(I_{j,i}) = h_j \cdot I_{j,i}, \qquad \forall (i, j), \tag{14}$$

where h_j denotes the inventory holding cost for facility j, and $h_j \leqslant h_{j+1}$.

As a result of these simplifying assumptions the optimal production schedules will
be nested [139]. Note also that these cost assumptions satisfy conditions (10) and
(11), for which theorem 3 holds.

4.1. A multi-level heuristic

Define a reorder period k as the last period with positive production at all facilities. Note that period 1 is always the first reorder period, assuming $r_1 > 0$. For each
facility and each time period a coefficient is computed, indicating whether a cost
reduction is possible by incorporating demands r_l, $l > k$ in a lot that has already
been scheduled in an earlier period. If all coefficients turn out to be negative for a
certain period i, $i > k$ then period i is considered the new reorder period and the
procedure is repeated.

The following coefficients will be used:

$$U_{j,i} = \sum_{l=1}^{j} S_l - C_{i-1} - h_j r_i(i - k), \qquad i = k + 1, k + 2, \dots$$

$$\forall j \leqslant j^0 \tag{15}$$

and

$$U_{j,i} = U_{j-1,i} + S_j - (h_j - h_{j-1}) \, r_i(i - p_j), \qquad i = k + 2, k + 3, \ldots$$

$$\forall j > j^0, \qquad\qquad\qquad\qquad\qquad\qquad\qquad\qquad (16)$$

where

C_{i-1} = the cumulative inventory holding costs incurred from reorder period k up to period $i - 1$, given the current order quantities.

p_j = the last period with positive production at facility j.

j^0 = the last facility for which $p_j = k$.

Coefficient (15) is a measure of the possible savings resulting from not scheduling production in facility j, period i, but instead adding r_i to the production lot of facility j in reorder period k — see fig. 4(a). Coefficient (16), on the other hand, is a measure of the possible benefits resulting from adding r_i to the production lot of facility j in period p_j instead of adding it to some previously defined plan — see fig. 4(b). Note from (15) that for a specific facility j we treat the facilities $1, 2, \ldots, j$ as a single facility with $\sum_{l=1}^{j} S_l$ and h_j as cost parameters. Figs. 4(a) and 4(b) illustrate the alternatives evaluated by (15) and (16) for $i = k + 2$ and $j^0 = 2$.

For a particular reorder period k the heuristic procedure can be summarized as follows:

Step 1. Let $p_j = k$, $\quad \forall j$
$\qquad A = \{1, 2, \ldots, m\}$
$\qquad i = k + 1$
$\qquad j^0 = m.$

Step 2. Check whether it is advantageous to include r_i in x_{j,p_j}, $j = 1, \ldots, m$ com-

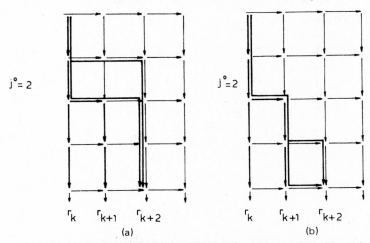

Fig. 4. (a) Alternatives evaluated by (15); (b) alternatives evaluated by (16).

puting the coefficients $U_{j,i}$, $j = 1, ..., m$ using (15) and (16). If $U_{j,i} < 0$, $\forall j$ go to step 4, otherwise go to step 3.

Step 3. Define j^* by $U_{j^*,i} = \max_j \{U_{j,i} \geqslant 0\}$ and update the current production plan and values of p_j. If $j^* \in A$ then, $j^0 = j^*$ and $A = \{1, 2, ..., j^0\}$; otherwise j^0 and A remain unchanged. Let $i = i + 1$ and return to step 2 if $i < n + 1$, otherwise stop.

Step 4(a). If $i \neq n$, then period i becomes a new reorder period. Let $k = i$ and return to step 1.

Step 4(b). If $i = n$, then r_n should be produced in all facilities in period n. In this case a backtracking procedure examines whether it is not profitable to include r_n into an earlier lot. We therefore compare the set-up costs which can be saved with the additional inventory holding costs which will be incurred by including r_n in x_{j,p_j}. Assuming savings do occur, r_n is added to the production lot of facility j, period p_j for which they are maximum.

A 7 facility, 7 period problem will be used to illustrate the above procedure.

Facility j	S_j	h_j	i	1	2	3	4	5	6	7
1	400	2	r_i	80	70	60	100	120	80	40
2	100	2								
3	100	3								
4	200	3								
5	300	3								
6	200	4								
7	100	5								

Reorder period $k = 1$.

· check $r_2, j^0 = 7, A = \{1, 2, ..., 7\}$

Formula (15) $\quad U_{12} = \quad 400 - 2 \times 70 = \quad 260$

$\quad\quad\quad\quad\quad\quad U_{22} = \quad 500 - 2 \times 70 = \quad 360$

$\quad\quad\quad\quad\quad\quad U_{32} = \quad 600 - 3 \times 70 = \quad 390$

$\quad\quad\quad\quad\quad\quad U_{42} = \quad 800 - 3 \times 70 = \quad 590$

$\quad\quad\quad\quad\quad\quad U_{52} = 1{,}100 - 3 \times 70 = \quad 890$

$\quad\quad\quad\quad\quad\quad U_{62} = 1{,}300 - 4 \times 70 = 1{,}020$

$\quad\quad\quad\quad\quad\quad U_{72} = 1{,}400 - 5 \times 70 = 1{,}050$

$\max_j \{U_{j,2}\} = U_{72} = 1{,}050 \rightarrow j^* = 7, j^* \in A, j^0 = 7$

$C_2 = 5 \times 70 = 350$.

check $r_3, j^0 = 7, A = \{1, 2, ..., 7\}$

Formula (15) $\quad U_{13} = \quad 400 - 350 - 2 \times 2 \times 60 = -190$

$\quad\quad\quad\quad\quad\quad U_{23} = \quad 500 - 350 - 2 \times 2 \times 60 = \quad -90$

$\quad\quad\quad\quad\quad\quad U_{33} = \quad 600 - 350 - 2 \times 3 \times 60 = -110$

$\quad\quad\quad\quad\quad\quad U_{43} = \quad 800 - 350 - 2 \times 3 \times 60 = \quad\quad 90$

$\quad\quad\quad\quad\quad\quad U_{53} = 1{,}100 - 350 - 2 \times 3 \times 60 = \quad 390$

$$U_{63} = 1{,}300 - 350 - 2 \times 4 \times 60 = \quad 470$$
$$U_{73} = 1{,}400 - 350 - 2 \times 5 \times 60 = \quad 450$$

$$\max_{j} \{U_{j3}\} = U_{63} = 470 \to j^* = 6,\, j^* \in A,\, j^0 = 6$$

$$C_3 = 350 + 2 \times 4 \times 60 = 830.$$

· check $r_4, j^0 = 6, A = \{1, 2, ..., 6\}$

Formula (15)
$$
\begin{aligned}
U_{14} &= \quad 400 - 830 - 3 \times 2 \times 100 = -1{,}030 \\
U_{24} &= \quad 500 - 830 - 3 \times 2 \times 100 = \quad -930 \\
U_{34} &= \quad 600 - 830 - 3 \times 3 \times 100 = -1{,}130 \\
U_{44} &= \quad 800 - 830 - 3 \times 3 \times 100 = \quad -930 \\
U_{54} &= 1{,}100 - 830 - 3 \times 3 \times 100 = \quad -630 \\
U_{66} &= 1{,}300 - 830 - 3 \times 4 \times 100 = \quad -730
\end{aligned}
$$

Formula (16)
$$
\begin{aligned}
U_{74} &= U_{64} + S_7 - (4 - 3) \cdot 100(5 - 4) \\
&= -730 + 100 - 100 = -730.
\end{aligned}
$$

Since all coefficients are negative we turn to the next reorder period $k = 4$.

The same procedure is repeated for the remaining 4 periods. The resulting solution is given below. The backtracking procedure explained in step 4(b) is used for period 7.

$x_{j,i}(I_{j,i})$

j \ i	1	2	3	4	5	6	7
1	210 (0)	0 (0)	0 (0)	340 (0)	0 (0)	0 (0)	0 (0)
2	210 (0)	0 (0)	0 (0)	340 (0)	0 (0)	0 (0)	0 (0)
3	210 (0)	0 (0)	0 (0)	340 (0)	0 (0)	0 (0)	0 (0)
4	210 (0)	0 (0)	0 (0)	340 (0)	0 (0)	0 (0)	0 (0)
5	210 (0)	0 (0)	0 (0)	340 (0)	0 (0)	0 (0)	0 (0)
6	210 (60)	0 (60)	0 (0)	340 (240)	0 (0)	0 (0)	0 (0)
7	150 (70)	0 (0)	60 (0)	100 (0)	240 (120)	0 (40)	0 (0)

Total cost: set-up costs   3,000
                   inventory costs 2,590

                   ─────
                   5,590

For this specific example total costs deviate by 1.27% from the optimal solution.

4.2. Level-by-level heuristics

Given the demand vector r_i, $i = 1, ..., n$ single-stage dynamic lot-size algorithms are used to compute a production program for the last facility, which in turn is then used as demand vector for computing a production plan for the preceding facility, etc. The following algorithms have been included in the analysis: Wagner–Whitin [243], Part-Period Balancing [52], Least Unit Cost [52], Silver-Metal [216], and Order Moment [146].

Concerning the set up cost for a specific facility j we distinguish three cases:

(1) The single setup cost version: S_j.
(2) The cumulative setup cost version: $S_j^* = \Sigma_{i=1}^j S_1$.
(3) The McLaren–Whybark [146] setup cost version

$$S_j' = S_j + \frac{\text{TBO}_j}{\text{TBO}_{j-1}} \cdot S_{j-1}$$

where $\text{TBO}_j = \left(\dfrac{2 \cdot S_j}{h_j \cdot \overline{R}}\right)^{1/2}$ and $\overline{R}$ is the average demand.

The inventory holding cost for each facility j is h_j.

Application of these heuristics is straightforward and needs no further explanation.

4.3. Computational results

The test problems used in our investigation were generated in the following way. The setup costs are found by drawing m numbers from a uniform distribution in the interval $[\epsilon, \epsilon + 500]$ (ϵ small positive number). The inventory holding costs are found by selecting m random numbers in the interval $[\epsilon, \epsilon + 1]$, multiplied by 10, and then arranged as a non-decreasing progression. The demand vectors are gene-

Table 1
Cost performance of the heuristics

Procedure	Cost performance		
Multi-level heuristic	101.84		
Level-by-level	Setup cost for facility j		
	S_j^*	S_j'	S_j
Wagner–Whitin	109.01	103.67	112.20
Order Moment	106.25	110.14	121.62
Part-Period Balancing	111.15	103.91	112.33
Silver-Meal	112.47	109.19	112.36
Least Unit Cost	117.92	106.90	114.56

Table 2
Influence of V_R and V_C on the cost performance of the multi-level and the level-by-level heuristics "Order-Moment" (with S_j^*) and "Wagner–Whitin" (with S_j')

V_R	V_C		
	0–1.5	1.5–3	>3
0 −0.15	M.L. = 100.75	M.L. = 100.73	M.L. = 101.27
	W.W.(S_j') = 106.11	W.W.(S_j') = 104.26	W.W.(S_j') = 100.20
	O.M.(S_j^*) = 101.28	O.M.(S_j^*) = 105.91	O.M.(S_j^*) = 111.99
0.15–0.30	M.L. = 102.20	M.L. = 101.78	M.L. = 102.50
	W.W.(S_j') = 104.49	W.W.(S_j') = 105.62	W.W.(S_j') = 101.37
	O.M.(S_j^*) = 108.25	O.M.(S_j') = 101.52	O.M.(S_j^*) = 108.33
>0.30	M.L. = 101.14	M.L. = 102.87	M.L. = 103.23
	W.W.(S_j') = 105.94	W.W.(S_j') = 102.97	W.W.(S_j') = 101.62
	O.M.(S_j^*) = 102.78	O.M.(S_j^*) = 103.33	O.M.(S_j^*) = 112.96

rated from a normal distribution with mean 100 and standard deviation 100α, with $\alpha = 0.1$ or 0.3. From this set we selected 72 problems with $4 \leqslant n \leqslant 10$ and $4 \leqslant m \leqslant 10$ and classified them with respect to the degree of demand variability and the degree of cost variation — see coefficients (17) and (18). The costs in tables 1 and 2 are expressed as percentages of the cost of the optimal solution which is set equal to 100.

Table 1 summarizes the average cost deviations and points out the superiority of the multi-level heuristic. Note that the multi-level approach resulted in the optimal solution for 34 of the 72 problems solved. Table 2 shows the average deviations as a function of the following measures of problem complexity: V_R, the coefficient of demand variation and V_C, a coefficient of cost variation, where

$$V_R = \frac{\sigma_R}{\bar{R}}, \tag{17}$$

$$V_C = \frac{1}{m-1} \sum_{j=2}^{m} \left\{ \left(\frac{h_j}{S_j}\right) \Big/ \left(\frac{h_{j-1}}{S_{j-1}}\right) \right\}. \tag{18}$$

As can be seen, the multi-level heuristic is superior to the Order Moment and Wagner–Whitin level-by-level heuristics for practically all values of V_C and V_R. For large values of V_C, the Wagner and Whitin level-by-level heuristic with the McLaren and Whybark setup cost consistently performs better than all other heuristics examined.

Finally, table 3 summarizes the CPU times for a number of selected cases. The

Table 3

Comparison of the CPU times of the multi-level heuristic and the optimal algorithm of Love

CPU times in msec; $n = 10$, $m = 4, 5, 6, 7, 8$

m	4	5	6	7	8
Multi-level heuristic	164	195	239	263	299
S. Love	939	1209	1471	1738	2028

CPU times in msec; $m = 5$, $n = 4, 5, 6, ..., 10$

n	4	5	6	7	8	9	10
Multi-level heuristic	102	126	137	149	174	185	195
S. Love	214	304	411	562	733	892	1209

computer times are significantly lower than the ones required by the optimal algorithm of Love. Moreover, the execution time is approximately linear both with respect to the number of facilities and the number of planning periods, whereas for optimal algorithms the execution time increases exponentially with the length of the planning horizon. The CPU times for the level-by-level procedures do not differ significantly from those required by the multi-level heuristic.

5. A facilities in series capacity constrained dynamic lot-size model: heuristic methods

The heuristics discussed in this section hold for the cost structure given in section 4. These assumptions satisfy conditions (10)–(12) such that theorem 3 holds. From a conceptual point of view, generalization to other cost structures poses no significant problems. It only increases the complexity of the computer programming required to evaluate their performance.

The heuristic procedures analysed are constructed as follows. An algorithm for generating all feasible production–inventory plans for a capacity constrained single-facility dynamic lot-size problem is used in connection with the previously discussed multi-level heuristic for solving unconstrained facilities in series dynamic lot-size problems. A major difference with the uncapacitated problem is that now information from all periods included in the horizon is needed to arrive at a solution. The proposed heuristics are compared to the optimal decomposition algorithm given in section 3.

5.1. Two multi-level heuristic procedures

The first step consists of generating all production schedules for the last facility which are candidates for an optimal solution, that is, production plans satisfying theorem 3. For a constant capacity structure ($c_{m,i} = c, \forall i$) and arbitrary production and inventory holding costs, both the Florian and Klein [77] and the Lambrecht and Vander Eecken [133] algorithms can be used. The latter also holds for time-varying capacities ($0 \leqslant x_{m,i} \leqslant c_{m,i}, i = 1, ..., n$). The very efficient Baker et al. [11] algorithm applies when the variable production and inventory holding costs are constant through time. It also handles varying capacity constraints.

Having obtained all candidate plans for the capacity constrained last facility, the next step involves solving a number of $(m - 1) \times (n)$ — uncapacitated facilities in series dynamic lot-size problems, using these plans as demand vectors for the reduced problems. A number of possibilities exist:

(1) Clearly, if all candidate schedules are considered and one of the optimal models of section 3 is used for solving the reduced problems, then the minimum cost solution will be found.
(2) If all candidate plans are considered and the multi-level heuristic of section 4 is used to solve the reduced problems, then sub-optimal solutions will be obtained.
(3) If only a subset of the candidate schedules is taken into consideration, then optimality cannot be guaranteed irrespective of the algorithm used to solve the reduced problems. This point is illustrated in appendix II.

The two heuristics that we have tested are of the third kind. Heuristic A only considers the best (minimum cost) production sequence for each pair of feasible regeneration points in computing feasible production plans s_k for the capacity constrained last facility. Suppose there are q such plans and denote their production—inventory holding costs by $C(s_k), k = 1, ..., q$. Let $K(s_k), k = 1, ..., q$ represent the total production—inventory holding costs of the solutions of the reduced uncapacitated problems obtained by using the multi-level heuristic. The cost of the selected production plan is then given by

$$\min_{k=1,...,q} \{C(s_k) + K(s_k)\} . \tag{19}$$

Heuristic B, on the other hand, only considers the best (minimum cost) last facility production program s_k^*, i.e.,

$$C(s_k^*) = \min_{s_k, k=1,...,q} \{C(s_k)\} . \tag{20}$$

With this plan as the demand vector, only one reduced uncapacitated problem is solved using the multi-level heuristic. Let $K(s_k^*)$ be the cost of this solution, then the total cost of the selected production plan is given by $C(s_k^*) + K(s_k^*)$.

The mechanics of these heuristics will be illustrated using the following example.

Table 4
Data of example 2

Period	1	2	3	4	5
$P_{m,i}(x)$	$5 + x_{m,1}$	$5 + x_{m,2}$	$5 + x_{m,3}$	$5 + x_{m,4}$	$5 + x_{m,5}$
$H_{m,i}(I)$	1	1	1	1	1
Capacity	12	15	10	9	11
Demand	10	6	7	8	12

Example 2.   Assume a 5-period problem with the following demand, capacities, and costs pertaining to the last facility (table 4). The network representing all feasible pairs of regeneration points is given in fig. 5. Clearly arcs (i, j) for which $\Sigma^j_{k=i+1} c_{m,k} < \Sigma^j_{k=i+1} r_k$ hold, are infeasible and can be eliminated. Moreover, if all arcs leaving node j are eliminated, then the incoming arcs in j may also be eliminated since they can never lead to a complete production plan. Here, arc $(4, 5)$ is infeasible since $c_{m,5} < r_{m,5}$ and as a consequence arcs $(0, 4)$, $(1, 4)$, $(2, 4)$, and $(3, 4)$ can be eliminated.

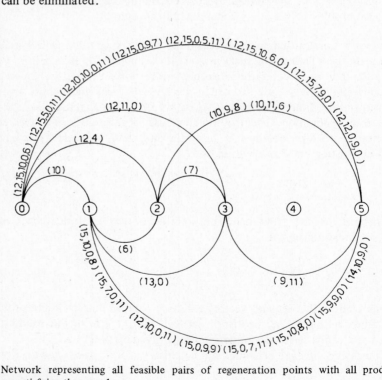

Fig. 5. Network representing all feasible pairs of regeneration points with all production sequences satisfying theorem 1.

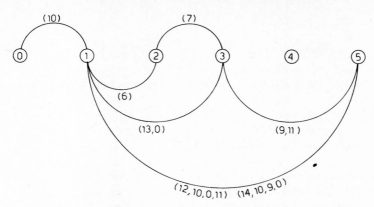

Fig. 6. Network representing only those pairs of regeneration points for which there exist production sequences satisfying theorem 3.

Retaining only those arcs for which there exist production sequences with the first period as partial production period (theorem 3) results in the reduced network shown in fig. 6. Observe that only four complete production–inventory plans remain. These plans are given in table 5. (Note that there are 22 plans satisfying theorem 1.)

To solve a facilities in series capacity constrained dynamic lot-size model for which the last facility is characterized as above, heuristic A computes $\min_{k=1,3,4}\{C(s_k) + K(s_k)\}$; s_2 is not considered because s_1 and s_2 are alternative production sequences for the feasible path $\{(0-1), (1-5)\}$, and $C(s_1) < C(s_2)$. Heuristic B, on the other hand, only computes $C(s_4) + K(s_4)$.

Observe that the optimal solution requires that four reduced problems with production schedules s_1, s_2, s_3, and s_4 as demand vectors are solved optimally (Love algorithm). If cost assumptions (10) and (11) do not hold, then 22 Zangwill problems must be solved to obtain the optimal production–inventory plan.

Table 5
Production–inventory plans satisfying theorem 3

s_i	$x_{m,i}$	$I_{m,1}$	$x_{m,2}$	$I_{m,2}$	$x_{m,3}$	$I_{m,3}$	$x_{m,4}$	$I_{m,4}$	$x_{m,5}$	$I_{m,5}$	Total costs
1	10	0	12	6	10	9	0	1	11	0	79
2	10	0	14	8	10	11	9	12	0	0	94
3	10	0	13	7	0	0	9	1	11	0	71
4	10	0	6	0	7	0	9	1	11	0	69

5.2. Computational results

The inventory holding costs, setup costs and the demand vectors for the 80 test problems were generated as described in section 4.3. Moreover, for each demand pattern several sets of capacity structures are generated using the following procedure:

$$c_{m,i} = \sum_{t=1}^{i} r_t - \sum_{t=1}^{i-1} c_{m,t} + \alpha \cdot x \, ,$$

with α = 50, 100 or 200,
   x = random number $[\epsilon, \epsilon + 1]$.

The selected 80 problems with $5 \leqslant n \leqslant 8$ and $m = 3$ or 6 were then classified with respect to the degree of variability in demand and costs and with respect to the ratio of total capacity over total demand. As before, costs are expressed as a percentage of the cost of the optimal solution which is set equal to 100.

Table 6 summarizes the cost performance of both procedures. As can be seen, both heuristics perform very well, with slightly better results for heuristic A: costs are on the average 101.09 for heuristic A and 101.56 for heuristic B. Further analysis did not show any significant correlation between the quality of the heuristics and the degree of problem complexity caused by factors such as demand variation, cost variation, and the total amount of excess capacity ($\sum_{i=1}^{n} c_{m,i} - \sum_{i=1}^{n} r_i$) which causes an increase in the number of last facility schedules to be taken into account.

Finally, table 7 summarizes the CPU times for the problem solved. A more detailed analysis shows that the execution times increase linearly with the number of facilities, and exponentially both with the number of periods and the amount of excess capacity in the last facility.

Table 6
Cost performance of both heuristics

		$n = 5$	$n = 6$	$n = 7$	$n = 8$	Average
$m = 3$	heur.B	101.09	102.13	100.72	100.62	101.14
	heur.A	101.09	101.54	100.29	100.62	100.89
$m = 6$	heur.B	101.98	102.47	102.60	100.83	101.97
	heur.A	101.98	100.57	102.03	100.54	101.28
Average	heur.B	101.54	102.30	101.66	100.73	101.56
	heur.A	101.54	101.06	101.16	100.58	101.09

Table 7
CPU times in msec for both heuristics

		$n = 5$	$n = 6$	$n = 7$	$n = 8$
$m = 3$	heur.A	186	330	528	909
	heur.B	170	309	446	790
$m = 6$	heur.A	258	430	640	1,067
	heur.B	217	357	492	835

6. Conclusions

Optimal and near optimal algorithms have been developed for capacitated and uncapacitated facilities in series dynamic lot-size problems. Our analysis shows that the heuristic procedures compare very favorably to the optimal models, both with respect to quality of the solutions obtained and the computer times they require.

Other capacitated multi-facility, multi-period problems have been studied [131]: problems in which the first facility is supposed to be a bottleneck operation and problems with capacity constraints on all facilities. The characterization of optimal production—inventory plans in such cases is extremely complex and so far no efficient optimal algorithms exist. Of course, some general-purpose algorithms such as branch and bound and fixed-charge transportation models can be used. We are convinced, however, that special-purpose — problem oriented — algorithms, such as the ones discussed in this paper, are more promising and therefore warrant further investigation.

Acknowledgements

This work is supported by the Research Fund of the Katholieke Universiteit Leuven, Grant OT/V/19. The authors gratefully acknowledge the comments and suggestions of two anonymous referees.

Appendix I

Theorem 3

> If at the last facility there is positive inventory carried over from a previous period, then production is either at capacity or zero; on the other hand, if there is positive production at a level less than capacity, then incoming inventory must be zero

This theorem holds under the cost assumptions (10) and (11).

This theorem means that for the facilities in series dynamic lot-size problems with capacity constraints on the last facility we will not forgo optimality by examining only those last facility production sequences for which the following property holds:

$$I_{m,i-1} \cdot (c_{m,i} - x_{m,i}) \cdot x_{m,i} = 0 , \qquad \forall i \tag{A1}$$

> Part I: For facility m, it is always possible to find production sequences satisfying (A1) and these programs dominate all other plans.

I(a) If for a pair of regeneration points (k, l), called a regeneration interval, it is impossible to have the partial production in period $(k + 1)$ because this results in a negative inventory level for some periods $t, k + 1 \leqslant t < l$, then the regeneration interval (k, l) can be divided into subregeneration intervals $(k, q), (q, s), ..., (j, l)$ for which the partial production period, if there is one, is always the first period of each subregeneration interval, that is, $(k + 1), (q + 1), ..., (j + 1)$.

Proof. Note that it is impossible to locate the partial production period in $(k + 1)$ for the regeneration interval (k, l) if for some period $t, t \geqslant k + 1$ the inventory becomes negative.

Consider the regeneration interval (k, l) and define period $j, k + 1 \leqslant j \leqslant l$ as the last period for which

$$F_{k+1}^{(k,l)} + \sum_{q=k+2}^{j} c_q < \sum_{q=k+1}^{j} r_q . \tag{A2}$$

(Since we are dealing with the last facility, we omit the index m.)

$F_{k+1}^{(k,l)}$: production quantity of period $k + 1$, for the regeneration interval (k, l) ,

with

$$F_{k+1}^{(k,l)} = c_{k+1} - \sum_{q=k+1}^{l} (c_q - r_q) .$$

For all periods $q, k + 1 \leqslant q \leqslant l$ with zero production we set $c_q = 0$. By definition, for $t \geqslant j + 1$

$$F_{k+1}^{(k,l)} + \sum_{q=k+2}^{t} c_q \geqslant \sum_{q=k+1}^{t} r_q ,$$

hence

$$\sum_{q=j+1}^{t} c_q > \sum_{q=j+1}^{t} r_q , \qquad \forall t \geq j + 1 . \tag{A3}$$

The above derivations prove that the regeneration interval (k, l) can be divided into two intervals (k, j) and (j, l). We next prove that for the regeneration interval (j, l) it is always possible to locate the partial production period in period $j + 1$. The proof is by contradiction. If this is not true, then there must exist a period t for which we have that

$$F_{j+1}^{(j,l)} + \sum_{q=j+2}^{t} c_q < \sum_{q=j+1}^{t} r_q ,$$

and as a consequence

$$\sum_{q=t+1}^{l} c_q > \sum_{q=t+1}^{l} r_q . \tag{A4}$$

But since $t > j$ we have by definition of period j [see (A2)] that

$$F_{k+1}^{(k,l)} + \sum_{q=k+2}^{t} c_q > \sum_{q=k+1}^{t} r_q ,$$

or

$$\sum_{q=t+1}^{l} c_q < \sum_{q=t+1}^{l} r_q , \tag{A5}$$

and (A5) is in contraction with (A4), so there does not exist such a period t.

We now still have the interval (k, j) which must eventually be further split up into subintervals; this can be done by following the above procedure. Note that the interval $(k, k + 1)$ exists, otherwise we should have that $c_{k+1} < r_{k+1}$ which means that the regeneration interval (k, l) is infeasible.

In this way the regeneration interval (k, l) can be divided into a finite number of regeneration intervals $(k, q), (q, s), ..., (j, l)$, each time having the partial production in the first period of each subinterval.

I(b) Production programs satisfying (A1) dominate with respect to costs all other plans, considering facility m by itself.

Consider the regeneration interval (k, l). If the partial production period is period $(k + 1)$ all other periods at capacity or zero, then this plan has lower costs compared with any other plan having the partial production period at $j, j > k + 1$.

For example

Plan I $\quad c_{k+1} \; c_{k+2}, \, ..., F_j, \, ..., c_l$

Plan II $\quad F_{k+1} \; c_{k+2}, \, ..., c_j, \, ..., c_l$

For plans I and II the total setup cost is the same. Furthermore we have that

$$\sum_{q=1}^{t} x_q^{(I)} \geqslant \sum_{q=1}^{t} x_q^{(II)} , \qquad t = k + 1, \, ..., l \qquad (A6)$$

so that, given the non-increasing variable production costs (assumption 11), total variable production costs of plan I will never be lower than the variable production costs of plan II.

Finally, given (A6), the inventory levels of plan II will never be higher than those of plan I.

This proves that plan II is always preferable to plan I (or any other plan having the partial production period at $j, j > k + 1$).

The reasoning is the same for the case in which the regeneration interval (k, l) must be divided into subregeneration intervals.

> Part II: In a multi-echelon (facilities in series) context, we will not forgo optimality by examining only those last facility production sequences satisfying (A1).

Consider a regeneration interval (k, l) and assume period $k + 1$ to be the partial production period.

Consider the following two last facility production programs:

Plan I $\quad c_{m,k+1}, \, ..., F_{m,t+1}^{(k,l)}, \, ..., c_{m,l}$

Plan II $\quad F_{m,k+1}^{(k,l)}, \, ..., c_{m,t+1}, \, ..., c_{m,l}$

For the remaining periods, both plans are identical.

Take any path of the production quantities of plan I through the remaining $(m - 1)$ facilities and assume that plan II follows the same path.

The setup costs are the same for both plans through facilities $1, \, ..., m$.

The variable production costs of plan II will never be higher than those of plan I, because of (10), (11) and (A7)

$$\sum_{i=1}^{q} x_{j,i}^{(I)} \geqslant \sum_{i=1}^{q} x_{j,i}^{(II)} , \qquad \begin{matrix} q = 1, \, ..., n \, , \\ j = 1, \, ..., m \, . \end{matrix} \qquad (A7)$$

For facility m, the inventory holding costs of plan II are lower than the inventory holding costs of plan I. This cost advantage equals

$$\Delta = a^{(k,l)} \cdot \sum_{q=k+1}^{t} h_{m,q} \, ,$$

where

$$a^{(k,l)} = c_{m,k+1} - F^{(k,l)}_{m,k+1} \, .$$

Since $F^{(k,l)}_{m,t+1} < c_{m,t+1}$, plan I will have a cost advantage (inventory holding costs) compared with plan II. Indeed, for plan I, a quantity $F^{(k,l)}_{m,t+1}$ must be shipped from facility 1 to facility m, period $t + 1$, whereas for plan II this quantity equals $c_{m,t+1}$. The difference between $c_{m,t+1}$ and $F^{(k,l)}_{m,t+1}$ equals $a^{(k,l)}$ and this quantity $a^{(k,l)}$ is penalized at a rate of $h_{j,i}, j = 1, ..., m - 1$ per unit. But since $h_{j,i} \cdot (a^{(k,l)}) \leqslant h_{m,i} \cdot (a^{(k,l)})$ for $j = 1, ..., m - 1$, and the fact that production schedules are nested, the cost advantage will never exceed Δ.

As a result, total costs of plan II will never be larger than those of plan I.

The same reasoning can be applied if the regeneration interval (k, l) must be divided in subintervals.

Appendix II

Theorem 3 says that optimality is guaranteed if all last facility production programs satisfying (A1) are considered as starting production plans in our multi-echelon structure.

If we only consider the least cost production program for each regeneration interval at the last facility, then optimality is not guaranteed. We prove this statement by means of a counter example.

Example

Period i	1	2	3	4
Demands r_i	8	7	5	13
Capacities c_i	17	7	8	9

Setup cost S_j	$S_1 = 650, S_2 = 100$
Inventory holding costs	$h_1 = 100, h_2 = 100$
Number of facilities	$m = 2$

For facility 2, we have three feasible schedules satisfying (A1):

Plan	$x_{2,i}$			
	1	2	3	4
I	9	7	8	9
II	16	0	8	9
III	17	7	0	9

These three plans are found by evaluating the regeneration interval $(0, 4)$.

Total cost for each plan, facility 2.

$$\text{Plan I} \ \ = 1{,}000$$

$$\text{Plan II} = 1{,}600$$

$$\text{Plan III} = 2{,}500$$

Suppose that we restrict our attention to plan I, the best production plan for facility 1 is then given by $x^1_{1,i} = \{9, 7, 8, 9\}$ and the total costs equal 3,600.

If, on the other hand, plan II is selected at facility 2, then $x^{II}_{1,i} = \{16, 0, 8, 9\}$ and total costs are 3,550.

This example proves that we have to consider all last facility schedules satisfying (A1) and not just the least cost one.

TIMS Studies in the Management Sciences 16 (1981) 95–110
© North-Holland Publishing Company

MULTI-STAGE LOT SIZING: AN ITERATIVE PROCEDURE *

Stephen C. GRAVES
Massachusetts Institute of Technology

This paper considers the lot-sizing problem in a multi-stage inventory system. External demand may occur at any stage, and is assumed to be known over a finite horizon. A heuristic, iterative procedure is proposed and tested for finding a periodic review schedule to minimize inventory and setup costs.

1. Introduction

In this paper we consider a dynamic lot-sizing problem for a multi-stage inventory system. The lot-sizing problem is to determine replenishment quantities for an inventory system which satisfy all demand requirements at minimum system cost. A multi-stage inventory system is a connected set of stages representing the steps for assembly and/or distribution for a family of products. Typically we may characterize a multi-stage inventory system as an acyclic, directed network; examples of such systems are given in fig. 1. A standard classification is to distinguish between assembly and distribution (or arborescent) inventory systems. For an assembly system, fig. 1(b), each stage has at most one immediate successor, while for a distribution system, fig. 1(c), each stage has at most one immediate predecessor. A serial system, fig. 1(a), is both a distribution and an assembly system, while a general multi-stage system need be neither a distribution nor an assembly system.

The objective of this paper is to propose and test a heuristic lot-sizing procedure for a general multi-stage, discrete-time inventory system. We assume that exogenous customer demand is known by period over a finite horizon, and must be satisfied from on-hand inventory without backordering. All lead times for supplying a stage from an immediate predecessor are fixed and, without loss of generality, are assumed to be zero. A lot-sizing procedure specifies a periodic schedule indicating the size and timing of inventory replenishments so that each stage satisfies the demand placed upon it by succeeding stages. The optimality criterion is to minimize total cost over the finite horizon where there are two types of costs at each stage: a fixed cost for placing an order, and an inventory holding cost which we assume to be proportional to the end-of-period inventory at each stage.

* Work supported in part by the Office of Naval Research under Contract N00014-75-C-0556.

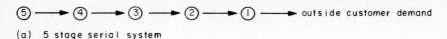

(a)   5 stage serial system

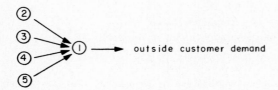

(b)   5 stage assembly system

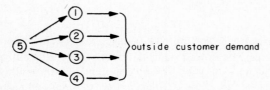

(c)   5 stage distribution system

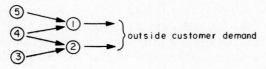

(d)   5 stage general system

Fig. 1. Examples of multi-stage inventory systems.

There has been a great amount of work done on dynamic lot-sizing problems, beginning with the classical work of Wagner and Whitin [243] for the single-stage problem. Significant extensions have been made by Wagner [240] to include dynamic cost functions, by Zabel [246], Eppen *et al.* [65], Kunreuther and Morton [126], [127], Blackburn and Kunreuther [17], and Lundin and Morton [140] to extend and generalize the planning horizon theorems, and by Zangwill [255] to include backlogging of demand.

For the dynamic multi-stage lot-sizing problem, Zangwill [255] has shown that for a serial system the optimal solution is contained in the set of extreme flows of a single-source network, and has given a dynamic programming recursion for calculating the optimal policies. Love [139] also considers a serial inventory problem, and gives an alternate algorithm, which exploits the nested property of the solution. The amount of computation for both procedures is bounded by a polynomial in the number of stages and the number of time periods.

Veinott [233], Crowston and Wagner [48], and Kalymon [108] have considered more general multi-stage problems, and have given algorithms for solving specific problems. However these algorithms are quite complex, with the amount of work required increasing exponentially with the number of stages, the number of time periods, or both.

Due to the complexity of the general multi-stage problem, many heuristic procedures have been proposed. The most common form of heuristic is to consider the stages sequentially, starting with the lowest echelon stages (those closest to the customer), and scheduling each stage with some single-stage procedure which may itself be a heuristic. Examples of such multi-stage heuristics are given in McLaren [145], McLaren and Whybark [146], Biggs *et al.* [16], and Blackburn and Millen [18]. For an *N*-stage system, the amount of work necessary for these heuristics, which we term *single-pass heuristics,* is comparable to that needed for solving *N* single-stage problems. All of the reported work has been restricted to assembly systems. From this work, the heuristic given in [145], [146] seems to give the best performance, although any conclusions are limited by the scope of the computational studies. This heuristic is discussed in greater detail in section 3.

The intent of this paper is to present and test a new type of heuristic, a *multi-pass heuristic* for the multi-stage lot-sizing problem. Whereas a single-pass heuristic sequentially schedules each stage and then stops, a multi-pass heuristic does not stop after the "single pass", but continues to revise the current schedule in an iterative fashion until no further improvements in the schedule are possible. Admittedly, multi-pass heuristics require more computational effort than single-pass heuristics, but hopefully much less than an optimal algorithm. The schedule performance of a multi-pass heuristic should likewise be bounded by that of a single-pass heuristic and an optimal algorithm.

The remainder of the paper is organized as follows: In the next section, a multi-pass heuristic is developed and is shown to be monotonic in cost and convergent. In section 3, we report and discuss our computational experiments comparing the multi-pass heuristic with two single-pass heuristics, and with an optimal algorithm. The last section discusses possible extensions, with particular focus on the capacitated lot-sizing problem.

2. The multi-pass heuristic

The multi-pass heuristic consists of two phases, one in which the current schedule is revised and the other in which various stages are "collapsed" into other

Fig. 2. A two-stage system.

stages based on the current schedule. The presentation in this section will first develop the logic for revision and then will consider the collapsing procedure; this development is motivated first by considering simple systems and then is generalized for more complex systems.

2.1. A revision procedure for a two-stage system

Consider a two-stage system as depicted in fig. 2, in which item 2 is the single component for item 1, the final product. This two-stage structure is the simplest multi-stage system, and is used here in order to simplify the presentation of the proposed heuristic. All results for this system can be generalized to more complex multi-stage structures.

Define the following:

d_{it} = external demand for item i in time period t,
S_i = setup cost for item i,
h_i = holding cost for item i,
v_{it} = variable production cost for item i in time period t,
T = length of scheduling horizon in periods, and
β = number of units of item 2 required for each unit of item 1.

We assume that the initial inventory for both items is zero, the production lead-time is zero, and $d_{11} > 0$. Also, item 2 may have external demand, independent of the demand imposed on it by item 1. For notational convenience, we will identify the single-stage problem with demand requirements d_t for $t = 1, ..., T$, setup cost S, holding cost h, and variable production cost v_t for $t = 1, ..., T$, as $WW[d_t, S, h, v_t]$, that is, the Wagner–Whitin problem. [1] Now the initial heuristic (H1) is as follows:

(1) Solve $WW[d_{1t}, S_1, h_1, v_{1t}]$. If x_{1t} is the production quantity of item 1 in time period t, then βx_{1t} is the demand imposed on item 2 by the production schedule of item 1.
(2) Set $\hat{d}_{2t} = d_{2t} + \beta x_{1t}$ = total demand for item 2 in period t. Solve $WW[\hat{d}_{2t}, S_2, h_2, v_{2t}]$. From this solution, determine γ_{2t} = the marginal cost of increasing demand for item 2 in period t by one unit.

---

[1] These problems are not truly "Wagner–Whitin" problems in that we allow a time-dependent variable production cost, whereas Wagner and Whitin [243] assumed constant marginal production costs. Indeed the solution procedure used is that given by Eppen *et al.* [65].

(3) Set $\hat{v}_{1t} = v_{1t} + \beta\gamma_{2t}$ = restated variable production cost in period t. Solve WW$[d_{1t}, S_1, h_1, \hat{v}_{1t}]$. If there is no change in the schedule for item 1, then stop; if there is a change, then return to step 2.

This procedure is an iterative procedure in which two single-stage problems are solved at each iteration. One might think of countless variations of (H1) in which any heuristic single-stage lot-sizing procedure is substituted for the optimal WW procedure; this paper focuses on (H1) primarily due to its convergence property. We will show that the procedure is nonincreasing in cost, and is convergent. First, though, we indicate how the marginal costs γ_{2t} are determined.

Define γ_{2t} to be the marginal cost of increasing by one unit the demand requirements of item 2 in time period t given a production schedule for item 2; γ_{2t} can be interpreted as a shadow price on demand for a fixed schedule for item 2. Let τ be the last time period prior to t in which there is production of item 2 (i.e., the setup cost is incurred). That is, if x_{2t} is the amount produced in time period t, then

$$x_{2\tau} > 0 ,$$

$$x_{2j} = 0 , \qquad \text{for } j = \tau + 1, ..., t ,$$

or

$$x_{2t} > 0 \quad \text{and} \quad t = \tau .$$

Now we specify γ_{2t} as

$$\gamma_{2t} = v_{2\tau} + (t - \tau) \cdot h_2$$

That is, if demand in period t is increased by one unit, production in period τ $(x_{2\tau})$ increases by one unit with an incremental cost consisting of the variable production cost in period τ, $v_{2\tau}$, plus the holding cost from period τ to t which is $(t - \tau) \cdot h_2$. Note that we assume τ always exists; this is true provided that there is no initial inventory and demand in the first period (external or induced) is nonzero.

We now show that the procedure converges. Define the following:

c_{in} = cost (using *original* costs S_i, h_i, v_{it}) for schedule of item i after the nth iteration,

$\{x_{it}^n\}$ = schedule for item i after nth iteration,

$\{\gamma_{2t}^n\}$ = marginal costs generated after nth iteration from $\{x_{2t}^n\}$, and

Δx_t = $x_{1t}^{n+1} - x_{1t}^n$ = change in schedule for item 1 in period t.

At the $n + 1$st iteration, for item 1 we solve the "revised" problem WW$[d_{1t}, S_1, h_1, \hat{v}_{1t}]$, where $\hat{v}_{1t} = v_{1t} + \beta\gamma_{2t}^n$, to obtain the schedule $\{x_{1t}^{n+1}\}$. If the cost for schedule $\{x_{1t}^{n+1}\}$ using the actual production costs v_{1t} is $c_{1,n+1}$, then the "revised" cost using $\hat{v}_{1t}$ is $c_{1,n+1} + \sum_{t=1}^{T} \gamma_{2t}^n(\beta x_{1t}^{n+1})$. Since $\{x_{1t}^{n+1}\}$ is the optimal schedule for the "revised" problem WW$[d_{1t}, S_1, h_1, \hat{v}_{1t}]$, we have

$$c_{1,n+1} + \sum_{t=1}^{T}\gamma_{2t}^n(\beta x_{1t}^{n+1}) \leqslant c_{1n} + \sum_{t=1}^{T}\gamma_{2t}^n(\beta x_{1t}^n) , \tag{1}$$

where the RHS is the cost for the "revised" problem using the schedule $\{x_{1t}^n\}$. We can rewrite (1) as

$$c_{1,n+1} \leq c_{1,n} - \sum_{t=1}^{T} \gamma_{2t}^n (\beta \Delta x_t) . \tag{2}$$

For item 2 at the $n + 1$st iteration, the demand is given by $\hat{d}_{2t}^{n+1} = d_{2t} + \beta x_{1t}^{n+1}$. The previous schedule $\{x_{2t}^n\}$ may be modified to satisfy this demand $\{\hat{d}_{2t}^{n+1}\}$ by just adjusting the positive order quantities (i.e., $x_{2t}^n > 0$); if $\{y_t\}$ is the modified schedule, we have

$$y_t = 0, \qquad \text{if } x_{2t}^n = 0 ,$$

and

$$y_t = x_{2t}^n + \sum_{j=t}^{\tau-1} (\hat{d}_{2j}^{n+1} - \hat{d}_{2j}^n)$$

$$= x_{2t}^n + \beta \sum_{j=t}^{\tau-1} \Delta x_j, \qquad \text{if } x_{2t}^n > 0 ,$$

where τ is defined such that $x_{2j}^n = 0$ for $j = t + 1, ..., \tau - 1$, and $x_{2\tau}^n > 0$, or $\tau = T + 1$. The cost for item 2 for the schedule $\{y_t\}$ can be shown to be equal to $c_{2n} + \beta \sum_{t=1}^{T} \gamma_{2t}^n (\Delta x_t)$; for $c_{2,n+1}$ being the cost for the optimal schedule, we have by definition

$$c_{2,n+1} \leq c_{2n} + \beta \sum_{t=1}^{T} \gamma_{2t}^n (\Delta x_t) . \tag{3}$$

Adding (2) and (3), we obtain

$$c_{1,n+1} + c_{2,n+1} \leq c_{1,n} + c_{2,n} . \tag{4}$$

Thus at each iteration, total cost is nonincreasing. If we ignore the possibility of cycling, the procedure converges since the single-stage (WW) problem considers only extreme point schedules, of which there are a finite number. Nevertheless, it may be possible for the solution to cycle; that is, the procedure cycles over a finite number of solutions with no cost improvement. This may be avoided by stopping the procedure if any solution is repeated, or by perturbing the data so that no two solutions have the same cost. One possible perturbation is to redefine the setup cost for stage 1 in time period t as $S_{1t} = S_1 + \epsilon^t$, where ϵ is a small positive constant.

2.2. Extension to more complex structures

The heuristic (H1) and its convergence properties are extendable to more complex structures. For instance, consider the following two-echelon, six-stage

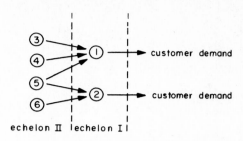

echelon II |echelon I|

Fig. 3. A six-stage, two-echelon system.

system (fig. 3). Define β_{ij} to be the number of units of item i needed for one unit of item j. Then (H1) is modified as follows:

(1) In step 1, the independent single-stage (WW) problems for the first echelon (items 1 and 2) are solved; these solutions determine the demand for echelon II items.
(2) In step 2, the independent WW problems for the second echelon (items 3–6) are solved. Note that for item 5, we have $\hat{d}_{5t} = d_{5t} + \beta_{51}x_{1t} + \beta_{52}x_{2t}$, where $\beta_{5i}x_{it}$ is the induced demand from the schedule for item i, $i = 1, 2$. For each item in echelon II, the marginal costs γ_{it} can be computed as before.
(3) Step 3 is identical to step 1 except that the "revised" WW problems are solved for items 1 and 2. Here the variable production costs are adjusted to reflect the effect of the higher echelon. For instance, we have $\hat{v}_{1t} = v_{1t} + \beta_{31}\gamma_{3t} + \beta_{41}\gamma_{4t} + \beta_{51}\gamma_{5t}$.

The proof of the convergence of this procedure is identical in structure to that given in the previous section.

The extension of the heuristic to more than two echelons is slightly more complex. The original heuristic is inherently geared for iterating between two echelons. With more than two echelons, we must decide in what order the procedure cycles over the echelons. This can best be illustrated by considering the following three-echelon, three-stage system (fig. 4). Here each stage corresponds to an echelon.

Again the revisions to (H1) are straightforward for this structure. Demand at the higher echelons, given schedules for the lower echelons, is

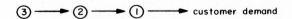

Fig. 4. A Three-stage serial system.

$$\hat{d}_{2t} = d_{2t} + \beta_{21} x_{1t} ,$$

$$\hat{d}_{3t} = d_{3t} + \beta_{32} x_{2t} .$$

The revised variable costs are computed as

$$\hat{v}_{1t} = v_{1t} + \beta_{21} \gamma_{2t} ,$$

where

$$\gamma_{2t} = \hat{v}_{2\tau} + (t - \tau) h_2$$

and

$$\hat{v}_{2\tau} = v_{2\tau} + \beta_{32} \gamma_{3\tau} ,$$

for τ being the last production period of item 2 prior to period t. Note that γ_{2t}, the marginal cost for item 2, reflects not only the incremental cost at stage 2, but also the incremental cost at stage 3.

Now, for this system two procedures suggest themselves for iterating over the echelons:

(a) echelon I → II → III → I → II ...
   Here a completely cyclic procedure is used; having scheduled the echelons from I to III, the procedure returns to echelon I and tries to improve the schedule.
(b) echelon I → II → III → II → III ... (until II and III converge) → I → II → III → II → III ...
   Here, given a schedule for echelon I, the two-echelon problem consisting of II III is completely solved. Given the solution to II and III, the procedure returns to I and revises its schedule. The procedure then repeats with the new schedule for I.

It is not clear which of these two procedures would be more effective. Preliminary computational tests on small examples suggest that the schedules are relatively insensitive to the procedure, but that procedure (b) requires more work than procedure (a).

Both procedures (a) and (b) can be shown to converge. The convergence proof for procedure (a) is given in the appendix. For procedure (b) the proof follows directly that given for the two-stage system; to see this, note that this procedure may be viewed as the solution to a nested series of two-stage problems, each of which is well behaved.

The m-echelon, N-stage problem $(M < N)$ is now just a combination of the previous two extensions. Again, for $M > 2$, we have the problem of deciding how to iterate over the echelons.

2.3. Additional improvements by stage collapsing

The heuristic (H1) is an improvement heuristic. Unfortunately examples can be easily constructed to show that it is not an optimal procedure. Indeed, it is possible for (H1) to give a schedule which not only is not optimal, but which can be easily improved. This section characterizes such situations and proposes a *collapsing routine* which is to be applied to the schedule generated by (H1).

Consider a two-stage system (i.e. fig. 2), and assume there is no external demand for item 2 ($d_{2t} = 0$). For this system it is quite possible for (H1) to give a schedule such that

$$x_{2t}^n = \beta x_{1t}^n , \qquad \text{for } t = 1, 2, ..., T .$$ (5)

That is, item 2 is simultaneously produced whenever item 1 is produced, and no inventory is ever kept for item 2. Note that if $\{x_{1t}^n\}$ is the schedule for item 1 after the nth iteration of (H1), and if $x_{2t}^n = \beta x_{1t}^n$, then we have $x_{1t}^{n+1} = x_{1t}^n$ which implies convergence for (H1). This will occur because at iteration $n + 1$ the "revised" variable production cost of item 1 in product t is unchanged if $x_{1t}^n > 0$, but is higher if $x_{1t}^n = 0$. Consequently, the new schedule for item 2 does not affect the scheduling of item 1.

An implication from (5) is that the two-stage problem may be restated as a single-stage WW problem with setup cost $S = S_1 + S_2$, holding cost $h = h_1$, variable production cost $v_t = v_{1t} + \beta v_{2t}$, and demand $d_t = d_{1t}$. The optimal solution of this single-stage problem must, by definition, be no worse than the schedule in (5). Thus, if (H1) generates a schedule satisfying (5), by collapsing stage 2 into stage 1, we can define a single-stage problem, from which an improved schedule may be found.

This improvement can be generalized for more complex N-stage problems as follows.

Suppose stage j is a successor to stage i. In an assembly system where j is the *unique* successor to i, we may collapse stage i into stage j if

$$x_{it}^n = \beta_{ij} x_{jt}^n , \qquad \text{for } t = 1, 2, ..., T .$$ (6)

That is, we redefine stage j to have setup cost $S = S_j + S_i$, holding cost $h = h_j$, and variable production cost $v_t = v_{jt} + \beta_{ij} v_{it}$. Note that immediate predecessors or inputs to stage i are now direct inputs to stage j.

For a distribution system, the procedure is complicated by the possibility that stage i may have more than one successor. For i being the unique predecessor to j, we need to require that the actual variable production cost at stage j be constant over time, and hence may be ignored. We will collapse stage j into stage i if stage j simultaneously produces with stage i; that is, $x_{jt}^n > 0$ if and only if $x_{it}^n > 0$ for $t = 1, 2, ..., T$. Here, we redefine stage i to have setup cost $S = S_i + S_j$, holding cost h_i and variable production cost v_{it}. All immediate successors to stage j are now immediate successors to stage i. In order to properly account for the inventory holding cost at stage j, all demand at stage i induced by stage j and its successors must be rescaled by the factor h_j/h_i.

After collapsing as many stages as possible, we may now reapply heuristic (H1) to find an improved schedule; the procedure stops when a schedule is found which cannot be improved by (H1), and from which no stages can be collapsed.

3. Computation tests

In order to test the performance of the proposed multi-pass heuristic, we tested the heuristic procedure on 50 test problems generated for each of five multi-stage assembly systems. Fig. 5 gives the five assembly systems each with five stages; these systems are the same as used in [145], [146]. Although all the test problems are for assembly systems, the multi-pass heuristic can be used for any multi-stage system.

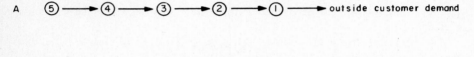

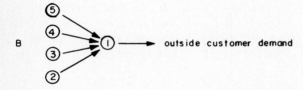

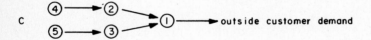

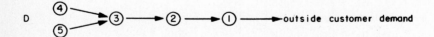

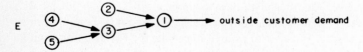

Fig. 5. Multi-stage assembly systems.

Assembly systems were chosen for the computational tests since most of the reported work in this area has focused on assembly systems. The multi-pass heuristic is to be compared with a single-pass heuristic proposed in [146] and with an optimal algorithm from [48] both of which *are* restricted to assembly systems. In generating the test problems, we normalized $h_5 = 1$; for $j = 1, ..., 4$ we set $h_j = e + \Sigma_{i \in B(j)} h_i$, where $B(j)$ is the set of immediate predecessors to j and $e = 0.1, 0.5, 1.0$, and 2.0, each with equal probability. Similarly, S_j is chosen with values 150, 300, 600, 1500; and d_{1t} with values $d_{1t} = 0, 10, 20, 30, 40, 100, 200, 400$. There was no other external demand ($d_{it} = 0$ for all t, and $i = 2, ..., 5$), all variable production costs v_{it} were zero, and the length of the horizon, T, was 12 periods.

For each test problem, we compared the multi-pass heuristic with two single-pass heuristics and with an optimal algorithm. The multi-pass heuristic (MP) that was implemented for these test problems iterated in a full cyclic fashion over the stages; that is, the procedure scheduled stages $1, 2, ..., 5$ using a Wagner–Whitin algorithm,

Table 1

Frequency of optimal schedules (out of 50 problems)

HEURISTIC

		SP-WW	SP-MW	MP
PROBLEM STRUCTURE	A	2	19	41
	B	4	42	48
	C	2	27	44
	D	2	20	46
	E	4	31	47

Table 2

Average percentage cost errors

HEURISTIC

		SP-WW	SP-MW	MP
PROBLEM STRUCTURE	A	8.64%	2.10%	0.58%
	B	3.27%	0.06%	0.05%
	C	5.12%	0.64%	0.26%
	D	7.45%	1.70%	0.31%
	E	4.76%	0.61%	0.26%

and then returned to stage 1 to begin the revisions. Alternative schemes were examined, but did not give significant improvements. The optimal schedule was found using the dynamic programming procedure of Crowston and Wagner [48]. One single-pass heuristic (SP–WW) was to schedule each stage using the Wagner–Whitin algorithm. The second single-pass heuristic (SP–MW) was that proposed by McLaren and Whybark [146]; here each stage is scheduled using the Wagner–Whitin algorithm, but with the stage's setup cost inflated to reflect the possible setups for preceding stages.

The primary results are given in tables 1 and 2; table 1 reports the number of times each heuristic obtained the optimal solution, while table 2 gives the average percentage cost penalty for the heuristics over the optimal procedure. From these tables, in the aggregate the SP–WW is dominated by the SP–MW which is dominated by the MP. However, for each problem structure there were exceptions to this domination such that on a few test problems SP–WW outperformed SP–MW, or SP–MW outperformed MP; SP–WW never did better than MP, since the multi-pass heuristic is an improvement routine which is initiated with the SP–WW schedule. We should note that even though the MP is optimal for about 90% of the test problems, compared with a rate of about 60% for SP–MW, both heuristics have miniscule average percentage cost errors. Also, the performance seemed to vary with the number of echelons in the system; the performance relative to the optimal procedure becomes poorer as the number of echelons grows. For the MP using the full cyclic iteration scheme, this behavior may be explained by the observation that the accuracy of the shadow prices seems to decrease as the number of echelons increases; this suggests that the alternative iteration scheme might be better suited for larger problems.

The computational effort required for the heuristics and for the optimal procedure was consistent with their respective performances. Both the SP–WW and the SP–MW heuristics solve one WW problem per stage, or five WW problems for each test problem; on a PRIME 400 minicomputer, the 250 test problems using the SP–MW heuristic were solved in 53 sec of CPU time (0.21 sec/problem). The multi-pass heuristic, due to its iterative nature, must solve a variable number of WW problems. It can be shown that a gross upper bound on the number of WW problems considered by the multi-pass heuristic, as implemented in this work, is $T \cdot N$, where T is the length of the horizon and N is the number of stages; since the WW problem can be solved efficiently, the multi-pass heuristic is an efficient procedure. For the 250 test problems, the average number of WW problems considered was slightly over 18 per test problem; the total CPU time for the 250 test problems was 115 sec (0.46 sec/problem). The optimal algorithm, as reported in [48], is an inefficient procedure in that the computational work grows exponentially with the length of the horizon; for the 250 test problems the optimal algorithm required 2077 sec of CPU time (8.31 sec/problem).

In summary, the multi-pass heuristic performs better than the leading single-pass heuristic, SP–MW, but requires more work. In light of the computational experience, we conjecture that the effort needed for the multi-pass heuristic will be proportional to that needed for a single-pass heuristic. Finally, we note that whereas the multi-pass heuristic is applicable to general multi-stage systems, both the SP–MW heuristic and the optimal algorithm are restricted to assembly systems.

4. Extension to capacitated problem

The problems addressed in this paper have ignored all possible capacity restrictions; in practice, this is not typically realistic. We believe, though, that the multipass heuristic and its underlying structure will be useful for developing solution procedures for the capacitated version of the multi-stage lot-sizing problem. We may conjecture here on the form of such extensions.

In the presence of capacity constraints, one possible extension to the multi-pass heuristic is to relax the constraints by means of Lagrange multipliers. This relaxation could then be solved using the multi-pass heuristic. Based on the current solution, the multipliers would be revised and the procedure would continue until a solution is obtained which satisfies some preset tolerance level. This type of procedure would be most appropriate when there is a single type of capacity to be shared over all stages.

An alternative procedure would be to try to incorporate the capacity restrictions into the framework of the multi-pass heuristic. In particular, the revision routine might be modified to allow for capacity constraints at each stage in the system. Here at each iteration, a capacitated lot-size problem with both demand and variable production cost being time-dependent, would have to be solved for each stage. Shadow prices for the higher echelons would be determined based on the current schedule, and would be used to revise the schedules for the stages in the lower echelons. However, due to the capacity limitations, the shadow prices, defined as incremental costs, would be valid only over certain ranges of the decision variables. Consequently, the revised schedule from the next iteration may not yield a cost improvement. Furthermore, the definition of the shadow price may be ambiguous when a capacity constraint is binding, in that the cost effect of an incremental change in demand may depend on the sign of the change. Despite these issues, the revision routine, using shadow price information, is still intuitively appealing, and should be explored. The collapsing routine would also seem to be applicable for the capacitated problem; in general, two connected stages may be considered as one stage when the two stages are assumed to produce simultaneously with each other. Here, care must be taken when collapsing stages to properly aggregate the available capacities for the two stages.

Appendix: Proof of convergence for three-stage serial system

Consider the three-stage system depicted in fig. 4. Assume that the revision procedure as outlined in section 2.2 has been applied where the iteration over the echelons is in a pure cyclic fashion (e.g., echelon $I \rightarrow II \rightarrow III \rightarrow I \rightarrow II$ ...). To show that the procedure converges, we will follow the arguments given in section 2.1 for the two-stage system. For notational ease we assume that $\beta_{32} = \beta_{21} = 1$. After the $n + 1$st iteration for $\{x_{1t}^{n+1}\}$ being the schedule for item 1 with actual cost $c_{1,n+1}$, the "revised" cost using $\hat{v}_{1t}$ is given by $c_{1,n+1} + \Sigma_{t=1}^{T} \gamma_{2t}^{n} x_{1t}^{n+1}$. Since $\{x_{1t}^{n+1}\}$ is optimal for the "revised" problem, we have

$$c_{1,n+1} + \sum_{t=1}^{T} \gamma_{2t}^{n} x_{1t}^{n+1} \leqslant c_{1n} + \sum_{t=1}^{T} \gamma_{2t}^{n} x_{1t}^{n} \tag{A1}$$

or

$$c_{1,n+1} \leqslant c_{1n} - \sum_{t=1}^{T} \gamma_{2t}^{n}(\Delta x_{1t}), \tag{A2}$$

where $\Delta x_{1t} = x_{1t}^{n+1} - x_{1t}^{n}$.

For item 2 at the $n + 1$st iteration, the demand is given by $\hat{d}_{2t}^{n+1} = d_{2t} + x_{1t}^{n+1}$. A feasible schedule $\{y_t\}$ may be derived from the previous schedule $\{x_{2t}^{n}\}$ as follows:

$$y_t = 0, \qquad \text{if } x_{2t}^{n} = 0 ,$$

and

$$y_t = x_{2t}^{n} + \sum_{j=t}^{\tau-1} \Delta x_{1j} , \qquad \text{if } x_{2t}^{n} > 0 ,$$

where τ is defined as the earliest period after t such that $x_{2\tau}^{n} > 0$. The cost associated with $\{y_t\}$ for the "revised" problem WW$[\hat{d}_{2t}, S_2, h_2, \hat{v}_{2t}]$ is

$$c_{2n} + \sum_{t=1}^{T} \gamma_{2t}^{n}(\Delta x_{1t}) + \sum_{t=1}^{T} \gamma_{3t}^{n} x_{2t}^{n} , \tag{A3}$$

where c_{2n} is the actual cost associated with schedule $\{x_{2t}^{n}\}$. To verify (A3), note that $c_{2n} + \Sigma_{t=1}^{T} \gamma_{3t}^{n} x_{2t}^{n}$ is the "revised" cost for schedule $\{x_{2t}^{n}\}$ assuming demand $\hat{d}_{2t}^{n} = d_{2t} + x_{1t}^{n}$. When the item's demand is restated as $\hat{d}_{2t}^{n+1} = \hat{d}_{2t}^{n} + \Delta x_{1t}$, schedule $\{x_{2t}^{n}\}$ need not be feasible; the feasible schedule $\{y_t\}$ derived from $\{x_{2t}^{n}\}$, has additional costs which are given by $\Sigma_{t=1}^{T} \gamma_{2t}^{n}(\Delta x_{1t})$, by definition of the marginal costs.

The cost for the optimal schedule $\{x_{2t}^{n+1}\}$ for the "revised" problem WW$[\hat{d}_{2t}, S_2, h_2, \hat{v}_{2t}]$ is

$$c_{2,n+1} + \sum_{t=1}^{T} \gamma_{3t}^{n} x_{2t}^{n+1} , \tag{A4}$$

where $c_{2,n+1}$ is the actual cost of the schedule. Due to the optimality of $\{x_{2t}^{n+1}\}$ we have that (A4) is less than or equal to (A3), which may be written as

$$c_{2,n+1} \leqslant c_{2n} + \sum_{t=1}^{T} \gamma_{2t}^{n}(\Delta x_{1t}) - \sum_{t=1}^{T} \gamma_{3t}^{n}(\Delta x_{2t}) . \tag{A5}$$

For item 3 at the $n+1$st iteration, the demand is given by $\hat{d}_{3t}^{n+1} = d_{3t} + x_{2t}^{n+1}$. The previous $\{x_{3t}^{n}\}$ may be modified to satisfy this demand in a similar fashion to the derivation of $\{y_t\}$ for item 2. The actual cost for this schedule can be shown to be equal to $c_{3n} + \sum_{t=1}^{T} \gamma_{3t}^{n}(\Delta x_{2t})$. If schedule $\{x_{3t}^{n+1}\}$ with cost $c_{3,n+1}$ is the optimal schedule to WW$[\hat{d}_{3t}, S_3, h_3, v_{3t}]$, then we must have

$$c_{3,n+1} \leqslant c_{3n} + \sum_{t=1}^{T} \gamma_{3t}^{n}(\Delta x_{2t}) \tag{A6}$$

due to the optimality of $\{x_{3t}^{n+1}\}$.

By combining the inequalities (A2), (A5), and (A6), we have

$$c_{1,n+1} + c_{2,n+1} + c_{3,n+1} \leqslant c_{1n} + c_{2n} + c_{3n} ,$$

which states that at each iteration total cost is nonincreasing. By similar reasoning to that given for the two-stage example, this result is sufficient to guarantee convergence.

To extend this result to an N-stage serial system is straightforward. Inequalities (A2) and (A6) can be shown true for stage (item) 1 and for stage (item) N, respectively. For stages 2, 3, ..., $N-1$, an inequality identical to (A5) can be established. By combining these inequalities the desired result is obtained.

For more general multi-stage systems, the convergence proof is similar in structure but is complicated by the notational needs. Essentially, for each echelon in the system an inequality similar to (A2), (A5), or (A6) is derived which relates the total actual costs of the echelon at the $n+1$st iteration to those costs at the nth iteration. The details of this proof have been omitted.

TIMS Studies in the Management Sciences 16 (1981) 111–125

HIERARCHICAL MACHINE LOAD PLANNING

James P. CAIE

General Motors Corporation

and

William L. MAXWELL

Cornell University

A combination of mathematical programming techniques is used to determine economic run quantities for each manufacturing stage of a multi-stage production process. The model considers capacities of machines and storage areas, feasible machine-tool-part assignments, bill-of-material relationships, and the economics of lot-size decisions. A previously developed model using subgradient optimization and binary integer assignment algorithms for solution of the tool-to-machine assignment within a manufacturing state is embedded within a dynamic programming approach for determining consistent lot sizes across manufacturing stages. The model is now being used in several plants; implementation issues as well as uses of the model are presented.

1. Introduction

Machine load planning is the process of scheduling the production of parts on a set of machines over a planning horizon. This involves consideration of part demand, a multi-level bill of material, available tools, available machine resources, available storage area capacity, the traditional economic lot-size costs, setup time, and the time phasing of production on a machine. The output of this process is a specification of how many units of each part are run on each tool and when each tool is mounted on various machines.

Machine load planning is now performed by planners using hand calculations in an attempt to arrive at one feasible solution: lot sizes and machine assignments that are consistent with resources available. These hand calculations currently require one person's full-time effort. The spirit of our approach is to replace this one-shot feasibility effort with a procedure that can also address issues of optimality and sensitivity to model parameters.

We develop a model for machine load planning subject to the following assumptions:

(1) The assignment of parts to tools is the responsibility of the user. Consequently we consider only tool-to-machine allocations rather than part-to-tool and tool-to-machine allocations. This assumption avoids the issue of how to assign several

parts of different colors (or different tool inserts of the same shape) to various tools that make the same shape.

(2) The model uses a multi-level *bill of tool* (a precedence structure for tools in the same sense that a bill of material is a precedence structure for the components of a part), derived from the bill of material for parts, to relate the production of components and associated subassemblies and assemblies. In a typical metal stamping plant, for example, level one of the bill of tool might consist of blanking operations, while level two might include forming, and level three, assembly operations. The production process must be consistent with the level make-up of the bill of tool; the machines can be logically grouped into levels so that all production operations of tools on parts move in one direction through the levels. The production process always starts at a low level, such as blanking, and proceeds to a higher level, such as forming. A part can neither stay at the same level nor return to a lower level when proceeding from one production operation to the next (see fig. 1).

(3) Over the planning horizon either a tool is not used or it must be mounted, perhaps several times, on one and only one machine. The same tool cannot be planned for mounting on two or more different machines.

(4) When the production of a part is completed, it must be stored in an in-process or finished goods area. Each storage area has a given capacity and can be associated with only one level of the bill of tool. For instance, a typical stamping plant might have an in-process storage area for blanks, one for formed components, and a final storage area for finished assemblies ready for shipment (see fig. 2).

(5) The planning horizon is logically divisible into a number of equal time periods. For example, the planning horizon could cover 16 weeks.

(6) For each tool and each machine applicable to the tool, the *production cycle* is the time between setups of a tool on a machine and is limited to some subset of 1, 2, 4, or 8 time periods. In practice, this usually amounts to saying that a tool is mounted every 5, 10, 20, or 40 working days. Based upon the work of Elmaghraby [62], there is strong theoretical justification for this assumption. Also, plant managers are familiar with this type of tool cycling, and support information systems are geared to these particular cycles.

(7) The cycles of all components and subassemblies should be consistent with the cycle of their successor(s). In our stamping plant example, the cycle of a particular blank is dependent on the cycle of its associated components and/or (sub)assemblies. Based on work done by Crowston *et al.* [49], an optimal production policy for a tool with one immediate successor occurs when the tool's cycle is an integral multiple of its immediate successor's cycle. This should be intuitively obvious since we do not want to incur more than one setup for the blank before it is used in its successor. If a particular blank has only one successor, the cycle of the blank is an integral multiple of its immediate successor's cycle. An example of this situation is shown in fig. 2, where tool B has a

two-week cycle and tool D-E has a four-week cycle. If a particular blank has several successors, the cycle of the blank is based on a demand weighted average of its immediate successors' cycles.

(8) The model trades off setup and holding costs. There are two types of setup costs: major and minor. Major setup costs include the expenses associated with removing the previous tool from a machine and mounting a new tool. Minor setup costs include the expense associated with changing a tool insert or changing the material to produce a new part without performing a major setup. The model assumes that all minor setups will take place in a predesignated order after the associated major setup is done.

(9) The model uses the concept of echelon holding costs. Using echelon holding cost allows us to compute holding costs for a tool at a particular level independent of the tool's predecessor and successor (see Appendix).

(10) The objective of the model is to determine the machine assignment and production cycle for each tool during the planning horizon that minimizes setup and holding costs and that is consistent with machine and warehouse capacity.

Section 2 of this paper covers the development of the model. The first portion of section 2 covers the relationship between part and tool data, while the last portion discusses actual model formulation. Section 3 describes how integer programming, subgradient optimization, and dynamic programming are used in solving the model. Section 4 discusses how the model was implemented in a stamping environment. Section 5 concludes the paper by discussing future development areas for the model. The appendix presents a detailed explanation of echelon holding cost calculations.

2. Development of the model

2.1. Preliminaries

The model assumes that the user preassigns each part to a tool. This preassignment process is simple in most stamping plant environments because a metal part usually can only be produced on a single tool. In a plastic manufacturing environment, however, we have found that the assignment of parts to tools may be a rather complicated process. Often several plastic parts of the same shape but different colors can be produced on one of several identical tools. The problem that planners often face is how to allocate colors among these identical tools. Since changing colors is a minor setup and relatively inexpensive, planners are usually more interested in generating a feasible part-to-tool assignment that satisfies demand requirements, rather than one which minimizes setup costs in addition to meeting demand. A planner's main objective is to level the load between identical tools so that no tool is overcapacitated and demand is satisfied. Planners will normally use a simple "greedy" approach, assigning "hot" colors (those with imminent initial inventory depletion) to alternative identical tools first, and then allocating remaining production in order to keep color contrast to a minimum on each tool. A planner sometimes finds it necessary to split a color between two tools in order to level tool capacities. This greedy approach, with the allowance of color splitting, gives the planner the ability of assigning colors to alternative identical tools without a complex algorithm.

Since the model allocates tools to machines and leaves the user the responsibility for assigning parts to tools, the model focuses attention at the tool level of detail, not the part. Much of the data for a particular tool is obtained by aggregating data for all parts being produced on the tool. For instance, a tool's storage cost is determined by a demand weighted average of the respective storage cost for each part produced on the tool. The machine time requirements for a tool, however, are more complicated to calculate because both simultaneous and sequential production must be considered. In simultaneous production, several parts associated with the same minor setup (e.g., color) are produced during a single closing of the tool. In sequential production, a batch of one color is followed by a batch of another color after a minor setup (color change) has taken place. A particular tool's total machine time requirement is calculated by summing the *largest* machine time requirement of all simultaneously produced parts associated with the same minor setup (color) over all sequential minor setup (colors) changes for the tool.

Another important tool data item related to parts is the bill of material (fig. 1). A bill of material specifies the material usage of each component part into its immediate successor assembly part. The nodes represent various parts which make up the assembly and the arcs represent the usage in pieces of a component into its successor subassembly or assembly. In fig. 2, assembly A is a finished part ready for ship-

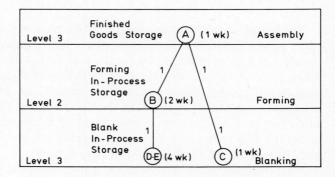

Fig. 1. A bill of material.   Fig. 2. A bill of tool generated from the bill of material in fig. 1.

ment. It consists of one unit each of subassembly B and component C, and sub-assembly B consists of one unit each of component D and component E.

In this model, we are interested in production-oriented relationships not material relationships. Therefore, the part-oriented bill of material is converted into a bill of tool. The bill of tool indicates the manufacturing routing required to produce each part and reflects each production operation of a part. Successive production operations on a part are normally separated by a storage activity. In current applications, the bill of tool is generated by replacing tools for parts in the bill of material, combining bill-of-material entries for parts made by the same tool.

Fig. 2 represents a bill of tool which was generated from the bill of material shown in fig. 1. There are several conceptual differences between the two bills. First, the nodes in fig. 2 represent tools not parts. There is only one node for tool D-E, not two, because tool D-E makes both part D and part E. Second, the arcs in the bill-of-tool diagram have several functions. Instead of indicating usage in pieces, the number on the bill-of-tool arc represents the number of tool closings required for a tool, such as tool B, to satisfy the demand requirements created by one tool closing of an immediate successor tool, such as tool A. The bill-of-tool arc also represents an in-process or final storage activity taking place after a production operation has been completed. Third, there are distinct levels associated with the bill of tool. These levels relate the production and storage of components from tools, such as tools D-E and C, to the production and storage of subassemblies from a tool, such as tool B, and assemblies from a tool, such as tool A. In the example, level 1 represents blanking parts D and E into flat square sheets by tool D-E and part C into round sheets by tool C, and the in-process storage of all blank parts after their production. Level 2 represents forming operations on blanks D and E by tool B to form subassembly B which in turn is stored in the forming in-process storage area. Level 3 represents welding operations by tool A to form assembly A which in turn is stored in the finished goods area.

2.2. Model formulation

In this section we develop a detailed mathematical statement of the problem.

Let t be the index for tools, t' the index for successor tools of a tool, m the index for machines, k the index for possible cycles, and l the index for levels. Level 1 corresponds to the initial processing operations and the highest level, L, to final assembly operations. The decision variables are:

$$x_{tmk} = \begin{cases} 1 \text{ if tool } t \text{ is set up on machine } m \text{ using the } k\text{th cycle}, \\ 0 \text{ otherwise}. \end{cases}$$

Let T_l be the set of tools at level l and M_l the set of machines at level l. As explained in section 2.1, a tool may have zero, one, or more successor tools at levels above the level of the tool. Let S_t be the set of successor tools of tool t. For $t' \in S_t$

let $u_{tt'}$ be the usage of tool t by successor tool t'; $u_{tt'}$ is the number of tool closings of tool t required to make the parts that are used in one closing of tool t'.

Based upon the demand (in tool closings) for a tool, the time required for a tool closing on a machine, the setup time and costs, the echelon inventory holding costs, and the part sizes and containers used for storage one can determine the following constants for the planning horizon (see Caie *et al.* [24] for details):

r_{tmk} = total hours required of machine m to satisfy the demand of tool t using the kth cycle,

f_{tmk} = the total floorspace required to hold the output of tool t when run on machine m using the kth cycle, and

c_{tmk} = the total setup and echelon holding costs when tool t is run machine m using the kth cycle.

Let R_m be the hours available on machine m (see Caie *et al.* [24] or Klingman *et al.* [21] on how overtime hours can be accommodated) and let F_l be the floorspace available for storing the output of level l.

It is convenient to introduce an intermediate variable, α_t, that represents the cycle length for tool t. If $k = 1$ corresponds to a cycle of one time period, $k = 2$ to 2 time periods, $k = 3$ to 4 time periods, and $k = 4$ to 8 time periods, then

$$\alpha_t = \sum_m \sum_{k=1}^{4} 2^{k-1} x_{tmk} . \qquad (*)$$

The problem is now stated as an integer programming problem:

$$\min \sum_t \sum_m \sum_k c_{tmk} x_{tmk} ,$$

subject to

$$\sum_m \sum_k x_{tmk} = 1 , \qquad\qquad \forall t, \qquad\qquad (1a)$$

$$\sum_t \sum_k r_{tmk} x_{tmk} \leqslant R_m , \qquad\qquad \forall m , \qquad\qquad (1b)$$

$$\sum_{t \in T_l} \sum_{m \in M_l} \sum_k f_{tmk} x_{tmk} \leqslant F_l , \qquad\qquad \forall l , \qquad\qquad (2)$$

$$x_{tmk} = 0 \text{ or } 1, \qquad\qquad \forall t, m, k , \qquad\qquad (3)$$

$$\alpha_{t'} \leqslant \alpha_t \quad t' \in S_t , \qquad\qquad \forall t , \qquad\qquad (4)$$

where α_t and $\alpha_{t'}$ are defined by (*) above.

Constraint (1a) ensures that a tool is run on only one machine using only one cycle, and constraint (1b) ensures that the machine hours available are not exceeded. Constraint (2) ensures that the floorspace available after each processing level is not overused. Constraint (3) is the integer programming requirement. Constraint (4) states the requirement that a successor tool's cycle length is not more than the tool's cycle length; this allows us to use the echelon holding cost rates, as explained in the appendix.

3. Solution technique

With only one level to the bill-of-tool ($L = 1$), constraint (4) disappears. Also without the floorspace constraint (2), the problem as posed is a generalized assignment problem which has been addressed by Ross and Soland [194] in the sense that an efficient branch and bound procedure exists. The added complexity of a floorspace constraint, but still with only one level, was addressed by Caie et al. [24]. The complexity introduced by several levels, that is, the consideration of the bill-of-tool constraint (4) appeared to us to exclude the potential of obtaining an overall optimal solution to the problem, since the special case of one level involves enumeration and approximate solution techniques.

If one relaxes the limited cycle possibilities, constraints (1a) and (3), and is not concerned with machine utilization, constraint (1b), or floorspace usage, constraint (2), the model reverts to one considered by Schwarz and Schrage [204]. Since they came to the conclusion that a heuristic solution procedure was desirable for their problem, we feel comfortable in suggesting an *ad hoc*, yet reasonable, overall approach to the solution of the problem.

The bill-of-tool constraint (4) along with the separable nature of the objective function suggests the use of a very simple dynamic programming recursion to resolve cycle conflicts between a tool t and its successor tool t'. Tool t "tells" tool t' what its total costs are for each possible cycle for it and then tool t' selects the best of these, consistent with constraint (4), where best is defined as the least total sum of the costs for tool t and tool t'. We note that without machine resource or floorspace constraints (1b) and (2), the dynamic programming approach will yield an optimal solution since the entire possible state space will be considered.

The solution technique developed thus involves satisfying constraint (4) by the use of dynamic programming over levels and the use of the Caie, Linden, Maxwell procedures for solution at a level.

Starting at level 1 (the initial processing operations), machine assignments and cycle values are obtained by solving

$$\min \sum_{t \in T_1} \sum_{m \in M_1} \sum_k c_{tmk} x_{tmk} \,,$$

subject to

$$\sum_{m \in M_1} \sum_k x_{tmk} = 1 \,, \qquad\qquad \forall t \in T_1 \,,$$

$$\sum_{t \in T_1} \sum_k r_{tmk} x_{tmk} \leqslant R_m \,, \qquad\qquad \forall m \in M_1 \,,$$

$$\sum_{t \in T_1} \sum_{m \in M_1} \sum_k f_{tmk} x_{tmk} \leqslant F_1 , \qquad \forall t \in T_1, \forall m \in M_1, \forall k ,$$

$$x_{tmk} = 0 \text{ or } 1 , \qquad \forall t \in T_1, \forall m \in M_1, \forall k .$$

This is solved using a subgradient approach for floorspace costing followed by a branch and bound procedure to do least cost resource constrained allocations.

The result of this step is a specification of a machine and a cycle for each tool at level 1; for tool t suppose the machine is m_t and the cycle is k_t (i.e., $x_{tm_t k_t} = 1$).

We propose using dynamic programming up through the levels for level 1 to level L. For a successor tool t' at level 2, which is a successor to tool t at level 1, we would like $c_{t'mk}$ to reflect not only the setup and echelon holding cost of successor tool t' at level 2 but also the least cost values for all tools t at level 1 which have as a successor the successor tool t'. The least cost value added by tool t is

$$\min_{j \geqslant k} c_{tm_t j} ,$$

where k is the cycle used by successor tool t', $j \geqslant k$ are the cycles possible for tool t, and m_t is the machine selected for use by tool t when level 1's resource allocation problem was solved. Unfortunately, in solving this problem, a specific value for the cycle of tool t, k_t, was also selected. To allow for other possible values of the cycle, j, we add the relative cost coefficient difference:

$$\gamma_{m_t}(r_{tm_t j} - r_{tm_t k_t}) + \delta(f_{tm_t j} - f_{tm_t k_t}) ,$$

where γ_{m_t} is the dual variable for the resource constraint equation for machine m_t and δ is the dual variable for the level 1 floorspace constraint equation. The dual variables are taken from the output of the subgradient algorithm.

The cost coefficient of $x_{t'mk}$ for successor tool t' at level 2 is

$$d_{t'mk} = c_{t'mk} + \min_{j \geqslant k} [c_{tm_t j} + \gamma_{m_t}(r_{tm_t j} - r_{tm_t k_t}) + \delta(f_{tm_t j} - f_{tm_t k_t})] .$$

This formula is the crux of the dynamic programming approach.

At level 2 we have a problem exactly like the problem of level 1, with cost coefficients d_{tmk}. This is solved in the same manner as the problem of level 1, resulting in machine and cycle specifications for the tools of level 2. The entire solution procedure then works up through the levels, leaving markers so that the nature of the solution can be recovered by backtracking down through the levels.

The above development assumes that a tool t at level 1 has only one successor tool at some level greater than level 1. Unfortunately this is often not the case: the set S_t of successor tools of tool t may contain several distinct successor tools, as in the case when a tool produces a part which has common usage across several different subassemblies. In this case, for $t' \in S_t$, $d_{t'mk}$ should reflect some allocation of the cost contribution of tool t. The allocation we chose to use is based upon the demands of the successor tools $t' \in S_t$; if D_t is the demand over the horizon for tool t in tool closings of tool t, $D_{t'}$, the demand over the horizon for successor tool t'

in tool closings, and $u_{tt'}$ the number of tool t closings needed to satisfy one tool closing of successor tool t' then

$$D_t = \sum_{t' \in S_t} u_{tt'} D_{t'} .$$

The fraction of the cost contribution of tool t allocated to the successor tool $t' \in S_t$ is denoted by $g_{tt'}$, where we take

$$g_{tt'} = u_{tt'} D_{t'} / D_t .$$

The cost coefficient of $x_{t'mk}$ for successor tool t' is then

$$d_{t'mk} = c_{t'mk}$$
$$+ \sum_t g_{tt'} \min_{j \geq k} [c_{tmtj} + \gamma_{mt}(r_{tmtj} - r_{tmtk_t}) + \delta(f_{tmtj} - f_{tmtk_t})] .$$

When working down through the levels during the backtracking stage of dynamic programming, one sometimes finds inconsistent and seemingly irreconcilable cycle length specifications for a tool t with several successor tools $t' \in S_t$. Consider a very simple example for $t = 5$ and $S_5 = \{6,10\}$. Successor tool $t' = 6$ is on a 4-period cycle and backtracking from $t' = 6$ indicates that tool 5 should be on a 4-period cycle. Successor tool $t' = 10$ is on a 1-period cycle and backtracking from $t' = 10$ indicates that tool 5 should be on a 2-period cycle.

If we choose $\alpha_5 = 4$ then $\alpha_6 \leq \alpha_5$ and $\alpha_{10} \leq \alpha_5$ but this may involve excessive buildups of the output of tool 5 to satisfy the demand of successor tool $t' = 10$. If we choose $\alpha_5 = 2$ then $\alpha_6 \leq \alpha_5$ is not satisfied, so that our echelon holding cost calculations are incorrect. One can, however, re-evaluate the holding costs and select the value of α_5 with the smallest total cost.

4. Implementation of the model

The model has been incorporated into the solution phase of a capacity planning system called the Machine Load Planning (MLP) System. We briefly describe the database generation and report phases of the system, since this constituted 90% of the computer programming effort. We also discuss how the system is being used to improve production planning in plastic and metal stamping environments in a large corporation.

4.1. Input data

The database generation phase obtains and edits data. The data needed can be categorized by part, tool, machine, part–tool, and tool–machine.

4.1.1. Part data

Part data includes information associated with the production and subsequent storage of a part at each production operation. Required part data includes part material and labor-added values to calculate unit holding costs; part standard containers, standard pack quantities, and storage locations to determine part storage capacity requirements; average part demand data over the planning horizon to determine total holding cost and machine time requirements of various production cycles over the planning horizon; shape data to designate which cavities of a tool can make a particular part; and a bill of material to specify the usage of each component into its successor.

4.1.2. Tool data

Tool data includes information associated with the setup and production policies of a tool. Required tool data includes major setup manhours to calculate a tool's setup cost on a machine; the elapsed time for setup to determine how long a machine is down for setup and unavailable for production; the available production cycles representing the candidate set of cycles; production rate for each tool stated in terms of attainable tool closings or hits per hour, taking into consideration all runtime and downtime allowances; and production manpower requirements stated as the number of people needed to produce parts on a specific tool.

4.1.3. Machine data

Machine data includes information on the status of availability of a machine. Required machine data includes location, configuration, and capacity information. Each machine must be assigned to a production area which in turn is ultimately uniquely associated with a level in the bill of tool. A machine may be specified as a single facility, part of a machine line, or an entire machine line. The capacity of a machine is stated in hours available over the planning horizon. A calendar is used to calculate the exact capacity available over the planning horizon, taking into consideration holidays, weekends, planned maintenance, regular time shifts, and overtime shifts.

4.1.4. Part–tool data

The system also needs part–tool assignment data to specify exactly which tools make each part. The number of cavities in a tool that can produce a particular part is required information to calculate the part's production rate in pieces per hour. The system has the ability to consider minor setup data for various parts on a tool to determine the cost and time of changing tool inserts or the various material types being processed.

4.1.5. Tool–machine data

The key data of the model is the tool–machine compatibility data which specifies all the potential tool–machine assignments. For each tool, users must indicate all the potential machines a tool can run on and the relative preference of each potential assignment. The users must consider such things as welding configurations, toggle press locations, material isolation problem, automation, and production rate efficiencies when generating the tool—machine compatibility.

In one application the MLP system is being used to load approximately 1500 dies on 300 presses. Because of the great amount of data involved in an MLP application such as this, it has been necessary to develop software to extract as much data as possible from existing plant files to minimize data maintenance. Data interface programs have been written to extract most of the required information from Production and Material Control, Accounting, and Industrial Engineering computer files, edit it, and reshape it into a format that is readable by the MLP system. The only exception to this mechanical data extraction has been the generation of the tool—machine compatibility data. In applications encountered to date, this compatibility data has never formally existed in a computer file. Because of the large amount of potential tool—machine combinations that have to be considered in most of our applications, several computer programs have been written to group logically similar machines together and help the user develop and maintain the compatibility data.

4.2. Reports

The MLP system generates a variety of reports. Most of these reports had to be geared to the managerial cost center organization of the plants. The machine load report displays the tools the system has allocated to each machine. For each tool on a machine the report shows the tool's recommended cycle and the setup and production time requirements over the planning horizon. The machine load summary report summarizes machine utilization by machine, tonnage, department, and plant. The warehouse reports display projected warehouse loads in square feet and the utilization of available storage space resulting from a MLP production plan. The container reports display container requirements by container type and the cost reports display storage, setup, and overtime cost information associated with a given production plane.

4.3. Use

The MLP system can be used for both short- and long-range planning. In short-range planning, the system can be used to support scheduling. In a plastics application, schedulers are using MLP results as a starting point for their scheduling decisions. Schedulers at the plastic plant are basing their schedules on the system's recommended machine assignment and cycle for each tool. They manually consider current inventory status, recent "hot" part lists, and resource balance constraints and manually sequence each of the tools on their designated machines. The MLP system has greatly simplified scheduling in this application. The schedulers are unable to follow the MLP load only about 5% of the time because of instances where MLP loaded too many hot parts on a single machine.

The MLP system can also be used for planning beyond the current week. In long-range planning, the system can be used to answer management "WHAT IF" type questions dealing with how fluctuating demands affect inventory and manpower levels, and capacity requirements for machines, containers, and storage. Several plants have used the system to determine the amount and type of additional machinery that is necessary to meet forecasted demands. Another plant dealing with the production of bulky parts has used the system to design their warehouse storage facilities. The MLP system does not take an excessive amount of computer time when it runs. In a typical application with 1500 tools and 300 presses, the system requires about one CPU minute on an IBM 370/168. Because of these short run times, the users of the system feel free to vary parameters and make several runs when answering management "WHAT IF" type questions.

5. Future developments

Our next development effort in machine load planning will be to extend the MLP system into a scheduling system. The extended MLP scheduling system will not only assign tools to machines and determine economic cycles, but also will specify when to mount a tool on a machine in order to meet production requirements on time. Some of the scheduling considerations will be stockout avoidance and hot part list reduction, balancing labor requirements from shift to shift, considering material availability when lot sizing, and ensuring components are produced before their associated subassemblies.

Our philosophy in developing a scheduling system will be to follow the MLP generated load as closely as possible and still meet demand. On the average, the MLP assignments and cycles will result in good economics and minimum machine and warehouse capacity problems. Since demand requirements for the metal stamping and plastic parts of most of our plants are relatively constant, it makes good sense to base the production schedule on the MLP generated machine load.

An important extension to MLP will be analytic techniques to discourage too many hot parts from being loaded on a single machine during the planning phase. After this is accomplished, our main challenge will be to determine methods to fit together MLP cycle patterns on each machine so that part demand and other scheduling considerations previously mentioned are met.

We have found that current production and material control systems primarily use the computer to perform bookkeeping functions, i.e. to keep track of inventory status and shipping requirements. This function is essential to coordinate production and shipping. There is a great potential, however, in using the power of the computer to analyze information provided by these bookkeeping systems and thereby reduce costs. Analytical systems such as MLP are being developed to assist in the complete process from initial capacity planning through daily scheduling of production runs. This will achieve a better balance between setup costs, machine and labor utilization, and inventory.

Appendix

Echelon holding costs

The holding costs for the inventory produced when a tool is run on a machine are a function of the inventory pattern for the tool. The inventory pattern is a joint function of additions to inventory and depletions from inventory. When a tool corresponds to a final assembly the inventory pattern is assumed to be the familiar sawtooth pattern of EOQ models (we ignore the production time effect) as shown in fig. A1.

If h_t is the holding cost/unit-year, d_t the demand per time period, α_t the cycle length, I_t the average inventory, then

$$I_t = \alpha_t d_t / 2 \ ,$$

and the holding cost is

$$h_t \alpha_t d_t / 2 \ .$$

When a tool corresponds to an intermediate stage of processing the set S_t of successor tools must be considered. First consider the case where S_t has only one member, t'.

If $\alpha_t \geqslant \alpha_{t'}$ then one lot of tool t is successively depleted in lot sizes for the successor tool t', as shown in fig. A2. There are $\alpha_t / \alpha_{t'}$ periods each of length $\alpha_{t'}$ between the production of tool t. The average inventory of tool t is

$$I_t = \tfrac{1}{2} (\alpha_t - \alpha_{t'}) d_t \ .$$

If $\alpha_t < \alpha_{t'}$ then lots of tool t are successively added in lot size for tool t until the entire inventory is depleted by one lot for the successor tool t', as shown in fig. A3. There are $\alpha_{t'} / \alpha_t$ periods each of length α_t between the production of successor

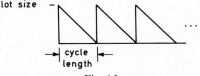

lot size

cycle length

Fig. A1.

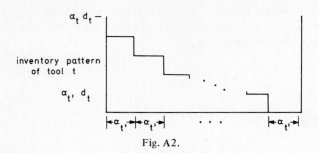

Fig. A2.

tool t'. The average inventory of tool t is

$$I_t = \tfrac{1}{2}(\alpha_{t'} - \alpha_t)d_t \ .$$

The general form is

$$I_t = \tfrac{1}{2}\,|\alpha_t - \alpha_{t'}|d_t \ .$$

If we assume that $\alpha_t \geqslant \alpha_{t'}$ is a requirement (see Crowston *et al.* [49] for a justification and "proof" of the necessity of this reasonable condition and Singer [223]
for arguments whereby this requirement does not always guarantee optimality),
then

$$I_t = \tfrac{1}{2}(\alpha_t - \alpha_{t'})d_t \ .$$

In the expression for total holding costs one would find $\alpha_t d_t/2$ multiplied by h_t
to account for the inventory pattern of tool t and also by $-u_{t''},_t h_{t''}$ for every tool t''
which is a direct predecessor of tool t (the $u_{t''},_t$ term stems from the fact that $d_{t''} =
u_{t''},_t d_t$). The echelon holding cost for tool t, e_t, is defined as

$$e_t = h_t - \Sigma u_{t''},_t h_{t''} \ , \qquad t'' \in \text{predecessors of tool } t \ .$$

The echelon holding cost allows us to compute holding costs as though tools

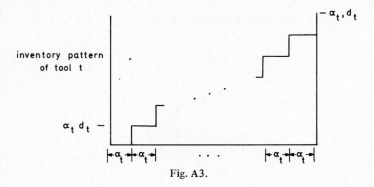

Fig. A3.

were independent of each other. The total value of holding costs will be correct as long as one maintains $\alpha_t \geqslant \alpha_{t'}$.

When a tool has more than one successor, as long as $\alpha_t \geqslant \alpha_{t'}$ for all $t' \in S_t$, the echelon holding cost computed in the above fashion is valid for every successor tool. If $\alpha_t \geqslant \alpha_{t'}$ for some $t' \in S_t$ and $\alpha_t < \alpha_{t'}$ for some other $t' \in S_t$, cost corrections must be made. This issue is addressed in section 3.

TIMS Studies in the Management Sciences 16 (1981) 127–143
© North-Holland Publishing Company

COORDINATION OF PRODUCTION SCHEDULES
WITH SHIPPING SCHEDULES

William L. MAXWELL and John A. MUCKSTADT

Cornell University

Scheduling logistics operations in a multi-echelon production system requires planning and coordination of production and transportation decisions. In this paper we show how these decisions can be made in an economical manner for a real situation involving: (1) limited capacity production lines in an automotive component plant; (2) limited rail car shipping capability at the component plant; and (3) meeting shipping requirements on time for several automobile assembly plants over a fixed planning horizon. The model employed is a special case of a multi-commodity network flow problem. A two-phase heuristic solution procedure is developed, first for weekly aggregate demand and then for shift-by-shift aggregate demand within the first week of the horizon. The straightforward details of disaggregating into production and shipping schedules for products are also presented.

1. Introduction

Scheduling logistics operations in a multi-echelon production system requires planning and coordinating production and transportation decisions for all facilities in the system. Our goal in this paper is to show how these decisions can be made in an actual multi-facility system operated by a large automotive manufacturer. The system consists of a component plant, at which components are produced, and a set of destinations, at which automobiles are assembled. An assembly schedule for automobiles is specified in advance for each week in the planning horizon for each of the destinations. In the real environment, the planning horizon is normally 12 weeks, and the assembly schedule is known for each week of the horizon. The component plant is required to ship the correct mix of products to each destination to meet the automobile assembly schedule on time, considering rail transit times between the component and assembly plants.

The component plant produces components on independent production lines. Certain components can be produced on each line. Only one component is produced on a given line at a time; different or the same components can be produced on different lines at the same time. Changing production from one product to another on a given line is accomplished quickly and at virtually zero cost. This occurs because the fixtures moving down a line are the same for each product on the line, and because every work station on the line simultaneously has all the parts and tools required for each component produced on the line. Production lines are designed to produce components used in the assembly of a limited number of types of automobiles. These production lines can be divided into separate groups so that lines in one *line group* are all capable of producing the same range of components and so that any component produced in a given line group cannot be produced in any other line group.

Only certain types of cars are assembled at each destination. Furthermore, the manner in which components have been assigned to production lines corresponds to the components used at the destinations. Consequently, destinations can be divided into groups such that each component produced in a line group goes to only one *destination group,* and the components used at any destination are produced on only one line group. This relationship is illustrated in fig. 1.

The components produced on all lines perform roughly the same function on each type of automobile (e.g., braking, heating). The production lines are designed to take advantage of the peculiarities of components manufacture that are dictated by the differences in the design of the automobiles. Due to the similarity in their

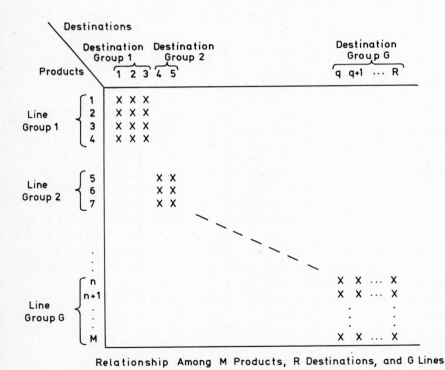

Relationship Among M Products, R Destinations, and G Lines

Fig. 1. X indicates a particular combination is possible; a blank indicates the combination is not possible.

basic design, the cost to manufacture each component on the same group of production lines is essentially the same. Once produced, the individual units are placed in containers which are transported to a warehouse for temporary storage prior to being shipped. The number of components produced on a particular production line is normally measured in container loads and the time required to produce a container load is essentially the same for all components.

Each week in the planning horizon is subdivided into shifts. During each shift container loads of products are loaded into rail cars, which are then sent to various destinations. A rail car is never partially loaded; only full rail cars are shipped. For any given destination, any mix of components can be loaded into a rail car. Also, any integral number of rail cars can be loaded for a particular destination, with no savings in freight cost for multiple rail car dispatching. One rail car goes to one and only one destination.

Assembly schedules can be expressed in terms of rail car equivalents. Thus a schedule can be stated in terms of the number of rail cars of each component that is needed at each destination by a specified week to carry out the planned assembly schedule. Due to the fact that each component is produced on one line group, which is, in turn, uniquely identified with a destination group, we can aggregate the requirements for each destination and express these requirements in terms of *rail car equivalents*. For example, we could state destination twenty's requirement as follows: by the end of week three we must have at least five rail cars shipped to destination twenty from its line group. The component plants can disaggregate this rail car plan by recognizing the exact mix of automobiles that will be assembled at each destination. Thus the production goals for each type of component can be established for each week in the horizon given a weekly rail car shipping schedule and the assembly requirements at each destination. Furthermore, these weekly production goals can then be systematically assigned by component and ultimate destination to each shift throughout a given week.

Other considerations in addition to the ones we have already mentioned must be taken into account when preparing a production and rail car shipping schedule. First, there are weekly and shift constraints on the number of rail cars that can be loaded and dispatched to destinations from the component plant. (These constraints arise from union restrictions on the activities of the rail car loading crews.) Second, a maximum number of container loads of components can be produced on a given line during a shift; however, this production capacity can be divided in any fashion among the components that can be produced on the line plus slack time, if any.

We have noted that production changeover costs are negligible at the component plant, and that the cost of producing a container load of any component is approximately the same. Also, the cost of production does not depend on the shipping schedule since there is adequate capacity on regular time to meet all demands at the component plant. (Overtime, in practice, is used only when an unforeseen shortage occurs for parts used in making the components, or a quality problem occurs at the component plant.) However, the manner in which production and shipping activities occur at the component plant do significantly affect inventory carrying costs at each location. If production takes place several weeks prior to the time that units are needed, then carrying costs are incurred. These units are sometimes stored at the component plant, but may be shipped by rail car to assembly plants in advance of the time they are needed and stored there. Normally if the units are stored at a destination, they are left in the rail cars. The cost of storing a unit, including the additional material handling cost at the component plant and the demurrage for a rail car used as a storage device at a destination, is assumed to be the same at either the component plant or a destination.

We ignore the pipeline inventory of units in rail cars traversing from the component plant to a destination; this time has been taken into account in the assembly schedule at the component plant for a destination.

The production and shipping scheduling problem we have discussed can be modelled in several ways. One possible model would have as decision variables the amount of each component produced on each shift at the component plant and the number of rail cars shipped to each destination during each shift throughout the entire planning horizon. Although this type of model is easy to develop, computational requirements for generating an optimal solution are substantial. For example, the real problem we examined involves 100 components, 10 production lines, 11 shifts per week, 12 weeks in the horizon, 40 assembly plants, 18 containers per rail car, and 20 rail cars shippable per shift. A frontal attack dealing with a container load as the basic unit of data requires solving a problem having 124,120 constraints and 10,810,800 integer variables!

Rather than tackling this computationally intractable detailed shift-by-shift problem for the entire horizon, we propose to separate the production and shipping scheduling problem into two parts. Since weekly assembly schedules are fixed at the destinations for many weeks in advance, we first propose to identify aggregate week-by-week production and shipping goals for the component plant. The aggregation scheme we propose is conceptually similar to the one proposed by Hax and Meal [97]. Aggregation is done over all components that are (a) produced on a given line group, and (b) shipped to a particular destination group. Thus, rather than being concerned with particular components, production and shipping requirements will be expressed in terms of rail car equivalents for each group of components at each group of destinations over the planning horizon. This aggregation is possible since production capacity in each line group is interchangeable among the components produced on those lines and each destination's requirements are produced on only one line group. The first model we develop will determine the number of rail car loads to produce and ship from the component plant to the destinations each week so that the only cost under control, the carrying cost at the plant and the destinations, is minimized while satisfying constraints on: (1) meeting aggregate component demand at each destination; (2) loading no more than a maximum number of rail cars each week at the component plant; and (3) producing no more than capacity allows each week on a group of production lines at the component plant. The model also must not allow a rail car to be sent to more than one destination. Thus, the solution to this problem, which we will call the *aggregate production and shipping scheduling* problem, will indicate the number of rail cars to ship each week to each destination so that overall inventory carrying costs will be minimized.

Given this plan, the second problem we propose to solve determines what components to produce and ship on each shift of the first week so that carrying costs are minimized over this period of time subject to satisfying the constraints on: (a) rail car loading capacity for each shift; (b) production capacity on each line in each shift, and (c) the weekly shipping schedule as established in the solution to the aggregate production and shipping scheduling problem. We also must ship only full rail cars, and individual rail cars can go to only one destination.

Rather than determining these detailed schedules for the entire horizon, we will establish them for only the first week of the horizon. A detailed schedule can be developed for a longer horizon if desired using the methods described.

As will be seen, each of the two problems has a special structure. In the next section we will state a mathematical model for the aggregate production and shipping scheduling problem, analyze the structure of this model, develop an algorithm which exploits this structure, and present an example problem. In the third section, we will show how the solution to the aggregate production and shipping scheduling problem can be disaggregated. In the final section we summarize our results and discuss some possible extensions to the model.

2. Analysis of the aggregate production and shipping scheduling problem

The aggregate production and shipping scheduling problem described above can be formulated as a mathematical programming problem. The model we present takes special advantage of the relationship between a line group and a destination group. Recall: (1) all production lines within a group can produce the same components; (2) components produced in one line group cannot be produced in any other line group; (3) each component produced in a line group is shipped to only one destination group; and (4) the components used at a destination are produced in only one line group. Hence there is a one-to-one correspondence between a line group and a destination group. The weekly production capacity for each line group can therefore be considered as the sum of the capacities of the lines within that group; also, the shipping requirements for all destinations within the same destination group can be aggregated. This relationship is expressed in fig. 2, which shows the flow of rail cars through production inventory, and consumption.

We assume the planning horizon is W weeks in length; the number of production line groups, and therefore the number of destination groups, is G; the demand, measured in rail car loads, for all components used in destination group g in week w is

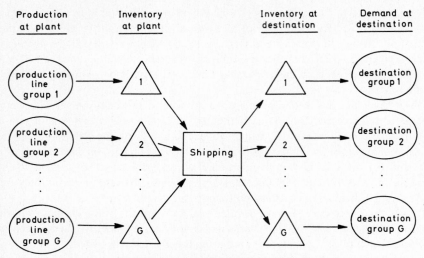

Fig. 2. Production and shipping flow process.

D_{gw} ($g = 1, ..., G$ and $w = 1, ..., W$); and the maximum number of rail car loads that can be shipped from the component plant during week w is L_w.

The decision variables used in the model are

P_{gw} = the number of rail cars of components produced on line group g during week w,

S_{gw} = the number of rail cars shipped from the component plant to destination group g in week w,

H_{gw} = the number of rail car loads of components produced on line group g in inventory at the component plant at the end of week w,

E_{gw} = the number of rail car loads of components on hand at the end of week w at destination group g,

U_{gw} = the slack production capacity for line group g during week w (measured in rail cars), and

V_w = the slack rail car loading capacity in week w.

Recall that the objective of the aggregate production and shipping scheduling problem is to determine: (a) the number of rail car loads to produce on each line group during each week of the planning horizon P_{gw}; and (b) the number of rail cars to send to each destination group each week of the horizon S_{gw}, so as to minimize system carrying charges while satisfying production and shipping limitations at the component plant, and demand requirements for each destination group. The carrying charges are proportional to the number of rail car equivalents worth of inventory carried in the system (excluding those in transit from the component plant to the destinations since there is no way to reduce this quantity). The model can be stated as

$$\min Z = \sum_g \sum_w H_{gw} + \sum_g \sum_w E_{gw} \qquad (1)$$

(minimize the total rail car loads of inventory carried at the component plant and the destinations), subject to

$$H_{g,w-1} + P_{gw} = H_{gw} + S_{gw} , \qquad (2)$$

inventory balance constraints at destination group g

$$E_{g,w-1} + S_{gw} = E_{gw} + D_{gw} , \qquad (3)$$

production capacity constraints at the component plant

$$P_{gw} + U_{gw} = C_{gw} , \qquad (4)$$

rail car loading constraints at the component plants

$$\sum_g S_{gw} + V_w = L_w , \qquad (5)$$

$P_{gw}, H_{gw}, E_{gw}, S_{gw}, U_{gw}, V_w \geq 0$, where $g = 1, ..., G$ and $w = 1, ..., W$ in all of the above cases, and all variables are integers.

The above problem is a near network problem. This can be seen by examining the graphical representation of the constraints given in fig. 3. First, we observe that by ignoring the rail car loading constraints the problem decomposes into G independent network problems, one for each production line group—destination group combination. Next, observe that the rail car loading constraint for week 1 states that the sum of the flows over the G arcs labelled 1 (encircled) cannot exceed L_1. In general, the rail car loading constraint for week w states that the sum of the flows over G arcs having encircled label w (flow is $\Sigma_g S_{gw}$ over these arcs) cannot exceed L_w. Constraints that cut across arcs in this fashion are often called "bundle constraints." The presence of these bundle constraints cause the problem to have a structure that is not a network flow structure. More precisely, the problem is a multi-commodity network flow problem [118], albeit one having a special structure.

We now discuss a heuristic algorithm for finding a solution to the problem, which is based on the problem's near network structure. The complicating rail car loading constraints are first relaxed to take advantage of the simplicity of the structure of the remaining problem. As we have stated, the remainder of the problem has the form of G independent problems. These G problems are all network flow problems that have the form of a linear production—distribution problem with upper bounds on production in each period. This type of problem was first discussed by Bowman [21]. The optimal solution to these individual problems is found by simply producing the destinations' requirements as late as possible. When destination requirements in the future are stochastic in nature, the myopic Bowman type

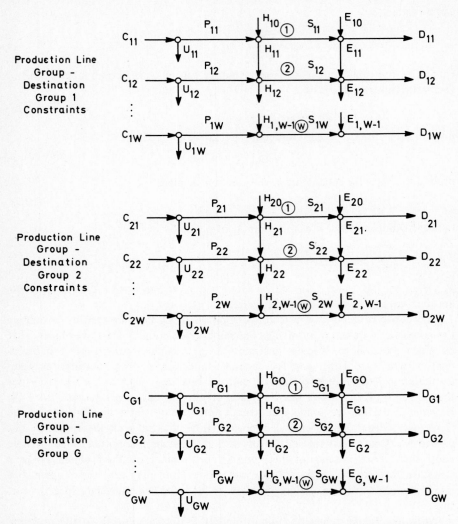

Fig. 3. Graphical representation of the constraints for the aggregate production and shipping scheduling problem.

approach may not be appropriate. We are not aware of any models that adequately address this issue. Once these solutions have been found, the rail car loading constraints that are violated by the solution obtained for the G independent problems are addressed one at a time. Inventory and production decisions are revised but remain as close as possible to the solution found when solving the G independent problems. Let us now formally state the algorithm.

2.1. Algorithm for solving the aggregate production and shipping scheduling problem

Step 1: Obtain the least cost production schedule for each group that satisfies production capacity constraints and demand requirements, ignoring the rail car loading constraints. In the solution, carry inventory only at the destinations. The algorithm used to determine the optimal production plan places production as close to the period in which it is consumed as possible. (A formal statement of this algorithm can be found in Wagner [241].)

Step 2: If all rail car loading constraints are satisfied by the solution found in step 1, then that solution is optimal. Otherwise, beginning with period 1, and proceeding period-by-period, resolve rail car loading infeasibilities by following in order step 2a and, if necessary, step 2b.

Step 2a: If $V_w < 0$, w^1 is the earlier period following w having a positive slack loading capacity ($V_{w^1} > 0$), and there is a destination group g having $E_{gj} > 0$ for $j = w, w + 1, ..., w^1 - 1$, then increase H_{gk} by $a = \min(-V_w, V_{w^1}, \sum_{j=w,...,w^1-1} E_{gj})$, $k = w, ..., w^1 - 1$. Next, adjust V_w, V_{w^1}, S_{gw} and S_{gw^1} to reflect the fact that car loads previously shipped in period w are now shipped in period w^1; also, decrement E_{gj}, $j = w, ..., w^1 - 1$, by a. Examine additional destinations until either $V_w = 0$, there are no destinations for which shipping can be moved into the future, or there is no slack car loading capacity in any future period.

Step 2b: If $V_w = 0$, then return to step 2a and examine the next period for which the car loading constraint is violated (if there are no future periods for which the car loading constraint is violated, then the algorithm terminates). If $V_w < 0$, then beginning with period $w - 1$, and moving back period-by-period as necessary, attempt to find a destination g for which $P_{gw} > 0$ (positive production at destination g in week w) and for which there exists a week $j < w$ for which $U_{gj} > 0$ (there is slack production capacity in week j) and a week k, $j \leqslant k < w$, in which $V_k > 0$ (excess car loading capacity exists in week k). Let

$$a = \min(U_{gj}, P_{gw}, -V_w, V_k) .$$

Then decrement U_{gj}, V_k, P_{gw}, S_{gw} by a and increment P_{gj}, S_{gk}, V_w, H_{gl}, $l = j, ..., k - 1$, E_{gl}, $l = k, ..., w - 1$ by a. Repeat until $V_w = 0$. If V_w cannot be increased to a value of zero, then no feasible solution exists.

The first step of the algorithm establishes the optimal production and shipping plan ignoring the rail car loading constraint. Step 2a adjusts the shipping schedule to eliminate infeasibilities in the rail car loading constraints without increasing the amount of inventory carried. If all infeasibilities are eliminated via these adjustments, then an optimal solution has clearly been obtained. If step 2b is invoked for a given week, inventory carrying costs are increased.

This algorithm does not necessarily reach an optimal solution when step 2b must be used. However, it is a reasonable, myopic type of greedy algorithm. We leave it

Table 1
Demand and capacity data

		Week (w)				
		1	2	3	4	5
Group 1	D_{1w}, demand	4	6	8	10	10
	C_{1w}, production capacity	6	8	8	8	8
Group 2	D_{2w}, demand	3	5	7	9	9
	C_{2w}, production capacity	6	6	8	8	8
	Rail car shipping capacity	10	15	13	16	17

to those interested in the performance of algorithms to address the issues of near-optimality.

We now illustrate the algorithm on an example problem. Assume there are two production line–destination group combinations ($G = 2$) and the planning horizon is five weeks long ($W = 5$). The demand, production capacity, and rail car shipping capacity data are given in table 1. We also assume all initial inventories are zero.

The solution to the production and shipping problem ignoring the rail car loading constraint is given in table 2; that is, the solution obtained from step 1 of the algorithm is given there. We see that this solution violates the rail car loading constraint in week 3. Therefore, we must invoke step 2a of the algorithm. Week 3

Table 2
Initial solution

		Week (w)				
		1	2	3	4	5
Group 1	P_{1w}, production	6	8	8	8	8
	S_{1w}, shipments	6	8	8	8	8
	H_{1w}, factory inventory	0	0	0	0	0
	E_{1w}, destination inventory	2	4	4	2	0
	U_{1w}, slack production	0	0	0	0	0
Group 2	P_{2w}, production	3	6	8	8	8
	S_{2w}, shipments	3	6	8	8	8
	H_{2w}, factory inventory	0	0	0	0	0
	E_{2w}, destination inventory	0	1	2	1	0
	U_{2w}, slack production	3	0	0	0	0
	V_w, slack rail car loading capacity	1	1	−3	0	1

is the first week, and in this example the only week, with a negative slack on rail car loading capacity. The first week following week 3 having positive slack rail car loading capacity is week 5 ($w^1 = 5$ and $V_{w1} = 1$). Destination 1 has positive inventory carried at the destination at the end of weeks 3 and 4 ($E_{13} = 4$ and $E_{14} = 2$). Instead of carrying one rail car load of inventory at destination 1 we can carry that one rail car load of inventory at the component plant. Formally, the algorithm states that the maximum increase in H_{13} and H_{14} is $a = \min \{-(-3), 1, \min(4,2)\} = 1$. Then V_w and S_{15} are increased by 1, and V_{w1}, E_{13}, S_{13} and E_{14} are all decreased by 1. The result of these calculations is given in table 3. Note that the total inventory carried is the same as it was at the end of step 1. Consequently, if the solution found after making these adjustments yields a feasible solution (that is, satisfies the rail car loading constraints), then that new solution is optimal.

Week 3 is still the first week with a negative slack on rail car loading capacity. Looking forward in time from week 3, it is not possible to delay any rail car shipping since there is no slack rail car shipping capacity in either week 4 or week 5. Therefore, we invoke step 2b of the algorithm. Thus we will now look back in time to see what changes need to be made to the production and shipping schedule.

Production lines in group 1 have no excess capacity in weeks 1, 2 or 3 ($U_{11} = U_{12} = U_{13} = 0$) so that no changes will be made to the production or shipping schedule for the production lines in group 1. There is additional capacity on production lines in group 2, however, since $U_{21} = 3$. Furthermore, in week 1 there is available rail car loading capacity ($V_1 = 1$). Thus we can reduce the production on lines in group 2 in week 3 by $a = \min(3, 8, -(-2), 1) = 1$. Then $U_{21} = 2$, $V_1 = 0$, $P_{23} = 7$, $S_{23} = 7$, $P_{21} = 4$, $S_{21} = 4$, $V_3 = -1$, $E_{11} = 1$, and $E_{12} = 2$. Since $V_3 = -1$,

Table 3
Results of first iteration

		Week (w)				
		1	2	3	4	5
Group 1	P_{1w}, production	6	8	8	8	8
	S_{1w}, shipments	6	8	7	8	9
	H_{1w}, factory inventory	0	0	1	1	0
	E_{1w}, destination inventory	2	4	3	1	0
	U_{1w}, slack production	0	0	0	0	0
Group 2	P_{2w}, production	3	6	8	8	8
	S_{2w}, shipments	3	6	8	8	8
	H_{2w}, factory inventory	0	0	0	0	0
	E_{2w}, destination inventory	0	1	2	1	0
	U_{2w}, slack production	3	0	0	0	0
	V_w, slack rail cars	1	1	-2	0	0

Table 4
Final solution

		Week (w)				
		1	2	3	4	5
Group 1	P_{1w}, production	6	8	8	8	8
	S_{1w}, shipments	6	8	7	8	9
	H_{1w}, factory inventory	0	0	1	1	0
	E_{1w}, destination inventory	2	4	3	1	0
	U_{1w}, slack production	0	0	0	0	0
Group 2	P_{2w}, production	5	6	6	8	8
	S_{2w}, shipments	4	7	6	8	8
	H_{2w}, factory inventory	1	0	0	0	0
	E_{2w}, destination inventory	1	3	2	1	0
	U_{2w}, slack production	1	0	2	0	0
	V_w, slack rail cars	0	0	0	0	0

we repeat step 2b. There is still additional production capacity for production lines in group 2 in week 1 ($U_{21} = 2$). We see that $V_2 = 1$, that is, there is excess car loading capacity in week 2. The production on lines in group 2 can therefore be reduced by $a = \min(2, 7, 1, 1) = 1$ in week 3. The results of applying step 2b are displayed in table 4. Since all of the rail car loading constraints are now satisfied, the solution displayed in table 4 is the final solution.

Initial values for inventory at a destination, E_{g0}, can be used to net out destination demand, so without loss of generality one can assume $E_{g0} = 0$. Any required values for inventory at the destination at the end of the horizon, E_{gT}, can be added to the demand, D_{gT}, so one can assume $E_{gT} = 0$.

Initial values for inventory of a group at the factory, I_{g0}, can in step 2 be assumed to be shipped in week 1 to the destination and then netted against demand. Step 2 may shift this inventory from the destination to the component plant, if necessary. Any required values for inventory at the component plant at the end of the horizon can be assumed to be produced on "a-latest-possible-week" basis. To do this one appropriately adjusts the capacities C_{gw}, netting final requirements backward in time.

3. Detailed production and shipping planning

The solution of the aggregate production and shipping scheduling problem discussed in section 2 is a plant that smooths weekly fluctuations in demand over the planning horizon subject to weekly constraints on rail car loadings and production line capacities. In particular, the solution determines what total production should be for each line group and what amounts should be shipped to each destination group in the first week, considering various capacity constraints in future weeks. Thus, the solution specifies the values of P_{g1}, the number of rail cars of components to produce on line group g during week 1, and S_{g1}, the number of rail cars to be shipped to destination group g during week 1. This aggregate plan can be accomplished in week 1 since $P_{g1} \leqslant C_{g1}$ (the production does not exceed production capacity) and $\Sigma_g S_{g1} \leqslant L_1$ (the number of rail car loadings is not greater than loading capacity in week 1).

The aggregate planning information must now be disaggregated to establish the detailed production and shipping plan for the first week. We will show how to disaggregate the quantities P_{g1} and S_{g1} at three levels. First, we disaggregate the first week's production and shipping plan by indicating production and shipping requirements for each of the T shifts during that week. At this stage no attempt is made to establish production and shipping goals by individual product or by specific destination location. All production quantities will be measured in rail car loads without regard for individual product requirements; the shipping requirements and plan will be stated in terms of the number of rail cars for each destination group. The second level of disaggregation specifies how the first week's shipments should be allocated among the individual destinations within each destination group. At this stage no attempt is made to disaggregate by individual product types. In the final level of disaggregation, the aggregate quantities of production and shipping determined in the first two levels of the disaggregation process are divided among the individual products made and shipped to each group.

The purpose of the three level disaggregation process is to determine what components, measured in container loads, should be produced on each group of production lines during each shift, what portion of a shift's production and the inventory on-hand at the beginning of each shift at the component plant should be loaded into rail cars and shipped during that shift to each destination, and what portion of a shift's production should be carried in inventory at the component plant into the next shift.

First, we will show how the first week's aggregate production and shipping schedule can be disaggregated into a shift-by-shift production and shipping schedule for the first week. Recall that the solution of the aggregate model specifies the number of rail car loads of components produced on production line group g in week 1 (P_{g1}), the number of rail car loads shipped to destination group g during week 1 (S_{g1}), the number of rail car loads of components produced in group g in inventory at the component plant at the end of week 1 (H_{g1}), and the number of rail car loads of inventory at destinations in group g at the end of week 1 (E_{g1}).

In addition to the weekly production and shipping goals, we have other data that are used to determine shift-by-shift production and shipping decisions. The capacity of group g during shift t is c_{gt}, which is measured in rail car loads. We assume $\Sigma_{t=1}^{T} c_{gt} = C_{g1}$. We also have the shipping capacity for each shift, l_t, which is also measured in rail car loads. We also assume $\Sigma_{t=1}^T l_t = L_1$.

The decision variables we will have in this first level disaggregation problem are:

P_{gt} = the production on line group g during shift t measured in rail car loads,

s_{gt} = the number of rail cars shipped to destination group g during shift t,

h_{gt} = the number of rail car loads produced in line group g remaining in inventory at the component plant at the end of shift t, and

e_{gt} = the number of rail car loads carried by destination group g corresponding to shipments from the component plant made prior to the end of shift t.

Using these data we can state the first level disaggregation problem as: find the aggregate (without regard to product types or destination within a group) production and shipping schedule that minimizes inventory holding cost at both the component plant and destination groups during week 1 subject to (1) meeting end of the week inventory goals at both the component plant and each destination group; (2) satisfying aggregate demand requirements for each destination group; and (3) not exceeding shift-by-shift production and rail car loading capacities. As before, we assume that the cost of holding a container load is the same for all products.

The mathematical statement of this first level disaggregation problem is

$$\min Z = \sum_g \sum_t h_{gt} + \sum_g \sum_t e_{gt} \tag{6}$$

subject to

$$h_{g,t-1} + p_{gt} = h_{gt} + s_{gt} , \tag{7}$$

$$e_{g,t-1} + s_{gt} = e_{gt} + d_{gt} , \tag{8}$$

$$p_{gt} + u_{gt} = c_{gt} , \tag{9}$$

$$\sum_g s_{gt} + v_t = l_t , \tag{10}$$

$$h_{gT} = H_{g1} , \tag{11}$$

$$e_{gT} = E_{g1} , \tag{12}$$

p_{gt}, h_{gt}, e_{gt}, s_{gt}, u_{gt}, $v_t \geq 0$, $g = 1, ..., G$ and $t = 1, ..., T$, where u_{gt} is the slack production capacity for line group g in shift t, v_t is the slack rail car shipping capacity for shift t, and $d_{gt} = 0$ for $t = 1, ..., T - 1$ and $d_{gT} = S_{g1}$, the aggregate shipment for destination group g in week 1. The reason for defining the d_{gt} as we have is obvious once we examine the structure of this problem.

Observe that this disaggregation problem (6)–(10) is mathematically equivalent to the aggregate production and shipping scheduling problem (1)–(5) discussed in section 2. Since this problem's structure is identical to that of the aggregate production and shipping scheduling problem, we can use the special algorithm developed in section 2 to find the optimal (or near optimal) values for each of the decision variables.

The second level of disaggregation involves assigning the rail car quantities of shipping and production by shift obtained in the first level of disaggregation to each of the specific destinations within a destination group. For group g, suppose there are I destinations, indexed by $i = 1, ..., I$. Let r_{iw} be the rail car demand at destination i in week w; the aggregate demand for group g in week w, D_{gw}, is $\Sigma_{i=1}^{I} r_{iw}$.

At the start of week 1 a total of E_{g0} rail cars are at the destination of group g and a total of H_{g0} rail cars of product are in inventory at the component plant. We will show shortly that the quantities E_{g0} and H_{g0} can be considered to be already disaggregated by destination by showing how the quantities E_{g1} and H_{g1} are disaggregated by destination.

Fig. 4 shows the essential features of the procedure for deciding to which specific destination rail cars are shipped in each shift and for which specific destination rail cars of components are produced in each shift. The top scale has the specific destination demand in rail cars ordered by week and then by destination. The aggregate relations $D_{g1} + E_{g1} = E_{g0} + S_{g1}$, and $S_{g1} + H_{g1} = H_{g0} + P_{g1}$ are shown. The disaggregation of D_{g1} into specific destination demands, of S_{g1} into shift shipping, and of P_{g1} into shift production are also shown.

To find to which destination the kth rail car of shift t (the kth unit of s_{gt}) is to be shipped, one simply projects to the top scale and finds the destination index. Similarly, to find for which destination the kth rail car of shift t (the kth unit of p_{gt}) is produced, one also projects to the top scale and finds the destination index.

The final level of disaggregation is to determine the number of container loads of each of the J components to ship in each rail car or to produce for each rail car. We

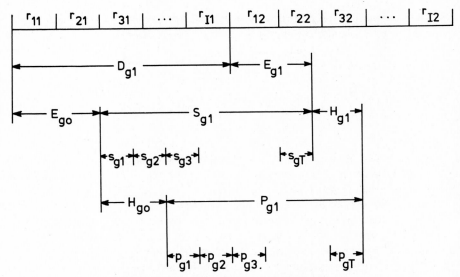

Fig. 4. Disaggregation of rail cars by destination.

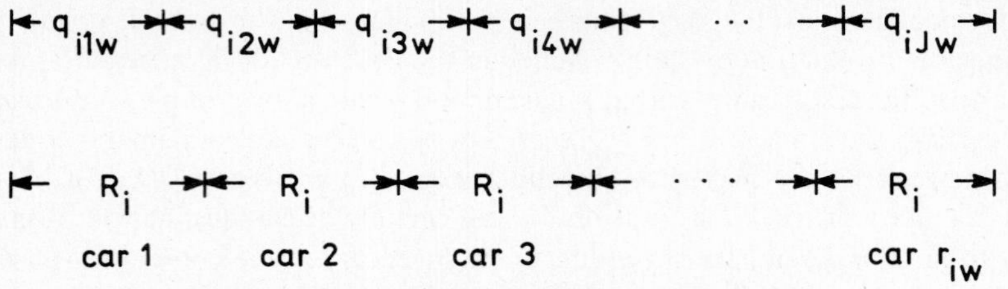

Fig. 5. Disaggregation of rail car loads into products.

show how to disaggregate r_{iw}, the rail car demand at destination in week w.

Let q_{ijw} be the container demand at destination i for product j in week w and R_i the number of containers that fit into a rail car going to destination i. By assumption, $\Sigma_j q_{ijw}/R_i = r_{iw}$.

Fig. 5 shows how this final level of disaggregation is accomplished. To find which product to put in the kth container of a rail car, one simply projects to the top scale and finds the product index. To find the shift of shipping and the shift of production one needs to project downward on fig. 4.

4. Extensions

The models and algorithms we have developed can be extended to other situations. If components produced on different groups of production lines cost different amounts to produce, then the objective function can be modified to reflect the difference in holding costs. Furthermore, the algorithms we presented can be modified so that adjustments to shipping and production decisions are made, in order, from highest to lowest holding costs for the production line group—destination group combinations.

Also, if holding costs are higher at destinations than at the component plant, the algorithm we presented for the aggregate scheduling problem can be modified so that initial inventory is all carried at the component plant rather than at the destinations. The shipping plan can be adjusted in the same general manner as described in the algorithm presented in section 2. The difference is that inventory is sent to the destinations as late as possible rather than as early as possible. Thus the roles of the destination and component plant in the algorithm stated in section 2 would be essentially reversed.

As we have previously stated, the production lines in the real environment involve a fixture for a product moving on a conveyor past a series of many piece part assembly stations. The velocity of the conveyor can be adjusted within limits. This adjustment requires rebalancing the work performed at each station on the assembly line so as to achieve the output rate dictated by the conveyor velocity. Given the position of the operator stations relative spacewise to the position of bins of piece parts, there is a maximum possible conveyor speed. Consequently, a maximum production capacity exists for a production line; this maximum production capacity is C_{gw} (or C_{gt}), since any demand requirements above this amount must be satisfied by production in prior weeks (or shifts). If the actual production requirements are $P_{gw} < C_{gw}$, then the production line can be rebalanced to meet the projected production requirements, P_{gw}.

There remains a very important managerial decision as to how to allocate a fixed labor force among the production lines so as to achieve maximum labor force utilization as well as meet required shipping schedules on time with minimum use of inventory. The model we have presented can be used to help make this decision.

Acknowledgments

This research was supported in part by the Office of Naval Research under Contract N00014-C-1172, Task NR 042-335.

We are grateful to the referees and the editor, whose extensive comments helped to improve substantially the content and exposition of this paper.

TIMS Studies in the Management Sciences 16 (1981) 145–161
© North-Holland Publishing Company

(s, S) POLICIES FOR A WHOLESALE INVENTORY SYSTEM

Richard A. EHRHARDT

The University of North Carolina at Chapel Hill

Carl R. SCHULTZ

The University of New Mexico at Albuquerque

and

Harvey M. WAGNER

The University of North Carolina at Chapel Hill

We consider inventory stockage rules for a warehouse facility whose demand is comprised of replenishment orders from other facilities that follow (s, S) policies. Such a demand process frequently experiences many consecutive periods of no demand; eventually, when demand *is* positive, it can be quite large. Furthermore, the demand process exhibits autocorrelation in that periods of high demand tend to be followed by several periods of low demand.

We confine our attention to warehouse policies of a stationary (s, S) form and, using simulation, find "best" (s, S) policies. We then evaluate easily computed *approximately* optimal policies. We show that policies that ignore the demand correlation perform poorly in that they tend to hold too much inventory and order too infrequently. Better performance is provided by a rule that is an adjustment of the Power Approximation of Ehrhardt [57] to an autocorrelated demand environment. The only demand information required by this rule is the single-period mean and variance and the variance over one lead time. We find that the policy is close to optimal when this information is known exactly, and reasonably close when statistical estimates are used.

1. Introduction

Many wholesale inventory systems exhibit erratic demand histories whose underlying generating process is difficult to characterize with textbook-type probability distributions. Specifically, the wholesale facility experiences several (sometimes many) consecutive periods of no demand; eventually, when demand *is* positive, it may be sizeable and vary within a wide range. One explanation for this observed behavior is that the wholesaler's total demand originates from other facilities which employ (s, S) type replenishment policies. When this explanation is valid, the wholesaler's demand tends to be highly correlated from one period to another.

In this paper, we consider the use of (s, S) replenishment policies for erratic, correlated demand histories that arise in a wholesale warehouse environment. We analyze a two-echelon inventory system consisting of a number of lower-echelon facilities (stores) filling exogenous customer demand and themselves acting as customers to a single upper-echelon facility (warehouse).

Most published research on two-echelon inventory control with stochastic demand (see Clark [34]) has established rules or policies which, when applied at the individual facilities, satisfy a prescribed *system-wide* performance objective, such as minimal *total* expected cost. The complexity of centralized system control makes the problem of determining optimal order and supply policies computationally intractable unless very restrictive assumptions are imposed on both the model and the policy forms. These assumptions seem over-restrictive relative to practical applications. In addition, centralized control over the entire system often is not possible in applied situations, particularly if the owner of the wholesale warehouse does not own the lower-echelon facilities.

In this investigation we depart from the traditional approach of system-wide inventory control and, instead, view the management of the warehouse as a single-facility control problem. The demand process at the warehouse is induced by the aggregated replenishment processes of the stores which, we assume, employ (s, S) type policies. Unlike the demand processes commonly studied in the single-facility inventory control problem, this demand process can be highly erratic and significantly correlated. Little prior research has dealt with dependent demands, and the existing results of Karlin and Fabens [110] are not applicable to this demand structure.

1.1. A wholesale warehouse inventory model

We consider inventory management for a wholesale warehouse, which is the upper-echelon facility of the two-echelon inventory environment, graphically represented in fig. 1. Basic demand enters the environment at a lower echelon comprised of N individually operated stores in parallel. The random basic demand at each store is independently and identically distributed. (In a real situation, the actual number of stores N may not be known to the wholesaler.) This basic demand at each store is filtered through a replenishment policy and, disallowing transshipments of items between the stores, is passed to the warehouse after being aggregated over all replenishment orders.

Specifically, let X_t^k represent the size of the replenishment order received from store k in period t. Then

$$Z_t = \sum_{k=1}^{N} X_t^k \qquad (1)$$

is the entire demand realized at the warehouse in period t. We assume that *at each facility* (warehouse and stores) demand is met as long as there is stock on hand at that location, and when a stockout occurs, unfilled demand is backlogged until sufficient replenishments arrive there. Items kept in inventory are assumed to be conserved, there being no losses by deterioration, obsolescence, or pilferage.

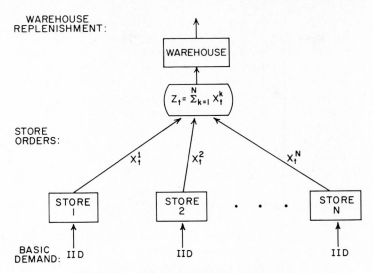

Fig. 1. A two-echelon inventory environment.

Inventory on hand at the end of a given period is the inventory from the previous period plus any replenishment that arrives, less demand in the given period. If inventory on hand is negative, its absolute value is the amount of backlogged demand. At the warehouse, the time sequence of events within any period is taken to be order, delivery, and demand.

We assume the cost structure at the warehouse to be of a simple form. At the end of each period, a unit holding cost h or a unit penalty cost p is incurred for each unit on hand or on back order, respectively, at the warehouse. The cost of a replenishment quantity is assumed to be linear with a fixed setup cost K, and replenishments are assumed to be delivered to the warehouse a fixed lead time L after being ordered by the wholesaler. The criterion for optimal inventory control at the warehouse is minimization of the wholesaler's undiscounted expected cost per period over an infinite horizon.

We assume that replenishment control at each facility (warehouse and stores) is exercised by an (s, S) type policy: whenever inventory x on hand and on order is less than or equal to the value s, an order is placed for a replenishment of size $S - x$. Given the economic assumptions for the wholesaler, an (s, S) policy would be optimal if warehouse demands were independently and identically distributed (Iglehart [102], [104]); methods for computing the optimal policies are developed by Veinott and Wagner [237]. When demands in successive periods are dependent, however, as is the case at the warehouse, an optimal policy is not of the (s, S) form. Nevertheless, in this study we confine our attention to warehouse replenishment policies of the (s, S) form because they are frequently used in applied situations.

1.2. An algorithm to set (s, S) with partial demand information

This paper develops a rule for determining the values of (s, S) in a warehouse environment. This rule is both cost effective and easy to compute. Furthermore, the rule utilizes only partial knowledge of the warehouse demand distribution. Such a rule, the Power Approximation, has been developed by Ehrhardt [57] for the situation where demands are independently and identically distributed. Here we show how to adapt this rule for the postulated warehouse demand process.

The Power Approximation employs asymptotic renewal theory to characterize the behavior of the optimal policy values as functions of the model parameters. Ehrhardt [57] uses these functions to construct regressions with coefficients that are calibrated with a grid of 288 known optimal policies as data. The resulting Power Approximation policies (formulas) are easy to compute and require only the mean and variance of demand. Extensive computational results in Ehrhardt [57] show that the approximation yields expected total costs that typically are well within 1% of optimal.

The Power Approximation is executed as follows. Let

$$D_p = (1.463)\,\mu^{0.364}(K/h)^{0.498}(\sigma_{L+1})^{0.1382}\,, \tag{2}$$

and

$$s_p = (L+1)\,\mu + (\sigma_{L+1})^{0.832}(\sigma^2/\mu)^{0.187}$$
$$\times\,(0.220/z + 1.142 - 2.866z)\,, \tag{3}$$

where

$$z = \{D_p/[(1+p/h)\,\sigma_{L+1}]\}^{0.5} \tag{4}$$

and

$$\sigma_{L+1}^2 = (L+1)\,\sigma^2\,. \tag{5}$$

If D_p/μ is greater than 1.5, let $s = s_p$ and $S = s_p + D_p$. Otherwise, use the empirical modification of Wagner [241]. The modification is based on the observation of Wagner *et al.* [242] that as μ grows large relative to K/h, the optimal policy converges to a single critical number. Therefore, when D_p/μ is sufficiently small, less than or equal to 1.5, S_p is compared with a single critical number that would be approximately optimal if K were equal to zero. The smaller of these two numbers is then used as S in the policy, thereby reducing the separation between S and s. The single critical number used is one that would be optimal if demand followed a normal distribution and K were equal to zero. Define S_0 as

$$S_0 = (L+1)\,\mu + \upsilon\sigma_{L+1}\,, \tag{6}$$

where υ is the solution to

$$\int_{-\infty}^{\upsilon} (2\pi)^{-0.5} \exp(-x^2/2)\,\mathrm{d}x = p/(p+h)\,. \tag{7}$$

The policy parameters are given by

$$s = \min(s_p, S_0) ,$$
$$S = \min(S_p, S_0) .$$

(8)

If demands are integer valued, then s_p, D_p, and S_0 are rounded to the nearest integer.

Since the Power Approximation is designed for independently and identically distributed demands, the term σ_{L+1}^2 given by (5) represents the variance of demand over $L + 1$ periods. Our adaptation of the Power Approximation adjusts this term to account for correlation in the warehouse demand process.

If the demand process is covariance-stationary, then the variance σ_{L+1}^2 of demand over $L + 1$ periods can be written as

$$\sigma_{L+1}^2 = \left[(L + 1) + 2 \sum_{j=1}^{L} (L + 1 - j) \rho(j) \right] \sigma^2 ,$$

(9)

where $\rho(j)$ is the correlation between demands separated by j periods. Thus our adaptation of the Power Approximation is the replacement of (5) with (9). (An analogous approach is successfully used by Kaufman [117] to adapt the Power Approximation to an environment with independent, but time-varying demand distributions.)

It is important to note that the Power Approximation does not rely on detailed information about the structure of the multi-echelon environment. It relies solely upon information about the demand process, as observed at the warehouse. Accordingly, in applying the Power Approximation, the values for μ, σ^2, and σ_{L+1}^2 are computed from known demand parameters, or, in most real situations, from statistical estimates of these quantities based on historical records of warehouse demand.

As the purpose of this study is to demonstrate the applicability of the Power Approximation to a warehouse demand process, we first report in depth on the effectiveness of the Power Approximation when the true values of the warehouse demand parameters are known. Afterwards, we summarize the analysis found in Schultz [202] that demonstrates the Power Approximation works effectively when the demand parameters are statistically estimated.

2. Evaluating the performance of warehouse inventory policies

In order to test the effectiveness of the Power Approximation as a replenishment rule at the warehouse, we must posit a reasonable *base case* for making the relative comparisons. Recall that our criterion for optimal warehouse inventory control is minimization of undiscounted expected cost per period over an infinite horizon. The complexity of the warehouse demand process makes the computation of a

truly optimal policy prohibitive. Even the form of an optimal policy is very difficult to characterize; in general, it will not be of a stationary (s, S) form. Nevertheless, we restrict our attention to (s, S) policies because of their simplicity and
widespread use.

But even if we restrict the cost minimization search to only those policies of a
stationary (s, S) form, severe computational difficulties remain. Therefore, our
base-case policies are themselves only approximately optimal; but, as we argue
below, the approximation is negligible.

We find *base-case* policies as follows. First we generate a history of 5,000 periods
of warehouse demands by simulating basic demands at the store level and aggregating the resulting store replenishments to the warehouse level. Then, using a
Fibonacci search process, we test trial values for $D \equiv S - s$, where for each trial D,
a value for S is found that minimizes total cost for the 5,000 periods of simulated
demand. The best (D, S) pair observed is our base case. The software package is
described in Kaufman [116]. (Because we employ a Fibonacci rather than an
exhaustive search on D, these could be another pair (D, S) that yields even lower
cost for the 5,000 period history.) What we seek from this procedure primarily is an
accurate estimate for expected cost per period. The testing that we have done with
this length of history leads us to believe that our cost estimates are highly accurate
(that is, negligibly little improvement in accuracy would result from a longer run
or an exhaustive search on D). We also are interested in the resulting values for D, S.
We do not seek the same accuracy for these values, however, because our prior
experience has shown that the expected cost function does not vary greatly when
the policy parameters deviate moderately from optimal values.

Kaufman's software provides the computation of cost per period for an
arbitrarily selected (s, S) policy, using the same 5,000 period history of warehouse
demands that yields the base-case policy. The program computes confidence
intervals for the obtained cost per period, thereby permitting a comparison among
alternative policy values.

As in Ehrhardt [57], we test the effectiveness of the Power Approximation by
means of a simulation experiment. The experimental design requires that we specify
the warehouse demand parameters, and the settings that we use are comparable to a
subset of those used in Ehrhardt [57].

We consider a set of 72 independent inventory items to be stocked at the warehouse; table 1 lists the warehouse parameters settings. The four values for mean
warehouse demand are 4, 8, 12, and 16. The variance-to-mean ratio of the warehouse demand process is 9. Three values, $L = 0, 2$, and 4, are assigned to leadtime.
The cost function is linear in the parameters K, h, and p; we normalize the value of
unit holding cost at unity. The penalty cost values are $p = 4, 9$, and 99. The setup
cost values are $K = 32$ and 64. Ehrhardt also examined other cases with lower
variance-to-mean ratios. The Power Approximation performs better when the
variance-to-mean ratio gets smaller; thus, the case in this paper provides a stringent
test.

Table 1
Warehouse parameters

Parameter	Parameter setting	Number of settings
Mean demand, μ_w	4, 8, 12, 16	4
Demand variance/mean σ_w^2/μ_w	9	1
Delivery leadtime, L	0, 2, 4	3
Unit holding cost, h	1	1
Unit penalty cost, p	4, 9, 99	3
Ordering setup cost, K	32, 64	2

The above parameter settings do not completely specify the warehouse demand process, as we have not yet described the erratic and correlated aspects of the process which derive from the replenishment process at the stores. We mentioned above that we actually simulate the demand and replenishment processes at the stores to provide the warehouse demand process. Thus, to complete the statement of our experimental design, we must make the proper connection between store-level parameters and the warehouse parameters.

2.1. The warehouse demand process

Consider a single store with a demand process, denoted by q_1, q_2, ...; that is, a sequence of non-negative, integer-valued, independently and identically distributed random variables having cumulative distribution $\Phi(\cdot)$ and probability mass function $\phi(\cdot)$. Let $\Phi^n(\cdot)$ and $\phi^n(\cdot)$ be, for $n \geq 1$, the n-fold convolutions of $\Phi(\cdot)$ and $\phi(\cdot)$. Let $\Phi^0(\cdot)$ represent the distribution whose full mass is located at zero.

We define the renewal functions

$$M(y) = \sum_{i=1}^{\infty} \Phi^i(y),$$ (10)

and

$$m(y) = \sum_{i=1}^{\infty} \phi^i(y).$$ (11)

Let μ_k and σ_k^2 denote, respectively, the mean and variance of the *demand* distribution for store k.

We assume that the store employs a stationary (s, S) replenishment policy. Let $D = S - s$ and note that the possible replenishment quantity values are $0, D + 1, D + 2 \ldots$.

Using the store assumptions given above, we analyze the properties of the store's replenishment-quantity process. Several important results from this analysis are given by the following proposition.

Let X_t represent the replenishment order quantity in period t. Then the stationary distribution of X_t is given by

$$\Pr[X_t = 0] = M(D)/[1 + M(D)] , \qquad (12)$$

and for $i = 0, 1, 2, ...,$

$$\Pr[X_t = D + i + 1] = [\phi(D + i + 1)$$

$$+ \sum_{j=0}^{D} \phi(j + i + 1) \, m(D - j)]/[1 + M(D)] ; \qquad (13)$$

the mean of the stationary distribution, denoted by μ_r, satisfies

$$\mu_r = \mu_k ; \qquad (14)$$

the variance of the stationary distribution, denoted by σ_r^2, satisfies

$$\sigma_r^2 = \sigma_k^2 + \left[2\mu_k \sum_{i=0}^{D} im(i) \right] \bigg/ [1 + M(D)] . \qquad (15)$$

The replenishment order quantity is asymptotically covariance stationary. The correlation between replenishment order quantities separated by j periods, denoted by $\rho_r(j)$, satisfies the recursive relationship

$$\rho_r(j) = \begin{cases} -\left[\mu_r \sum_{i=0}^{D} i\phi(i) \right] \bigg/ \sigma_r^2 , & j = 1 \\[4mm] -\left[\mu_r \sum_{i=0}^{D} i\phi^j(i) \right] \bigg/ \sigma_r^2 - \sum_{l=1}^{j-1} \Phi^{j-l}(D) \, \rho_r(l) , & j > 1 . \end{cases} \qquad (16)$$

Proofs for the above are given in Schultz [202].

Note that the first-order autocorrelation $\rho_r(1)$ is negative and becomes more negative as D increases. Both of these observations are intuitive considering the nature of (s, S) policies. A replenishment order in one period is likely to be followed by several periods without orders, and as D becomes larger, replenishment orders become less likely.

We now proceed to examine properties of the warehouse demand process as functions of store parameters. We can derive simple expressions for the mean, variance, and autocorrelation function of the warehouse demand process in terms of their counterparts for the single-store replenishment processes.

Consider the two-echelon environment in fig. 1, and let $\mu_{r,k}$, $\sigma_{r,k}^2$, and $\gamma_{r,k}(\cdot)$ be, respectively, the mean, variance, and autocovariance function of the *replenishment* process at store k. Let μ_w, σ_w^2, and $\rho_w(\cdot)$ be, respectively, the mean, variance, and autocorrelation function of the demand process at the warehouse. Several important properties of the warehouse demand process are given in the following proposition.

If all stores operate individually and have independent demand distributions, then

$$\mu_w = \sum_{k=1}^{N} \mu_{r,k} , \tag{17}$$

$$\sigma_w^2 = \sum_{k=1}^{N} \sigma_{r,k}^2 , \tag{18}$$

$$\rho_w(j) = \sum_{k=1}^{N} \gamma_{r,k}(j) \bigg/ \sum_{k=1}^{N} \sigma_{r,k}^2 , \qquad \text{for } j = 1, 2, 3, \dots ; \tag{19}$$

if all stores have identical demand distributions and replenishment policies, then

$$\mu_w = N\mu_r = N\mu_k , \tag{20}$$

$$\sigma_w^2 = N\sigma_r^2 , \tag{21}$$

$$\rho_w(j) = \rho_r(j), \qquad \text{for } j = 1, 2, 3, \dots . \tag{22}$$

Proof is given in Schultz [202].

We use the above propositions to set store parameters (μ_k, σ_k^2, D) so that we obtain the values of μ_w and σ_w^2/μ_w specified in table 1. Specifically, for each store we let $D = 8$, and assume that the basic demand is given by a negative binomial distribution. We investigate two different parameter settings for the mean of the store's demand. We let each $\mu_k = 1$ for one setting, and each $\mu_k = 4$ for the other. Since the warehouse values of μ_w are given (table 1), it follows from (20) that N is four times as large when $\mu_k = 1$ than when $\mu_k = 4$. Hence, we label the first situation as a *many-stores* environment and, by way of contrast, the second situation as a *few-stores* environment. Thus, warehouse mean demand values of 4, 8, 12, and 16 correspond to $N = 1, 2, 3,$ and 4 for the few-stores environment and correspond to $N = 4, 8, 12,$ and 16 in the many-stores environment. Similarly, it follows from (21) that σ_r^2 is 36 in the few-stores environment and 9 in the many-stores environment. The appropriate values for σ_k^2 must be found through numerical methods using (15) as the determining relation. Finally, (16) and (22) yield $\rho_w(j)$. Table 2

Table 2

Environment parameters

($D = 8$, negative binomial demand distribution at each store)

Demand environment	N	μ_k	σ_k^2	σ_r^2	$\rho_w(1)$	$\rho_w(2)$	$\rho_w(3)$	$\rho_w(3)$
Few stores	$\mu_w/4$	4	12.80	36	−0.30	−0.05	+0.03	+0.01
Many stores	μ_w	1	1.70	9	−0.11	−0.10	−0.09	−0.07

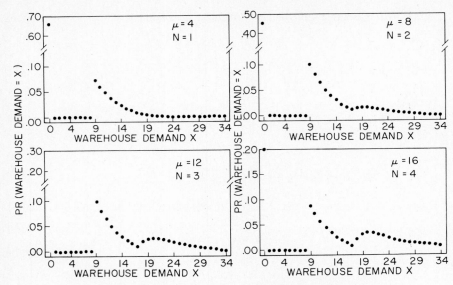

Fig. 2. Probability mass functions for the few-stores environment.

summarizes all the store parameter settings and indicates the implied warehouse autocorrelations.

Observe in table 2 for the few-stores environment that the autocorrelation function has a value of −0.30 at lag one and rapidly approaches zero for lags greater than one. For the many-stores environment the autocorrelation function has a value of −0.11 at lag one and slowly goes to zero as the lag number increases. The difference between the autocorrelation functions arises from the different values for the mean and variance of the store's demand distribution.

Fig. 2 plots the warehouse demand distribution for each of the four values of mean demand in the few-stores environment. The distributions are quite erratic; that is, demand is most likely to be zero, but when it is positive, it tends to be large.

Note for $N = 1$ the high probability of zero demand and the monotonically decreasing curve for demand values beyond $D + 1$. Note for $N = 2$ a slight increase in the probability mass begins at $2(D + 1)$. This is the effect of the second store. For $N = 3$ and $N = 4$ we still observe this bulge which begins at $2(D + 1)$; however, it becomes more pronounced when $N = 4$. The effect of more stores is to shift more mass into the tail of the distribution.

3. I.I.D. optimal policy in a warehouse environment

Here we address the question of what happens in determining (s, S) polices for the warehouse if the autocorrelation component in the demand process is ignored.

How far would the system be from operating at minimum expected cost?

To explore this question, we examine (s, S) policies that would be optimal if, contrary to fact, the warehouse demands were independently and identically distributed, with mean μ_w and variance-to-mean ratio $\sigma_w^2/\mu_w = 9$. We further postulate, also contrary to fact, that the distribution form of the demand process is negative binomial. Then using the algorithm of Veinott and Wagner [237], as programmed by Kaufman [116], we compute an (s, S) policy, which we designate here as the I.I.D. optimal policy. We compare the I.I.D. optimal policies with our base-case policies, using the experimental design given in the preceding section.

Table 3 summarizes the performance of I.I.D. optimal policies in both warehouse demand environments by aggregating cost components over each of the 72-item systems. We compare these policies with the base-case policies by listing the increase in aggregate costs over the costs associated with the base-case policies. The total cost performance of the I.I.D. optimal policies is 8.8% and 7.1% higher than the base-case values for the few-stores environment and the many-stores environment, respectively. The statistical error in the cost estimates in table 3 (as well as those in table 4 later) is negligible. A 95% confidence interval for any average total cost we derive has limits that are between 8 and 19 units of the total shown. For example, in the few-stores environment, the 95% confidence interval for the base-case policies is 3,081 ± 19, and for the I.I.D. optimal policies is 3,351 ± 8.

The degradation in total cost performance is clearly the result of holding too much inventory. Specifically, 31% more inventory is held in the few-stores environment, and 25% more in the many-stores environment.

In addition, inventory costs account for approximately two-thirds of the total cost in both environments. Observe that backlog and replenishment costs are significantly lower in both environments; however, the savings over base-case values

Table 3

Summary of the performance of I.I.D. optimal policies for two 72-item warehouse inventory systems

Cost component	Few-stores environment		Many-stores environment	
	Average costs per period [a]	Increase over base-case values [b]	Average costs per period	Increase over base-case values
Inventory	2,288 (68.3)	541 [31.0]	2,297 (67.2)	462 [25.1]
Backlog	311 (9.3)	−155 [−33.4]	369 (10.8)	−112 [−23.3]
Replenishment	752 (22.5)	−116 [−13.3]	752 (22.0)	−122 [−14.0]
Total	3,351 (100.0)	270 [8.8]	3,417 (100.0)	227 [7.1]

[a] Numbers in parentheses are percentages of total cost.
[b] Numbers in brackets are percentage differences in cost components over base-case values.

are not substantial enough to offset the substantial rise in inventory holding costs.

The I.I.D. optimal policies are unsatisfactory, especially for those items with a high penalty cost or a long lead time. In general, the I.I.D. optimal policies hold too much inventory and order too infrequently. It is not surprising that performance is especially poor for long lead times and high penalty costs. A long lead time causes a severe overestimate of lead time demand variance, an error which is particularly serious when the unit penalty cost is large. Hence it can be very costly to ignore the erratic and correlated nature of the warehouse demand process. We discuss next a policy that adjusts for correlation in the warehouse demand process.

4. The Power Approximation in a warehouse environment

In the previous section we observed that the correlated and erratic nature of the warehouse demand process cannot be overlooked without serious degradation in system performance. Klincewicz [120] studied the effectiveness of the Power Approximation in a particular sporadic demand environment in which demands are independently and identically distributed. He studied demand distributions that have considerable probability of no demand in a period and also have a high variance-to-mean ratio. His results indicate that the Power Approximation performance in such an environment is close to optimal. The erratic effect in the warehouse demand environment is similar, and, for this reason, we have concentrated on the effects of correlation in the warehouse demand process.

We present an adaptation of the Power Approximation to a correlated demand environment; it requires only knowledge of the mean, variance, and autocorrelation function up to lag L. Its performance is close to that of the base-case policies. Specifically, for the few-stores and many-stores environments the policies yield aggregate total costs of only 2.6% and 3.4%, respectively, above expected costs for the base-case policies, as we show below.

In the Power Approximation expressions (2), (3), and (4) for s and D, we find the term

$$\sigma_{L+1}^2 = (L + 1)\, \sigma^2 \,, \tag{23}$$

where σ^2 represents the variance of the demand process. Since the Power Approximation was derived for independently and identically distributed demands, the term σ_{L+1}^2 represents the variance of demand over $L + 1$ periods. We modify the Power Approximation by simply replacing (23) with the more general expression

$$\sigma_{L+1}^2 = \left[(L + 1) + 2 \sum_{j=1}^{L} (L + 1 - j)\, \rho(j) \right] \sigma^2 \,, \tag{24}$$

where $\rho(j)$ is the autocorrelation of the process at lag j. We refer to the Power Approximation with (24) replacing (23) as the Correlation-Adjusted Power Approximation.

Upon examination of the autocorrelation functions for both demand environments, it is clear that the correlation-adjusted variance over $L + 1$ periods will be
less than $(L + 1)\ \sigma^2$. For example, in the few-stores environment for $L = 4$, the
reductions are 40–50%.

4.1. The performance of Correlation-Adjusted Power Approximation policies

Table 4 summarizes the performance of the Correlation-Adjusted Power Approximation policies for both warehouse demand environments. The data are generated
by the simulation program described in section 2. The components of aggregate
average total cost per period are listed and are compared with the corresponding
costs when the systems are controlled by base-case policies. Note the total cost
component is only 2.6% above base-case policy performance for the few-stores
environment and 3.4% above for the many-stores environment. Inventory holding
costs are above base-case values, whereas backlog and replenishment costs are below
base-case values. The I.I.D. optimal policies displayed the same characteristics; however, here the differences are less severe. Substantial improvement has been made
in the inventory cost component due to lower values for S. In particular, inventory
costs for the few-stores environment are down from 31% to 10.5% above base-case
values. Replenishment costs for both environments are, respectively, 11.5% and
12.5% below base-case values. Since D is virtually unchanged, these percentages are
only slightly smaller than the corresponding percentages when using the I.I.D.
optimal policies. Backlog costs are, respectively, 1% and 5.5% below base-case
values for the few-stores environment and the many-stores environment, and are
much closer to base-case values than the corresponding backlog costs using the
I.I.D. optimal policies. This can be attributed to the lower values of s. The improvement over I.I.D. optimal policies is particularly noticeable for those items with large

Table 4
Summary of the performance of Correlation-Adjusted Power Approximation policies for two
72-item warehouse inventory systems

Cost component	Few-stores environment		Many-stores environment	
	Average costs per period [a]	Increase over base-case values [b]	Average costs per period	Increase over base-case values
Inventory	1,930 (61.1)	183 [10.5]	2,080 (63.1)	225 [13.3]
Backlog	461 (14.6)	−5 [−1.0]	454 (13.8)	−27 [−5.5]
Replenishment	768 (24.3)	−100 [−11.5]	765 (23.2)	−109 [−12.5]
Total	3,160 (100.0)	79 [2.6]	3,299 (100.0)	109 [3.4]

[a] Numbers in parentheses are percentages of total cost.
[b] Numbers in brackets are percentage differences in cost components over base-case values.

Table 5

Percentage above base-case costs per period for a 72-item warehouse inventory system

Cost component	Total	Input parameters											
		Penalty			Setup		Lead time			Mean			
		4	9	99	32	64	0	2	4	4	8	12	16
Few-stores:													
Inventory	10.5	−4.0	3.2	20.9	15.1	6.5	9.2	11.0	11.1	12.0	12.5	8.4	10.3
Backlog	−1.0	20.3	12.6	−49.5	−14.1	11.8	7.3	−1.8	−6.4	1.8	4.5	−3.2	−4.6
Replenishment	−11.5	−5.4	−10.0	−18.2	−13.1	−10.5	−10.8	−12.4	−11.4	−11.7	−15.8	−8.0	−11.3
Total	2.6	0.9	0.9	4.8	3.2	2.0	2.6	2.5	2.6	4.1	3.0	2.1	1.9
Many-stores:													
Inventory	13.3	−1.7	5.7	24.1	17.5	9.6	11.1	13.0	15.2	18.5	16.7	8.4	12.7
Backlog	−5.5	17.4	9.1	−60.0	−14.6	3.4	2.2	−6.0	−11.7	−13.3	−3.1	−0.2	−8.1
Replenishment	−12.5	−7.2	−13.2	−16.5	−15.6	−10.3	−14.5	−11.8	−10.9	−13.2	−18.3	−7.9	−11.5
Total	3.4	0.7	0.7	7.1	4.1	2.8	1.4	3.7	4.8	5.2	3.6	2.9	2.9

lead times. For example, total cost for the group of items with a lead time of 4 in the few-stores environment is down from 12.6% to 2.6% above base-case values.

Table 5 shows percentages above base-case values for each cost component and parameter setting using the Correlation-Adjusted Power Approximation policies. The total cost component reveals that, with the exception of those items with high penalty cost, the Correlation-Adjusted Power Approximation performance is close to base-case performance.

We pointed out above that our selection of parameters for the 72-item test system is motivated by earlier research on the Power Approximation, and the test items used here represent a stringent set, in our opinion. Schultz [202] has examined another 72-item system where the assumption that all the stores have the same demand process and replenishment rule ($D = 8$) is dropped. Schultz found the performance of the Correlation-Adjusted Power Approximation to be as good as or better than that for the identical stores environment reported here.

4.2. Estimated demand

In most real warehouse environments, the values for μ_w and σ_{L+1}^2 are not known exactly. They must be estimated from historical data. Schultz [202] has examined in depth the performance of the Correlation-Adjusted Power Approximation policies when statistical estimates are used. We present only a summary of those results here.

The statistics required are the estimators of the mean, variance, and variance of demand over one leadtime, denoted $\hat{\mu}_w$, $\hat{\sigma}_w^2$, and $\hat{\sigma}_{L+1}^2$, respectively. Let T be the number of observations of past warehouse demands, and let $t(\geqslant T)$ be the period in which a policy revision is to be made. Then, estimate the mean μ_w of the warehouse demand process $\{Z_i, i \geqslant 1\}$ by

$$\hat{\mu}_w = T^{-1} \sum_{\tau=1}^{T} Z_{t-\tau} , \tag{25}$$

the variance σ_w^2 by

$$\hat{\sigma}_w^2 = (T - 1)^{-1} \sum_{\tau=1}^{T} (Z_{t-\tau} - \hat{\mu}_w)^2 , \tag{26}$$

and the variance of demand over one leadtime σ_{L+1}^2 by

$$\hat{\sigma}_{L+1}^2 = \left[(L + 1) + 2 \sum_{j=1}^{L} (L + 1 - j) \hat{\rho}_w(j) \right] \hat{\sigma}_w^2 , \tag{27}$$

where

$$\hat{\rho}_w(j) = \left[\sum_{\tau=1}^{T-j} (Z_{t-\tau} - \hat{\mu}_w)(Z_{t-\tau-j} - \hat{\mu}_w) \right] \Big/ [(T - j - 1) \hat{\sigma}_w^2] \tag{28}$$

is the estimate of the correlation between two warehouse demands separated by j periods.

In some applied settings, especially in those where the number of inventoried items is quite large, the computational burden and data storage requirements of estimating L autocorrelation coefficients for each inventoried item can be large. In addition, if T is small, estimates of higher-order autocorrelation coefficients may be unstable. For these reasons, we also consider an alternative estimate of σ_{L+1}^2 which uses only the first-order autocorrelation coefficient estimate $\hat{\rho}_w(1)$ and sets all the estimates of higher-order autocorrelation coefficients equal to zero. This alternate estimate for σ_{L+1}^2 is given by

$$\hat{\sigma}_{L+1}^2 = [L(1 + 2\hat{\rho}_w(1)) + 1] \, \hat{\sigma}_w^2, \tag{29}$$

and is termed the truncated leadtime-demand variance estimator.

Our approach to testing the impact on system performance of using statistical estimates is as follows. We simulate the 72-item system in our experimental design by assuming that a history of $T = 26$ demands is used in setting the warehouse policy to be employed over the subsequent $T = 26$ periods, and that during this interval of $2T$ periods, the warehouse demand process remains unchanged. The statistical estimates above are calculated and substituted as appropriate into the Power Approximation. We make 200 replications of this statistical policy computation for each item in the 72-item system.

We find total costs under statistical demand information are only 7.8% and 10.9% above base-case total cost for the few-stores and many-stores environments, respectively. Recall that under full information total costs are, respectively, 2.6% and 3.4% above base-case costs. From a practitioner's viewpoint, the results under statistical demand information are encouraging in that total costs are within 11% of base-case values and are within 7.5% of performance levels with known demand parameters using a relatively small demand history of 26 periods. The results are comparable to those obtained in Ehrhardt [57], in which demand was independently and identically distributed. In that study, total costs were found to be 11.5% above optimal costs for a similar 72-item inventory system with a demand variance-to-mean ratio of 9 and a demand history of 26 periods controlled by the Statistical Power Approximation.

When only the first-order autocorrelation coefficient is estimated, the total costs under statistical demand information are 8.4% and 12.6% above base-case total cost for the few-stores and many-stores environments, respectively. Hence, only negligible deterioration occurs when the first-order autocorrelation coefficient is estimated instead of all L coefficients.

5. Summary

The practical implication of the research reported here is simple to state. The context of this investigation is a wholesaler's inventory replenishment situation in which warehouse demand, being observed for only a limited number of periods, looks erratic in that there is no demand in several consecutive periods, but eventually, a large demand occurs. This pattern is hypothesized as resulting from facilities at a lower echelon using (s, S) type replenishment policies, and thereby introducing autocorrelation in the warehouse demand process.

In this situation, an attractive replenishment policy for the warehouse is (2), (3), and (4), where (25), (26), (28), and (29) are used as statistical estimates.

If, instead, the warehouse replenishment policy ignores the autocorrelation, then the resulting inventory investment will be excessive and only partially offset by the associated improvement in service.

Acknowledgement

This research was supported by the Office of Naval Research, Grant N00014-78-C-0467.

We appreciate the helpful suggestions of the referees and the editor.

TIMS Studies in the Management Sciences 16 (1981) 163–193
© North-Holland Publishing Company

A MODEL FOR THE ANALYSIS OF SYSTEM SERVICE LEVEL
IN WAREHOUSE–RETAILER DISTRIBUTION SYSTEMS:
THE IDENTICAL RETAILER CASE

Bryan L. DEUERMEYER

Texas A&M University

and

Leroy B. SCHWARZ

Purdue University

This paper presents and tests an analytical model for estimating the expected service level (e.g., fill rates and backorders) of a one-warehouse N-retailer distribution system as a function of that system's parameters; e.g., warehouse and retailer lot sizes, nominal fixed lead times, and known stochastic demand parameters. The system examined here is one involving N identical retailers facing stationary Poisson demand (with a known mean) and operating with stationary (Q, r) replenishment policies. The model developed is a generalization of the exact single-facility (Q, r) model of Hadley and Whitin. The model is tested via computer simulation on a set of problems representing a wide range of "reasonable" operating parameters. The model's estimates very closely approximate the empirically observed service levels of the systems simulated.

1. Introduction

Multi-level distribution systems are commonly found in practice and frequently modeled in the management science literature, but, in fact, very little is known in general about the service level performance of these systems (e.g., fill rates, expected backorders, etc.) as a function of their parameters. Most real world distribution systems are managed — at best — using the results of single stocking location, or stocking point, models — see [4] and [191], for example. Such models ignore the demand, lot sizing, and/or reorder point interactions among the various stocking points. Such interactions can be quite significant.

Published research has been limited mostly to: (1) models for important special circumstances; e.g., $(S - 1, S)$ policies for reparable items (see [210] or [151]) or; (2) formulas for determining *inventory position* (on-hand plus on-order less backorders) — see [156]. Although the latter are interesting in themselves, they are of limited value to managers of multi-level distribution systems given that in general there is no direct relationship between inventory position and either service level or inventory related costs; e.g., holding costs depend on inventory on-hand; penalty costs, on backorders or lost sales. Moreover, the formulas are complex computationally, which poses difficulty for either sensitivity analysis or optimization. Muckstadt [153] derives the steady-state distribution for the number of backorders at each retailer for two warehouse–retailer systems: (a) two identical retailers, and (b) a "large" number of identical retailers (where "large" means a number sufficient to ensure that the warehouse demand process is approximately Poisson). Although these formulas are also computationally complex they could be used to validate special cases (two retailers, non-negative reorder points) of the model presented below.

The goal of the research described here is the development of analytical models for predicting the service level of multi-level distribution systems (e.g., warehouse–retailer systems) operating under (Q, r) policies in a stationary stochastic demand environment. The general system under examination is one warehouse (depot) supplying N retailers (bases), which, in turn, supply external stochastic unit demand. The order policy at the jth stocking point is (Q_j, r_j): when *inventory position* (on-hand plus on-order less backorders) at j falls to or below r_j, an order for Q_j is placed. Retailers order only from the warehouse; there is no transshipment. The warehouse orders from a supplier outside the system. Demand in excess of on-hand supply at each retailer is backordered. Excess demand at the warehouse is also backordered and filled FIFO (first-in first-out). Lot sizes, reorder points, warehouse lead time, and nominal retailer lead times (assuming no delay due to warehouse out-of-stock conditions) are assumed fixed and known. External demand is independent between retailers, and the retailer demand parameters are fixed and known.

The service level measures of interest are expected fill rate, or *fill rate,* and *expected backorders.* The fill rate at j, F_j, is the fraction of demand filled immediately from inventory on hand. Expected backorders at j, B_j, sometimes expressed as backorder-time/time, is the time-weighted average number of backorders at j. An additional service level measure, *expected delay* at j, T_j, is the demand-weighted average time (including zero) that a unit demand must wait before being satisfied. It is easily shown that in steady state $B_j = T_j \cdot \lambda_j$, where λ_j is the expected demand rate per unit time at j (see [137]). Expected system fill rate, or *system fill rate, F_s,* is the demand-rate-weighted fill rate across all retailers, $F_s = \Sigma_{j=1}^{N}(\lambda_j \cdot F_j)/\Sigma_{j=1}^{N}\lambda_j$. F_s is the fraction of the time an average system customer has its demand filled immediately. *Expected system backorders, B_s,* is the sum of expected backorders at all customer demand points, $B_s = \Sigma_{j=1}^{N}B_j$. Since the system service level depends only on the retailers' ability to satisfy external customer demand, the fill rate and expected backorders at the warehouse are omitted in determining B_s and F_s. This is because backorders at the warehouse only affect system performance indirectly by increasing retailer lead times beyond their fixed nominal values. Such delays only affect system performance if backorders at one or more retailers are a consequence, in which case they are reflected in the corresponding F_j and B_j values.

The particular system presented and analyzed here is a specialized one: external demand is Poisson with identical mean λ_R at all retailers, $\lambda_j = \lambda_R$, $j = 1, ..., N$. The nominal lead time to the retailer is also identical for all retailers, L_R. Further, the retailers follow identical order policies; i.e., $Q_j = Q_R$ and $r_j = r_R$, $j = 1, ..., N$. We require the warehouse lot size, Q_W, to be an integer multiple of Q_R, and prohibit warehouse *lot splitting;* that is, if the warehouse is unable to fill a given retailer order for Q_R *in full*, the entire retailer order is backordered until it can be filled in full. Relaxation of these assumptions poses no serious obstacles to the models presented, validated, and analyzed below, although minor modifications (outlined below and detailed in a sequel) must be incorporated. The Poisson assumption can be relaxed to cover other common probability distributions; e.g., normal, etc. Non-identical demand rates and/or retailer lot sizes require modification and reinterpretation of the approximate model of the warehouse demand process presented below. The no-lot-splitting assumption is in line with system policy for a number of real world systems.

The outline of the paper and its principal results are as follows: section 2 surveys the relevant literature; in section 3 we formally state the problem analyzed here and derive the formulas for predicting service level as a function of system parameters. Its development has three important components: (1) the exact (Q, r) model of Hadley and Whitin and its computational approximation [95], which is extended in one minor way here; (2) an analysis of the warehouse demand process, its approximation, and tests of that approximation; and (3) analysis of the effective retailer lead time, $\mathcal{L}_R$. This effective lead time is the fixed nominal lead time, L_R, plus any out-of-stock time remaining between the warehouse's receipt of the retailer's order and receipt of sufficient inventory to satisfy that order (after filling all previous outstanding retailer backorders). We approximate $\mathcal{L}_R$ by its expectation. In section 4 we describe the construction of a simulation model used to test the approximations presented in section 3; These approximations are shown to be remarkably good. Extensions are outlined in section 5.

2. Literature review

Continuous review inventory systems with stochastic demand have been studied in various ways and a large literature has been published. For our purposes, it is convenient to divide the relevant literature into three categories: empirical research, single-level theory, and multi-level theory and heuristics.

2.1. Empirical research

An important question that comes to mind when thinking about multi-level inventory models is: are such models really necessary? Why not model such systems by treating each stocking point independently and sequentially? It is conceivable that in some situations this method might work fairly well; and there is no question as to the simplicity of the approach. Recently, Muckstadt and Thomas [160] performed an empirical study to examine this question. They investigated two real systems (one system from the private sector and one from the military) which manage high cost–low demand items under a $(S - 1, S)$ (one-for-one) inventory policy. They conclude that substantially better performance can be obtained from simple multi-level models than single-level models. In another study, Schwarz [203] performed a simulation investigation of the procedure currently used by the United States Air Force to manage its depot-base inventory system for consumable spares. The current (Q, r) policy was shown to be inferior to two multi-level (Q, r) heuristics.

2.2. Single-level theory

Probably the best known (Q, r) model is that of Hadley and Whitin [95], which assumes Poisson unit demand, fixed lead times, and a positive reorder point. Results of this model are utilized in the analysis of the retailer demands process below. Simon [221] and Sivazlian [224] have shown that inventory position in a continuous review (s, S) system is uniformly distributed if unit demands arrive according to a stationary renewal process. This result generalizes the same result in [95] for a (Q, r) model with Poisson demand, since for unit demands (s, S) and (Q, r) policies are equivalent. Sahin [196] and Shanker [205] extended this model to permit non-unit demands occurring according to a stationary renewal process. Kruse [123] determined the expected delay in this model. Feeney and Sherbrooke [73] have examined an $(S - 1, S)$ system with compound Poisson demand, generalizing Palm's theorem [170] to characterize the distribution of the number of units in resupply.

In all of the above papers either an (s, S) or (Q, r) policy is assumed. In general, little appears to be known about the optimality of these policies. However, in certain cases it can be shown that (s, S) policies are indeed optimal. For example, Weiss and Pliska [244] applied a stopping-time analysis to establish this result for a class of continuous review systems.

2.3. Multi-level continuous review systems: theory and heuristics

The classic model of a continuous review multi-level system is METRIC, developed by Sherbrooke [210]. This model assumes a two level structure where customer level demands are Poisson and all locations use an $(S - 1, S)$ policy. Units fail after some time in service; routine repair is done at the base, and more serious repair is done at the depot. The model can be used to obtain the policy which minimizes expected backorders at the bases subject to a constraint on system investment, or evaluate the expected backorders for any distribution of inventory. The METRIC model assumes that the number of units in base resupply is approximately Poisson, an assumption which Shanker [205] examines in some detail. An important generalization of METRIC, called MOD-METRIC, was developed by

Muckstadt [151]. MOD-METRIC permits the modeling of inventory items and their components or subassemblies (e.g., aircraft engines and component modules, respectively). Optimal inventory and distribution policies are determined at each level for both assemblies and subassemblies. As in METRIC only $(S - 1, S)$ policies are considered.

The desirability of extending METRIC and MOD-METRIC type models to permit more general policies than $(S - 1, S)$ is well recognized. However, analysis of these extensions is *quite* difficult. For example, in a (Q, r) system with $Q > 1$, Palm's important result (or extensions thereof) cannot be applied. Muckstadt [156] studied the problem of characterizing the steady-state distribution of inventory position at the warehouse in a one-warehouse N-retailer system. He obtains a generalization of the well-known [224] result that this distribution is the discrete uniform. Muckstadt [153] applied these results to derive the steady-state distribution of the number of backorders at each retailer for two warehouse–retailer systems: (a) two identical retailers, and (b) a "large" number of identical retailers (where "large" is a number sufficient to ensure that the warehouse demand process is approximately Poisson).

One of the first papers to consider heuristic models of the multi-echelon N-retailer–warehouse system is Rosenbaum [191]. Rosenbaum assumes that warehouse demands are normally distributed and that lead times are fixed. Measures of service level are heuristically derived. Methods for computing policies are discussed.

3. Model definitions, assumptions, and analysis

The purpose of the model developed here is to provide approximations to the service level measures of a one-warehouse N-retailer inventory system as a function of that system's parameters. We consider three basic measures of service level: fill rate, expected backorders, and expected delay. These measures are computed for each retailer, for the warehouse, and for the system as a whole.

The basis for the model is direct analysis of the steady-state stochastic behavior of the system. There are three basic classes of stochastic processes which must be examined: (1) the net inventory process at each retailer; (2) the warehouse demand process; and (3) the net inventory process at the warehouse. Our model employs an exact representation of the retailer net inventory process (for Poisson demand and fixed lead times), approximations to the warehouse demand process and the warehouse inventory process, and a synthesis of these three processes.

3.1. Notation and assumptions

The following list summarizes most of the notation used in the paper; the precise definitions of some variables are deferred until they are used.

N = number of retailers, $1 \leqslant N < \infty$, integer,

j	= subscript used to identify a particular retailer, $j = 1, ..., N$,
R	= subscript used to identify any retailer,
W	= subscript used to identify the warehouse,
Q_j	= lot size (integer valued and > 0), $j = W, 1, ..., N$,
r_j	= reorder point, $-Q_j < r_j < \infty$, integer, $j = w, 1, ..., N$,
λ_j	= Poisson demand rate at retailer j, $j = 1, ..., N$,
L_j	= fixed, nonnegative lead time to location j, $j = W, 1, ..., N$,
Q_R, L_R, λ_R, r_R	= the values of the retailer parameters when the retailers are identical,
D_j	= expected delay from warehouse to retailer j due to inadequate warehouse stock, $j = 1, ..., N$,
$\mathcal{L}_j$	= expected effective lead time to retailer j $(\mathcal{L}_j = L_j + D_j)$,
T_j	= expected delay at location j, $j = W, 1, ..., N$,
F_j	= expected fill rate at location j, $j = W, 1, ..., N$,
B_j	= expected backorders at location j, $j = W, 1, ..., N$,
μ_W	= expected warehouse lead time demand, and
σ_W^2	= variance of the warehouse lead time demand.

We make the following additional assumptions:

(1) The customer demand process at retailer j is a stationary Poisson process, independent of all other customer demand processes.
(2) All unsatisfied demand is backlogged at each location.
(3) Warehouse lot size, Q_W, is an integer multiple of the largest common divisor of the Q_j, $j = 1, ..., N$.
(4) There is no lot splitting at the warehouse.

3.2. Retailer analysis

In this section, the service level measures for the retailers are derived. We assume, for notational ease, that there is only one retailer, so the identification subscript can be deleted. We assume further that this retailer places its orders on a warehouse which is always in stock (i.e., the warehouse has sufficient inventory to meet all demands). The lead time observed by the retailer is a constant $\mathcal{L} = L + D$, where L is the fixed lead time (the usual lead time concept) and D is a fixed and known additional delay at the warehouse. This nonstandard notation allows a smooth notational transition from the results obtained below and their subsequent use in formulating the final model, wherein the retailers' orders may experience random delays at the warehouse.

Given a (Q, r) policy and that times between unit demands form a renewal process, the inventory position at the retailer is uniformly distributed on the set $\{r + 1, ..., r + Q\}$ and inventory position and lead time demand are independent in steady state. See [221], [231], [54], [196], and [205]. In each of the following four propositions, part 1 due to Hadley and Whitin [95]. Proofs of part 2 can be found in appendix I. For readability subscripts have been deleted.

Proposition R1

$$(1)\ F(Q, r) = 1 - [\alpha(r) - \alpha(r + Q)]/Q, \qquad\qquad r \geqslant -1 \ ,$$

$$(2)\ F(Q, r) = 1 - [\alpha(0) - \alpha(r + Q)]/Q + \frac{r}{Q}, \qquad -Q \leqslant r \leqslant -1 \tag{1}$$

where

$$\alpha(v) = (\lambda \cdot \mathcal{L}) \, P(v; \lambda \cdot \mathcal{L}) - v P(v + 1; \lambda \cdot \mathcal{L})$$

and $P(\cdot; \lambda \cdot \mathcal{L})$ is the complementary cumulative Poisson distribution; $P(v; \lambda \cdot \mathcal{L}) = 1$, $v < 0$. Intuitively, $\alpha(v)$ may be viewed as expected lead time demand in excess of v. Hence $[\alpha(r) - \alpha(r + Q)]$ is the expected number of backorders attributable to one retailer order cycle (during which time Q units are demanded).

By using the normal approximation to the Poisson, one can derive approximations to parts 1 and 2 of proposition R1 which are more convenient computationally.

Proposition R1 * (normal approximations)

$$(1)\ F^*(Q, r) = 1 - [\alpha^*(r) - \alpha^*(r + Q)]/Q, \qquad\qquad r \geqslant 0 \ ,$$

$$(2)\ F^*(Q, r) = 1 - [\alpha^*(0) - \alpha^*(r + Q)]/Q + \frac{r}{Q}, \qquad -Q \leqslant r < 0 \tag{1*}$$

where

$$\alpha^*(v) = \sigma \phi \left(\frac{v - \mu}{\sigma} \right) - (v - \mu) \, \Phi \left(\frac{v - \mu}{\sigma} \right)$$

with $\sigma = \mu^{1/2}$ and $\mu = \lambda \mathcal{L}$, for Poisson unit demand; $\phi(\cdot)$ and $\Phi(\cdot)$ are the standard normal density and complementary distribution, respectively.

Proposition R2

$$(1)\ B(Q, r) = \frac{1}{Q} [\beta(r) - \beta(r + Q)], \qquad r \geqslant 1 \ ,$$

$$(2)\ B(Q, r) = \frac{1}{Q} [\beta(0) - \beta(r + Q)] + \frac{r}{Q} \left[\frac{(r + 1)}{2} - \alpha(0) \right], \tag{2}$$

$$\text{for } -Q \leqslant r < -1$$

where

$$\beta(v) = \frac{(\lambda \cdot \mathcal{L})^2}{2} P(v-1;\lambda \cdot \mathcal{L}) - (\lambda \cdot \mathcal{L}) vP(v;\lambda \cdot \mathcal{L})$$

$$+ \frac{v(v+1)}{2} P(v+1;\lambda \cdot \mathcal{L}).$$

Intuitively, $\beta(v)$ may be viewed as the time-weighted backorders arising from lead time demand in excess of v. Hence $[\beta(r) - \beta(r+Q)]$ is the expected time-weighted backorders attributable to one retailer order cycle.

Once again the normal distribution can be used to derive approximations.

Proposition R2*

$$(1) B^*(Q,r) = \frac{1}{Q} [\beta^*(r) - \beta^*(r+Q)], \qquad r \geq 0 ,$$

$$(2) B^*(Q,r) = \frac{1}{Q} [\beta^*(0) - \beta^*(r+Q)] + \frac{r}{Q}\left[\frac{r}{2} - \alpha^*(0)\right],$$

(2*)

$$\text{for } -Q \leq r < 0$$

where

$$\beta^*(v) = \tfrac{1}{2} [\sigma^2 + (v-\mu)^2] \Phi\left(\frac{v-\mu}{\sigma}\right) - \frac{\sigma}{2}(v-\mu)\phi\left(\frac{v-\mu}{\sigma}\right)$$

Finally, we use [137] to determine the expected time out of stock:

$$T(Q,r) = \lambda^{-1} B(Q,r) .$$

(3)

The results just obtained are correct, of course, only when the effective lead time, $\mathcal{L}$, is fixed and demand is Poisson. When retailer demand is other than Poisson distributed, R1* and R2* may be used to approximate fill rate and expected back-orders with μ and σ^2 suitably chosen to fit the given distribution. For variable $\mathcal{L}$, these results are not strictly applicable if the warehouse experiences backorders. However, by interpreting D as the average time the warehouse is out of stock, one can use the above expressions as approximations. This line of reasoning is employed to formulate the final model.

3.3. The warehouse demand process

This section provides two exact characterizations of the warehouse demand process: (1) as a superposition of N independent renewal processes, and (2) as a Markov renewal process. The first characterization demonstrates that the warehouse demand process is, in general, a nonstationary renewal process and is used to motivate our approximate model. The second characterization provides a framework for doing exact computations, but, at this time, is not a practical approach.

The first method for modeling the warehouse demand process views it as the superposition of the retailer ordering processes. Let $N_j(t)$ be the number of orders placed by retailer j, $j = 1, 2, ..., N$ during $[0, t]$. For the sake of simplicity, assume that each retailer placed an order at time 0. Then, the times between orders from retailer j, $j = 1, ..., N$ will have the Erlang-Q_j distribution with mean time between orders Q_j/λ_j. That is, the inter-order times from retailer j have the common distribution $G_j(\cdot)$ given by

$$G_j(\tau) = 1 - \sum_{k=0}^{Q_j-1} \frac{(\lambda_j \tau)^k e^{-\lambda_j \tau}}{k!}, \qquad \tau \geq 0 .$$

Now, let $N_W(t)$ be the number of retailer orders on the warehouse during $[0, t]$, and let $\{T_n\}_0^\infty$ be the times at which these orders occur. Then,

$$N_W(t) = \sum_{j=1}^{N} N_j(t) , \qquad t \geq 0 .$$

It is easily established that the times between orders from retailer j form a renewal process for customer demands given by a renewal process. It follows that the times between demand occurrences at the warehouse form another renewal process, $(N_W) = \{N_W(t)\}_{t \geq 0}$. (N_W) is the superposition of the N retailer ordering processes. Unfortunately, (N_W) is nonstationary — see Cinlar [31] for a comprehensive summary of results concerning the superposition of renewal processes. However, there are two special cases when (N_W) is stationary. If $Q_j = 1, j = 1, ..., N$, each of the retailer order processes [1] will be Poisson. In this case one can apply the well-known result that the superposition of independent stationary Poisson processes is again a stationary Poisson process (see Cinlar [29]). When this applies, (N_W) is a Poisson process. In the second case, it is known (see Feller [72] and Cinlar [30]) that (N_W) is approximately Poisson for N large and t sufficiently large. [2] Except for these two cases, however, the warehouse demand process will be nonstationary. Fortunately, this nonstationarity turns out to be relatively minor. We exploit this below. The reason for the nonstationarity is interesting and merits a brief discussion. In order to be a stationary renewal process, the times $\{T_n - T_{n-1}\}$ would necessarily have to be identically distributed for $n \geq 2$ (we do not need to force $T_1 - T_0$ to have the same distribution). The warehouse demand epochs are caused by an order placed by one retailer. At any one of these epochs, the inventory position of the other retailer inventory processes reside at an intermediate point in their

[1] This corresponds to an $(S - 1, S)$ policy at each retailer.
[2] In addition, certain other 'regularity' conditions must be satisfied.

respective order cycles. The time of the next warehouse demand is the minimum of the time-to-order of *all* N retailers. Obviously, this time depends upon the inventory position of all N retailers. Since there are several possible values for the collection of inventory positions (except in the case $Q_j = 1$, $j = 1, 2, ..., N$), the times $\{T_n - T_{n-1}\}$ cannot be identically distributed. By taking this additional information regarding the inventory positions into account, we can precisely characterize the warehouse demand process. The vehicle for accomplishing this formulation is the Markov renewal process, which we now discuss.

Let X_{jn} be the inventory position of retailer j at warehouse demand epoch T_n, $j = 1, 2, ..., N$. Then, the interval $[r_j + 1, r_j + Q_j]$ is the state space of the random variable X_{jn}. Also, define $X_n = (X_{1n}, ..., X_{Nn})$, which specifies the inventory position at each retailer at the time T_n. Theorem 1 which follows is easily established using the definition of the Markov renewal process given in Cinlar [29] and [30].

Theorem 1. The stochastic process $(X, T) = \{(X_n, T_n): n = 0, 1, ...\}$ is a Markov renewal process with state space $E \times \mathbb{R}_+$, where $\mathbb{R}_+ = [0, \infty)$ and $E = \{(X_1, ..., X_N);$ $X_j = r_j + Q_j$ for at least one j and $r_k + 1 \leqslant X_k \leqslant r_k + Q_k - 1$ for all other $k\}$.

Remarks. The warehouse demand at time T_n is caused by an order placed by exactly one retailer, call it j. At T_n it is possible that the inventory position at some other retailer, say i, is at $r_i + Q_i$. This will occur when no demands occur at that retailer between the time it placed an order and T_n. The other retailers are at an intermediate point in their reorder cycle, so that $r_k + 1 \leqslant X_k \leqslant r_k + Q_k - 1$, for all other k.

Consequently, the state space E is substantially smaller than the naive choice of $E_1 \times E_2 \times ... \times E_N$, where $E_j = \{x_j; r_j + 1 \leqslant X_j \leqslant r_j + Q_j\}$, $j = 1, 2, ..., N$.

The importance of this theorem is that the theory of Markov renewal processes is complete; transient and steady-state results are known (see Cinlar [29]). Therefore, one could use the theorem above to exactly characterize the warehouse demand process. This approach is very complex computationally.

The process (N_W) can be closely approximated by a renewal process. In the discussion to follow, we assume that $Q_j = Q_R$, $j = 1, 2, ..., N$. What we propose is to replace the N independent Poisson customer arrival processes by an aggregated Poisson process (alternatively, think of this aggregated process as the superposition of the N customer processes: the result will be another Poisson process). We interpret this new process as the customer arrival process to an artificial retailer who, in turn, places orders on the warehouse. This approximation yields a stationary renewal process that is easy to work with and at the same time is sufficiently accurate. See appendix II for comparisons between the actual and approximate warehouse processes.

The arrival rate for the aggregate process is

$$\lambda_W = \sum_{j=1}^{N} \lambda_j .$$

The lot size used by the artificial retailer will also be Q_R. Therefore, the times between orders from this retailer, after the placement of its first order, are independent and have the common distribution function

$$G(\tau) = 1 - \sum_{k=0}^{Q_R - 1} \frac{(\lambda_W \tau)^k e^{-\lambda \tau}}{k!}, \qquad r \geq 0 ; \tag{4}$$

that is, G is the Erlang-Q with mean Q/λ_W. Let $(N) = \{N(t): t \in \mathbb{R}_+\}$ be the order process for this artificial warehouse. Let the renewal function associated with (N) be $R(t)$. Then $R(t)$, the expected number of renewals (retailer orders) in the interval $[0, t]$ has the representation

$$R(t) = \sum_{n=0}^{\infty} G^{*n}(t)$$

if we include the order at the origin as a renewal, and

$$R(t) = \sum_{n=1}^{\infty} G^{*n}(t)$$

if we choose not to count this order, where G^{*n} is the n-fold convolution of G with itself. We use the latter in our analysis for the reason that the warehouse lead time, L_W, is initiated by a retailer order which reduces the warehouse inventory position to or below r_W. Warehouse lead time demand consequently consists of all orders except the first during time $t = L_W$.

Upon using the specific $G(\cdot)$ in (4), we can specialize some well-known properties of renewal processes.

Theorem 2 (see Feller [72], pp. 361, 366, 386)

$$\text{(a)} \ R(t + a) - R(t) \rightarrow \frac{\lambda_W a}{Q_R}, \qquad t \rightarrow \infty ,$$

$$\text{(b)} \ R(t) - \frac{\lambda_W t}{Q_R} \rightarrow \frac{1 - Q_R}{2Q_R}, \qquad t \rightarrow \infty ,$$

$$\text{(c)} \ \mathrm{var}\,[N(t)] = 2R^* R(t) - R(t) - (R(t))^2 ,$$

$$\text{(d)} \ \mathrm{var}\,[N(t)] \rightarrow \frac{\lambda_W t}{Q_R^2} , \qquad t \rightarrow \infty .$$

We use this theorem to approximate the mean and variance of customer orders on the warehouse during its lead time, L_W, as: [3]

---

[3] There are alternative methods for approximating the renewal function by a linear function. An interesting approach is taken by Marshall in [144]. For Erlang-generated renewal processes, his bounds yield our estimate, (5).

$$\mu_W = E[N(L_W)] = \frac{\lambda_W L_W}{Q_R} + \frac{1 - Q_R}{2Q_R} \tag{5}$$

and

$$\sigma_W^2 = \mathrm{var}[N(L_W)] = \frac{\lambda_W L_W}{Q_R^2} . \tag{6}$$

If $Q_R = 1$, these two approximations are exact for all $t \geqslant 0$. We use the normal distribution with μ_W given by (5) and σ_W^2 given by (6) to approximate the distribution of $N(t = L_W)$, the number of retailer orders during the warehouse lead time L_W.

3.4. Warehouse inventory process: the identical retailer lot-size case

In this section we specify the model used to estimate the warehouse expected backorders, fill rate, and customer delay. This model uses the approximate warehouse demand model described immediately above and the Hadley–Whitin [95] model described prior to that. If one checks through most of Hadley and Whitin's proof, it is clear that the demand process need not be Poisson, provided the demand during the lead time and inventory position are independent in steady state. This has been established in a variety of settings — (see [123], [160] and [196]). The Poisson is important, however, in that closed form expressions for $\alpha(\cdot)$ and $\beta(\cdot)$ (see above) can be obtained. We circumvent this problem by using the normal distribution to approximate the distribution of warehouse demand during its lead time.

Therefore, we use the following expressions.

Proposition W1

$(1)\ B_W(Q_W, r_W; \mu_W, \sigma_W^2)$

$$= \begin{cases} \dfrac{1}{Q_W} [\hat{\beta}(r_W) - \hat{\beta}(r_W + Q_W)] , & r_W \geqslant 0 , \\[4mm] \dfrac{1}{Q_W} [\hat{\beta}(0) - \hat{\beta}(r_W + Q_W)] + \dfrac{r_W}{Q_W} \left[\dfrac{r_W}{2} - \hat{\alpha}(0) \right] , & -Q_W \leqslant r_W < 0 , \end{cases} \tag{7}$$

$(2)\ F_W(Q_W, r_W; \mu_W, \sigma_W^2)$

$$= \begin{cases} 1 - \dfrac{1}{Q_W} [\hat{\alpha}(r_W) - \hat{\alpha}(r_W + Q_W)] , & r_W \geqslant 0 , \\[4mm] 1 - \dfrac{1}{Q_W} [\hat{\alpha}(0) - \hat{\alpha}(r_W + Q_W)] + \dfrac{r_W}{Q_W} , & -Q_W \leqslant r_W < 0 , \end{cases} \tag{8}$$

where

$$\hat{\alpha}(v) = \sigma_W \phi\left(\frac{v - \mu_W}{\sigma_W}\right) - (v - \mu_W) \, \Phi\left(\frac{v - \mu_W}{\sigma_W}\right), \tag{9}$$

$$\hat{\beta}(v) = \tfrac{1}{2}[\sigma_W^2 + (v - \mu_W)^2] \, \Phi\left(\frac{v - \mu_W}{\sigma_W}\right) - \frac{\sigma_W}{2}(v - \mu_W)$$

$$\times \phi\left(\frac{v - \mu_W}{\sigma_W}\right), \tag{10}$$

and μ_W and σ_W^2 given by equations (5) and (6).

Notice that the arguments of $B_W(\cdot)$ and $F_W(\cdot)$ include μ_W and σ_W^2 to emphasize the dependence on the retailer processes.

Finally,

$$T_W(Q_W, r_W; \mu_W, \sigma_W^2) = \lambda_W^{-1} \, B_W(Q_W, r_W; \mu_W, \sigma_W^2) . \tag{11}$$

3.5. Synthesis

Having analyzed the three stochastic processes relevant to the operation of the warehouse N-retailer system, we now assemble these processes into a single model for the system as a whole. Prerequisite for accomplishing this task is a basic understanding of the three principal interrelations among the inventory processes at each of the $N + 1$ system locations. First, there is the effect of the retailers on the warehouse process; second, there is the effect of the warehouse on each of the retailers; and third, there is the interrelation between and among the retailers themselves.

The retailers affect the warehouse through their combined ordering processes. We demonstrated above exactly how the warehouse demand process is constructed. It was also shown how each retailer ordering process is defined by its customer demand processes and its inventory (ordering) policy. We also proposed an approximation to the warehouse demand process which results from aggregating all of the customer demands.

The warehouse has an effect on the retailers through its shipments (including backordered shipments) in response to retailer orders: the warehouse may run out of stock and be forced to backorder retailer orders while waiting for its own order(s) to be received. This causes a delay before the order can be shipped back to the retailer. The effect is to increase the retailer lead time by a random amount. Mathematically, the effective lead time corresponding to the mth order placed by retailer j is

$$\mathcal{L}_{jm} = L_j + d_{jm} , \tag{12}$$

where $d_{jm} \geq 0$. Note that $d_{jm} > 0$ iff the warehouse is in a backordered condition when the mth order is received by the warehouse or if warehouse inventory on-hand is smaller than Q_j.

The stochastic processes $\{d_{jm}\}_{m=1}^{\infty}$, $j = 1, ..., N$ are very complex and their behavior depends upon a number of factors: the number of backorders at the warehouse at the instant order m is placed by retailer j, the number of orders placed by the warehouse still outstanding, the number of total retailer demands prior to this order, etc. It is through $\{d_{jm}\}$ that the warehouse affects retailers and also how the retailers can affect one another.

The retailers interact with one another in an indirect way by the sequencing and number of their orders through the warehouse demand process. Thus, retailer j may place an order after the other retailers have forced the warehouse into a backorder position.

The approach taken here to couple the separate models together involves the previously discussed approximation of the warehouse demand process and a deterministic approximation to the retailer effective lead times. This approach is similar to that of Sherbrooke in METRIC [210] and Muckstadt in MOD-METRIC [151].

The effective lead time of the mth order placed by retailer j was defined in (12). We define

$$\mathcal{L}_j = L_j + D , \tag{13}$$

where

$$D = E[d] = T_W(Q_W, r_W; \mu_W, \sigma_W^2) . \tag{14}$$

D is interpreted as the average length of time that an order placed at random on the warehouse will wait before it can be shipped. Thus, $\mathcal{L}_j$, the expected effective lead time for any order placed by retailer $j, j = 1, 2, ..., N$, is assumed to be deterministic and fixed. We use this value for the lead time ($\mathcal{L}$) in the retailer model above.

There are two important points to consider in justifying the use of $\mathcal{L}_j$ as computed in (13) in the retailer model. First, this method ignores the FIFO sequencing of backordered retailer orders at the warehouse. Second, the same adjustment, D, is used in computing all the effective retailer lead times. The following view of the warehouse gives rise to our approximation, and addresses both points.

Suppose when a retailer places an order it phones the warehouse and a warehouse clerk records the fact that someone has just placed an order, but does not identify this retailer. In response to this order, the clerk checks the inventory to see if the order can be filled (recall that no partial filling is permitted). If it can be filled, the clerk has the completed order immediately put out on the delivery dock. If necessary, the clerk places an order to its supplier and readjusts the warehouse inventory position. If the order cannot be filled, the clerk increases the number of backorders. It is important to stress that all this while, there is no retailer identity associated with an order placed on the warehouse. At the same time that the clerk records the order, the retailer placing the order sends a messenger to make the pick-up, the trip taking zero time units.

As soon as the clerk has put an order on the dock, one of the messengers, say from retailer j, will pick this order up and make a delivery to retailer j, L_j units of time later.

The messengers appear the instant the retailers place orders. Each messenger is identified with a specific retailer. If a messenger from, say, retailer j arrives at the warehouse and there are other messengers from retailer j already waiting, he gets in line behind those messengers. In effect, there will be N-FIFO queues at the dock, each containing some (or no) messengers.

When a completed order is placed on the dock, only the first messenger in each queue can make the pickup; and, in our approximation, each such messenger has an equal probability of making this pickup.

In this setup, the average length of time a messenger waits is D and the corresponding average length of time (the effective lead time) before the retailer receives its order is $\mathcal{L}_j = L_j + D$.

Our model of the complete system is determined as follows.

(1) Specify $\lambda_j = \lambda_R$, $Q_j = Q_R$, $r_j = r_R$, and $L_j = L_R$ for the retailers.
(2) Specify Q_W, r_W, and L_W for the warehouse such that Q_W and r_W are integer multiples of Q_R, and let $\lambda_W = N\lambda_R$.
(3) Estimate the mean and variance of the warehouse lead time demand (μ_W and σ_W^2) according to

$$\mu_W = \frac{N\lambda_R L_W}{Q_R} + \frac{1 - Q_R}{2Q_R} \tag{15}$$

and

$$\sigma_W^2 = \frac{N\lambda_R L_W}{Q_R^2}. \tag{16}$$

Note that μ_w and σ_w are expressed in units of Q_R.
(4) Apply the warehouse model described above to obtain $B_W(Q_W, r_W; \mu_W, \sigma_W^2)$, $F_W(Q_W, r_W; \mu_W, \sigma_W^2)$ and $T_W(Q_W, r_W; \mu_W, \sigma_W^2)$ using (7)–(11).
(5) Compute $\mathcal{L}$ according to

$$\mathcal{L} = L_R + T_W(Q_W, r_W; \mu_W, \sigma_W^2). \tag{17}$$

(6) Apply the retailer model above to obtain $B_R(Q_R, r_R), F_R(Q_R, r_R)$ and $T_R(Q_R, r_R)$ using (1) or (1*), (2) or (2*), and (3).

4. Model validation

4.1. A computer simulation model

A computer simulation model was carefully constructed in order to validate the approximate model presented above. The purpose of this model was the generation of point and interval estimates of the system service level of a real system operating under the assumptions of section 1. In what follows, we outline the most salient aspects of the simulation model. Next we describe the parameter ranges of the problems used for validation, the validation tests conducted, and the outcome of those tests.

The inputs to the simulation model are: the number of retailers, the demand rates, lot sizes, nominal lead times, and safety stock; and the number and size of the sampling intervals to be used for the given run. Reorder points at each stocking point j are computed by the program to be expected nominal lead time demand plus safety stock, S_j: $r_j = \lambda_j \cdot L_j + S_j$, $j = W, 1, ..., N$. The *sampling interval* is the simulated time over which the output statistics are collected. All sampling intervals are equal in length and contiguous in time. Several pilot runs were conducted to verify that the sampling intervals chosen were adequate to ensure independence between intervals. [4] In every case a sampling interval of at least three *system cycles* was used in the validation tests which followed. A *system cycle*, SC, is defined to be the approximate time taken by a random item to move through the entire distribution system:

$$SC = L_W + Q_W/\lambda_W + L_R + Q_R/\lambda_R$$

$$= \text{Warehouse pipeline time}$$
$$+$$
$$\text{Warehouse cycle inventory time} \qquad (18)$$
$$+$$
$$\text{Retailer pipeline time}$$
$$+$$
$$\text{Retailer cycle inventory time .}$$

The simulated system is initialized with inventory on hand at stage j of $Q_j + r_j$, $j = W, 1, ..., N$, zero backorders, and zero inventory on order. [5] The simulation then proceeds, processing each transaction in order, using a variable-time-increment clock. Upon the occurrence of each transaction, counters are updated to reflect demand, inventory position, inventory on-hand, pipeline inventory, backorders, time in-stock, time out-of-stock, etc., since the last event. At the end of each

---

[4] Two tests were used: (1) a simple test on lagged correlation coefficients, and (2) the Fishman [75] test.

[5] This corresponds to setting inventory on-hand equal to inventory position, and setting inventory position equal to what it would be immediately upon placing an order at each stage j, $j = 1, ..., N, W$. Although this initialization of on-hand inventory *may* be quite unrepresentative of what on-hand inventory would ever be in the system's real world counterpart (especially for systems with short inventory cycle times and long order pipelines), the long sampling intervals used in the validation tests eliminate this initialization bias. Indeed, sensitivity analysis on initial on-hand inventory failed to show *any* consistent difference between initialization as described above and initialization at zero on-hand inventories after two sampling intervals.

sampling interval the following is written on an output file: demand rate (units demanded ÷ sampling interval); fill rate (1-unit backorders ÷ unit demand); average backorders (accumulated backorder-time ÷ sampling interval); average time out of stock per occurrence (total time out of stock ÷ number of out-of-stock occurrences); average time in stock per occurrence; average time in stock per order cycle (accumulated time between out of stock occurrences ÷ number of orders placed); and average time out of stock per order cycle at each stocking point j. Then all of the counters are zeroed and the processing of events resumes. The output file is then processed by a computer program which performs tests of independence and computes point and interval estimates of all output variables. In our validation tests 36 observations (sampling intervals) were made on each measure of interest, the first six being discarded for possible initialization bias.

4.2. Validation of the model using the simulation

Having verified that the simulation program provided statistically useful (stationary and independent) measures of system performance, the output of the program was then used to test the accuracy of the formulas derived in section 3. The purposes of these tests were: (1) to determine the overall accuracy of the formulas given a set of "realistic" system parameters, and (2) to determine the accuracy of the formulas, as a function of specific system parameters (e.g., warehouse lead times). Systematic tests were made on $N = 2$ and $N = 5$ retailer problems, with additional exploratory tests for the $N = 10$ retailer problem. For these tests demand rates at each retailer were fixed at one of three levels, 10 (low), 100 (medium), and 300 (high) per unit time, and all other parameters were based on these values.

Retailer lot size, Q_R. Q_R values in the interval $[\lambda_R/50, \lambda_R]$ were used, corresponding to a pattern of retailer orders ranging from weekly, $\lambda_R/50$, to annually, λ_R, assuming one-year time units. Systematic tests were conducted at approximately the 25th, 50th, and 75th percentiles of this range, corresponding to $Q_R = 0.05\lambda_R$ (low), $0.15\lambda_R$ (medium), and $0.4\lambda_R$ (high), with additional exploratory tests at both intermediate and more extreme values.

Warehouse lot size, Q_W. Q_W values in the interval $[Q_R, 16Q_R]$ were used, with systematic tests at $Q_W = 4Q_R$ (low), $6Q_R$ (medium), and $10Q_R$ (high), and additional exploratory tests at both higher and lower values.

Retailer lead time, L_R. Retailer lead times in the interval $[0.1Q_R/\lambda_R, 6Q_R/\lambda_R]$ were used, corresponding approximately to a retailer order pipeline containing between one-tenth and six retailer orders. Systematic tests were conducted at $L_R = 0.25Q_R/\lambda_R$ (low), $0.8Q_R/\lambda_R$ (medium), and $2Q_R/\lambda_R$ (high), with additional exploratory tests at higher and lower values.

Warehouse lead time, Q_W. Warehouse lead times in the interval $[0.1Q_W/\lambda_W, 10Q_W/$

Table 1
Parameter sets for systematic tests
(L = low; M = medium; H = high)

Parameter	Parameter set									
	1	2	3	4	5	6	7	8	9	10
Q_R	L	M	H	M	M	M	M	M	L	H
L_R	H	H	H	H	L	H	H	L	H	L
Q_W	L	M	H	M	M	H	L	M	H	L
L_W	H	H	H	L	H	H	H	L	L	H

λ_W] were used. Systematic tests were conducted at $L_W = 0.25 Q_W/\lambda_W$ (low), $0.4 Q_W/\lambda_W$ (medium), and Q_W/λ_W (high), with additional exploratory tests at higher values.

For the systematic tests the above parameters were combined to create 10 *parameter sets* as detailed in table 1. These particular sets were chosen so that data would be available to determine the sensitivity of the model's accuracy to the system's parameters. For example, results for parameter sets 1–3 were compared to determine sensitivity to overall lot size; parameter sets 2, 4, and 5 were compared to determine sensitivity to lead time differentials, etc.

Each parameter set was tested on three demand levels (10, 100, and 300 units/ time) at a variety of safety stock values and positions. For each parameter set and demand level the model was used to compute warehouse and system fill rates and backorders for a wide range of safety stock values (from $-2Q_j$ to $2Q_j$ in increments of Q_j). Particular *test problems* (a combination of parameter set, demand level, and safety stock position and value) were selected to test the model based on these calculations. In general, the selected test problems had warehouse fill rates between 0.4 and 0.9 (although in some cases more extreme values were tested) and system fill rates between 0.1 and 0.95. Higher warehouse and/or system fill rates fail to rigorously test this or any other model, although they are accurately predicted by the model.

Test problems were simulated as described above. In accordance with our tests on the simulation model, a sampling interval of at least three system cycles was used (actually, the smallest integer larger than three times the system cycle); and 36 sampling intervals constituted a run. For estimation purposes, data from the first six sampling intervals was ignored. The means and standard deviations of the remaining 30 observations of warehouse and retailer fill rates and backorders were computed to obtain point estimates [6] of the mean and variance of the "true" system service level measures. These estimates were used to measure the accuracy of our formulas.

---

[6] Normality was assumed.

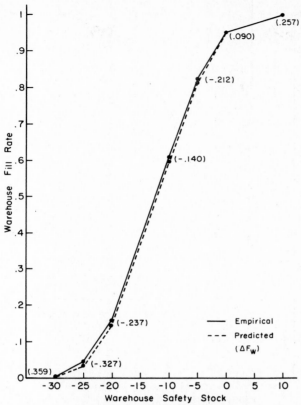

Fig. 1A. Comparison between predicted and simulated fill rate (parameter set 1; λ_R = 100; N = 2).

4.3. Results

Approximately 300 test problems were simulated and the results compared with those predicted by the model. Model accuracy, Δ, was measured as the difference between the point estimate of the mean from the simulation and the model's prediction, expressed in terms of the standard error of the mean [7] (estimated from the simulation). The Δ subscript codes are as follows: F_S = system fill rate; B_S = system backorders; F_W = warehouse fill rate; B_W = warehouse backorders.

The overall fit of the model over a wide range of demand levels, numbers of

[7] For example, if the model predicted system fill rate is 0.90 and the simulation estimate of system fill rate is 0.88 with a variance of 0.04, then ΔF_S = (0.90 − 0.88)/0.2 = 1.

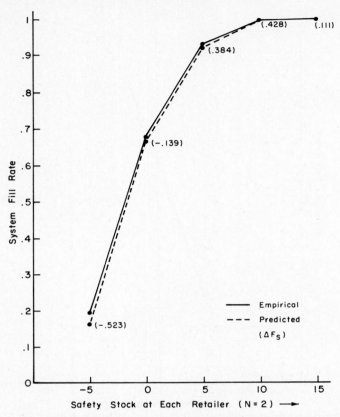

Fig. 1B. Comparison of predicted and simulated system fill rate (parameter set 1; $\lambda_R = 100$; $S_W = -10$).

retailers, safety stock values, and positions is quite good. The warehouse model is extremely good, as might be expected from the analysis in appendix II: except in cases involving extremely low safety stocks for *some* parameter sets, the absolute values of ΔF_W and ΔB_W, $|\Delta F_W|$ and $|\Delta B_W|$, never exceed 1.5 and averaged less than 1 — see fig. 1(A) for example. In addition the predictions appear to be un-biased: both positive and negative values of ΔF_W and ΔB_W are observed in no particular pattern, except, as expected, ΔF_W and ΔB_W usually have opposite signs. It also appears that $|\Delta B_W| < |\Delta F_W|$ for any given test problem and, holding all other parameters equal, $|\Delta F_W|$ decreases somewhat for increasing N, the number of retailers. The overall model is also quite good: again the predictions appear to be unbiased, $|\Delta B_S| < |\Delta F_S|$, $|\Delta F_S|$ appears to decrease with increasing N, and on an overal basis ΔF_S and ΔB_S are small. In approximately 90% of the problems tested $|\Delta F_S| < 1$, most of the rest were between 1 and 2 — see fig. 1(B). However, there is a tendency for $|\Delta F_S|$ and $|\Delta B_S|$ to increase as the warehouse fill rate decreases, and for *some* parameter sets the model provides inaccurate predictions when the warehouse fill rate falls below 50%. For example, in parameter set 4 with $\lambda_R = 100$, $S_W = -75$, and $S_R = 0$, a simulated warehouse fill rate of 0.124 is obtained with $\Delta F_W = 0.45$, $F_S = 0.114$, and $\Delta F_S = -3.84$.

Note that in this instance, and in most others for which the model becomes inaccurate, the warehouse "fit" is quite good ($\Delta F_W = 0.454$). This suggests that the model inaccuracy lies in the use of the mean delay, D, at the warehouse as a proxy for the random delay, d_{jm}, in the retailer model – see (12) and (14). It is quite plausible that, as the warehouse fill rate decreases, the variance in the delay process increases. Consequently, random drawings from the delay distribution might be expected to differ more from the mean than when warehouse fill rates are higher. This issue is presently under investigation.

5. Extensions

On the basis of the results summarized above we believe that a basic model for predicting system service level in a one-warehouse N-retailer (Q, r) system is at hand. Of course, much still remains to be done. These extensions fall into three categories: (1) analysis and interpretation; (2) application; and (3) generalization. In the following paragraphs we outline the most important ones.

5.1. Analysis and interpretation

The model presented above provides remarkably good estimates of system service level for "reasonable" parameterizations of the system under study. However, more analysis is required in order to better understand the limits of the approximations.

5.2. Application

The model presented here will provide estimates of system service level given a set of system parameters. This is very useful in itself. For example, a manager may use the model to evaluate the trade-off between system service level and system safety stock. Or, given a budgeted system safety stock, the model may be used to evaluate alternative safety stock positioning (distribution among stages) alternatives, etc. However, the model's full potential will not be utilized until a companion optimization scheme is developed. Such a scheme would, for example, determine optimal safety stock position given a budgeted safety stock and/or determine appropriate trade-offs in system design; e.g., the appropriate values of the system parameters.

5.3. Generalization

The simple system analyzed here should also be generalized in a variety of important ways. First, and perhaps most important, the model should be extended to non-identical retailer lot sizes and demand rates. This will require modification of the approximation to the warehouse demand process and order process. Second, the model should be extended to non-identical retailer reorder points and lead times. Third, the model should be extended to allow partial shipments of retailer lot sizes from the warehouse under appropriate circumstances; e.g., ship all available stock, or ration dwindling warehouse stocks among the retailers. A number of additional extensions are also worth while, among them, bulk (non-unit) demand at the retailers, non-Poisson order arrivals at the retailers, stochastic nominal warehouse and retailer lead times, nonstationary demand at the retailers, correlated demand among the retailers, etc.

Some of these extensions are presently being pursued; the remainder will be subsequently pursued.

Appendix I

In this appendix we provide the proofs for part (2) of propositions R1, R1*, R2, and R2*, found in section 3.

Let Y be the random variable representing the number of backorders on-hand at any time t. As in Hadley and Whitin [95], we let $\Psi_2(y)$ be the probability function of Y. We want to derive $\Psi_2(y)$ where the recorder point, r, can take on negative values. Hadley and Whitin [95] have established this distribution for $r \geqslant -1$. We now consider $-Q \leqslant r < -1$.

Two cases need to be considered: (1) $0 \leqslant y \leqslant -(r+1)$, and (2) $y > -(r+1)$. The proof follows the same line of argument as in [95].

Lemma 1. Suppose $-Q \leqslant r < -1$. Then,

$$
\Psi_2(y) = \begin{cases}
\dfrac{1}{Q}\left[1 - P(r + Q + y + 1; \mu)\right], \\[0.5em]
\quad \text{for } 0 \leqslant y \leqslant -(r+1), \\[1em]
\dfrac{1}{Q}\left[P(r + y + 1; \mu) - P(r + Q + y + 1; \mu)\right], \\[0.5em]
\quad \text{for } y > -(r+1),
\end{cases}
$$

where $\mu = \lambda \cdot \mathcal{L}$.

Proof

Case 1 $(r + 1 \leqslant -y \leqslant 0)$. Suppose at time t there are exactly y backorders. Then, at time $t - \mathcal{L}$ the inventory position must be one of the values $\{-y, -y + 1, ..., r + Q\}$. The probability assigned to each of these values is $1/Q$. Therefore,

$$\Psi_2(y) = \frac{1}{Q} \sum_{j=-y}^{r+Q} p(y + j; \mu)$$

$$= \frac{1}{Q} \sum_{j=0}^{r+Q+y} p(j; \mu)$$

$$= \frac{1}{Q} [P(0; \mu) - P(r + Q + y + 1; \mu)]$$

$$= \frac{1}{Q} [1 - P(r + Q + y + 1; \mu)] .$$

Case 2. $(-y < r + 1)$. Using the same reasoning, we obtain

$$\Psi_2(y) = \frac{1}{Q} \sum_{j=r+1}^{r+Q} p(y + j; \mu)$$

$$= \frac{1}{Q} \sum_{j=r+y+1}^{r+Q+y} p(j; \mu)$$

$$= \frac{1}{Q} [P(r + y + 1; \mu) - P(r + Q + y + 1; \mu)] .$$

In lemma 2 we establish an approximation, $\Psi_2^*(\cdot)$, to $\Psi_2(\cdot)$ based on the normal approximation to the Poisson.

Lemma 2.   Let $r < -1$. Then,

$$\Psi_2^*(y) = \begin{cases} \dfrac{1}{Q} \displaystyle\int_{-y}^{r+Q} \dfrac{1}{\sigma} \phi\left(\dfrac{x + y - \mu}{\sigma}\right) \mathrm{d}x , & 0 \leqslant y \leqslant -r , \\[4mm] \dfrac{1}{Q} \displaystyle\int_{r}^{r+Q} \dfrac{1}{\sigma} \phi\left(\dfrac{x + y - \mu}{\sigma}\right) \mathrm{d}x, & y > -r . \end{cases}$$

Proof. We proof this lemma by approximating the $p(x; u)$ by $\phi((x - \mu)/\sigma)$ in the proof of lemma 1. In that proof,

$$
\Psi_2(y) = \begin{cases} \dfrac{1}{Q} \displaystyle\sum_{x=0}^{r+Q+y} p(x;\mu), & 0 \leqslant y \leqslant -(r+1), \\[18pt] \dfrac{1}{Q} \displaystyle\sum_{x=r+y+1}^{r+Q+y} p(x;\mu), & y > -(r+1). \end{cases}
$$

Hence, with $\Psi_2^*(y)$ representing the normal approximations to $\Psi_2(y)$, we obtain

$$
\Psi_2^*(y) = \begin{cases} \dfrac{1}{Q} \displaystyle\int_y^{r+Q} \dfrac{1}{\sigma} \phi\!\left(\dfrac{x+y-\mu}{\sigma}\right) dx, & 0 \leqslant y \leqslant -r, \\[18pt] \dfrac{1}{Q} \displaystyle\int_r^{r+Q} \dfrac{1}{\sigma} \phi\!\left(\dfrac{x+y-\mu}{\sigma}\right) dx, & y > -r. \end{cases}
$$

Therefore,

$$
\Psi_2(y) = \begin{cases} \dfrac{1}{Q}\left[1 - \Phi\!\left(\dfrac{r+Q+y-\mu}{\sigma}\right)\right], & 0 \leqslant y \leqslant -r \\[18pt] \dfrac{1}{Q}\left[\Phi\!\left(\dfrac{r+y-\mu}{\sigma}\right) - \Phi\!\left(\dfrac{r+y+Q-\mu}{\sigma}\right)\right], & y > -r. \end{cases}
$$

Proof of proposition R1, part (2). Let P_{out} be the probability that the system is out of stock, at any point in time. Then,

$$
P_{\text{out}} = \sum_{y=0}^{\infty} \Psi_2(y)
$$

$$
= \frac{1}{Q} \sum_{y=0}^{-(r+1)} [1 - P(Q+r+y+1;\mu)]
$$

$$
+ \frac{1}{Q} \sum_{y=-r}^{\infty} [P(r+y+1;\mu) - P(r+Q+y+1;\mu)]
$$

$$
= \frac{1}{Q}\left[\sum_{y=0}^{-(r+1)} 1 + \sum_{y=-r}^{\infty} P(r+y+1;\mu) \right.
$$

$$
\left. - \sum_{y=0}^{\infty} P(r+Q+y;\mu) \right]
$$

$$
= -r/Q + [\alpha(0) - \alpha(r+Q)]/Q .
$$

The final result is obtained from the identity $F(r, Q) = 1 - P_{out}$.

Proof of proposition R1*, part (2). Let P_{out}^* be the approximation to P_{out}. Then,

$$P_{out}^* = \int_0^\infty \Psi_2^*(y)\, dy$$

$$= \frac{1}{Q} \int_0^{-r} \left[1 - \Phi\left(\frac{r + Q + y - \mu}{\sigma}\right) \right] dy$$

$$+ \frac{1}{Q} \int_{-r}^\infty \left[\Phi\left(\frac{r + y - \mu}{\sigma}\right) - \Phi\left(\frac{r + Q + y - \mu}{\sigma}\right) \right] dy$$

$$= \frac{1}{Q} \int_0^{-r} dy + \frac{1}{Q} \int_{-r}^\infty \Phi\left(\frac{r + y - \mu}{\sigma}\right) dy$$

$$- \frac{1}{Q} \int_0^\infty \Phi\left(\frac{r + Q + y - \mu}{\sigma}\right) dy$$

$$= -r/Q + [\alpha^*(0) - \alpha^*(r + Q)]/Q$$

Proof of proposition R2, part (2)

$$E[Y] = \sum_{y=0}^\infty y\Psi_2(y)$$

$$= \frac{1}{Q} \left[\sum_{y=0}^{-(r+1)} y[1 - P(r + Q + y + 1; \mu)] \right.$$

$$\left. + \sum_{y=0}^\infty y[P(r + y + 1; \mu) - P(r + Q + y + 1; \mu)] \right]$$

$$= \frac{1}{Q} \left[\sum_{y=0}^{-(r+1)} y + \sum_{y=-r}^\infty yP(r + y + 1; \mu) \right.$$

$$\left. - \sum_{y=0}^\infty y[P(r + Q + y + 1; \mu)] \right]$$

$$= r(r + 1)/2Q + [\beta(0) - \beta(r + Q)]/Q - \alpha(0)\, r/Q .$$

Proof of proposition R2*, part (2). We approximate $E[Y]$ by using $\Psi_2(\cdot)$ developed in lemma 2. Thus,

$$E[Y]^* = \int_0^\infty y\Psi_2^*(y)\,dy$$

$$= \frac{1}{Q}\int_0^{-r} y\left[1 - \Phi\left(\frac{r+Q+y-\mu}{\sigma}\right)\right]dy$$

$$+ \frac{1}{Q}\int_{-r}^\infty \left[\Phi\left(\frac{r+y-\mu}{\sigma}\right) - \Phi\left(\frac{r+Q+y-\mu}{\sigma\ \sigma}\right)\right]dy$$

$$= \frac{1}{Q}\int_0^{-r} y\,dy + \frac{1}{Q}\int_{-r}^\infty y\Phi\left(\frac{r+y-\mu}{\sigma}\right)dy$$

$$- \frac{1}{Q}\int_0^\infty y\Phi\left(\frac{r+Q+y-\mu}{\sigma}\right)dy$$

$$= \frac{r^2}{2Q} + [\beta^*(0) - \beta^*(r+Q)]/Q - r\alpha^*(0)/Q .$$

Appendix II

In section 3 the warehouse process was characterized as a Markov renewal process. In our model this process is approximated by an Erlang-Q renewal process with mean time between renewals $\mu = Q/(N\lambda)$. The purpose of this appendix is to demonstrate that these two processes have nearly identical means and very similar variances for the time intervals $[0, t]$ corresponding to the warehouse lead times considered here. It is not difficult to show that these processes will have the same mean and variance for extremely wide intervals (i.e., $t \to \infty$). The point here is to show that they are almost equivalent for small intervals. The method of analysis involves the simulation of each process and statistical analysis of the resulting means and variances.

Data generation

Consider an arbitrary renewal process $(\tilde{N})$. Let $\tilde{R}(t) = E[\tilde{N}(t)]$ and $\tilde{V}(t) = \text{var}(\tilde{N}(t))$ be the mean and variance of the number of renewals in $[0, t]$. Given m independent observations of this process, let $n_i(t)$ be the observed number of renewals in the interval $[0, t]$ for the ith observation, $i = 1, 2, ..., m$. Then, $\tilde{R}(t)$ and $\tilde{V}(t)$ may be estimated by

$$\tilde{R}(t) = \frac{1}{m} \sum_{i=1}^{m} n_j(t)$$

and

$$\tilde{V}(t) = \frac{1}{m} \sum_{i=1}^{m} n_j^2(t) - m(\tilde{R}(t))^2.$$

In this manner, estimates of the mean and variance of the Erlang-Q approximation $R'(t)$ and $V'(t)$, respectively, can be obtained. A similar procedure can be applied to the warehouse process.

In what follows, the time interval $[0, t]$ represents the warehouse lead time. Time $t = 0$ is interpreted as the instant the warehouse places an order with its supplier and t represents the warehouse lead time. Using the notation of section 3, let $x = (x_1, ..., x_n)$ represent the state of the warehouse demand process at time $t = 0$, where x_j is the inventory position at retailer j. Then, let $R(t; x)$ and $V(t; x)$ be the mean and the variance of the number of demands at the warehouse during $[0, t]$, given the initial condition x. By definition, $x_j = r + Q$ for some j, $j = 1, ..., N$ and for $k \neq j$, $x_k \in S = \{r + 1, ..., r + Q\}$. In the simulation, $j = 1$ was arbitrarily assigned so that $x_1 = r + Q$ (as if retailer 1's order caused the warehouse to order at time $t = 0$) and x_j, $j = 2, 3, ..., Q$ was drawn at random from the set S. This selection is based on the fact that the retailer inventory position is uniformly distributed over S. For a particular set of parameters (Q, N), the same value of x was used to simulate the n replications required to estimate $R(t; x)$ and $V(t; x)$. This method of randomization eliminates any effect of the initial condition on the statistical analysis.

Comparison of means

It is well known (see Cinlar [29] or Feller [72]) that any arbitrary renewal function $\tilde{R}(t)$ can be closely approximated by $(1/\mu)t$, where μ is the mean time between renewals for t large. More generally, one can accurately approximate $\tilde{R}(t)$ by a linear function of the form $\tilde{R}(t) = a + bt$ (see Marshall [144] for a similar approach), for large values of t. Consequently, it was not surprising that estimates of $R(t; x)$ and $R'(t)$ for "large" t were both linear and virtually identical. The question remained: how closely do $R(t; x)$ and $R'(t)$ compare for "small" t values? The following methodology was adopted to determine the correspondence between $R(t; x)$ and $R'(t)$ for $0 \leqslant t \leqslant T_{max}$, where T_{max} is the largest value of t considered. (1) Use the simulation to estimate $R(t; x)$ and $R'(t)$ at times t_i, $t_i = i \cdot (T_{max}/100)$, $i = 1, ..., 100$ based on $m = 20$ observations. These estimates yield the data $\{(t_i, R(t_i; x)\}_{i=1}^{100}$ and $\{(t_i, R'(t_i))\}_{i=1}^{100}$. (2) Estimate the parameters (a, b) and (α, β) for the linear representation $R(t; x) = a + bt + \epsilon$ and $R'(t) = \alpha + \beta t + \gamma$, using linear regression on the data generated in (1). (3) Compare (a, b) and (α, β).

In the analysis, Q and N were varied with Q taking on the values $Q = 1, 5$, and 10, and N taking on the values $N = 1, 2$, and 5. To standardize the results the Erlang-Q renewal process, used as the approximation, was constructed to have an asymptotic mean rate of 100 renewals per unit time, regardless of the problem parameters. Then, the warehouse process was constructed from the superposition of retailer Erlang-Q processes, each having an asymptotic rate of $\mu = 100Q/N$. In this manner, the asymptotic mean rate of the warehouse process would also be 100. For example, suppose a particular case has $Q = 5$ and $N = 2$. Then, the approximation process would be an Erlang-5 with a steady-state rate of 100 orders per unit time and the individual retailer processes would each be Erlang-5 with $\mu = (100)(5)/2 = 250$ orders per unit time. Then, for t sufficiently large, $R(t, x) \cong R'(t) \cong 100t$.

The results of simulation/regression analysis are presented in table AII.1 for $T_{max} = 0.5$ (i.e., a maximum of $L_W = 0.5$ year) and in table AII.2 for $T_{max} = 0.1$. Results for $T_{max} > 0.5$ show that both $R(t; x)$ and $R'(t)$ are linear with slopes statistically equal to 100. Comparison of tables AII.1 and AII.2 show the sensitivity of fit to T_{max}. In all cases the linear model provides a representation of both means $(R^2 \cong 0.99)$, and the corresponding values (a, α) and (b, β) are quite close. The differences between the intercepts show that the superposition (warehouse) process is rather sensitive to extremely small time intervals. Put another way, the warehouse process starts differently than the approximation process, but the difference is quickly made up. In general, the difference between the two means is less than 1 renewal (order). For example, for $N = 2$, $Q = 5$ and $t = 0.02$, and using the estimators from table AII.1, $R(t; x) = 2.1615$ and $R'(t) = 2.3406$.

Table AII.1
Results of regression analysis [a]
(T_{max} = 0.5 year)

N	Q	Superposition			Approximation		
		a	b	r^2	α	β	r^2
1	1	1.0482	98.2853	0.9996	1.0482	98.2853	0.9996
1	5	0.2986	102.1001	0.9998	0.2986	102.1001	0.9998
1	10	0.4588	101.7571	0.9999	0.4588	101.7571	0.9999
2	1	0.9838	98.3928	0.9997	1.0482	98.2853	0.9996
2	5	0.1213	102.0104	0.9998	0.2986	102.1001	0.9998
2	10	0.3173	101.7621	0.9998	0.4588	101.7571	0.9999
5	1	0.9385	98.4789	0.9996	1.0482	98.2853	0.9996
5	5	0.1365	101.9888	0.9997	0.2986	102.1001	0.9998
5	10	0.2898	101.6166	0.9998	0.4588	101.7571	0.9999

[a] Based on intervals of length $\Delta = 0.005$ years.

Table AII.2
Results of regression analysis [a]
$(T_{max} = 0.1$ year)

N	Q	Superposition			Approximation		
		a	b	r^2	α	β	r^2
1	1	1.2773	97.0512	0.9932	1.2773	97.0512	0.9932
1	5	0.6186	98.0891	0.9985	0.6186	98.0891	0.9985
1	10	0.4939	100.2666	0.9987	0.4939	100.2666	0.9987
2	1	1.2104	96.7080	0.9931	1.2773	97.0512	0.9932
2	5	0.4129	97.6093	0.9976	0.6186	98.0891	0.9985
2	10	0.3380	100.2858	0.9965	0.4939	100.2666	0.9987
5	1	1.3678	91.4264	0.9933	1.2773	97.0512	0.9932
5	5	0.5573	95.4003	0.9981	0.6186	98.0891	0.9985
5	10	0.3526	99.7150	0.9962	0.4939	100.2666	0.9987

[a] Based on intervals of length $\Delta = 0.001$ years.

Comparison of variances

The same simulation runs provide estimates of $V(t; x)$ and $V'(t)$. Unfortunately, it is difficult to formulate a basis for comparison in this case since the asymptotic properties of the variance of a renewal process are not as useful as their counterparts for the mean. Although it is expected, from theory, that both $V(t; x)$ and $V'(t)$ will become linear for t sufficiently large (see [12]), it turns out that t has to be very large before this property is observed. For this reason, it is difficult to obtain meaningful representations (i.e., linear or other type of function) for $V(t; x)$ and $V'(t)$ to facilitate comparisons. Nonetheless, one can examine the properties of the estimates of $V(t; x)$ and $V'(t)$ graphically as in figs. AII.1–AII.3. From fig. AII.1 it is easy to see that the behavior of both variances are quite similar. Also, it is apparent that both variances are becoming linear, but this convergence is much slower than for the means.

Fig. AII.2 illustrates the behavior of $V(t; x)$ for fixed $N(=2)$ as a function of Q. As expected, the variance decreases as Q increases. In addition, convergence to the linear form is much more rapid for increasing Q. Fig. AII.3 illustrates the relative insensitivity of $V(t; x)$ to N for fixed Q.

Conclusion

The evidence above suggests that, while not perfect, the approximation proposed and used in section 3 is a very good one.

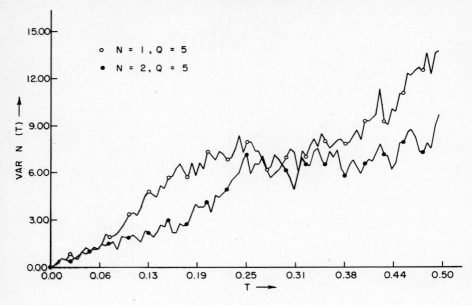

Fig. AII.1.

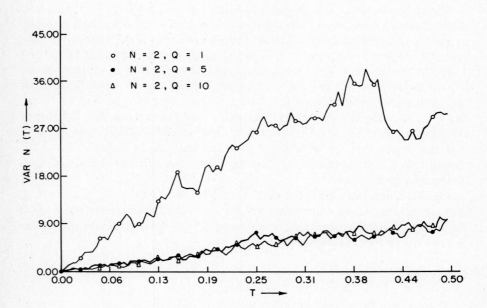

Fig. AII.2.

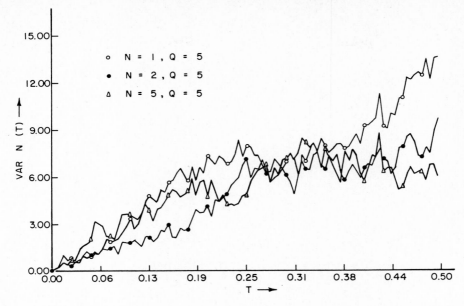

Fig. AII.3.

TIMS Studies in the Management Sciences 16 (1981) 195–207
© North-Holland Publishing Company

INVENTORY PLACEMENT IN A TWO-ECHELON
INVENTORY SYSTEM: AN APPLICATION

Barbara Amdur ROSENBAUM

Eastman Kodak Company

This paper deals with the application of a heuristic model which was developed to aid in determining safety-stock placement in the Eastman Kodak Company's two-level finished goods inventory systems. Within the company's inventory control systems, safety-stock quantities are based upon service levels which are individually set at each location. The heuristic model was developed to compute that combination of location service levels which minimizes total company safety-stock inventory while ensuring that a specified percentage of customer demand will be filled from on-hand inventory at the location where the demand occurs. The heuristic was recently tested on a sample of products at Kodak over a period of six months. This paper concentrates on a discussion of the field test and its results.

1. Introduction

The Eastman Kodak Company is a major manufacturer and worldwide distributor of chemicals, film, photographic paper and equipment. This paper deals

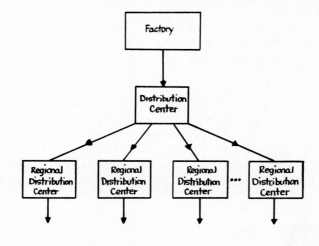

Customers

Fig. 1.

specifically with the distribution of its high-volume products in the United States. A two-level distribution system is in operation consisting of two central distribution centers (DCs) ordering from the factory, and up to seven regional distribution centers (RDCs) ordering from the DCs (see fig. 1). One inventory control system is in operation at each DC and a second inventory control system is in operation at each RDC. Both systems operate in accordance with an item-by-item service-level approach where the RDC and DC service levels are set independently of one another. A study was initiated several years ago at Kodak to coordinate the service-level values at the two echelons, and in so doing, coordinate safety-stock policy. It was felt that better customer service could be provided with the same amount of inventory, or perhaps even less, if the interaction of the service levels in the two systems was considered.

No exact solution to the question of determining optimal safety-stock placement in a two-echelon system similar to Kodak's is presently available. Previous publications on this subject include an article by Lawrence in *Interfaces* [134] discussing the implementation of an approximate solution to a similar question, and a variety of papers discussing exact solutions to special cases with characteristics inapplicable to this problem. For example, Sherbrooke [210] and Muckstadt [151] consider $(S-1, S)$ ordering policies at each location and Deuermeyer and Schwarz [56, chapter 8] assume identical demand rates, reorder points and lead times at each RDC. Due to the difficulty in obtaining an exact solution to the problem, a heuristic solution, which is described in detail in an unpublished paper by the author [192], was developed. For each item, the heuristic computes that combination of DC and RDC service levels which minimizes total company safety-stock inventory for that item while ensuring that a specified percentage of customer demand will be filled from on-hand inventory at the RDC. In [192], a comparison of simulated values with values calculated from the heuristic is presented, and demonstrates that the heuristic model is effectively representing the service-level relationships for high demand, low-variability items. Subsequent to the presentation of these initial results to Kodak's management, it was decided to test the heuristic on a sample of products over a period of six months.

This paper concentrates on a discussion of the real-world situation which resulted in the need for the model, and the subsequent field test and results. A detailed discussion of the mathematics and assumptions of the heuristic model can be found in [192]. Section 2 of the paper describes the DC and RDC inventory systems, the resulting problem, and a brief overview of the heuristic solution. Section 3 presents the details and results of the test implementation of the heuristic.

2. Problem and heuristic solution

Kodak's distribution network consists of two central distribution centers (DCs) which receive product from the factories and supply product to seven regional distribution centers (RDCs). The regional distribution centers fill direct customer orders. Because each product stocked in each RDC has one DC designated as its unique source of supply, and the analysis is performed on an item-by-item basis, the distribution network can be modeled for each item as two networks each consisting of one DC and n RDCs. Since transshipments between RDCs are minimal, this option is ignored. A periodic review, "order-up-to" system is in operation to determine DC orders on the factory, and an EOQ/reorder point system controls RDC orders on the DC. The item-level order-up-to quantity at the DC, S, is computed as the solution to

$$1 - DSL = \frac{\int_{S}^{\infty} (a - S) f_A(a) \, da}{E[\text{Demand over the review time}]} \quad (1)$$

where DSL is the item-level DC service level representing the percentage of RDC demand on the DC which will be filled from on-hand inventory, and $f_A(a)$ is the probability density function of demand on the DC over the DC review time + production lead time.

The system at RDC_i ($i = 1, ..., n$) calculates EOQ_i based on the standard Wilson square-root formula and then calculates a reorder point (R_i) as the solution to

$$1 - RSL_i = \frac{\int_{R_i}^{\infty} (b - R_i) f_{B_i}(b) \, db}{EOQ_i} \quad (2)$$

where RSL_i represents the percentage of customer demand on RDC_i which would be filled from on-hand inventory at RDC_i if the DC supplied 100% service to the RDCs, and $f_{B_i}(b)$ is the probability density of demand on RDC_i over the RDC_i lead time, assuming that the DC always has stock to fill RDC_i orders. The RDC_i lead time includes order processing and travel time but no allowance for a delay due to a backorder condition at the DC. Therefore, any value of DSL less than 100% will reduce the actual service that the customer receives to a level below RSL_i. The lower the value of DSL, the greater the decrease in customer service. Thus, the actual customer service at RDC_i, denoted by CSL_i and defined as the percentage of customer demand filled from on-hand inventory at RDC_i, is a function of both RSL_i and DSL.

Presently, item level values of DSL and $RSL_1, ..., RSL_n$ are manually input by inventory planners, each of whom has responsibility for a specific group of products. Decisions are based upon past experience and judgement. The problems that arise in using this method of determining service levels are three-fold:

(1) There is no direct computable relationship between the service levels input to the systems and the actual service level that the customers receive.

(2) It is not known how to optimally divide safety stock amongst the locations (i.e., how to set the service level at each location) so as to minimize inventory while maintaining a specified level of customer service.
(3) It is a time-consuming task to set and maintain service levels for thousands of stock items, each of which may be located in 2 DCs and 7 RDCs.

In response to these three needs, a heuristic model was developed which can analyze the interaction of RSL_i and DSL and determine what value of CSL_i results from any combination of RSL_i and DSL. The heuristic is used as follows in a system which was given the acronym TIBS (The Inventory Balance System). First, inventory planners set a customer service-level goal, CSL, by product group. Although the model will allow a different value of CSL at each RDC, in reality the company requires the same level of service at each location. A large number of $(DSL/RSL_1, RSL_2, ..., RSL_n)$ combinations will achieve any given customer service-level goal. In order to find a range of these combinations, TIBS considers a range of DSLs and then uses a binary search technique along with the heuristic model to find, for each DSL value, the required value of RSL in each region. Empirically we have found that the average total company safety stock inventory required for the resulting $(DSL/RSL_1, ..., RSL_n)$ combinations is a convex function of DSL. Thus, a second search can easily find the minimum inventory $(DSL/RSL_1, ..., RSL_n)$ combination which achieves the specified level of CSL. With this procedure, TIBS has the mechanism to determine, for each product, that service level combination, and correspondingly that level of safety stock at each location, which will minimize total company safety stock inventory while maintaining the specified level of customer service. The item level computed values for DSL and $RSL_1, ..., RSL_n$ can then be automatically input to the DC and RDC inventory control systems, respectively.

There are two major elements of the present RDC and DC inventory control systems which, in part, define the nature of the heuristic model in TIBS which determines CSL_i given DSL and RSL_i. In the RDC inventory control system, demand over the RDC_i lead time, $f_{B_i}(b)$, is assumed to be normally distributed with zero probability that demand is less than zero, and in the DC inventory control system, the same assumption is made for demand over the production lead time + review time, $f_A(a)$. For high volume, low variability items, the normality assumption at the RDC is quite accurate because of the large number of orders placed on each RDC each day. Sand shows in [197, Chapter 9] that demand on the DC over the production lead time + review time is also quite accurately described by a normal distribution for high volume, low variability items. Because of these normality assumptions, the RDC and DC inventory control systems are primarily applicable to the high volume, low variability items which account for a large majority of the company's sales volume. The remaining items, which are classified as C items, are handled with manual control points or a simple weeks' supply concept. The heuristic, which coordinates the service levels in the two systems, makes use of the same normality assumptions, and was therefore also designed for high volume, low variability items. Because there is a definite relationship between demand volume and variability, that is, as demand volume increases, variability tends to decrease, the ratio of the mean absolute deviation (MAD) of daily demand to expected daily demand can be considered as an indication of demand volume as well as variability. Previous simulation results [192] determined that the model provides an acceptable approximation for items with daily MAD/mean < 1.0.

The second element of the present systems which affects the heuristic is the service-level definition. In the existing inventory management systems, service level is defined in terms of an item-level fill rate. A service level is set for each item at each location to indicate the percentage of that item's demand which will be filled from on-hand inventory at that location. In order to maintain consistency with the current systems, the customer service level in TIBS is also defined in terms of an item-level fill rate. In the initial studies, the average length of a customer backorder had been used as a criterion to consider in conjunction with total company safety stock inventory when selecting a $(DC/RDC_1, ..., RDC_n)$ service-level combination. However, it was found that at the high customer service levels at which Kodak operates, the calculated backorder duration was typically very short and insensitive over the range of $(DSL/RSL_1, ..., RSL_n)$ values which were at or near the minimum levels of total company inventory. Therefore, it was decided to eliminate from consideration the duration of a customer backorder.

A brief explanation of the heuristic model which computes CSL_i given RSL_i and DSL will now be presented. For a more rigorous analytical description of the assumptions and the mathematics, see [192]. For simplicity, subscripts will be eliminated during the discussion. All of the analysis is done on an item-by-item basis considering each RDC independently of all other RDCs, but in conjunction with the DC. Thus, all values are for any given item stocked at the DC and any given RDC. Customer service level, CSL, is defined, as previously discussed, as the percentage of annual customer demand on the RDC met from on-hand inventory at the RDC. That is,

$$CSL = 1 - \frac{\text{Expected annual backorders at the RDC}}{\text{Expected annual demand at the RDC}}$$

By assumption, all backorders at the RDC occur during the RDC's lead time. Therefore, the expected annual backorders at the RDC consist of the sum of (a) expected backorders which occur during "normal" RDC lead times involving no delays at the DC due to out of stock conditions, and (b) expected backorders which occur during RDC lead times which are lengthened by an out-of-stock condition at the DC. If the RDC places an order on the DC which can be only partially filled, we consider that order as two orders. That portion which can be filled immediately has a "normal" lead time and is handled in case (a), and that portion which cannot be filled immediately has an extended lead time due to the DC stock-out condition and thus is handled in case (b). We assume that the lead time for the unfilled portion of the order begins after a quantity equal to the filled portion of the order has been depleted at the RDC.

For case (a) we need to compute (the expected number of lead times per year with a "normal" lead time) × (the expected number of backorders per "normal" lead time). Recall that $(1 - \text{RSL})$ is computed as (the expected number of lead times per year given that every lead time is a "normal" one) × (the expected number of backorders per "normal" lead time). Also recall that DSL represents the expected percentage of the year during which the DC has stock, that is, the percentage of the year during which "normal" lead times occur. Thus, the expected number of backorders per year occurring during "normal" lead times is simply $(1 - \text{RSL}) \times \text{DSL} \times E$ (annual demand at the RDC).

The formulation of case (b) is similar, except that we are dealing here with "long" lead times which are lengthened by an out-of-stock condition at the DC. The first value needed is the number of "long" lead times per year. We make the assumption that when the DC receives a replenishment order, that order will be of sufficient quantity to fill all outstanding backorders. Therefore, all orders placed on the DC while the DC is in a zero-stock situation will be filled at the same time — the time when the DC receives a replenishment order. Thus, we need only consider the first lead time beginning after the DC depletes its stock. All other lead times occurring during the zero stock situation are completely contained within the first. Therefore, there is a maximum of one lead time each time the DC is in a zero stock situation, and the number of "long" lead times per year can be expressed as (# DC lead times per year) × Pr (DC depletes its inventory during its lead time and the RDC places an order while the DC is in a zero stock situation). The second expression needed in formulating case (b) is the expected number of backorders occurring during a "long" lead time. We assume that demand over the "long" lead time is normally distributed and, therefore, given the expected value and variance of the

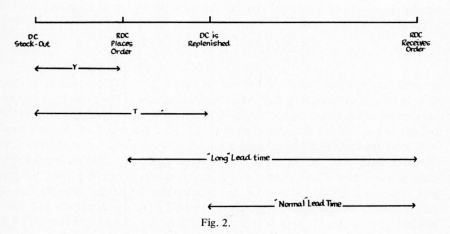

Fig. 2.

length of the "long" lead time, we can easily compute the expected number of backorders over that period of time.

The values that are needed to complete the calculations in case (b) are (i) Pr (DC depletes its inventory during its lead time and the RDC places an order while the DC is in a zero stock situation), and (ii) the expected value and variance of the "long" lead time. Fig. 2 helps to graphically depict these two values. Note that value (i) is equal to Pr $(Y < T)$ and value (ii) is equal to the length of the "normal" lead time + $(T - Y | Y < T)$. For low variability items, easily computable approximations for these values have been developed. The computer simulation analysis described in [192] has shown that the heuristic, which uses these approximations to compute CSL as a function of DSL and RSL, is quite good.

Due to the effectiveness of the heuristic in the simulated situation, management requested that TIBS, which uses this heuristic in setting item-level location service levels, be tested in a live situation on a sample of products. The next section will describe the resulting field test.

3. Field test

The purpose of the field test of TIBS was two-fold. Firstly, it was to determine if the theoretical results of the system reflect reality, and secondly, it was to determine if TIBS could provide significant improvement, either in terms of decreased inventory or better customer service, over the existing methods. Recall that existing item/location service levels were manually set, based upon inventory planners' subjective judgement and experience.

Four planners, representing two product areas, were selected by management to participate in the field test. In order to accomplish the test goals, a sample of products was selected for use in testing TIBS over a six-month period. The average inventory levels and backorder rates of these sample items were measured over the test period and compared with historical, as well as theoretical, values. The process involved in conducting the field test in conjunction with the planners can be divided into the following four steps, each of which will be discussed in detail: (1) training, (2) product selection, (3) implementation and data collection, and (4) analysis.

3.1. Training

The first, and perhaps most important, element of the field test consisted of training for the planners assigned to the project. The planners have the ultimate responsibility for the inventory management of the products assigned to them. They work with the inventory management systems in carrying out their responsibility and must deal with monitoring and adjusting system values and determining when a system value should be overriden. Thus, although it was not essential for them to understand in detail each system calculation, it was essential for them to understand the basic concepts of the system so that they could intelligently work with it. Past experience has demonstrated that, in general, the more a user understands a system, the more likely he is to use it and use it effectively. The first aspect of the training involved an explanation of the system's objectives and, conceptually, how it meets those objectives. Included here was an interpretation of the assumptions such that the planners were aware of the system's limitations. Of particular importance was the fact that the system's applicability is limited to high volume, low variability items. Secondly, the training focused on a discussion of the input parameter values, where they are obtained, and how each of them impacts the system. Finally, the training dealt with the output of the system, that is, DC and RDC service levels, and how these values serve to meet the objectives of the system.

3.2. Product selection

Once a basic understanding of the system and its applicability were established, the next step was to select the items to be used in the test. As previously discussed, the model's applicability is limited to items with a daily MAD/mean ratio in each region of less than 1. Given this restriction, approximately 20 items from each of the two product areas were selected. An effort was made to choose items with a variety of characteristics in terms of volume, demand variability and EOQ. In addition, the planners requested that the model be tested on a sample of high variability items in order to ascertain with certainty that it is in fact inapplicable to these items. Therefore, a smaller sample consisting of a total of 11 high variability C items was also selected.

The test began with a total of 50 products. However, two situations arose during its course which forced us to eliminate some of the products from consideration. The first situation involved a change in manufacturing and DC warehouse location for seven products. Since the test was taking place during the transition period, we were unable to consistently control these items with the TIBS parameters. Thus, we found it necessary to eliminate them from consideration. The second situation involved manufacturing considerations which made us unable, during a portion of the trial, to obtain enough inventory to reach the TIBS recommended inventory goals for the 22 high volume items in one of the two product areas. Rather than eliminate the 22 items, which constituted a large portion of the total sample, we felt it would be meaningful to compare the test group data with data from a control group composed of similar products with the same short supply situation, but which did not have TIBS determined service levels. In this way we could make a comparison of the TIBS system and existing procedures during a short supply situation. For 13 of the 22 test items we were able to find a product for the control group which exhibited very similar characteristics. For the other nine items, no similar product was available. Therefore, a control group and an experimental group of 13 items each were established, and the remaining nine items from the original experimental group were eliminated. Thus, at the end of the trial, we had a total of 34 experimental items.

3.3. Implementation and monitoring

The mechanics of the actual implementation involved loading TIBS with the appropriate input parameters for the trial items, running the system, and then inputting the resulting DC and RDC service levels into the appropriate inventory control systems.

The input required to perform the TIBS calculations include the following:

(a) The mean and standard deviation of the DC lead time, and the mean and standard deviation of the RDC lead time in each region given that RDC orders are not delayed by an out-of-stock condition at the DC.
(b) The mean and standard deviation of daily demand at the DC and each RDC.
(c) The EOQ value at each RDC.
(d) The desired value for CSL.

Values for (a), (b), and (c) were easily obtainable from the existing DC and RDC inventory systems. The mean and MAD of demand and lead time are exponentially smoothed, and EOQ is calculated from the standard Wilson square-root formula. The fourth item, (d), is a matter of management policy and it was the responsibility of the planners to set this value for their items. They examined historical backorder rates and set a customer service level that was greater than or equal to the historical value, as we hoped to demonstrate in the study that we could equal or better the historical backorder rates while achieving a reduction in overall company inventory. Some experimentation with various customer service levels was needed before deciding upon a value, in order to ascertain what various customer service levels implied in terms of total company safety-stock inventory.

The output of TIBS for each item consisted of recommended service levels for the DC and each RDC. These service levels represented that $(DC/RDC_1, RDC_2, ..., RDC_n)$ service-level combination which achieved the customer service-level goal at each location with the least amount of total company safety stock inventory. These values were then input to the DC and RDC inventory control systems and the planners agreed to allow the systems to run for six months with no manual intervention or overrides unless a problem situation arose. As previously discussed, 16 items were eliminated from consideration due to circumstances which arose during the trial. The remaining 34 items experienced no planner intervention during the six-month period.

Fig. 3 presents, for a sample product, the theoretical levels of total company inventory associated with the range of $(DC/RDC_1, ..., RDC_n)$ service-level combinations which, according to the heuristic calculations, achieve the specified level of customer service in each region. For this sample product, customer service level,

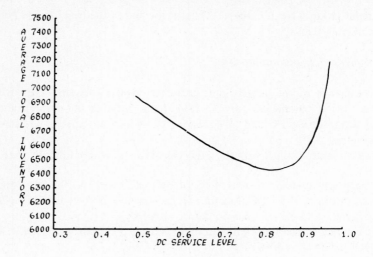

Fig. 3. DC service level versus average total inventory for a sample product.

CSL, was set at 99.5%. Although the scale of the graph shows only DC service level, DSL, associated with each value of DSL are the different values of RDC service (RSL₁, RSL₂, ..., RSL$_n$) calculated for each region. The value of CSL in each region was identical. However, the required value of RSL varied in each region due to differences in demand, lead time and EOQ. Because of the high value of CSL used for this item, the range of minimum inventory values fell within the range of DSL between 80% and 90%. If a lower value for CSL had been specified, the range of minimum inventory values would have fallen into a lower range of DSLs. Table 1 presents the values of RSL in each region for DSL = 85%. It also presents the EOQ and average "normal" lead time values (i.e., the RDC lead time when the DC has stock) for each region. Demand variability in each region was approximately the same. All other things being equal, we found that the RDCs with the smallest value of "normal" lead time required the largest value of RSL. This phenomenon occurs because the RDCs with the shortest in-transit times have the least amount of safety stock to cover variations in lead time and, therefore, require the most additional protection to buffer against any increase in the lead time due to a zero stock situation at the DC. The EOQ value in each RDC also has a significant effect on the recommended values of RSL. The longer the average time between order placements at an RDC, the lower the value of RSL that was required in that region. If order placements are infrequent, the probability that the RDC will order while the DC is in a backorder situation decreases, and therefore, the effect on customer service also decreases.

During the six-month test period, backorder rates and daily inventory levels at

Table 1
A sample of service level values (CSL = 99.5%; DSL = 85%)

	Average lead time (days)	EOQ (days' supply)	RSL
RDC 1	5.0	8.8	99.998%
RDC 2	6.0	10.2	99.968%
RDC 3	8.0	6.0	99.996%
RDC 4	10.0	7.6	99.966%
RDC 5	12.5	14.2	99.910%
RDC 6	9.5	10.8	99.948%
RDC 7	7.0	7.2	99.995%

each location were monitored. In addition, data on backorder rates and inventory levels for these same products during the identical six-month period in the previous year were obtained. When the control group was introduced, we also obtained inventory and backorder values for these control items during the test period. Backorder rates for all items were easily obtainable as the company has a very accurate backorder monitoring system which records backorders by location and cause. We eliminated from consideration all backorders caused by a warehouse error when the product was in fact available. In order to monitor average inventory levels, we obtained daily reports indicating the amount of product at each location, as well as in-transit. Product in-transit to any RDC was included as a part of that region's inventory. The daily inventory values were then averaged to obtain average on-hand inventory over the six-month period. Historical inventory levels were obtained in a similar fashion from the previous year's reports. Thus, at the end of the six-month trial period, we were able to compare the actual performance of the test products against the theoretical values as well as against historical or control group performance. The comparison with theoretical values was important in order to determine the accuracy of the model assumptions, while the comparison with historical or control data was important to management in determining the worth of the system with respect to its ability to improve upon the present procedures.

3.4. Analysis

The results of the field test are summarized in tables 2 and 3. All inventory values have been stated in terms of weeks' supply coverage of forecasted demand in order to eliminate inventory differences due to changes in demand.

Table 2 presents the data for the group of high volume items for which we compared test period data with historical data. One can see that with these products we were very effective in meeting the recommended TIBS inventory levels, and the resulting backorder rate is very close to the value calculated from the heuristic. In addition, average total company inventory for these products over the six-month

Table 2
Product group 1: low variability items

	Historical data	Trial period data	Analytical model goals
Average total RDC inventory (weeks' supply)	3.5	3.9	3.8
Average DC inventory (weeks' supply)	5.4	3.0	2.5
Total average inventory (weeks' supply)	8.9	6.9	6.3
Backorder rate	2.1%	0.7%	0.5%

period was reduced 22% over what it had been in the previous year. The data indicates that we experienced a substantial decrease in DC inventory (37%) accompanied by a smaller increase in total RDC inventory (11%), thus resulting in a net decrease in average total company inventory for these products. What is not obvious from the total RDC inventory value, is that a redistribution of inventory within the RDCs occurred. Previous to the study, for a given item, the value of RSL in each region was typically the same. As discussed above, various characteristics in each RDC, particularly the EOQ and the average lead time values, cause each RDC to have different RDC service-level requirements given that we want to maintain the same level of customer service at each RDC. Thus, TIBS is effective in determining a DC–RDC inventory split as well as in balancing inventory amongst the regions themselves.

Table 3 presents data for the sample of high volume products for which we compared experimental data with control group data during the test period. In this product area, we experienced the temporary short supply situation discussed above, where manufacturing was unable to fill all order requirements within the normal production lead time. By examining table 3, one can see that the experimental items experienced a lower backorder rate, with a smaller amount of total company inventory, than the control group. TIBS items had a lower level of inventory than

Table 3
Product group 2: low variability items

	Control group	Trial group	Analytical model goals
Avg total RDC inventory (weeks' supply)	3.9	3.7	4.0
Average DC inventory (weeks' supply)	2.9	1.5	2.2
Total average inventory (weeks' supply)	6.8	5.2	6.2
Backorder rate	1.0%	0.4%	0.1%

the control group during the short supply situation because the DC service level was set lower for these items and product allocation was based, in part, upon the system calculated "order-up-to" quantity. The data in table 3 serves to answer a very important management question with regard to how TIBS-calculated service levels affect the backorder rates during a short supply situation. By showing that TIBS performed better than existing systems, in spite of the fact that it had less inventory to work with, we demonstrated that TIBS is a useful tool in determining proper inventory placement and that larger quantities of inventory result in no increase in customer service if they are not properly placed.

Finally, in our analysis with the 11 low demand, high variability items, we found, as expected, that the system does not effectively model these items. Backorder rates were substantially higher (3–4%) than the theoretical values, and also higher than historical values, as inventory had been reduced during the trial period.

Several conclusions can be drawn from the above test results. First, from the table 2 data, it appears that TIBS does provide a reasonably accurate model of reality for low variability, high demand products, as over the trial period we were able to achieve a backorder rate close to the rate calculated by the heuristic for these test items. Secondly, for this group of products, the system does appear to offer an improvement over the present methods, as inventory as well as backorder rates were lower when TIBS was in effect. We cannot conclude, however, that a general application of the system to all low variability items in this product group would reduce backorders and inventory to the same extent as we experienced in the trial. TIBS only accounts for normal fluctuations in demand and lead times, and over time, inventory and backorders are affected by the anticipation and occurrence, respectively, of unusual circumstances. In addition, fluctuations in inventory above its minimum required value often occur at various times of the year due to manufacturing considerations. Thus, from the table 2 test results we can conclude that a reduction in inventory and/or backorder rates should result from use of the system in this product group, but we cannot conclude the exact long-term magnitude of the benefits. The total impact to the company in terms of inventory and/or backorder reductions that would result from applying TIBS to the many other product groups in the company would of course depend upon the existing and suggested inventory levels for each group. Table 3 demonstrates a third conclusion by showing the effectiveness of TIBS in one non-normal situation. It shows that TIBS helps to minimize the effects of a temporary short supply situation by properly placing available inventory. Finally, we demonstrated that TIBS is not an effective tool for dealing with high variability, low demand items. Research efforts are now continuing in the direction of finding a method to deal with those types of items.

TIMS Studies in the Management Sciences 16 (1981) 209–223
© North-Holland Publishing Company

PREDICTING DEMAND ON THE SECONDARY ECHELON:
A CASE STUDY

Gene SAND

Eastman Kodak Company

In multi-echelon inventory systems, there are multiple levels of demand. First is the primary demand on the lowest echelon; then the secondary demand from the lowest echelon on the next level, and so on. This paper considers an inventory system with two echelons and the problem of forecasting demand on the secondary level. The primary level has from one to seven stocking locations that experience independent, non-identical demands with backordering and no lost sales. No transshipments are allowed between primary locations. The inventory position (on hand + on order − backorders) is reviewed daily and orders are placed in multiples of economic order quantities. For various planning purposes, such as providing specified service levels, it is necessary to know the distribution of demand on the secondary echelon during a designated time period, such as a random lead time. This paper discusses two methods for predicting the demand on the secondary echelon, and compares the results to data obtained from simulations of Kodak products.

1. Introduction

The Eastman Kodak Company has a large nationwide distribution system. The plant in Rochester transfers finished product to a central distribution center (DC) nearby. From the DC, the product is shipped to n regional distribution centers (RDCs) (see fig. 1).

The inventory at each RDC_i ($i = 1, 2, ..., n$) is controlled by an inventory system that orders an EOQ_i of product from the DC at the end of the day if the RDC_i inventory position (on hand + on order − backorders) is at or below the reorder level R_i. Demand on RDC_i that cannot be filled from on-hand inventory is backordered (no sales are lost). Also, each RDC is supplied directly from the DC; there are no transshipments between RDCs. The DC uses a periodic review system. This study considers color and black-and-white paper items for which the time between reviews is one week. There are about 2,000 stock items in this weekly review system. (Other items, such as film and cameras, are reviewed once every four weeks. In other respects, film, cameras, and paper items share a common distribution system.) At the beginning of each week, the DC has the opportunity to place an order on the plant. The plant then schedules the manufacturing and finishing operations and transfers the finished goods to the DC. The time from order placement to the arrival of the product at the DC is random and is assumed to be normally distributed.

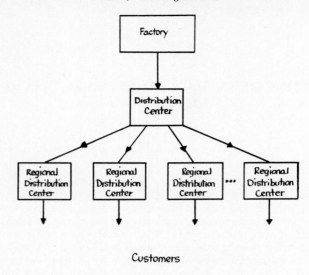

Figure 1.

Recently at Kodak, a new inventory management system for paper items at the DC was designed. Each week the DC calculates an "order up to" inventory level using demand forecasts and the current inventory position I_{0i} at each RDC$_i$. The RDC inventory position is available from inventory management systems. The objective of the DC inventory is to provide a minimum level of service that is specified as an input parameter. (Rosenbaum [191] discusses how to set the DC service level in conjunction with an RDC service level to achieve a specified system service level and to minimize inventory costs.) In order to have inventory levels that provide this service, it is necessary to know the distribution of demand on the DC during the time between reviews (one week) plus the time from the order placement to the arrival of the product. In the rest of the paper, the term lead time will refer to the DC review time plus the time from order placement to arrival at the DC. As a result of the previous assumption, the lead time is normally distributed.

Demand on the DC is directly related to demand on the RDCs. The daily demand on RDC$_i$ is most accurately modeled by a compound distribution consisting of binomial probabilities of demand occurring on any day and normally distributed quantities when demand occurs. An important consideration for this study is demand on RDC$_i$ during a DC lead time because this is the source of the demand that is placed on the DC. During sufficiently long lead times, the demand on the DC will be approximately equal to the demand on the RDCs, because all RDC demand will ultimately be passed on to the higher echelon. But over a short lead time, there could be large differences between the demand on the RDCs and on the

DC. Consider a simple low volume item. The inventory position for the item at one RDC at the beginning of the lead time is $R + EOQ/4$. If the actual demand on the RDC during the lead time is $EOQ/2$ units, then the inventory position will drop below R once and the demand on the DC will be EOQ units; that is, twice the demand on the RDC. If the initial inventory position were $R + EOQ$ and the demand during the lead time were $EOQ/2$ units, then no orders would have been placed on the DC during the lead time.

There are several ways to model demand on the DC. Two of them will be described in sections 2 and 3. Model A is a nearly precise method for describing all of the factors involved in the demand activity. It differs from the process described above only in its assumption of normal demand on the RDC during the DC lead time. This assumption will be justified. The drawback of model A is the complicated calculation that must be made to compute even the expected value of demand on the DC during its lead time. Today's modern computers are capable of handling the calculation, but for a weekly production environment it is desirable to find a method of computing inventory control points in as short a time as possible. Model B is the result of that constraint. Section 4 shows empirical evidence that supports the suitability of model B for a large percentage of Kodak's volume.

An unpublished paper by Kaplan[107] investigated four methods of estimating the mean of demand on an upper echelon. Method I is a semi-analytic simulation, method II is the same as the mean of model B. Method III is a deterministic version of model A. Method IV weights the means obtained from methods II and III. He suggests that, with appropriate weights, method IV may give superior results for all items, the difference being most apparent for low volume items.

2. Model A

For medium and high volume items, the probability of demand occurring any day is close to 1. Therefore, the demand for these items on each RDC_i during the DC lead time is approximately normal because the lead time is normal and each RDC_i experiences normal demand almost daily. Model A assumes normal demand on RDC_i during the DC lead time. Define the following symbols:

n = number of RDCs,

D_{Ri} = demand on RDC_i during the lead time, $i = 1, 2, ..., n$,

D_{Ci} = demand on the DC from RDC_i during the lead time,

$$D_C = \sum_{i=1}^{n} D_{Ci},$$

I_{0i} = inventory position at RDC_i at the beginning of the lead time, and

R_i, EOQ_i = reorder level and EOQ at RDC_i.

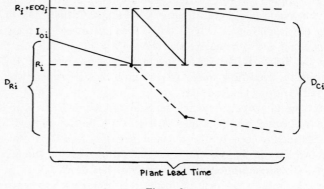

Figure 2.

A graph of the inventory position at RDC_i may look as given in fig. 2. The demand from the RDC on the DC is equal to two EOQs in this case. The demand on the DC from RDC_i can be expressed as a function of EOQ_i. The inventory position at the end of the lead time would be at $I_{oi} - D_{Ri}$ if no orders had been placed on the DC. Orders are placed to bring inventory position up to but not more than $R_i + EOQ_i$, and orders are only in multiples of EOQ_i. Therefore

$$D_{Ci} = \left[\frac{R_i + EOQ_i - (I_{oi} - D_{Ri})}{EOQ_i} \right]_g \times EOQ_i , \tag{1}$$

where $[x]_g$ is the greatest integer less than or equal to x. The only random variable on the right-hand side of this expression is D_{Ri}.

The expression for the probability density function (p.d.f.) of D_{Ci} can be derived as shown. Let

μ_{Ri}, σ^2_{Ri} = mean and variance of D_{Ri}; computed from three random processes: occurrence of demand each day, quantity of demand when it occurs, and lead time.

$f_{Ri}(x)$ = p.d.f. of $D_{Ri} = \dfrac{1}{\sigma_{Ri} \sqrt{(2\pi)}} \exp\left(\dfrac{-(x - \mu_{Ri})^2}{2\sigma^2_{Ri}} \right) .$

$\phi(x)$ = standard normal p.d.f. $= \dfrac{1}{\sqrt{(2\pi)}} \exp\left(\dfrac{-x^2}{2} \right) .$

$\Phi(x)$ = $\displaystyle\int_{-\infty}^{x} \phi(t)\, dt .$

p_{ik} = probability that RDC_i orders k EOQ_is from the DC.

$P(D = x)$ = probability that the random variable D takes on the value x.

Then

$$p_{ik} = P(D_{Ci} = k \times \mathrm{EOQ}_i), \qquad k = 1, 2, \ldots$$

$$= p\left(k \leqslant \frac{R_i + \mathrm{EOQ}_i - (I_{0i} - D_{Ri})}{\mathrm{EOQ}_i} < k + 1\right)$$

$$= P((k - 1) \times \mathrm{EOQ}_i + I_{0i} - R_i \leqslant D_{Ri} < k \times \mathrm{EOQ}_i + I_{0i} - R_i). \quad (2)$$

Let $r(i, k) = k \times \mathrm{EOQ}_i + I_{0i} - R_i$:

$$p_{ik} = \int_{r(i, k-1)}^{r(i,k)} f_{Ri}(x) \, \mathrm{d}x ,$$

$$p_{i0} = \int_{-\infty}^{r(i,0)} f_{Ri}(x) \, \mathrm{d}x .$$

Graphically, p_{ik} looks as shown in fig. 3 for an item with μ_{ri} approximately equal to three EOQ_is, where $a_i = I_{0i} - R_i$.

Continuing from (2) and standardizing D_{Ri}:

$$p_{ik} = P\left(\frac{(k - 1) \times \mathrm{EOQ}_i + I_{0i} - R_i - \mu_{Ri}}{\sigma_{Ri}} \leqslant \frac{D_{Ri} - \mu_{Ri}}{\sigma_{Ri}}\right.$$

$$\left. < \frac{k \times \mathrm{EOQ}_i + I_{0i} - R_i - \mu_R}{\sigma_{Ri}}\right).$$

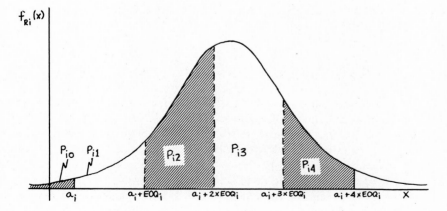

Figure 3.

Let $h_i = R_i - I_{0i} + \mu_{Ri}$:

$$p_{ik} = P\left(\frac{(k-1) - (h_i/\text{EOQ}_i)}{\sigma_{Ri}/\text{EOQ}_i} \leqslant \frac{D_{Ri} - \mu_{Ri}}{\sigma_{Ri}} < \frac{k - (h_i/\text{EOQ}_i)}{\sigma_{Ri}/\text{EOQ}_i}\right)$$

$$= \Phi\left(\frac{k - (h_i/\text{EOQ}_i)}{\sigma_{Ri}/\text{EOQ}_i}\right) - \Phi\left(\frac{(k-1) - (h_i/\text{EOQ}_i)}{\sigma_{Ri}/\text{EOQ}_i}\right),$$

$$p_{io} = \Phi\left(\frac{-h_i/\text{EOQ}_i}{\sigma_{Ri}/\text{EOQ}_i}\right).$$

Thus, the p.d.f. of D_{Ci} is discrete with two parameters, h_i/EOQ_i and σ_{Ri}/EOQ_i.

Since $D_C = \Sigma_{i=1}^{n} D_{Ci}$, the p.d.f. of D_C is the convolution of the n p.d.f.s of the D_{Ci}. Since the D_{Ci}s are independent,

$$E(D_C) = \sum_{i=1}^{n} E(D_{Ci}),$$

$$V(D_C) = \sum_{i=1}^{n} V(D_{Ci}).$$

The disadvantages of model A are that the computations are time consuming for large h_i/EOQ_i and large n and that μ_{Ri} and σ_{Ri} for individual RDCs are required.

3. Model B

The following statement is seen to be true by referring to fig. 2:

I_{Li} = inventory position at RDC$_i$ at the end of the DC lead time
    $= I_{0i} - D_{Ri} + D_{Ci}$.

Therefore,

$$D_{Ci} = D_{Ri} + I_{Li} - I_{0i}.$$

I_{0i} is known from inventory systems records, and I_{Li} is a random variable that is dependent on I_{0i}, D_{Ri}, and EOQ_i. The assumption of this model is that I_{Li} is independent of D_{Ri} and I_{0i}. Of course, this is not theoretically precise. However, Kaplan [107] has identified three factors that reduce the impact of initial inventory position on ending inventory position: (i) increased variability of demand, (ii) decreased EOQ size, and (iii) increased DC lead time.

In other words, there are some items for which the amount of activity during the lead time is sufficient to mask any effects of initial inventory position. Model A considered the complicating effects of the dependency between beginning and ending inventory. The purpose of model B is to hypothesize a more streamlined approach to determining the distribution of demand on the DC.

In the appendix, it is shown that after the review and ordering process at the end of the day at RDC_i, the inventory position is uniformly distributed between $R_i + 1$ and $R_i + EOQ_i$. Therefore, $E(I_{Li}) = R_i + EOQ_i/2$ and $V(I_{Li}) = EOQ_i/12$. (It is assumed that EOQ_i is large enough that the effect of integer-only inventory levels is negligible and, therefore, the continuous mean and variance are used.)

Using the symbol definitions of the previous section,

$$E(D_C) = \sum_{i=1}^{n} E(D_{Ci}) = \sum_{i=1}^{n} \mu_{Ri} + R_i + (EOQ_i/2) - I_{0i} \,,$$

$$V(D_C) = \sum_{i=1}^{n} V(D_{Ci}) = \sum_{i=1}^{n} \sigma_{Ri}^2 + (EOQ_i^2/12) \,.$$

The pdf of D_C is the convolution of the nD_{Ci}'s, which are convolutions of D_{Ri} and I_{Li}. Fortunately, the central limit theorem of probability theory suggests that if n is large, the distribution of D_C is approximately normal. Model B assumes that n is large enough for this to be true.

The advantage that model B has over model A is that μ_{Ri} and σ_{Ri}^2 need not be known for each individual RDC_i and there are no tedious computations for the pdf of D_C.

4. Statistical results

Since model B is simple with few calculations, it is the more practical one to use. However, statistical tests were needed to determine if the approximations were satisfactory for Kodak's paper products.

Fourteen items were selected with a variety of demand volumes and EOQs. Some items were stocked at only one RDC; others were stocked at as many as seven RDCs. Table 1 shows the results of calculations that are described below.

Demand on the DC during its lead time was generated using a Monte Carlo simulation of demand on the RDCs for each item. Daily demand on each RDC was simulated using the compound distribution consisting of binomial probabilities of occurrences of demand and normally distributed quantities when demand occurs. The demand on the RDCs was filled from simulated inventory. The initial inventory position I_{0i} was taken from the inventory records for an arbitrary day. At the end of each day, if the inventory position had fallen to or below the reorder level R, an order was placed on the DC, thus creating a demand on the DC. The number of days in the DC lead time was randomly generated according to a normal distribution. One hundred lead times were simulated for each item.

Table 1
Results of simulation and calculations

Item	RDC	EOQ_i	$I_{0i} - R_i$	D_{Ri}		Model A	
				μ_{Ri}	σ_{Ri}	$E(D_{Ci})$	$\sqrt{[V(D_{Ci})]}$
A	1	400	145	832.2	237.5	887.0	265.0
	2	260	206	463.8	137.7	387.8	157.8
	3	400	169	490.3	173.2	518.3	210.7
	4	160	31	143.7	66.9	191.2	80.2
	5	400	85	471.4	190.5	586.1	226.7
	6	120	−93	401.6	162.3	554.6	165.9
	7	400	399	601.3	178.2	402.3	205.0
	Total			3,404.2	451.9	3,527.3	516.1
B	1	100	70	399.3	134.8	174.4	137.6
	2	60	3	12.9	18.3	42.5	27.7
	3	40	18	144.8	60.4	146.9	61.1
	4	60	33	230.0	91.5	227.2	92.7
	5	180	30	133.6	66.7	191.8	76.8
	6	400	81	456.6	148.3	572.4	204.3
	7	100	8	129.8	61.1	171.8	67.5
	Total			1,506.8	246.4	1,732.0	290.2
C	1	60	11	169.9	98.2	189.8	97.5
	2	20	10	31.4	41.0	36.5	33.9
	3	45	20	45.3	41.2	49.9	39.5
	4	80	36	217.9	119.4	223.2	118.6
	5	40	2	73.0	55.9	92.0	54.8
	6	100	87	139.9	76.6	105.2	77.2
	7	20	13	26.3	35.1	28.5	28.3
	Total			703.6	193.6	725.1	189.9
D	1	400	252	752.4	213.2	700.9	242.5
	2	60	50	115.0	53.8	95.6	55.1
	3	120	115	332.2	156.2	279.3	155.4
	4	60	28	106.1	88.1	112.5	82.0
	5	120	154	300.8	119.6	208.4	120.9
	6	100	−202	390.9	164.2	642.9	166.7
	7	100	45	193.2	86.1	198.2	90.8
	Total			2,190.7	359.4	2,237.8	378.6

Model B		Simulated D_{Ci}		Power at 5% tolerance	t-stat: model B	Chi-square
$E(D_{Ci})$	$\sqrt{[V(D_{Ci})]}$	$E(D_{Ci})$	$\sqrt{[V(D_{Ci})]}$			
887.2	264.1	888.0	274.7			
387.8	156.1	392.6	158.1			
521.3	208.2	524.0	209.3			
192.7	81.3	187.2	78.2			
586.4	222.7	588.0	229.5			
554.6	166.0	553.2	172.7			
402.3	212.3	408.0	211.5			
3,532.2	516.2	3,541.0	522.5	0.98	0.17	18.0
379.3	137.8	380.0	134.2			
39.9	25.2	25.2	32.0			
146.8	61.5	147.6	63.4			
227.0	93.2	228.6	93.2			
193.6	84.5	196.2	67.8			
575.6	188.0	568.0	213.0			
171.8	67.6	173.0	69.1			
1,733.8	281.3	1,718.6	294.1	0.95	0.51	12.8
188.9	99.7	190.2	98.2			
31.4	41.4	32.4	41.3			
47.8	43.2	50.0	44.5			
221.9	121.6	224.0	122.9			
91.0	57.0	87.6	59.3			
102.9	81.9	104.0	76.1			
23.3	35.6	25.6	34.3			
707.1	198.8	713.8	197.3	0.69	0.34	32.4
700.4	242.5	712.0	243.8			
95.0	56.5	96.0	57.6			
277.2	160.0	274.8	163.0			
112.5	82.0	108.0	91.8			
206.8	124.5	204.0	123.0			
642.9	166.7	644.0	164.5			
198.2	90.8	201.0	93.3			
2,228.7	383.6	2,239.8	385.5	0.94	0.29	11.6

G. Sand, Predicting demand

Table 1 (*continued*)

Item	RDC	EOQ_i	$I_{0i} - R_i$	D_{Ri}		Model A	
				μ_{Ri}	σ_{Ri}	$E(D_{Ci})$	$\sqrt{[V(D_{Ci})]}$
E	1	80	78	129.3	84.6	96.6	78.6
	3	100	14	199.7	86.9	235.8	91.4
	4	100	86	249.0	124.7	214.9	123.8
	5	120	48	120.7	52.0	132.1	60.6
	6	120	116	218.3	101.3	164.1	103.3
	7	30	12	30.6	24.8	30.0	23.0
	Total			947.6	209.4	873.5	211.5
F	1	60	52	222.8	76.7	200.9	79.3
	3	250	220	294.5	106.0	202.0	125.8
	4	60	42	142.8	63.6	121.2	65.0
	5	40	5	36.8	32.9	51.8	34.8
	6	60	2	245.3	93.8	273.4	95.3
	7	60	17	226.8	68.9	239.8	71.1
	Total			1,169.0	189.2	1,099.1	203.8
G	2	20	20	27.9	24.9	21.2	20.9
	4	20	13	10.2	13.2	9.2	11.6
	5	60	50	36.8	23.9	17.4	27.4
	6	100	92	220.9	102.3	180.2	103.3
	7	20	16	51.3	28.7	46.2	28.0
	Total			347.3	112.5	274.2	113.0
H	1	24	23	17.7	15.9	9.6	13.3
	6	40	40	49.9	45.0	36.2	37.4
	7	24	31	8.8	15.6	1.9	6.6
	Total			76.4	50.2	47.7	40.2
I	3	48	35	93.8	108.4	96.4	89.4
	5	40	22	31.9	34.4	33.1	31.3
	6	20	3	18.4	24.0	27.0	22.0
	Total			144.1	116.2	156.5	97.2
J	1	20	7	21.2	27.8	24.0	21.9
	4	20	1	54.6	46.0	57.1	41.4
	Total			75.8	55.8	81.1	46.8
K	5	24	22	22.1	19.1	8.2	13.3
	6	18	51	11.2	19.1	0.4	2.7
	Total			23.3	27.1	8.6	13.6

Model B		Simulated D_{Ci}		Power at 5% tolerance	t-stat: model B	Chi-square
$E(D_{Ci})$	$\sqrt{[V(D_{Ci})]}$	$E(D_{Ci})$	$\sqrt{[V(D_{Ci})]}$			
91.3	87.7	91.2	84.7			
235.7	91.6	233.0	97.0			
213.0	128.0	219.0	126.3			
132.7	62.5	130.8	59.0			
162.3	107.1	166.8	104.5			
28.6	25.5	28.8	24.9			
863.6	220.2	869.6	218.1	0.75	0.27	45.2
200.8	78.6	201.6	80.7			
199.5	128.2	212.5	124.4			
130.8	65.9	132.6	65.9			
51.8	34.8	50.0	36.8			
273.3	95.4	275.4	96.0			
239.8	71.1	240.6	68.1			
1,096.0	205.7	1,112.7	203.8	0.92	0.82	17.6
17.9	25.6	19.8	22.5			
7.2	14.4	8.2	12.4			
16.8	29.5	16.8	28.2			
178.9	106.3	179.0	106.1			
45.6	29.2	46.0	29.1			
266.3	117.8	269.8	116.4	0.45	0.30	24.4
6.7	17.3	9.8	14.4			
29.9	46.4	37.6	39.5			
−10.2	17.1	4.1	10.8			
26.4	52.4	51.5	43.4	0.22	5.75	154.4
82.8	109.2	85.4	104.9			
29.9	36.3	32.4	35.2			
25.4	24.7	22.2	27.7			
138.1	117.7	140.0	114.1	0.28	0.17	62.8
21.4	25.8	20.0	27.1			
54.7	45.6	53.4	46.1			
76.1	52.4	73.4	53.5	0.30	−0.50	160
2.1	20.4	8.4	15.7			
−30.8	19.8	1.6	6.3			
−28.7	28.4	10.0	16.9	0.34	22.78	984

Table 1 (*continued*)

Item	RDC	EOQ_i	$I_{0i} - R_i$	D_{Ri}		Model A	
				μ_{Ri}	σ_{Ri}	$E(D_{Ci})$	$\sqrt{[V(D_{Ci})]}$
L	5	400	385	784.4	262.9	564.1	285.3
	6	30	2	7.1	12.6	15.5	13.0
	Total			755.5	263.2	579.6	285.6
M	1	24	20	12.3	19.0	9.4	14.0
N	2	10	2	9.4	16.1	14.4	13.5

In table 1, the items are identified by letters in the first column. The column "RDC" lists the stocking locations for each item. For example, items A to D are stocked at all seven RDCs; item E is not stocked in RDC_2. The column "$I_{0i} - R_i$" shows for each item–RDC the quantity by which inventory position exceeded the reorder level at the beginning of each of the 100 lead times. There are two instances in which this quantity is negative, even though in inventory theory $I_{0i} > R_i$. Both models handle the situation easily because the models themselves do not require I_{0i} to be greater than R_i. The column "D_{Ri}" shows the mean and standard deviation of 100 lead time demands that were randomly generated using the process described above. The columns for model A and model B are results of calculations described in sections 2 and 3. The column "simulated D_{Ci}" shows the estimates of the mean and standard deviation of the samples of demand on the DC.

Two statistical tests were conducted. The first was a test of the suitability of the mean of model B for estimating the mean of the simulated demand. The null hypothesis is that the mean given by model B is the true mean. The test statistic t is given by $(x - \mu) \cdot \sqrt{(n - 1)}/S$, where x and S are the simulated (sample) mean and standard deviation of the demand, μ is $E(D_C)$ from the model B, and n is the sample size of 100. For a sample of this size, t is approximately normally distributed. The significance level $\alpha = 20\%$ was chosen to demonstrate that even with a large probability of rejecting the null hypothesis when it is true, it is rejected infrequently, and reasons for rejection can be given. The power β was computed for an alternative hypothesis that the true mean is 5% less than (or greater than) the null hypothesis. The distribution of the sample mean was assumed to be normal with known standard deviation equal to the sample estimate. For items with large variability, the power is not adequate for accepting the null hypothesis since there is a large probability of accepting the mean from model B when in fact the true mean is 5% different from the mean from model B. In order to further investigate higher variability items such as H to N, simulations with larger sample sizes should be run.

Model B		Simulated D_{Ci}		Power at 5% tolerance	t-stat: model B	Chi-square
$E(D_{Ci})$	$\sqrt{[V(D_{Ci})]}$	$E(D_{Ci})$	$\sqrt{[V(D_{Ci})]}$			
563.4	287.2	552.0	281.6			
15.1	13.6	7.2	15.1			
578.5	287.5	561.2	282.0	0.40	−0.61	385
4.3	20.2	9.1	17.9	0.20	2.67	953
12.4	16.3	10.8	17.7	0.22	−0.90	751

The critical value of $|t|$ is 1.29. If $|t| > 1.29$, then the null hypothesis is rejected. The t-statistic is shown in the appropriate column of table 1.

The null hypothesis is accepted for 11 of the 14 items. The power of items A through F indicate that there is small probability of an alternative being true. These are high volume items that are stocked in six or seven RDCs. The medium volume items G, I, and L also have acceptable t-statistics, but there is a greater risk of a type II error when the power is computed at 5% margin for the alternative.

The remaining items, low volume, showed mixed results. Items H and K each have one location that shows negative $E(D_{Ci})$. In practice, there is never a return from the RDC to the DC (negative demand on the DC) and so for testing the means these $E(D_{Ci})$s should be zero. If zero were used, then the total $E(D_C)$ would be 36.6 and 2.1 for H and K, respectively, and the t-statistics would be 3.42 and 4.65. These statistics are smaller, but they still indicate rejection of the null hypothesis. The null hypothesis is also rejected for item M.

The items H, K, and M are similar in that orders for only one or no EOQs are placed from each region; thus, the ending inventory I_{Li} is not uniformly distributed but rather is highly dependent on the relationships among inventory, demand, and the EOQ size. The t-statistic for item H using the mean of model A is 0.87. For items K and M it is 0.82 and −0.17. These results indicate that model A is more appropriate, but the assumptions of model B are not appropriate for these items.

The second test is the chi-square goodness-of-fit between the simulated sample and a normal distribution with the same parameters. The observed demands were grouped into 20 intervals such that if the demand were normal, one would expect five observations in each interval. Letting O_j be the number of observations in interval j, the test statistic is

$$\chi^2 = \sum_{j=1}^{20}(O_j - 5)^2/5 .$$

If $\chi^2 = 118.5$, the hypothesis that the demand is normally distributed is rejected with 10% probability when the hypothesis is true. The hypothesis is accepted for all of the high volume items and for G and I of the medium volume items. The hypothesis is rejected for the remaining six items. These six items are stocked in three RDCs or less. Therefore, it would seem that $n = 3$ is not large enough to satisfy the conditions of the central limit theorem for approximation to the normal distribution. High volume items, however, are always stocked in almost all seven RDCs, so that the normal assumption is appropriate for them.

5. Conclusions

The normal distribution with the mean and variance of model B is a good model for high and medium volume items that are stocked at several RDCs. Low volume items and those stocked at only a few RDCs are not reliably approximated by this model. However, if the lead time were two or three items longer, then more orders would be placed on the DC, and model B would probably be suitable even for items H, K, and M. This possibility needs to be investigated further if the conclusions are to be extended to other applications.

Appendix

For each RDC_i, let $W_i(j, q)$ be the probability that the inventory position after ordering is $R_i + j$ one day and $R_i + q$ the next day; $j, q = 1, 2, ..., EOQ_i$. Let D_i be the random variable representing one day's demand on RDC_i. The subscript i will not be shown again in the appendix, but all parameters are related to RDC_i.

The distribution of D, as described in the main body of the paper, is compound: binomial occurrences and normal quantity. Since orders actually occur only in integer quantities, the assumption of normal is an approximation to an underlying discrete distribution. The characteristic of D that is required for this proof is the positive probability that D takes on any non-negative integer value, and that daily demands are identically and independently distributed.

$$w(j, q) = \sum_{k=1}^{\infty} P(D = k \times EOQ + j - q), \qquad \text{for } j < q,$$

$$w(j, q) = \sum_{k=0}^{\infty} P(D = k \times EOQ + j - q), \qquad \text{for } j \geqslant q.$$

Let $w(j, q)$ be the element in row j and column q of matrix W. W is the transition matrix for a Markov process. The rows sum to one. The columns also sum to one, as shown:

$$\sum_{j=1}^{EOQ} w(j, q) = \sum_{j=1}^{q-1} \sum_{k=1}^{\infty} P(D = k \times EOQ + j - q)$$

$$+ \sum_{j=q}^{EOQ} \sum_{k=0}^{\infty} P(D = k \times EOQ + j - q)$$

$$= \sum_{k=0}^{\infty} \left(\sum_{j=1+EOQ-q}^{EOQ-1} P(D = k \times EOQ + j) + \sum_{j=0}^{EOQ-q} P(D = k \times EOQ + j) \right)$$

$$= \sum_{k=0}^{\infty} \sum_{j=0}^{EOQ-1} P(D = k \times EOQ + j) = \sum_{m=0}^{\infty} P(D = m) = 1 .$$

It is easy to show that $\Pi^0 = (1/EOQ, 1/EOQ, ..., 1/EOQ)$ is the steady-state distribution of the inventory position after ordering. The transition matrix W is doubly stochastic. Since D can take the value of any non-zero integer, W is also irreducible and aperiodic; therefore, there is a unique steady-state Π that can be achieved from any initial state. By definition of steady-state, $\Pi = \Pi W$. This is satisfied by Π^0, since

$$\Pi_q = (\Pi W)_q = \sum_{j=1}^{EOQ} \frac{1}{EOQ} w(j, q) = \frac{1}{EOQ} \sum_{j=1}^{EOQ} w(j, q) = \frac{1}{EOQ} .$$

The author first saw this proof in an Eastman Kodak Company working paper by Furber dated 1967 [81]. The same concept is used in Hillier and Lieberman's book [100].

TIMS Studies in the Management Sciences 16 (1981) 225–251
© North-Holland Publishing Company

STATISTICAL PROBLEMS IN THE CONTROL OF MULTI-ECHELON INVENTORY SYSTEMS

Shelemyahu ZACKS *

Case Western Reserve University †

The robustness of adaptive control procedures is of high practical and theoretical importance. This paper studies the robustness of the Bayes adaptive control of two-echelon inventory systems when erroneous assumptions are made concerning: (1) the initial control parameters; (2) the stationarity of the demand distribution; and (3) the nature of the demand distribution. In general, the procedures appear to be robust.

1. Introduction

In a series of papers on two-echelon multi-station inventory systems [248,250, 251,252], optimal ordering procedures were developed for systems modeled towards possible naval applications. In these models we assumed that ordering at the lower-echelon stations and at the upper-echelon depot is done periodically (at the beginning of every month) and that the lead times are fixed, one month from the depot to the lower-echelon stations and two months from the wholesale supply centers to the depot. We further assumed that the monthly demand at each lower-echelon station is a random variable having a Poisson distribution, stationary in time. Moreover, the demand variables at different lower-echelon stations were assumed to be mutually independent. The means of the corresponding demand distributions were assumed, however, to be unknown. Adaptive Bayes ordering policies were developed in [251,252] and proved in [248] to be optimal for the specific cost functions and objectives specified. These Bayes procedures were based on the assumption that the unknown means of the Poisson distributions are a priori independent, having prior gamma distributions. The assumption about the prior independence of the means was essential to the development. On the other hand, the assumption concerning their prior gamma distribution is not essential but advantageous, since the gamma distribution is a conjugate prior to the Poisson distribution.

* Supported by the Office of Naval Research, Contract N00014-75-C-0729, Project NR 347-020, at the Program In Logistics, The George Washington University.
† Presently in the Department of Mathematical Sciences, State University of New York at Binghamton, Binghamton, New York 13901.

The present study investigates certain robustness or sensitivity questions related to these Bayes control procedures for one-station two-echelon systems. First, it is interesting to evaluate the sensitivity of the system to the choice of the initial prior parameters. Second, it is important to investigate the effects on the system of possible changes in the intensity of the demand distributions (the Poisson means) which may occur at unknown time points. Third, it is worth while to study the robustness of the control procedures to deviations of the demand distributions from the assumed Poisson distributions. Assuming that the demand distributions are indeed Poisson, or very close to Poisson, we may expect that the control procedures will adjust the ordering levels quickly to the optimal ones for known λ, provided the choice of the prior parameters is such that the prior means are close to the true values of the Poisson means and the prior variances are small. The Bayes procedures are optimal in the sense of minimizing the prior risk under the assumed prior parameters. However, for the sensitivity analysis we compare the procedures by simulating certain realizations of the system over a large number of periods, determining the moving averages of the accrued costs.

If the demand process is not stationary, the sequence of moving averages will fluctuate, reflecting this lack of stability. However, we will demonstrate that even in such nonstationary cases, the Bayes adaptive control performs better than the optimal control which assumes a complete knowledge of the demand distribution.

One can probably attain a similar degree of effectiveness by non-Bayes adaptive procedures, like the ones based on the maximum-likelihood estimation of the unknown parameters. We have not, however, compared Bayes and non-Bayes procedures.

Finally, for the purpose of showing the possible effect on the moving averages of the monthly costs of pronounced deviation of the demand distribution from the Poisson, we studied the behavior of the Bayes control procedures when the demand distribution is a compound Poisson, with mean at each month randomly determined according to a uniform distribution on some finite range. There is a strong indication in the results that the Bayes adaptive procedures adjust quite rapidly to possible changes in the underlying demand distributions, and provide effective controls. We also show that the approximate procedures [251,252] are effective only if the initial state of the system is not too unfavorable. The reader is referred to section 6 for a summary and conclusions based on certain simulations.

2. The two-echelon system and its statistical control

The system under consideration is comprised of a lower-echelon station, E, and an upper-echelon depot, D. Customers arrive at random at E and demand a random number of units of a specified item. Let X_i (i = 1, 2, ...) designate the total number of items demanded from E during the ith month. It is assumed that X_i has a Poisson distribution with mean λ_i (i = 1, 2, ...), and $X_1, X_2, ...$ are mutually indepen-

dent given λ_1, λ_2, ... Let Q_i denote the number of units in stock at E at the beginning of the ith month. At the beginning of the ith month E places an order on D for
Y_i units, $-Q_i \leqslant Y_i \leqslant S_i - Q_i$, where S_i denotes the total number of units in the system. A negative Y means that units are sent back to D. The lead-time for the flow
of stock between E and D is $L_1 < 1$ month. At the beginning of the ith month the
depot, D, places an order for Z_i units to be purchased from outside sources. It is
assumed that the lead-time for this replenishment is $L_2 = 2$ months. The procurement cost for new units is C^* [\$/unit]. A unit demanded at E can be supplied to the
customer at any time during the month. Unsatisfied demand at the end of a month
is lost, with penalty for shortage of H[\$/unit]; (no backlogging). Units which are
left at E undemanded accrue a carrying cost of C[\$/item]. The variables $(Q_i, S_i, X_i,$
$Y_i, Z_{i-1}, Z_i)$, $i = 1, ..., k$, designate the state of the system during the ith month.
The following recursive relations hold:

$$Q_{i+1} = (Q_i + Y_i - X_i)^+ ,$$
$$S_{i+1} = (S_i + Z_{i-1} - Y_i)^+ , \qquad i = 0, 1, ... \qquad (1)$$

where S_0 and Q_0 are the initial stock levels, $X_0 \equiv 0$, $Y_0 \equiv 0$, Z_{-1} and Z_0 are the
prior pending procurement orders, and $a^+ = \max(0, a)$.

In [251,252] we adopted the criterion of determining Y_i so as to minimize the
expected cost to the lower echelon, due to surplus or shortages during the $(i + 1)$st
month. Furthermore, it was suggested that the ordering policy of the upper echelon
will be the minimum required to guarantee that the probability of shortage at the D
will not exceed a specified risk level β, $0 < \beta < 1$. As shown in [251], if $\lambda_1 = \lambda_2 =$
$... = \lambda$, then the "desired" ordering level of E is $Y^0(\lambda, Q) = k^0(\lambda) - Q$, where

$$k^0(\lambda) = \textit{least non-negative integer } k$$
$$\textit{satisfying}: \text{Pos}(k|2\lambda) - R \cdot \text{Pos}(k|\lambda) \geqslant 0 , \qquad (2)$$

where $R = H/(C + H)$ and $\text{Pos}(k|\mu)$ designates the c.d.f. of a Poisson distribution
with mean μ. $k^0(\lambda)$ is known as the "order up to" level.

Let $G(1/\tau, \nu)$ designate a gamma distribution, with scale parameter τ and shape
parameter ν. If λ is unknown and one applies the Bayes adaptive procedure, with
prior gamma $G(1/\tau, \nu)$ distribution, then the "desired" ordering level at the beginning of the ith month is

$$K^0(T_{i-1}) - Q_i , \qquad \text{where } T_{i-1} = \sum_{j=0}^{i-1} X_j , \qquad \text{and}$$

$$K_i^0(T_{i-1}) = \textit{least non-negative integer } k$$
$$\textit{satisfying}: G(k|2\psi_{i+1}, \nu + T_{i-1}) - R \cdot G(k|\psi_i, \nu + T_{i-1}) \geqslant 0 , \qquad (3)$$

in which $G(k|\psi, \nu)$ designates the c.d.f. of a negative-binomial distribution with p.d.f.

$$g(j|\psi, \nu) = \binom{\nu + j - 1}{\nu} \psi^j (1 - \psi)^\nu, \qquad j = 0, 1, \dots \tag{4}$$

$0 < \psi < 1$, and where $\psi_i = \tau/(1 + i\tau)$. The "desired" ordering level cannot always be obtained since S_i may be smaller than $K^0(T_{i-1})$. We thus define

$$Y_i^0 = \min(K^0(T_{i-1}), S_i) - Q_i, \qquad i = 1, 2, \dots. \tag{5}$$

The upper-echelon ordering policy is defined as the least non-negative integer Z such that the predictive probability of $\{(S_i + Z_{i-1} - X_i)^+ - X_{i+1} + Z \geqslant K_{i+2}(T_{i-1} + X_i + X_{i+1})\}$, given T_{i-1}, is at least $\gamma = 1 - \beta$. We have established in [251] that the Bayes adaptive ordering policy of the upper echelon satisfying the above requirement is

$$Z_i^0(T_{i-1}) = \textit{least non-negative integer } Z \textit{ satisfying:}$$

$$G(Z - K_i^0(T_{i-1})|\psi_i, \nu + T_{i-1}) + \sum_{j=0}^{S_{i-1}^*} g(j|\psi_i, \nu + T_{i-1})$$

$$\times [G(Z - K_i^0(T_{i-1}) + S_i^* - j|\psi_{i+1}, \nu + T_{i+1} + j)$$

$$- G(Z - K_i^0(T_{i-1})|\psi_{i+1}, \nu + T_{i-1} + j)] \geqslant \gamma, \tag{6}$$

where

$$S_i^* = S_i + Z_{i-1}, \qquad i = 1, 2, \dots.$$

In table 1 we present a simulated two-echelon system with parameters $Z_0 = 0$, $\lambda = 10$, $\nu = 9.75$, $\tau = 1.1$, $C = 0.5[\$]$, $H = 10.0[\$]$, $C^* = 5.0[\$]$ and $\gamma = 0.85$. We denote by IQ, IS, and IX the values of Q_i, S_i, and X_i. KOP designates $K_i^0(T_{i-1})$; IOR designates Y_i^0 defined in (3), and IZN is equal to $Z_i^0(T_{i-1})$ defined in (6). The cost is designated by CST and is equal to $C^* \cdot \text{IZN} + C \cdot \max(0, \text{IQ} - \text{IX}) - H \cdot \min(0, \text{IQ} - \text{IX})$. Fig. 1 shows a (computer) graph of the moving-averages of the simulated monthly cost, CST. It is interesting to note that the initial stock level $Q_1 = 5$ and $S_1 = 10$ are small compared to the desired stock level, which is $k^0(10) = 28$. Although λ is unknown there is a relatively quick convergence of $K_i^0(T_{i-1})$ to $k^0(10)$. There is also an immediate correction of the stock level S_1 by a large order $Z_1 = 52$. As seen in fig. 1, the moving-averages of CST converge rapidly to the limit of their expectations. As shown in the appendix, if the system's stock level S_i stabilizes on a level higher than $k^0(\lambda)$ the limiting value of the average monthly cost is approximately

$$\bar{C} = \lambda C^* + (C + H)[\bar{Q} \, \text{Pos}(\bar{Q}|\lambda) - \lambda \, \text{Pos}(\bar{Q} - 1|\lambda)] - H(\bar{Q} - \lambda), \tag{7}$$

where $\bar{Q} = k^0(\lambda) - \lambda$. For the parameters of table 1, $\bar{Q} = 18$ and $\bar{C} = 54.93$.

As discussed in [251], there is a high correlation in the simulated data between the order level Z_i and the demand in the previous month, X_{i-1}. Indeed, in table 1

Table 1

Simulated two-echelon system under Poisson demand, $\lambda = 10$, Bayes control $\nu = 9.75$, $\tau = 1.1$, $\gamma = 0.85$; $C = 0.5(\$)$, $C^* = 5.0(\$)$, $H = 10.0(\$)$; exact upper-echelon ordering

I	IQ	IS	IX	KOP	IOR	IZN	CST
1	5	10	4	37	5	52	260.50
2	6	6	6	24	0	0	0.00
3	0	52	14	22	22	0	140.00
4	8	38	14	26	18	11	115.00
5	12	24	10	28	12	18	91.00
6	14	25	10	28	11	10	52.00
7	15	33	11	28	13	10	52.00
8	17	32	15	28	11	11	56.00
9	13	27	13	30	14	18	90.00
10	14	25	6	30	11	14	74.00
11	19	37	10	29	10	4	24.50
12	19	41	12	29	10	10	53.50
13	17	33	7	29	12	12	65.00
14	22	36	10	28	6	5	31.00
15	18	38	13	28	10	10	52.50
16	15	30	9	29	14	15	78.00
17	20	31	5	29	9	9	52.50
18	24	41	7	28	4	3	23.50
19	21	43	10	27	6	5	30.50
20	17	36	10	27	10	10	53.50
21	17	31	13	27	10	11	57.00
22	14	28	10	28	14	14	72.00
23	18	29	14	28	10	10	52.00
24	14	29	13	28	14	14	70.50
25	15	26	13	28	11	13	66.00
26	13	27	8	29	14	15	77.50
27	19	32	14	28	9	6	32.50
28	14	33	10	29	15	16	82.00
29	19	29	6	29	10	10	56.50
30	23	39	8	28	5	4	27.50
31	20	41	11	28	8	8	44.50
32	17	34	8	28	11	11	59.50
33	20	34	10	28	8	8	45.00
34	18	35	10	28	10	10	54.00
35	18	33	10	28	10	10	54.00
36	18	33	10	28	10	10	54.00
37	18	33	7	28	10	10	55.50
38	21	36	10	28	7	7	40.50
39	18	36	7	28	10	10	55.50
40	21	36	13	28	7	7	39.00

Table 1 (continued)

I	IQ	IS	IX	KOP	IOR	IZN	CST
41	15	33	11	28	13	13	67.00
42	17	29	10	28	11	11	58.50
43	18	32	16	28	10	10	51.00
44	12	27	9	28	15	16	81.50
45	18	28	3	28	10	9	52.50
46	25	41	7	28	3	3	24.00
47	21	43	8	27	6	6	36.50
48	19	38	8	27	8	8	45.50
49	19	36	19	27	8	7	35.00
50	8	25	6	28	17	21	106.00
51	19	26	3	28	7	6	38.00
52	23	44	10	27	4	1	11.50
53	17	40	10	27	10	10	53.50
54	17	31	6	27	10	10	55.50
55	21	35	10	27	6	6	35.50
56	17	35	12	27	10	10	52.50
57	15	29	13	27	12	12	61.00
58	14	26	11	27	12	13	66.50

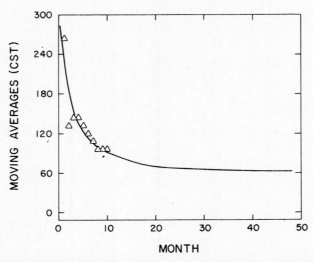

Fig. 1. Moving averages of monthly cost; Bayes control, $\nu = 9.75$, $\tau = 1.1$, $H = 10(\$)$, $C = 0.5(\$)$, $C^* = 5(\$)$; exact upper-echelon ordering.

Table 2
Simulated two-echelon system under Poisson demand, $\lambda = 1.1$, Bayes control $\nu = 9.75$, $\tau = 1.1$, $\gamma = 0.85$; $C = 0.5(\$)$, $C^* = 5.0(\$)$, $H = 10.0(\$)$; approximate upper-echelon ordering

I	IQ	IS	IX	KOP	IOR	IZN	CST
1	5	10	4	37	5	52	260.50
2	6	6	6	24	0	0	0.00
3	0	52	14	22	22	6	170.00
4	8	38	14	26	18	14	130.00
5	12	30	10	28	16	14	71.00
6	18	34	10	28	10	10	54.00
7	18	38	11	28	10	10	53.50
8	17	37	15	28	11	11	56.00
9	13	32	13	30	17	15	75.00
10	17	30	6	30	13	13	70.50
11	24	39	10	29	5	6	37.00
12	19	42	12	29	10	10	53.50
13	17	36	7	29	12	12	65.00
14	22	39	10	28	6	7	41.00
15	18	41	13	28	10	10	52.50
16	15	35	9	29	14	13	68.00
17	20	36	5	29	9	9	52.50
18	24	44	7	28	4	5	33.50
19	21	46	10	27	6	7	40.50
20	17	41	10	27	10	10	53.50
21	17	38	13	27	10	10	52.00
22	14	35	10	28	14	13	67.00
23	18	35	14	28	10	10	52.00
24	14	34	13	28	14	14	70.50
25	15	31	13	28	13	13	66.00
26	15	32	8	29	14	13	68.50
27	21	37	14	28	7	8	43.50
28	14	36	10	29	15	14	72.00
29	19	34	6	29	10	10	56.50
30	23	42	8	28	5	6	37.50
31	20	44	11	28	8	8	44.50
32	17	39	8	28	11	11	59.50
33	20	39	10	28	8	8	45.00
34	18	40	10	28	10	10	54.00
35	18	38	10	28	10	10	54.00
36	18	38	10	28	10	10	54.00
37	18	38	7	28	10	10	55.50
38	21	40	10	28	7	7	40.50
39	18	40	7	28	10	10	55.50
40	21	40	13	28	7	7	39.00

Table 2 (continued)

I	IQ	IS	IX	KOP	IOR	IZN	CST
41	15	37	11	28	13	13	67.00
42	17	33	10	28	11	11	58.50
43	18	36	16	28	10	10	51.00
44	12	31	9	28	16	16	81.50
45	19	32	3	28	9	9	53.00
46	25	45	7	28	3	3	24.00
47	21	47	8	27	6	7	41.50
48	19	42	8	27	8	8	45.50
49	19	41	19	27	8	8	40.00
50	8	30	6	28	20	19	96.00
51	22	32	3	28	6	6	39.50
52	25	48	10	27	2	3	22.50
53	17	44	10	27	10	10	53.50
54	17	37	6	27	10	10	55.50
55	21	41	10	27	6	6	35.50
56	17	41	12	27	10	10	52.50
57	15	35	13	27	12	12	61.00
58	14	32	11	27	13	13	66.50

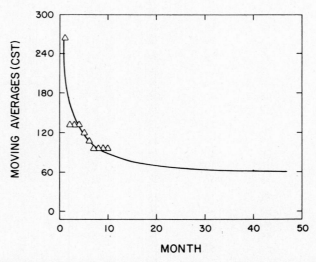

Fig. 2. Moving averages of monthly cost; Bayes control, $\nu = 9.75$, $\tau = 1.1$, $H = 10(\$)$, $C = 0.5(\$)$, $C^* = 5(\$)$; approximate upper-echelon ordering.

Table 3
Simulated two-echelon system under Poisson demand, $\lambda = 10$, Bayes control $\nu = 1.0$, $\tau = 1.1$, $\gamma = 0.85$; $C = 0.5(\$)$, $C^* = 5.0(\$)$, $H = 10(\$)$; exact upper-echelon ordering

I	IQ	IS	IX	KOP	IOR	IZN	CST
1	5	10	4	7	2	2	10.50
2	3	6	6	11	3	12	90.00
3	0	2	14	14	2	11	195.00
4	0	0	14	20	0	26	270.00
5	0	0	10	24	0	19	195.00
6	0	16	10	24	16	10	150.00
7	6	25	11	25	19	12	110.00
8	14	24	15	26	10	13	75.00
9	9	21	13	27	12	17	125.00
10	8	21	6	28	13	15	76.00
11	15	32	10	27	12	4	22.50
12	17	37	12	27	10	10	52.50
13	15	29	7	27	12	12	64.00
14	20	32	10	27	7	7	40.00
15	17	34	13	27	10	10	52.00
16	14	28	9	27	13	13	67.50
17	18	29	5	27	9	9	51.50
18	22	37	7	27	5	5	32.50
19	20	39	10	26	6	5	30.00
20	16	34	10	26	10	11	58.00
21	16	29	13	26	10	10	51.50
22	13	27	10	27	14	14	71.50
23	17	27	14	27	10	10	51.50
24	13	27	13	27	14	14	70.00
25	14	24	13	28	10	15	75.50
26	11	25	8	28	14	13	66.50
27	17	32	14	28	11	8	41.50
28	14	31	10	28	14	14	72.00
29	18	29	6	28	10	10	56.00
30	22	37	8	28	6	6	37.00
31	20	39	11	27	7	7	39.50
32	16	34	8	28	12	12	64.00
33	20	33	10	27	7	7	40.00
34	17	35	10	27	10	10	53.50
35	17	32	10	27	10	10	53.50
36	17	32	10	27	10	10	53.50
37	17	32	7	27	10	10	55.00
38	20	35	10	27	7	6	35.00
39	17	35	7	27	10	10	55.00
40	20	34	13	27	7	7	38.50

Table 3 (continued)

I	IQ	IS	IX	KOP	IOR	IZN	CST
41	14	31	11	27	13	13	66.50
42	16	27	10	27	11	11	58.00
43	17	30	16	27	10	10	50.50
44	11	25	9	28	14	18	91.00
45	16	26	3	28	10	9	51.50
46	23	41	7	27	4	1	13.00
47	20	43	8	27	7	7	41.00
48	19	36	8	27	8	8	45.50
49	19	35	19	27	8	8	40.00
50	8	24	6	27	16	19	96.00
51	18	26	3	27	8	6	37.50
52	23	42	10	27	4	3	21.50
53	17	38	10	27	10	10	53.50
54	17	31	6	27	10	10	55.50
55	21	35	10	27	6	6	35.50
56	17	35	12	27	10	10	52.50
57	15	29	13	27	12	12	61.00
58	14	26	11	27	12	13	66.50

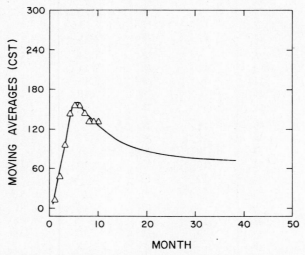

Fig. 3. Moving averages of monthly cost; Bayes control, $\nu = 1$, $\tau = 1.1$, $\gamma = 0.85$, $H = 10(\$)$, $C = 0.5(\$)$, $C^* = 5(\$)$; exact upper-echelon ordering.

the correlation between Z_i and X_{i-1} for all $i \geqslant 3$ is 0.954. It is therefore desirable (see [251] to determine Z_1 and Z_2 exactly (according to (6)) and to set $Z_i = X_{i-1}$ for every $i \geqslant 3$. This policy will be called the "approximate upper-echelon ordering policy". In table 2 and fig. 2 we present the simulated system for the same demand values as in table 1 but with the approximate upper-echelon policy. We see that the results are quite similar and the moving-averages of CST converge to the same limit. The convergence is however somewhat slower. The graph in fig. 2 is above that of fig. 1 for $i \leqslant 40$.

3. The effects of the prior parameter

In this section we study the effect of the prior parameters on the control procedure. In order to demonstrate the possible effect of a wrong choice of the prior parameter, we have performed a simulation run similar to that of tables 1 and 2, but with the prior parameter $\nu = 1.0$ rather than $\nu = 9.75$.

In table 3 we present the results using the exact upper-echelon policy, while in table 4 we show the influence of the approximate upper-echelon policy. As seen in table 3 and fig. 3, the inventory system adjusts itself very rapidly to the difference between the assumed prior expectation of λ (which is 1.1) and the actual value of λ. The moving averages of CST converge to the same limiting value as those of tables 1 and 2. This is not the case, however, when we apply the approximate upper-echelon policy, as shown in table 4 and fig. 4. One has to apply the exact upper-echelon policy for about $n = 10$ months before switching to the approximate policy, namely using X_{i-1} for Z_i. Exact ordering for $n = 2$ months is insufficient due to the effect of the low initial stocks and relatively high demand. As a result, the Q_i values in table 4 are often close to zero. The general conclusion is that as long as the stock levels Q_i and S_i are small, one should apply the exact Bayes ordering policy of the upper-echelon. Once the system stabilizes with S_i values greater than $K_i(T_{i-1})$ values, one can switch to the approximate policy.

4. The effects of non-stationarity

Non-stationarity can manifest itself in different forms. Here we investigate the effects of sudden unexpected changes in the intensity, λ, of the Poisson process of demand. More specifically, we present in table 5 a simulation of an inventory system with $\lambda_i = 10$ for $1 \leqslant i \leqslant 19$, $\lambda_i = 15$ for $20 \leqslant i \leqslant 39$, and $\lambda_i = 20$ for $40 \leqslant i$. Notice that when the mean λ_i changes, so does the variance. Thus, the sequence obtained in the present example is not even covariance stationary. The statistician, however, is unaware of these abrupt changes in λ and continues to use the Bayes adaptive policy, with an approximate upper-echelon ordering.

As expected, since the Bayes procedure is adaptive, it reacts gradually to the fact

Table 4
Simulated two-echelon system under Poisson demand, $\lambda = 10$; Bayes control $\nu = 1.0$, $\tau = 1.1$, $\gamma = 0.85$; $C = 0.5(\$)$, $C^* = 5.0(\$)$, $H = 10.0(\$)$; approximate upper-echelon ordering

I	IQ	IS	IX	KOP	IOR	IZN	CST
1	5	10	4	7	2	2	10.50
2	3	6	6	11	3	12	90.00
3	0	2	14	14	2	6	170.00
4	0	0	14	20	0	14	210.00
5	0	0	10	24	0	14	170.00
6	0	4	10	24	4	10	150.00
7	0	8	11	25	8	10	160.00
8	0	7	15	26	7	11	205.00
9	0	2	13	27	2	15	205.00
10	0	0	6	28	0	13	125.00
11	0	9	10	27	9	6	130.00
12	0	12	12	27	12	10	170.00
13	0	6	7	27	6	12	130.00
14	0	9	10	27	9	7	135.00
15	0	11	13	27	11	10	180.00
16	0	5	9	27	5	13	155.00
17	0	6	5	27	6	9	95.00
18	1	14	7	27	13	5	85.00
19	7	16	10	26	9	7	65.00
20	6	11	10	26	5	10	90.00
21	1	8	13	26	7	10	170.00
22	0	5	10	27	5	13	165.00
23	0	5	14	27	5	10	190.00
24	0	4	13	27	4	14	200.00
25	0	1	13	28	1	13	195.00
26	0	2	8	28	2	13	145.00
27	0	7	14	28	7	8	180.00
28	0	6	10	28	6	14	170.00
29	0	4	6	28	4	10	110.00
30	0	12	8	28	12	6	110.00
31	4	14	11	27	10	8	110.00
32	3	9	8	28	6	11	105.00
33	1	9	10	27	8	8	130.00
34	0	10	10	27	10	10	150.00
35	0	8	10	27	8	10	150.00
36	0	8	10	27	8	10	150.00
37	0	8	7	27	8	10	120.00
38	1	11	10	27	10	7	125.00
39	1	11	7	27	10	10	110.00
40	4	11	13	27	7	7	125.00

Table 4 (*continued*)

I	IQ	IS	IX	KOP	IOR	IZN	CST
41	0	8	11	27	8	13	175.00
42	0	4	10	27	4	11	155.00
43	0	7	16	27	7	10	210.00
44	0	2	9	28	2	16	170.00
45	0	3	3	28	3	9	75.00
46	0	16	7	27	16	3	85.00
47	9	18	8	27	9	7	35.50
48	10	13	8	27	3	8	41.00
49	5	12	19	27	7	8	180.00
50	0	1	6	27	1	19	155.00
51	0	3	3	27	3	6	60.00
52	0	19	10	27	19	3	115.00
53	9	15	10	27	6	10	60.00
54	5	8	6	27	3	10	60.00
55	2	12	10	27	10	6	110.00
56	2	12	12	27	10	10	150.00
57	0	6	13	27	6	12	190.00
58	0	3	11	27	3	13	175.00

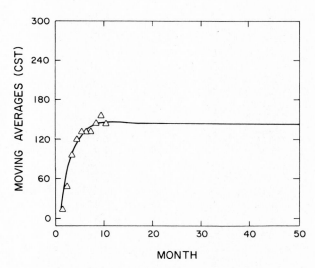

Fig. 4. Moving averages of monthly cost; Bayes control, $\nu = 1$, $\tau = 1.1$, $H = 10(\$)$, $C = 0.5(\$)$, $C^* = 5(\$)$; exact upper-echelon ordering.

Table 5
Simulated two-echelon system under Poisson demand with increasing intensity; $\lambda_i = 10(i \leqslant 19)$, $\lambda_i = 15(20 \leqslant i \leqslant 39)$, $\lambda_i = 20(i \geqslant 40)$; Bayes control $\nu = 9.75$, $\tau = 1.1$, $\gamma = 0.85$; $C = 0.5(\$)$, $C^* = 5.0(\$)$, $H = 10.0(\$)$; approximate upper-echelon ordering

I	IQ	IS	IX	KOP	IOR	IZN	CST
1	5	10	4	37	5	52	260.50
2	6	6	6	24	0	0	0.00
3	0	52	14	22	22	6	170.00
4	8	38	14	26	18	14	130.00
5	12	30	10	28	16	14	71.00
6	18	34	10	28	10	10	54.00
7	18	38	11	28	10	10	53.50
8	17	37	15	28	11	11	56.00
9	13	32	13	30	17	15	75.00
10	17	30	6	30	13	13	70.50
11	24	39	10	29	5	6	37.00
12	19	42	12	29	10	10	53.50
13	17	36	7	29	12	12	65.00
14	22	39	10	28	6	7	41.00
15	18	41	13	28	10	10	52.50
16	15	35	9	29	14	13	68.00
17	20	36	5	29	9	9	52.50
18	24	44	7	28	4	5	33.50
19	21	46	10	27	6	7	40.50
20	17	41	18	27	10	10	60.00
21	9	30	15	28	19	18	150.00
22	13	25	19	29	12	15	135.00
23	6	24	22	30	18	19	255.00
24	2	17	14	31	15	22	230.00
25	3	22	17	31	19	14	210.00
26	5	27	12	32	22	17	155.00
27	15	29	12	32	14	12	61.50
28	17	34	15	32	15	12	61.00
29	17	31	14	32	14	15	76.50
30	17	29	17	32	12	14	70.00
31	12	27	16	32	15	17	125.00
32	11	25	12	33	14	16	90.00
33	13	30	18	33	17	12	110.00
34	12	28	16	33	16	18	130.00
35	12	24	23	33	12	16	190.00
36	1	19	12	34	18	23	225.00
37	7	23	14	34	16	12	130.00
38	9	32	11	34	23	14	90.00
39	21	33	22	34	12	11	65.00
40	11	25	10	34	14	22	110.50

Table 5 (continued)

I	IQ	IS	IX	KOP	IOR	IZN	CST
41	15	26	20	34	11	10	100.00
42	6	28	17	35	22	20	210.00
43	11	21	24	35	10	17	215.00
44	0	17	25	35	17	24	370.00
45	0	9	23	36	9	25	355.00
46	0	10	25	37	10	23	365.00
47	0	10	19	37	10	25	315.00
48	0	14	17	37	14	19	265.00
49	0	22	17	37	22	17	255.00
50	5	24	17	38	19	17	205.00
51	7	24	19	38	17	17	205.00
52	5	22	19	38	17	19	235.00
53	3	20	23	38	17	19	295.00
54	0	16	31	38	16	23	425.00
55	0	4	14	39	4	31	295.00
56	0	13	22	39	13	14	290.00
57	0	22	23	39	22	22	340.00
58	0	13	18	40	13	23	295.00

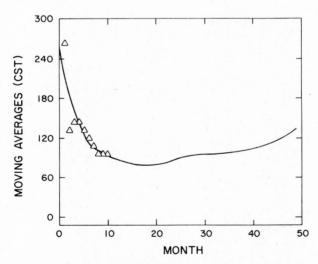

Fig. 5. Moving averages of monthly cost; Bayes control, $\nu = 9.75$; $\tau = 1.1$, $\gamma = 0.85$; $H = 10(\$)$, $C = 0.5(\$)$, $C^* = 5(\$)$; Poisson demand with increasing intensity; approximate upper-echelon ordering.

Table 6

Simulated two-echelon system under Poisson demand with increasing intensity; $\lambda_i = 10 (i \leq 19)$, $\lambda_i = 15 (20 \leq i \leq 39)$, $\lambda_i = 20 (i \geq 40)$; lower echelon control optimal for Poisson with $\lambda = 10$; $C = 0.5(\$)$, $C^* = 5.0(\$)$, $H = 10.0(\$)$; approximate upper-echelon control

I	IQ	IS	IX	KOP	IOR	IZN	CST
1	5	10	4	28	5	43	215.50
2	6	6	6	28	0	0	0.00
3	0	43	14	28	28	6	170.00
4	14	29	14	28	14	14	70.00
5	14	21	10	28	7	14	72.00
6	11	25	10	28	14	10	50.50
7	15	29	11	28	13	10	52.00
8	17	28	15	28	11	11	56.00
9	13	23	13	28	10	15	75.00
10	10	21	6	28	11	13	67.00
11	15	30	10	28	13	6	32.50
12	18	33	12	28	10	10	53.00
13	16	27	7	28	11	12	64.50
14	20	30	10	28	8	7	40.00
15	18	32	13	28	10	10	52.50
16	15	26	9	28	11	13	68.00
17	17	27	5	28	10	9	51.00
18	22	35	7	28	6	5	32.50
19	21	37	10	28	7	7	40.50
20	18	32	18	28	10	10	50.00
21	10	21	15	28	11	18	140.00
22	6	16	19	28	10	15	205.00
23	0	15	22	28	15	19	315.00
24	0	8	14	28	8	22	250.00
25	0	13	17	28	13	14	240.00
26	0	18	12	28	18	17	205.00
27	6	20	12	28	14	12	120.00
28	8	25	15	28	17	12	130.00
29	10	22	14	28	12	15	115.00
30	8	20	17	28	12	14	160.00
31	3	18	16	28	15	17	215.00
32	2	16	12	28	14	16	180.00
33	4	21	18	28	17	12	200.00
34	3	19	16	28	16	18	220.00
35	3	15	23	28	12	16	280.00
36	0	10	12	28	10	23	235.00
37	0	14	14	28	14	12	200.00
38	0	23	11	28	23	14	180.00
39	12	24	22	28	12	11	155.00
40	2	16	10	28	14	22	190.00

Table 6 (*continued*)

I	IQ	IS	IX	KOP	IOR	IZN	CST
41	6	17	20	28	11	10	190.00
42	0	19	17	28	19	20	270.00
43	2	12	24	28	10	17	305.00
44	0	8	25	28	8	24	370.00
45	0	0	23	28	0	25	355.00
46	0	1	25	28	1	23	365.00
47	0	1	19	28	1	25	315.00
48	0	5	17	28	5	19	265.00
49	0	13	17	28	13	17	255.00
50	0	15	17	28	15	17	255.00
51	0	15	19	28	15	17	275.00
52	0	13	19	28	13	19	285.00
53	0	11	23	28	11	19	325.00
54	0	7	31	28	7	23	425.00
55	0	0	14	28	0	31	295.00
56	0	9	22	28	9	14	290.00
57	0	18	23	28	18	22	340.00
58	0	9	18	28	9	23	295.00

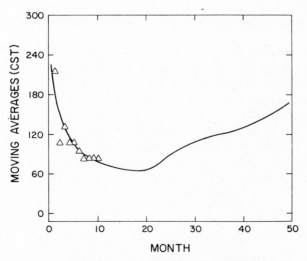

Fig. 6. Moving averages of monthly cost; fixed control under Poisson demand with increasing intensity.

that the observed demand is larger after the change in λ than before. As a consequence the $K_i(T_{i-1})$ values increase steadily after $i = 20$. They do not, however, reach the optimal values $k^0(15) = 41$ and $k^0(20) = 50$. Fig. 5 presents the graph of the moving average of monthly cost, CST. We cannot compare this graph with that of fig. 2 when $i \geqslant 20$ because the expected monthly costs associated with the optimal policy, based on a complete knowledge of the epochs and magnitude of change in λ, jumps at every epoch of change to a new steady-state limit. We can compare, however, the results presented in table 5 and fig. 5 to those obtained when the statistician knows the initial value of λ but is not aware of possible changes in λ. In other words, the same optimal policy, based on the exact initial λ, is employed all the time. In table 6 and fig. 6 we present the simulation results of such a case.

Fig. 6 shows that the moving averages, CST, are below those of fig. 5 for $1 \leqslant i \leqslant 20$ (as expected), but for $i > 20$ the adaptive Bayes procedure performs better. This indicates that when there is a possibility of non-stationarity, a non-adaptive optimal policy based on the assumption of stationarity is likely to perform worse than the adaptive procedure, which corrects itself according to the observations on the actual demand. We remark here that, as seen in table 5, the Bayes adaptive policy applied reacts rather slowly to unanticipated, abrupt changes in λ. Indeed, this policy is not optimal in such situations; it was designed for stationary cases in which λ is unknown but fixed. The derivation of a Bayes adaptive policy for cases of abrupt changes in λ, at unknown epochs, is an important subject for future research.

5. The effect of erroneous demand models

One of the important components of the parametric control model is the form of the demand distribution. In the previous sections we studied various characteristics of control procedures derived for the model of Poisson distribution of demand. It is interesting to investigate how robust these adaptive control procedures are against deviations from the Poisson model. An exhaustive study of the sensitivity of the Bayes adaptive procedures requires more development in terms of various alternatives to the Poisson distribution than what we present here. We focus attention only on the following alternative: we consider a compound Poisson distribution in which the mean, λ, is uniformly distributed over the interval [10, 20]. This provides a discrete distribution with a p.d.f.

$$f(j) = \frac{1}{10 \cdot j!} \int_{10}^{20} e^{-\lambda} \lambda^j \, d\lambda$$

$$= \tfrac{1}{10} [\text{Pos}(j \,|\, 10) - \text{Pos}(j \,|\, 20)] , \qquad j = 0, 1, \dots . \tag{8}$$

Notice that $\Sigma_{j=0}^{\infty}(1 - \text{Pos}(j|\lambda))$ is the expected value, λ, of the Poisson random variable. Hence, $\Sigma_{j=0}^{\infty} f(j) = 1$. Moreover, the expected value and variance of a random variable, J, having the above p.d.f. is $E\{\Lambda\} = 15$ and

$$
\begin{aligned}
\text{Var}\{J\} &= E\{\text{Var}\{J|\Lambda\}\} + \text{Var}\{E\{J|\Lambda\}\} \\
&= E\{\Lambda\} + \text{Var}\{\Lambda\} \\
&= 15 + \tfrac{100}{12} = 23.33 \ldots .
\end{aligned}
\tag{9}
$$

Accordingly, we may try to compare the behavior of the Bayes adaptive control procedure, for a Poisson distribution under a demand distribution specified by (8) to that of a Poisson with mean $\lambda = 15$.

In table 7 and fig. 7 we see the performance of the Bayes adaptive control under the compound Poisson demand distribution and the exact upper-echelon ordering. We see that $K_i(T_{i-1})$ approaches, indeed, $k^0(15) = 41$. The upper-echelon policy of exact Bayes adaptive control, according to (6), guarantees that the system stock level, S_i, is generally above the "desirable" level $K_i(T_{i-1})$. The moving average of the monthly cost, CST, converges consequently to a limiting expected cost of approximately 100.5. Note that if the demand distribution were Poisson with mean $\lambda = 15$, then the limiting expected cost, according to (7) would be $\bar{C} = 81.71$. Thus, there is a 25% increase in the limiting expected cost due to the fact that the actual demand distribution is not Poisson. It is of interest to test how the approximate upper-echelon ordering policy would perform in the present case, compared to that of the exact upper-echelon policy.

In table 8 and fig. 8 we present a simulation with the approximate policy, parallel to that of table 7. We see that in the case of an approximate upper-echelon policy the system stock levels, S_i, are generally below the "desirable" one, and shortages in the lower echelon are prevalent. The limiting expected monthly cost is increased, as seen in fig. 8, to 135. This is about a 35% increase over that of the exact upper-echelon policy. The indication is that the approximate upper-echelon ordering policy is not robust against considerable deviations of the actual demand distribution from the assumed one. It is safer to use the exact policy.

6. Summary and discussion

The following general trends were indicated in the present study:
(1) The exact Bayes adaptive ordering procedures adjust very quickly to the actual demand, even if the initial prior parameters are incorrectly chosen or if the initial stock values are inappropriate. The moving averages of the actual monthly costs rapidly converge, in the stationary case, to the limiting expected monthly cost.
(2) When the system stock level, S_i, is above the "desired" stock level $K_i(T_{i-1})$, the approximate upper-echelon ordering, $Z_i = X_{i-1}$, provides an effective sim-

Table 7

Simulated two-echelon system under compound Poisson demand with random uniform inten-
sity ($10 \leqslant \lambda \leqslant 20$); Bayes control $\nu = 9.75$, $\tau = 1.1$, $\gamma = 0.85$; $C = 0.5(\$)$, $C^* = 5.0(\$)$, $H = 10.0$
($\$$); exact upper-echelon ordering

I	IQ	IS	IX	KOP	IOR	IZN	CST
1	5	10	6	7	2	2	20.00
2	1	4	16	15	3	20	250.00
3	0	0	18	24	0	25	305.00
4	0	2	13	30	2	30	280.00
5	0	14	12	31	14	15	195.00
6	2	32	15	31	29	12	190.00
7	16	32	13	33	16	18	91.50
8	19	31	18	33	12	13	65.50
9	13	31	16	34	18	21	135.00
10	15	28	13	35	13	18	91.00
11	15	36	17	35	20	13	85.00
12	18	37	6	36	18	18	96.00
13	30	44	10	34	4	3	25.00
14	24	52	21	34	10	10	51.50
15	13	34	18	35	21	23	165.00
16	16	26	21	36	10	19	145.00
17	5	28	22	37	23	23	285.00
18	6	25	12	38	19	24	180.00
19	13	36	14	38	23	12	70.00
20	22	46	11	38	16	14	75.50
21	27	47	12	37	10	10	57.50
22	25	49	17	37	12	12	64.00
23	20	42	19	37	17	17	85.50
24	18	35	15	38	17	20	101.50
25	20	37	14	38	17	15	78.00
26	23	43	11	38	15	14	76.00
27	27	47	21	38	11	11	58.00
28	17	40	25	38	21	22	190.00
29	13	26	10	39	13	26	131.50
30	16	38	13	39	22	10	51.50
31	25	51	13	38	13	12	66.00
32	25	48	20	38	13	13	67.50
33	18	40	7	39	21	21	110.50
34	32	46	17	38	6	6	37.50
35	21	50	11	38	17	17	90.00
36	27	45	23	38	11	11	57.00
37	15	39	17	39	24	24	140.00
38	22	33	15	39	11	17	88.50
39	18	42	27	39	21	15	165.00
40	12	32	16	39	20	28	180.00

Table 7 (*continued*)

I	IQ	IS	IX	KOP	IOR	IZN	CST
41	16	31	12	39	15	16	82.00
42	19	47	13	39	20	12	63.00
43	26	50	7	39	13	13	74.50
44	32	55	10	39	7	6	41.00
45	29	58	18	39	10	10	55.50
46	21	46	11	39	18	18	95.00
47	28	45	10	39	11	11	64.00
48	29	53	13	38	9	9	53.00
49	25	51	8	38	13	13	73.50
50	30	52	20	38	8	7	40.00
51	18	45	25	38	20	21	175.00
52	13	27	10	39	14	26	131.50
53	17	38	11	38	21	9	48.00
54	27	53	13	38	11	11	62.00
55	25	49	17	38	13	13	69.00
56	21	43	17	38	17	17	87.00
57	21	39	8	38	17	17	91.50
58	30	48	21	38	8	8	44.50

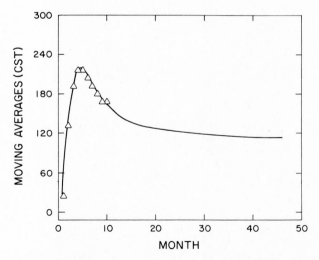

Fig. 7. Moving averages of monthly cost; compound Poisson demand; Bayes control, $\nu = 9.75$, $\tau = 1.1$, $\gamma = 0.85$, $H = 10(\$)$, $C = 0.5(\$)$, $C^* = 5(\$)$; exact upper-echelon ordering.

Table 8

Simulated two-echelon system under compound Poisson demand with random uniform intensity ($10 \leqslant \lambda \leqslant 20$); Bayes control $\nu = 9.75$, $\tau = 1.1$, $\gamma = 0.85$; $C = 0.5(\$)$, $C^* = 5.0(\$)$, $H = 10.0$ ($\$$); approximate upper-echelon ordering

I	IQ	IS	IX	KOP	IOR	IZN	CST
1	5	10	6	37	5	52	270.00
2	4	4	16	27	0	0	120.00
3	0	40	18	32	32	16	260.00
4	14	22	13	36	8	18	90.50
5	9	25	12	36	16	13	95.00
6	13	31	15	35	18	12	80.00
7	16	29	13	36	13	15	76.50
8	16	28	18	36	12	13	85.00
9	10	25	16	37	15	18	150.00
10	9	22	13	37	13	16	120.00
11	9	27	17	37	18	13	145.00
12	10	26	6	38	16	17	87.00
13	20	33	10	36	13	6	35.00
14	23	40	21	35	12	10	51.00
15	14	25	18	37	11	21	145.00
16	7	17	21	37	10	18	230.00
17	0	17	22	38	17	21	325.00
18	0	13	12	39	13	22	230.00
19	1	22	14	39	21	12	190.00
20	8	30	11	39	22	14	100.00
21	19	31	12	38	12	11	58.50
22	19	33	17	38	14	12	61.00
23	16	27	19	38	11	17	115.00
24	8	20	15	39	12	19	165.00
25	5	22	14	39	17	15	165.00
26	8	27	11	39	19	14	100.00
27	16	31	21	38	15	11	105.00
28	10	24	25	39	14	21	255.00
29	0	10	10	40	10	25	225.00
30	0	21	13	39	21	10	180.00
31	8	33	13	39	25	13	115.00
32	20	30	20	39	10	13	65.00
33	10	23	7	39	13	20	101.50
34	16	29	17	39	13	7	45.00
35	12	32	11	39	20	17	85.50
36	21	28	23	39	7	11	75.00
37	5	22	17	39	17	23	235.00
38	5	16	15	39	11	17	185.00
39	1	24	27	39	23	15	335.00
40	0	14	16	40	14	27	295.00

Table 8 (*continued*)

I	IQ	IS	IX	KOP	IOR	IZN	CST
41	0	13	12	40	13	16	200.00
42	1	28	13	40	27	12	180.00
43	15	31	7	40	16	13	69.00
44	24	36	10	39	12	7	42.00
45	26	39	18	39	13	10	54.00
46	21	28	11	39	7	18	95.00
47	17	27	10	39	10	11	58.50
48	17	35	13	39	18	10	52.00
49	22	33	8	39	11	13	72.00
50	25	35	20	38	10	8	42.50
51	15	28	25	39	13	20	200.00
52	3	11	10	39	8	25	195.00
53	1	21	11	39	20	10	150.00
54	10	35	13	39	25	11	85.00
55	22	32	17	39	10	13	67.50
56	15	26	17	39	11	17	105.00
57	9	22	8	39	13	17	85.50
58	14	31	21	38	17	8	110.00

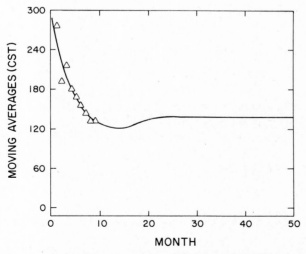

Fig. 8. Moving averages of monthly cost; compound Poisson demand; Bayes control, $\nu = 9.75$, $\tau = 1.1$, $\gamma = 0.85$, $H = 10(\$)$, $C = 0.5(\$)$, $C^* = 5(\$)$; approximate upper-echelon ordering.

plification without much additional cost. On the other hand, if the system stock level, S_i, is too low the upper-echelon ordering should be according to the exact Bayes predictive policy.
(3) In cases of possible abrupt changes in the demand distributions at unknown time points, it is better to apply adaptive procedures than optimal procedures based on the assumption of stationarity of demand.
(4) The exact Bayes ordering policy protects better than the approximate one against possible discrepancy between the model and the actual demand distribution.

The above trends in the performance of the adaptive control procedures were observed in a rather restricted range of parameters in the simulated systems. We expect that in stationary cases similar trends will be manifested in a wide range of parameters, excluding maybe unrealistic cases of cost components. On the other hand, in non-stationary cases the trends indicated here may not hold. The adaptive procedures which are good (optimal) for stationary cases may react too slowly to abrupt changes in the parameters of the demand distributions or to changes in the entire structure of these distributions. The objective of the present paper is to indicate problem areas and the need for further research on the performance of inventory control procedures under non-stationary demand.

Appendix

Derivation of the limiting average cost

The expected monthly cost associated with Y_i^0 and Z_i^0 is

$$E\{CST\} = C^* E\{Z_i^0\} + E\{C[(Q_i + Y_i^0 - X_i)^+ - X_{i+1}]^+ \\ - H[(Q_i + Y_i^0 - X_i)^+ - X_{i+1}]^-\} , \tag{A1}$$

where $a^+ = \max(0, a)$ and $a^- = \min(0, a)$. If $S_i \geqslant K_i(T_{i-1})$ then $Q_i + Y_i^0 = K_i(T_{i-1})$. Furthermore, we have seen that after the system adjusts itself, $Z_i^0 \approx X_{i-1}$ and $K_i(T_{i-1}) \approx k^0(\lambda)$. Accordingly, the limiting expected monthly cost is approximately

$$M(\lambda) = C^* \lambda + E\{C[(k^0(\lambda) - X_i)^+ - X_{i+1}]^+ \\ - H[(k^0(\lambda) - X_i)^+ - X_{i+1}]^-\} . \tag{A2}$$

If we replace $k^0(\lambda) - X_i$ in (A2) by its expectation, $\bar{Q} = k^0(\lambda) - \lambda$, we obtain formula (6); namely

$$\bar{C} = \lambda(C^* + H) + (C + H)[\bar{Q} \, \mathrm{Pos}(\bar{Q}|\lambda) - \lambda \, \mathrm{Pos}(\bar{Q} - 1|\lambda)] - H\bar{Q} . \tag{A3}$$

To evaluate this approximation we develop the formula of $M(\lambda)$. From (A2) we obtain

$$M(\lambda) = C^*\lambda + C\sum_{j=0}^{k^0} p(j|\lambda) \sum_{i=0}^{k^0-j} p(i|\lambda)(k^0 - j - i)$$

$$+ H\sum_{j=0}^{k^0} p(j|\lambda) \sum_{i=k^0-j+1}^{\infty} p(i|\lambda)(i - k^0 + j) + \lambda H \sum_{j=k^0+1}^{\infty} p(j|\lambda), \quad \text{(A4)}$$

where $k^0 = k^0(\lambda)$ and $p(j|\lambda)$ is the p.d.f. of the Poisson distribution at $J = j$ and mean λ. Notice that for each integer $k \geqslant 1$,

$$\sum_{i=1}^{k} p(i|\lambda)(k - i) = k\,\text{Pos}(k|\lambda) - \lambda\,\text{Pos}(k - 1|\lambda)$$

$$= (k - \lambda)\,\text{Pos}(k - 1|\lambda) + kp(k|\lambda) \quad \text{(A5)}$$

and

$$\sum_{i=k+1}^{\infty} (i - k)\,p(i|\lambda) = (\lambda - k) - (\lambda - k)\,\text{Pos}(k - 1|\lambda) + kp(k|\lambda). \quad \text{(A6)}$$

Hence, (A4) obtains the form

$$M(\lambda) = (C^* + H)\,\lambda + (C + H)\sum_{j=0}^{k^0-1} p(j|\lambda)\,[(k^0 - j - \lambda)$$

$$\cdot \text{Pos}(k^0 - j - 1|\lambda) + (k^0 - j)\,p(k^0 - j|\lambda)] \quad \text{(A7)}$$

$$- p\,[(k^0 - \lambda)\,\text{Pos}(k^0 - 1|\lambda) + k^0 p(k^0|\lambda)].$$

Finally, we notice that

$$\sum_{j=0}^{k^0-1} p(j|\lambda)\,\text{Pos}(k^0 - j - 1|\lambda) = P\{X_1 + X_2 \leqslant k^0 - 1\}$$

$$= \text{Pos}(k^0 - 1|2\lambda), \quad \text{(A8)}$$

where X_1 and X_2 are independent identically distributed Poisson r.v.'s with mean λ. Similarly,

$$\sum_{j=0}^{k^0-1} jp(j|\lambda)\,\text{Pos}(k^0 - j - 1|\lambda) = \lambda \sum_{j=0}^{k^0-2} p(j|\lambda)\,\text{Pos}(k^0 - 2 - j|\lambda)$$

$$= \lambda\,\text{Pos}(k^0 - 2|2\lambda). \quad \text{(A9)}$$

Accordingly, from (A8) and (A9) we prove that

$$M(\lambda) = \lambda(C^* + H)$$
$$+ (C + H)\left[(k^0 - 2\lambda)\,\text{Pos}(k^0 - 2|2\lambda) + (k^0 - \lambda)\,p(k^0 - 1|2\lambda)\right]$$
$$+ (C + H)\left[k^0 p(k^0|2\lambda) - k^0 p(0|\lambda)\,p(k^0|\lambda) - \lambda p(k^0 - 1|2\lambda)\right.$$
$$+ \lambda p(0|\lambda)\,p(k^0 - 1|\lambda)\big] - H(k^0 - \lambda)\,\text{Pos}(k^0 - 1|\lambda) - H k^0 p(k^0|\lambda)\,.$$
$$\text{(A10)}$$

This function is considerably more complicated than $\bar{C}$ given by (6) or (A3). In table A1 we give a few numerical comparisons between $\bar{C}$ and $M(\lambda)$. We see that for λ not exceeding 10, the approximation to $M(\lambda)$ given by $\bar{C}$ is very good. For values of λ greater than 10 the approximation is not as good, but the relative error for $\lambda \geqslant 20$ is less than 2%. Since (A3) is considerably simpler than (A10), it seems justifiable in many circumstances.

The limiting behavior of the moving averages of monthly costs under stationary demand

In this appendix we show that when the demand is stationary the moving averages of the monthly costs, CST, under the exact or approximate Bayes procedures converge (in mean-square) to the limiting value of the expected monthly cost, $M(\lambda)$, given in the previous section. We start with a definition and some results from the theory of time-series.

Generally, let $\{W_t; t \geqslant 1\}$ be a sequence of random variables having finite variances σ_t^2, $t \geqslant 1$; and let $\mu_t = E\{W_t\}$. Assume that $\lim \mu_t = \mu$ is finite. Let $\bar{W}_n = (1/n)\sum_{t=1}^{n} W_t$, $n \geqslant 1$, be a corresponding sequence of moving averages. $\{W_t; t \geqslant 1\}$ is said to be ergodic in the mean (see Fuller [1, p. 230]) if $\lim E\{[W_n - \mu]^2\} = 0$. A sufficient condition for a sequence to be ergodic in the mean is that $\lim \text{cov}(\bar{W}_n, W_n) = 0$ (see Fuller [1, p. 231]). We wish to show that the sequence $W_t = C^* Z_t + C[Q_t + Y_t^0 - X_t]^+ - H[Q_t + Y_t^0 - X_t]^-$, $t \geqslant 1$, is ergodic in the mean, when $\{X_t;$

Table A1
Numerical comparison of $\bar{C}$ and $M(\lambda)$ for $\lambda = 5(5)\ 30$ and $C^* = 5$, $C = 0.5$ and $H = 10$

λ	$\bar{C}$	$M(\lambda)$
5	28.57448	28.08917
10	54.92688	54.14090
15	81.70587	79.75215
20	107.50767	105.69582
25	133.29885	131.40261
30	159.00808	156.94519

$t \geqslant 1\}$ is a stationary sequence of demand variables. We notice first that since ergodic in the mean is a limiting property, we can consider the behavior of W_t for large t values. First, we can replace $Q_t + Y_t^0$ by $k^0(\lambda)$, since under stationarity of $\{X_t; t \geqslant 1\}$, $Q_t + Y_t^0 = K_t^0(T_{t-1}) \to k^0(\lambda)$ with probability 1. Furthermore, for large t values, $Z_t \approx X_{t-1}$. Notice that

$$\mathrm{cov}(\overline{W}_n, W_n) = \frac{1}{n} \sum_{t=1}^{n} \mathrm{cov}(W_t, W_n) , \tag{A11}$$

but, for large values of n,

$$\mathrm{cov}(W_t, W_n) \cong \mathrm{cov}(C^* Z_t + C(K_t^0(T_{t-1}) - X_t)^+ - H(K_t^0(T_{t-1}) - X_t)^- ,$$
$$C^* X_{n-1} + C(k^0(\lambda) - X_n)^+ - H(k^0(\lambda) - X_n)^-) . \tag{A12}$$

The r.h.s. of (A12) is zero for all $t < n - 1$, since $\{X_t\}$ is a sequence of independent r.v.'s. Hence, for large values of n,

$$\mathrm{cov}(\overline{W}_n, W_n) \cong \frac{1}{n} \left[\mathrm{cov}(W_{n-2}, W_n) + \mathrm{cov}(W_{n-1}, W_n) + \mathrm{cov}(W_n, W_n) \right] \to 0$$

as $n \to \infty$, since $\mathrm{Var}\{W_n\}$ is bounded by a function independent of n.

TIMS Studies in the Management Sciences 16 (1981) 253–277
© North-Holland Publishing Company

MANAGING REPARABLE ITEM INVENTORY SYSTEMS: A REVIEW

Steven NAHMIAS *†

University of Santa Clara

This paper reviews various mathematical models that have appeared in the literature for determining stocking levels for reparable item inventory systems. We classify existing models into three general classes: continuous review, periodic review, and models based on cyclic queueing systems. We primarily consider papers that have appeared in the open literature and concentrate on outlining the analytical approach used in éach case.

1. Introduction

The purpose of this paper is to provide a reasonably comprehensive review of the existing literature on managing inventory systems where items can be recovered through repair. The vast majority of classical inventory models have assumed that units are completely consumable; that is, once having satisfied demand, they leave the system for ever. However, in many supply systems involving spare parts, especially in the military, items that fail can be repaired and hence can cycle through the system indefinitely. It is generally the high value items that are more economical to repair than to replace, and although there may be fewer reparable than consumable items in any particular system, the reparables can account for a considerable portion of the inventory investment. Sherbrooke [210] estimated that approximately 52% of the total investment in spare parts in the Air Force was in recoverable items, which at that time (1968) amounted to about ten billion dollars. By 1975 the percentage had risen to about 65% [151]. Schrady [201] estimates that the Navy's investment in recoverables is approximately 58% of their total dollar investment in inventory.

Many reparable item inventory models can be considered to be a special type of multi-echelon model. One of the early models of a multi-echelon inventory system is due to Clark and Scarf [39] who assumed that the echelons were arranged in series with external random demand occurring at one or more of the echelons. This

---

* This researach was sponsored by the Air Force Office of Scientific Research, AFSC/USAF under Grant AFOSR 78-3494.

† This paper was prepared while the author was visiting the Departments of Operations Research and Industrial Engineering at Stanford University.

paper is significant because it introduces the concepts of system stock and implied shortage costs to demonstrate the optimality of a simple ordering rule. Extensions of these results to general arborescent structures (unidirected trees), using a different mode of analysis, was accomplished by Bessler and Veinott [15]. Other work along these lines is discussed in an informal review article by Clark [34]. Although models which treat only acyclic networks have dominated the literature on multi-echelon inventory theory, the peculiar nature of the reparable item problem, in which items cycle through the system, is not captured by an acyclic network.

Our review is organized in the following manner: in section 2 we discuss the theory of one-for-one, $(S - 1, S)$, ordering systems and their importance in manag-reparable items; in section 3 we discuss the METRIC model of stock allocation and its extensions; in section 4 we discuss other continuous review models that have been proposed, including both models for deterministic and random demand; in section 5 we treat periodic review models under random demand. In the final section we give a review of recent approaches based on queueing models. We will attempt in each case to highlight the essential thread of the analysis while also keeping in mind the potential applicability of the model to an actual operating environment.

2. One-for-one $(S - 1, S)$ ordering policies

Many of the reparable item models to be discussed are descriptions of a two-echelon system which operates in the following manner. Items fail at the base level (echelon 2). They are either repaired at the base or shipped to a central depot (echelon 1) if the repair is too complex to be carried out at the base. The base replaces the failed item from base-level stock (if it is available) and when shipping an item to the depot immediately places an order for a replacement from the depot. Define the inventory position at the base as the total number of units on hand plus units due in from base and depot repair minus backorders. The base maintains its inventory position at a fixed level, S, operating according to an $(S - 1, S)$ policy: each time one or more units is demanded, the inventory position drops below S and an order for an equal number of units is placed. Note that net inventory (on-hand minus backorders) becomes negative when a backorder condition exists.

For this reason, the theory of $(S - 1, S)$ inventory models plays a central role in many of the reparable item models to be discussed. The earliest work on this problem appears to be due to Scarf [198] who identified the analogy between this model and the theory of infinite server queues. At each placement of an order, one may think of a customer entering service in a system with an infinite number of servers. The number of busy servers corresponds to the number of outstanding orders (i.e., units in repair). Palm's [170] classic result says that if customers arrive according to a stationary Poisson process and service times are independent identically distributed random variables with a finite mean, then the steady-state probability distribution of the number of busy servers is Poisson, independent of the form of the service distribution. In the inventory problem this implies that if customer demands are generated by a stationary Poisson process, the steady-state number of outstanding orders (i.e., units in repair) is a random variable having a Poisson distribution, regardless of the distribution of lead-times (i.e., resupply times for units sent to repair) as long as lead-times are independent. That is,

$$P\{x \text{ orders outstanding}\} = P\{\text{net inventory} = S - x\}$$

$$= e^{-\lambda\tau}(\lambda\tau)^x/x , \qquad x = 0, 1, 2, \dots ,$$

where λ = mean number of units demanded per unit time and τ = expected lead-time.

This result is based on the assumption that excess demand is backordered. In the case of lost sales, a similar result holds except that the Poisson distribution is truncated at S. (See Scarf [198], Galliher et al. [83] and Haldey and Whitin [95] for further discussion of this case.)

An important generalization of Palm's theorem was obtained by Feeney and Sherbrooke [73] who showed that the distribution of outstanding orders is still Poisson when demands are generated by a stationary compound Poisson process. That is, the times of demand occurrences still follows a Poisson process with rate λ, but at each demand occurrence the number of units demanded is a random variable with an arbitrary discrete distribution on $\{0, 1, 2, \dots\}$. (Their result, however, is strictly true only when each of the units in a demand is repaired in the same time.) The importance of this extension to real inventory problems lies primarily in the fact that by proper choice of the compounding distribution, one may obtain any variance-to-mean ratio greater than or equal to one for the number of units demanded in a time t. Assuming demands are generated by a simple Poisson process gives a variance-to-mean ratio of 1.0. Actual data indicates the ratio is generally considerably larger than one (Sherbrooke [210] suggests some possible reasons for this phenomenon).

Traditional types of inventory models involving steady-state cost minimization have been treated by Galliher et al. [83] and Hadley and Whitin [73]. However, in the context of a reparable item system it is more common to use one of two types of service level criteria. The first service level criterion is commonly known as *fill rate* which is $1 - P_{\text{out}}$, where P_{out} is the probability of being out of stock at a random point in time. The other is based upon looking at the number of backorders on the books at a random point in time. Because of the importance of these measures and their interpretation in the context of the problem being considered, we will illustrate their meaning with a simple example.

Suppose net inventory (on hand minus backorders) in one particular cycle is given by fig. 1(a). The value of P_{out} for the time interval t_c is obtained by forming the ratio of the total time spent out of stock ($t_0 + \dots + t_4$) and t_c. If λ is the demand

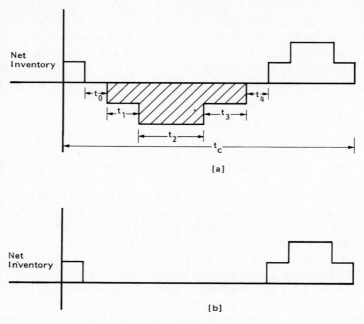

Fig. 1. Comparison of service level criteria.

rate, then λP_{out} can be interpreted as the average number of backorders incurred per unit time. This can be demonstrated using the following example: since the total number of units backordered during time t_c is two, the average number of backorders incurred during that time is $2/t_c$. As t_c grows large, the ratio of the number of units demanded when the system is out of stock divided by the time spent out of stock approaches λ. In the example, this is $2/(t_0 + ... + t_4) \approx \lambda$. Hence $\lambda P_{\text{out}} \approx [2/(t_0 + ... + t_4)] \cdot [(t_0 + ... + t_4)/t_c] = 2/t_c$ as required.

Using $1 - P_{\text{out}}$ as a measure of effectiveness (or levying a shortage cost against λP_{out}), however, completely ignores the amount of time a backorder stays on the books. For example, suppose that the net inventory is as in fig. 1(b) — it remains at zero during the time backorders are incurred in fig. 1(a). Then the value obtained for P_{out} during time t_c would be the same. Yet clearly, the sample path depicted in fig. 1(a) represents a less desirable situation than that of fig. 1(b). In order to account for this, *time-weighted backorders per unit time* is computed as the time average of the net inventory when it is negative. In the example of fig. 1(a), the first backorder stays on the books $t_1 + t_2$ units of time while the second $t_2 + t_3$ units of time. The average number of backorders on the books during t_c is then $(t_1 + 2 t_2 + t_3)/t_c$. The numerator is simply the area of the shaded portion of fig. 1(a). Note that when using a measure of effectiveness based on the average unit-years of shortage per year, a stockout of one unit for ten days is considered to be equivalent to a stockout of ten units for one day.

When demands are generated by a Poisson process with rate λ and the lead-time is fixed at τ, Hadley and Whitin [95] show that the average unit years of back-orders per year when following an $(S - 1, S)$ policy, $B(S)$, is given by

$$B(S) = \sum_{u=S}^{\infty} (u - S)\, p(u; \lambda\tau) \,,$$

where $p(u; \lambda\tau) =$ probability of exactly u demands in time τ when λ is the demand rate and τ is the lead-time (repair time).

Feeney and Sherbrooke [73] show that when lead-times are random and demands are generated by a compound Poisson process, the form of $B(S)$ remains the same except that $p(u; \lambda\tau)$ is a compound Poisson distribution and τ is inter-preted as the expected lead-time. Computational issues regarding various forms of the compound Poisson distribution are discussed by Sherbrooke [210].

An important consideration for using average backorders, $B(S)$ (as opposed to the fill rate, $1 - P_{out}$), as a measure of effectiveness in two-echelon inventory sys-tems is what happens when optimization indicates not carrying stock at the base level, as might be the case for a very low demand item. Since the fill-rate, which is based upon the incidence of shortage, will not be improved in such a case by stocking the unit at the depot level, there will be no advantage to holding depot stock and depot stock for this item will be zero as well. However, this will not be the case when using a time-weighted criterion such as $B(S)$.

There have been a number of other studies of $(S - 1, S)$ policies, none of which, to the best of our knowledge, has been incorporated into a multi-echelon model. Gross and Harris [91] considered a system in which the instantaneous probability of an order being filled depends upon the number of orders outstanding. They develop a cost model to find the optimal value of S. It appears that it would be dif-ficult to incorporate their generalization into the optimization of the multi-echelon models discussed below since explicit expressions for expected backorders are not derived. Rose [190] assumed that demands are generated by a sequence of indepen-dent and identically distributed random variables, and derives expressions for a variety of service measures. More recently, Das [51] analyzed the case where lead-times are exponential random variables and customers whose orders are not filled within some fixed time become impatient and cancel their orders. Sherbrooke [221], Higa et al. [99] and Kruse [124] considered the problem of determining the expected waiting time required to fill an order for a customer arriving at random to the system.

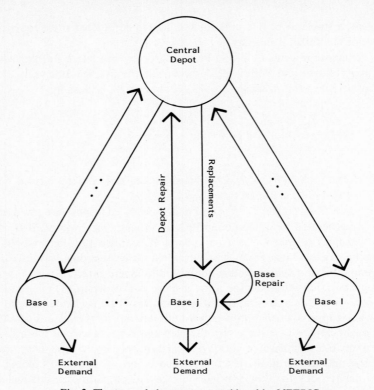

Fig. 2. The two-echelon system considered by METRIC.

3. METRIC-based models

3.1. METRIC

The METRIC model was developed over a period of years by a research group at the RAND Corporation and reported in the literature by Sherbrooke [210]. It is important in that it appears to capture many of the significant features of the problem of determining suitable spares levels in a large-scale reparable item inventory system, and, as a result, it is one of the few multi-echelon inventory models to be implemented. [1]

The model is applicable to a two-echelon system as pictured in fig. 2. Each of I

---

[1] Actually, the models which have reached the level of implementation differ slightly from the original version of METRIC. For example, in the Air Force version, stock levels are constrained to be as large as expected lead-time demand and all bases are assumed to be identical.

bases stock J spare parts. At the occurrence of a demand (that is, failure of one or more items in the field), the following takes place: the demand is either satisfied from available base stock or backordered and the failed item is inspected to determine the extent of the repair required. If the repair can be made at the base the unrepaired item enters base repair. If the item cannot be repaired at the base level it is shipped to the depot. Simultaneously with shipping the item (or items) to the depot, the base places an order for a replacement (or replacements), so that the inventory position for item i at base j is a fixed constant, S_{ij}. The model assumes that demand requests are filled by the depot in the same order that they are received. The goal is to find values for S_{ij} at the bases and the depot that minimize the total expected level of backorders for spare parts at a random point in time subject to a constraint on the total dollar investment available. The following assumptions are made:

(1) Demands for item i at base j are generated by a stationary compound Poisson process with rate λ_{ij} and compounding distribution with mean f_{ij}.
(2) With probability r_{ij} a failed item of type i at base j can be repaired at the base. With probability $(1 - r_{ij})$ the item must be repaired at the depot.
(3) The expected base repair time, A_{ij}, the expected order-and-ship time from the depot to base j, O_{ij}, and the expected depot repair time, D_i, for item i are known constants.
(4) All items can be repaired. That is, the system is completely conservative with no condemnations allowed.
(5) There is no lateral resupply (transshipment) among bases.
(6) Successive repair times are independent identically distributed random variables.

Assumption 4 says that all items which fail can be repaired at either the base or the depot. In actuality, some items cannot be repaired and are condemned, and leave the system. Hence, the true system is not completely conservative and eventually outside procurements are required to replace condemned items. Sherbrooke [210] argues that since the condemnation rate is only around 5% and procurement decisions are determined separately from levels for spares, assuming a zero condemnation rate should be satisfactory.

Assumption 6 is equivalent to requiring that there is no queueing at the repair stations. This is basically the same as saying that there are infinitely many servers at the repair channels. The infinite server assumption appears to be fairly reasonable when there are a number of parallel service channels. This assumption can be inaccurate, however, when there are substantial queues at the service areas.

The principal computation requires obtaining an expression for the expected number of backorders on the books for item i at base j at a random point in time. This requires knowledge of the expected lead-time for replenishment. For convenience we drop the subscripts i and j. A unit is sent to base repair with probability r and the expected lead-time is the mean base repair cycle time, A.

The computation of the expected lead-time when items are shipped to the depot (the depot resupply time) is affected by a direct application of the classic formula $L = \lambda W$ from queueing theory, which says that the expected queue length is the product of the arrival rate and the expected waiting time of an entering customer, independent of the form of the interarrival or service distribution (see, for example, Little [137] or Eilon [58]). The expected waiting time at the depot for an arriving order is the expected number of backorders (expected queue length of backorders) divided by the expected rate of demand on the depot. The total demand on the depot is compound Poisson with rate $\lambda = \Sigma_{i=1}^{J}\lambda_j(1 - r_j)$ and compounding distribution with mean $f = \Sigma_{j=1}^{J} f_j(1 - r_j)$, since it is the superposition of the demand process at the bases. Since the number of busy servers has distribution $p(x|\lambda D)$ (by Feeney and Sherbrooke's [73] extension of Palm's theorem), the expected number of unfilled requests at the depot at a random point in time when depot stock is S_0 is

$$B(S_0|\lambda D) = \sum_{x=S_0+1}^{\infty} (x - S_0)\, p(x|\lambda D)\,.$$

The total expected depot demand per unit time is λf or $B(0|\lambda D)/D$. It follows from $L = \lambda W$ that the expected waiting time per demand at the deposit is $D \cdot B(S_0|\lambda D)/B(0|\lambda D)$ or $\delta(S_0)D$, where $\delta(S_0) = B(S_0|\lambda D)/B(0|\lambda D)$. Hence, the total expected resupply time for an item shipped to the depot is $0 + \delta(S_0)D$.

Combining this with the computation of the expected base resupply time and including subscripts for clarity, it follows that the expected lead-time (resupply time) for item i at base j, say $T_{ij}(S_{i0})$, is given by

$$T_{ij}(S_{i0}) = r_{ij}A_{ij} + (1 - r_{ij}) \cdot [O_{ij} + \delta(S_{i0})\, D_i]\,.$$

By applying Feeney and Sherbrooke's extension of Palm's theorem, the expected number of backorders of item i at base j at a random point in time when depot stock for item i is S_{i0} and base stock is S_{ij} is given by $\beta_{ij}(S_{i0}, S_{ij})$, where

$$\beta_{ij}(S_{i0}, S_{ij}) = \sum_{x=S_{ij}}^{\infty} (x - S_{ij})\, p[x|\lambda_{ij} T_{ij}(S_{i0})]\,.$$

It should be pointed out that this expression for expected backorders will be exact only if resupply times (lead-times) are independent random variables. However, since orders from the bases are assumed to be filled in the same sequence in which they were placed, successive resupply times will generally be correlated. (Fox and Landi [79], however, state that simulation experiments indicate that this expression gives relatively good agreement with backorder levels occurring in actual application.)

Suppose c_i is the cost of item i and C the total number of dollars available. The optimization problem is: find S_{ij}, $1 \leqslant i \leqslant I$, $0 \leqslant j \leqslant J$ to

$$\min \sum_{i=1}^{I} \sum_{j=1}^{J} \beta_{ij}(S_{i0}, S_{ij}),$$

$$\text{subject to } \sum_{i=1}^{I} c_i \sum_{j=0}^{J} S_{ij} \leqslant C,$$

$$S_{ij} \geqslant 0, \qquad 0 \leqslant i \leqslant I, \qquad 0 \leqslant j \leqslant J.$$

Sherbrooke develops a two-phase marginal allocation algorithm to solve the optimization problem. Subsequently, Fox and Landi [79] have proposed a Lagrangian algorithm of solution. More recently, Muckstadt [157] considers approximating the objective function by an exponential tail which depends on S_{ij} through the sum $\sum_{j=1}^{J} S_{ij}$ only. Muckstadt compares and contrasts these three computational techniques using actual operating data.

The METRIC model is significant in a number of respects. It provides an example of a model which was developed with the goal of ultimate implementation and one which captures the types of tradeoffs that can be achieved by proper allocation of stock to both items and echelons. However, it can also be criticized on a variety of different grounds. The infinite server assumption at the depot does not account for the manner in which units are scheduled for repair. A problem that arises in applying the model is that the results are obtained by assuming the system is in steady state. During the start-up phase of a program one must deal with problems of initial procurement. Furthermore, engineering design changes can cause failure rates to be higher initially. Even in steady state, when dealing with a relatively small total number of units, the system failure rate will depend upon the number of units that are actually operating at any point in time. Models which deal with some of these shortcomings will be discussed below.

3.2. Multi-indenture models

One important aspect of the spare parts inventory problem that is not taken into account by METRIC is the relationship between end items and their components, or modules. To be specific, consider an aircraft engine whose failure is the result of the failure of a particular replaceable module within the engine. Since the goal is to return the engine to working order, a lack of availability for modules is significant only in that it results in additional delay in the repair of the engine. It is backorders of the engines rather than the modules that is of direct concern to the system. The METRIC model ignores the indenture relationship between end items and modules in that the expected backorders of both modules and end items are

MULTI-INDENTURE CONCEPT

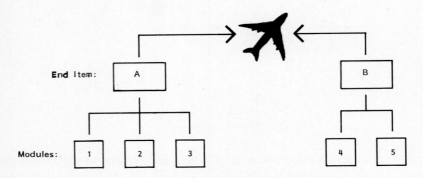

Minimizes backorders of End Items only.

METRIC CONCEPT

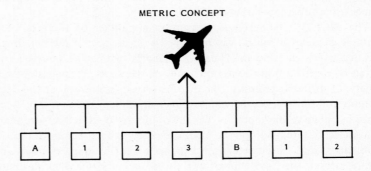

Minimizes backorders of both end items and modules without differentiation.

Fig. 3.

minimized. A schematic which indicates the difference between METRIC and a multi-indenture system is pictured in fig. 3.

Sherbrooke [209] was apparently the first to consider the multi-indenture relationship between modules and end items explicitly. Suppose an end item contains n replaceable modules or subassemblies. Demand for the end item follows a stationary Poisson process with rate λ. Suppose further that the failure of the end item is due to at most one module (and the probability that the ith module causes the failure is p_i) or that the failure is due to some other cause occurs with probability $p_0 (\sum_{i=0}^{n} p_i = 1)$.

Under the assumption of an infinite number of repair channels and complete cannibalization he shows, by applying Erlang's formula, that $P(x)$, the probability that x end items are being checked out, has a Poisson distribution with mean which depends upon p_0, λ and the system checkout and resupply times.

He then shows that $R(x)$, the probability that x or fewer end items are unavailable because they lack modules, is given by

$$R(x) = \prod_{i=1}^{n} \left(\sum_{k=0}^{S_i + a_i x} \frac{e^{-\lambda_i} \lambda_i^k}{k!} \right),$$

where S_i is the stock level of module i and a_i is the number of subassemblies of type i required per end item. The λ_i are the failure rates of the modules. The term in parentheses is simply the probability that the demand for module i does not exceed the total available spares plus the number in operation. Defining S_0 as the stock level of the end item, he obtains the stationary distribution of the probability that b or fewer end items are backordered, $\phi(b)$, as

$$\phi(b) = \sum_{y=0}^{S_0+b} \sum_{x=0}^{y} P(x) \, Q(y - x) \,,$$

where $Q(x) = R(x) - R(x - 1)$.

The difficulty one has with trying to use these results is that the expression obtained for the expected end item backorders is not separable in the decision variables $(S_0, ..., S_n)$. However, Silver [214] has noted that if the spares level of end items, S_0, is set to zero, then the problem of finding $(S_1, ..., S_n)$ to maximize availability subject to a budget constraint *is* separable in the decision variables. Three computational methods of solution are discussed including dynamic programming, marginal allocation, and Lagrange multipliers.

Demmy [53] has also considered a multi-indenture system, but does not allow cannibalization of modules. Suppose that S_i is the level of spares, λ_i the failure rate, and t_i the expected repair and resupply time of module i. Then the expected number of backorders of module i is given by

$$\beta_i(S_i, \lambda_i t_i) = \sum_{x=S_i+1}^{\infty} (x - S_i) \, p(x | \lambda_i t_i)$$

using assumptions and arguments similar to those used by Sherbrooke above.

The expected delay experienced due to shortages of module i can be found by again utilizing an argument based on the result $L = \lambda W$, that is, the expected delay for item i, say W_i, is

$$W_i = \beta_i(S_i, \lambda_i t_i)/\lambda_i \,.$$

From this Demmy develops an expression for the total expected lead-time for the end item, which can be used (as in METRIC) to determine the expected end item backorders at a random point in time. This is then minimized subject to a budget constraint. He formulates the optimization as a dynamic program and suggests using Kettelle's [119] algorithm in the suboptimization.

A similar approach was reported by Muckstadt [151] who extends the two-echelon METRIC model to include the multi-indenture relationship between modules and end items. Our notation differs from Muckstadt's in order to be consistent with Sherbrooke's. The significant difference between METRIC and MOD-METRIC (as Muckstadt has called it) is in the manner in which one computes the mean base repair cycle time for the end item at base j, say A_j. This can be expressed as $R_j + \Delta_j$, where R_j is the average repair time when modules are available and Δ_j is the average delay due to the unavailability of modules at base j. By utilizing $L = \lambda W$ as above, the expected delay (i.e., waiting time) at base j due specifically to the unavailability of module i, say Δ_{ij}, is given by

$$\Delta_{ij} = \beta_{ij}(S_{i0}, S_{ij})/\lambda_{ij} ,$$

where λ_{ij} is the failure rate of module i at base j. The total expected delay per demand at base j due to shortages in all modules is then

$$\Delta_j = \frac{1}{r_j \lambda_j} \sum_{i=1}^{I} \lambda_{ij} \Delta_{ij} ,$$

where λ_j is the failure rate of engines at base j and r_j is the likelihood that an engine can be repaired at base j. One now substitutes this form of A_j into the expression for the average resupply time at base j, T_j, in METRIC. Muckstadt discusses the optimization problem, which is considerably more complex than with METRIC due to the incorporation of the multi-indenture aspect of the problem. This model was implemented by the Air Force in determining stocking levels of spare parts for the F-15 weapons system.

3.3. Real-Time METRIC

Another extension of METRIC has been proposed by Miller [147]. In both METRIC and MOD-METRIC, demands upon the depot are assumed to be filled in the same sequence that they were placed originally. In Real Time METRIC (the name was used in the original RAND memorandum but not in the subsequently published version [147]), this restriction is not placed upon the depot. Instead, as each item completes depot repair, the depot has the prerogative of determining to which base the item will be shipped.

Miller assumes that demands for the item on the depot are generated by independent Poisson processes with respective rates λ_j. The time required at the depot to repair each item is independent of the repair times for other items, and repair times are exponentially distributed with mean $1/\mu$ days. In addition, he assumes that it requires T_j days to ship the item from the depot to base j, where the T_j's are known constants.

As each item completes repair, the rule he suggests is to ship the item to that base whose marginal decrease in expected backorders will be greatest at time T_j days into the future.

Miller shows this rule to be optimal for a slightly modified version of the recoverable item problem (a different modification is considered more recently in [148]) and claims that simulation of some tests resulted in considerable decreases in the levels of expected backorders observed when using METRIC. The assumptions required are quite stringent. Demands are assumed to be generated by simple Poisson processes and repair times are assumed to be independent exponential random variables. In order to implement a policy of this type, one would need to keep track of the disposition of stock levels at the bases as well as the number and destination of all spares in transit on a continuous basis. Clearly, this would not be feasible for all parts in a large-scale system such as is managed by the military. However, for high cost, high demand items, the improvement realized in system performance might justify the additional cost of information.

4. Other continuous review models

A number of other continuous review models for a reparable item inventory have appeared in the literature. Schrady [201] considers a stationary model with a deterministic failure pattern which is interesting in that it explicitly treats the interaction between the repair and procurement functions. He assumes that items fail at a fixed rate d and of those items that fail, a fraction $(1 - r)$ $(0 < r < 1)$ are condemned. A schematic of the system is pictured in fig. 4. The arrows indicate the rates at which items are shipped from one location to the other. It should be noted that both repairs (shipments from repair to supply depot) and external procurements are in batches.

Basically, the assumptions are that no shortages are allowed and both repairs and procurements are made in fixed batch sizes, say Q_p and Q_r. Fixed costs of A_r and A_p are assessed at the initiation of a repair batch or at the placement of an outside order, respectively, and holding costs are charged at h_1 per unit of repaired stock held per unit time and h_2 per unit of unrepaired stock held per unit time. He shows that the optimal procurement and repair batches that minimize the total cost per unit time of operating the system, say Q_p and Q_r, are given by

$$Q_p = \sqrt{\left(\frac{2A_p d(1 - r)}{h_1(1 - r) + h_2 r}\right)}$$

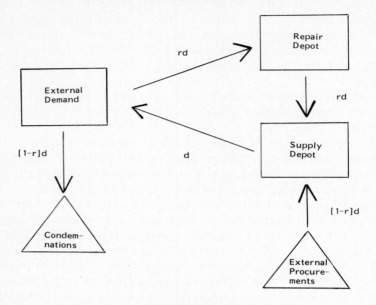

Fig. 4. A schematic representation of Schrady's deterministic model.

and

$$Q_r = \sqrt{\left(\frac{2A_r d}{h_1 + h_2}\right)}.$$

It is interesting to note how closely these expressions agree with the simple EOQ formula.

An extension of this model to the case where items are repaired at a finite rate is considered by Nahmias and Rivera [168]. They show that Q_p remains unchanged but Q_r is modified to incorporate a finite repair rate in the same way the simple EOQ model is modified to account for a finite rate of production (see Hadley and Whitin [95], page 52). It is unlikely that models of this type would ever be used since it is the underlying randomness of failure patterns which creates the problem. However, deterministic models can often be useful in pointing out potential underlying relationships in the system that can be generalized to random demand.

Simon and D'Esopo [222] consider a reparable item system which stocks a single type of item. At each occurrence of a demand, a unit is returned for which repair may or may not be possible. The total number of reparable and non-reparable demands are assumed to follow stationary independent stochastic processes. Reparable failures are sent to a repair facility, where they emerge in serviceable condition after a fixed time. Outside procurements are controlled by a stationary

(nQ, r) policy. That is, when the inventory position falls to or below r, an order is placed for that multiple of Q which returns the inventory position to a value between $r + 1$ and $r + Q$. The authors show that the well-known result in the non-reparable case that the stationary distribution of the inventory position is uniform (see Hadley and Whitin [95]) follows here as well. Using this result, they derive an expression for the stationary expected number of backorders. Explicit results are obtained for the case where the reparable and non-reparable demand processes are Poisson with respective rates $p\lambda$ and $(1 - p)\lambda$. (It should be noted that this paper generalizes and corrects an earlier version by Allen and D'Esopo [8].)

An interesting continuous review model was developed by Simon [220] which treats the same base/depot supply system considered in METRIC. Simon's model is more general than METRIC in that both a positive condemnation rate and external procurements at the depot level are allowed, but less general in that item demands at the bases are assumed to be generated by simple Poisson processes and all resupply times are assumed deterministic. As with METRIC, it is assumed that each base follows a continuous review ($S - 1, S$) policy. For an item which fails at base j, there is a probability of r_j that the item will be base reparable and a probability p that an item which is not base reparable will be depot reparable. Hence $(1 - r_j)$ $(1 - p)$ is the probability that an item which fails at base j must be condemned. Because the system is no longer conservative, outside replenishments are required. This is accomplished by assuming that the depot follows a continuous review (s_0, S_0) policy. Since demands occur one at a time, this is equivalent to assuming that an order for $Q = S_0 + s_0$ units is placed whenever the depot inventory position hits s_0.

Simon derives explicit expressions for the expected number of backorders at each base and at the depot as well as the expected level of positive stock at these locations as functions of S_j, S_0, and Q. These expressions may then be used to optimize the system stocking levels, although the specifics of the optimization are not discussed. Excluding the possible difficulties with computing the optimal stocking levels, Simon's model is of less value than METRIC due to the assumption that the failures at each base occur according to a simple Poisson process. If the true variance to mean ratio of demand is considerably larger than one, as it appears to be in many real environments, then Simon's model could seriously underestimate expected backorders. However, it should be point out that Simon's expression for expected backorders is exact while that developed in METRIC is only approximate.

In [125], Kruse and Kaplan claim that Simon's argument used to derive the stationary distribution for the backorders at base j is incorrect and provide an alternative expression for this quantity. However, in a later note Kruse [122] indicates that Simon was, in fact, correct and the two apparently different expressions are identical. However, as Kruse and Kaplan indicate, the argument used in [125] can be extended to allow the probability that an item can be repaired to be base dependent.

Shanker [205] considered an extension of Simon's model to allow for compound Poisson demand. One of the significant aspects of Shanker's work is that it gives exact results for the situation considered in METRIC except that repair times must be deterministic. Hence Shanker could use his results to evaluate the effectiveness of the approximations which are employed in METRIC. From the analysis of specific test cases, he concludes that the approximation is effective as long as the depot stock level exceeds expected demand during the mean depot repair cycle time. It is unlikely that Shanker's model would be used directly in a real system, since exact calculation of expected backorders is quite complex.

Richards [186] considers a model similar to those of Simon and D'Esopo [222] and Simon [220]. He assumes that external replenishments are controlled by an (nQ, r) policy which is based on the total stock on hand, in repair and on order (which he calls the inventory position) and allows repair times and procurement leadtimes to be random. This type of policy leads to the well-known result that the inventory position is uniformly distributed in the steady state, which is important in subsequent analyses. He shows that there is a simple relationship between net inventory and unserviceable inventory. The most notable contribution of this study is that the steady-state distribution of the net inventory is derived assuming failures are generated by a compound Poisson process. However, explicit expressions for the various measures of effectiveness of the system are obtained only for the case where failures are generated by a simple Poisson process.

Porteus and Lansdowne [179] consider a model in which a failure can be one of K types and, in addition, include the expected repair times as decision variables. Again, failures are assumed to occur according to simple Poisson processes.

The optimization problem is to find S_{ij} and T_{ijk} for $1 \leqslant i \leqslant I, 1 \leqslant j \leqslant J, 1 \leqslant k \leqslant K$ to

$$\min \sum_i \sum_j W_{ij} S_{ij}(s_{ij}, T_{ij1}, ..., T_{ijk}),$$

$$\text{subject to} \sum_i \sum_j C_{ij}^S(s_{ij}) + \sum_i \sum_j \sum_k C_{ijk}^R(T_{ijk}) \leqslant b,$$

where $S_{ij}(s_{ij}, T_{ij1}, ..., T_{ijk})$ is the expected backorders of item i at base j when the level of stock is s_{ij}; $T_{ij1}, ..., T_{ijk}$ are the expected repair times for each type of repair; W^{ij} is a weight, reflecting item essentiality; $C_{ij}^S(s_{ij})$ is the cost of stocking s_{ij} spares; $C_{ijk}^R(T_{ijk})$ is the cost of implementing an expected repair time of T_{ijk} for item i at base j for repair type k; and b is the total budget available. The expression used for the expected backorders is exactly the same as for the simple $(S-1, S)$ policy, $B(S)$ given above in section 2, except that $T_{ij} = \Sigma_k p_k T_{ijk}$ would be the corresponding lead-time. The optimization is discussed in detail for a number of special forms of the cost functions and sample computations are presented in each case.

Simpson [217] treats a heuristic model developed along lines somewhat similar to the approximate lot-size reorder-point models considered by Hadley and Whitin

[95, Chapter 4]. He assumes that item demand and repair per unit time are independent random variables with given continuous probability densities. This model would not be appropriate for inventory systems in which demands are created by the failure of reparable items as are most of the systems discussed here, since in such a case it is clear that the demand and repair processes are highly dependent. This type of phenomenon apparently does occur in certain large-scale telephone leasing systems. Simpson provides a heuristic solution for the best level of the inventory position just after the placement of an order.

A similar model was considered by Heyman [98]. Heyman assumed that both positive and negative demands (returns) could occur and are governed by independent Poisson processes with respective rates λ and μ. The goal is to characterize and compute optimal policies for returning stock to a central warehouse when stock levels become too large. It is assumed that outside procurements can be made instantaneously when on-hand stock reaches zero. He proves that the policy which minimizes the long-run average cost per unit time (where costs of returning shipping and holding are included in the model) is to return $b - a$ items when the stock level reaches b, where $0 < a < b$. Computational techniques are discussed which are based on Markov renewal programming algorithms.

Recent work on the returns problem is considered by Muckstadt and Isaac [158], [159]. In [158] they treat the case of a single item at a single location and assume that outside procurements are controlled by a continuous review (Q, r) policy. Simple approximations for the optimal procurement quantity and the optimal reorder point are derived using an analysis similar to that of Hadley and Whitin [95]. The authors extend this model in [159] to a two-echelon (retailer/warehouse) system. Approximate policies are developed for the multi-echelon model by assuming that the number of units in resupply at retailer j is approximately Poisson.

5. Periodic review models

All of the models considered thus far assume that inventory levels are reviewed continuously and, in the case of the stochastic models, are based strongly on the theory of one-for-one, $(S - 1, S)$, ordering policies. An alternative approach to treating random demands is to assume that inventory levels are reviewed periodically and that total demand in a period is a random variable with some specified distribution function, $F(t)$, and density $f(t)$. The methods of analysis and the nature of the results obtained are quite different under the periodic review assumption.

The prototype periodic review model for a reparable item inventory is due to Phelps [172]. The model is based on a two-dimensional dynamic program whose state variables at each stage, x_s and x_r, represent the amount of serviceable and reparable stock on hand, respectively, at the start of the current period. (The term serviceable here refers to items that have been repaired or procured from outside.

Reparable items are those which can be repaired and returned to serviceable condition. It does not include items which must be condemned.)

The decisions at each stage require specifying: (a) the number of items to procure from outside; (b) the number of reparables to repair; (c) the number of reparables and/or serviceables to scrap for salvage.

It turns out that only two decision variables are required; y, the number of serviceables and z, the number of reparables on hand after all decisions have been made. The model is formulated in terms of maximizing total expected return where the one-period return function allows for procurement, repair, and salvage. Let $W(x_s, x_r, y, z)$ be the total expected return in a single period when the starting stock of serviceables and reparables is (x_s, x_r) and the ending stock is (y, z). Phelps assumed that costs of penalty (which may be interpreted as a selling price in the context of the model considered), procurement, and returns for salvage of both reparable and nonreparable items are included in W. See [172] for a description of the specific form of W.

The functional equations defining an optimal policy for the multi-period version of the problem are given by

$$
\begin{aligned}
C_n(x_s, x_r) = \max_{\substack{y \geqslant 0 \\ 0 \leqslant z \leqslant x_r}} \Big\{ & W(x_s, x_r, y, z) + \alpha \int_0^y C_{n-1}(y - t, z + kt) f(t)\, \mathrm{d}t \\
& + \alpha C_{n-1}(0, z + ky)\, [1 - F(y)] \Big\}
\end{aligned}
$$

where $C_n(x_s, x_r)$ has the usual interpretation as the maximum expected discounted return when n planning periods remain and $f(t)$ and $F(t)$ are the density and distribution functions of one period's demand, respectively. Interpret k as the fraction of failures which can be repaired. Then the transfer equation arises in the following manner: if t units are demanded, then t units are also turned in for repair, only kt of which can be repaired. If $t < y$, then the level of serviceables decreases to $y - t$ and the level of reparables increases to $z + kt$. Since this particular model assumes lost sales, when $t > y$ the level of serviceables is reduced to zero and exactly y reparables are turned in.

Phelps analyzes both the single-period problem [whose return function differs slightly from $W(x_s, x_r, y, z)$] and the infinite horizon problem and shows that the optimal policy is specified by seven regions in the (x_s, x_r) plane as given in fig. 5. Since the region boundaries are quite difficult to determine it is unlikely the model would actually be implemented. However, it provides a structure for analyzing this problem and also yields some interesting qualitative properties of an optimal solution. One interesting point is that there exist some dispositions of starting stock for which an optimal policy calls for scrapping only serviceables and not reparables.

Simpson [217] also considers a two-dimensional dynamic programming formulation of a periodic review reparable item problem. However, his formulation of the

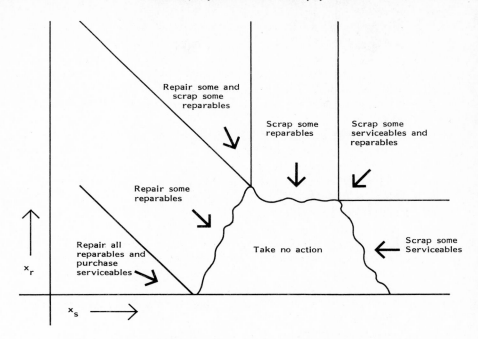

Fig. 5. The seven regions indicating the stationary solution to Phelps' model.

model differs from that of Phelps in a number of respects. The most significant is that he assumes that there is a joint probability density, say $f(t, u)$, of the random variables giving the number of serviceables demanded, t, and the number of reparables returned, u. In addition, he assumes a somewhat more conventional cost structure and backordering of excess demand. Let $L(y)$ be the expected holding and shortage cost when the level of serviceables at the start of the period is y and s is the cost of holding one unit of unrepaired stock for one period. Assume the other costs are as given above, and define the three decision variables: z = the number of serviceables purchased, w = the number of reparables repaired, and v = the number of reparables scrapped at zero salvage value. Then the functional equations defining an optimal policy are:

$$C_n(x_s, x_r) = \min_{\substack{v, w, z \geqslant 0 \\ v+w \leqslant x_r}} \left\{ cz + bw + s(x_r - w - v) + L(x_s + w + z) \right.$$

$$\left. + \alpha \int_0^\infty \int_0^\infty C_{n-1}(x_s + w + z - t, x_r - w - v + u) f(t, u) \, dt \, du \right\}.$$

Analyzing these functional equations, Simpson goes on to show that the optimal policy for an n-period problem has a structure similar to that obtained by Phelps in that there are also seven regions describing the optimal number of items to procure, repair and scrap. However, there is one important difference: in Simpson's case the n period solution is completely determined by three constants whose values depend on n. Determining the exact values of these constants appears to be difficult, however.

Veinott [236] discovered a formulation of the infinite horizon version of this model for which an optimal policy is fairly simple. Let x_s be defined as above, but let x_t be the number of serviceables plus reparables ($x_t = x_s + x_r$) on hand at the start of any period. It costs c_1 to repair a reparable and $c_1 + c_2$ to purchase a serviceable with $c_2 > 0$. Suppose D_1 is the demand for serviceables (and hence the input of reparables) and D_2 that portion of D_1 which cannot be repaired ($0 \leqslant D_2 \leqslant D_1$).

The decision variables, y and z, are the total number of serviceables on hand after procurement and repair and the total number of both serviceables and reparables. The total cost of both procurement and repair is then given by $c_1(y - x_s) + c_2(z - x_t)$.

Assuming a penalty cost $p > c_1 + c_2$, a holding cost h levied against each unit stored, and a discount factor $0 \leqslant \alpha \leqslant 1$, the "modified" one period cost function (which derives from the forward approach developed by Veinott [235]) is

$$G(y, z) = c_1(1 - \alpha) y + c_2(1 - \alpha) z + p \int_y^\infty (t - y) f_1(t) \, dt$$

$$+ h \int_0^z (z - t) f_2(t) \, dt + \alpha c_1 \mu_1 + \alpha c_2 \mu_2 \, ,$$

where f_1 is the density of D_1, f_2 the density of D_2, and μ_1 and μ_2 their respective means. Basically, the idea is that if it is possible to order to the minimum of $G(y, z)$ every period, then that solution is optimal. Since G is increasing in z the minimum of G over the set $z \geqslant y$ will occur at $z = y = y^*$, say. Suppose initially $x_s < y^*$. Then the optimal policy is to move to the point (y^*, y^*) which means all reparables should be repaired and $y^* - x_t$ items should be procured. Since after demand, x_s will again be less than y^* the same policy is optimal in the subsequent period and hence in every period thereafter. If $x_s > y^*$ then one either repairs a portion of available reparables (determined from a nonlinear function $W(x_t)$) or takes no action.

A somewhat more comprehensive model was developed along similar lines by Prawda and Wright [184]. They also treat a periodic review model and assume that outside procurements arrive λ periods after an order is placed and that items require η periods for repair where $0 \leqslant \eta \leqslant \lambda$. The demand in period t, say D_t, is the sum

$F_t + R_t$, where F_t are the non-reparable failures and R_t are the reparable failures. The state variable in period t, say x_t, is the total stock on hand, plus in repair, plus on order. By defining the state variable in this fashion, the dynamic problem can be formulated along the lines of Veinott's [235] approach as well.

The authors assume that the cost of holding is charged at the end of each period against the stock on hand and in repair according to the function $h(\cdot)$. The cost of shortage is given by $p(\cdot)$ and is charged against the excess demand at the end of the period. All excess demand is backordered.

Let y_t be the total stock on hand, on order and in repair *after* ordering (so that the order quantity in period t is $y_t - x_t$). One can then show that total stock on hand plus in repair at the end of period $t + \lambda$ is $y_t - \Sigma_{j=t}^{t+\lambda} F_j$ and the net inventory (on hand minus backorders) at the end of period $t + \lambda$ is $y_t - \Sigma_{j=t}^{t+\lambda} D_j + \Sigma_{j=t}^{t+\lambda-\eta} R_j$. It follows that

$$L(y_t) = E\left\{ h\left(y_t - \sum_{j=t}^{t+\lambda} F_j\right) + p\left(\sum_{j=t}^{t+\lambda} D_j - \sum_{j=t}^{t+\lambda-\eta} R_j - y_t\right)\right\}$$

is the expected holding and shortage cost incurred in period $t + \lambda$. If future costs are discounted by $0 < \alpha \leqslant 1$, then an "effective" one period cost function in period t (assuming the planning horizon extends to at least period $t + \lambda$) is $G(y_t) = c(1 - \alpha)y_t + \alpha^\lambda L(y_t)$. The stationary solution is simply to order to y^* where y^* solves $c(1 - \alpha) + \alpha^\lambda L'(y^*) = 0$. We should note that although the form of this equation is identical to the classical lead-time problem with full backordering (see [10] page 168), the actual expression for $L(y)$ will be different in this case. The authors also discuss the extension to allow for a fixed cost K for ordering.

One of the assumptions required in this model is that the number of units on hand, in repair and on order are known by the inventory manager at the start of each period. However, in some systems, the knowledge of stock levels in repair may not be available. This can occur when the repair depot is at a separate location from the supply depot. Cohen et al. [42] consider a model which assumes that inventory decisions are made based on knowledge of the on-hand inventory only. The repair process is then equivalent to a feedback system where a fraction of items issued to satisfy demand recycle back into stock after λ period (here λ corresponds to the number of periods required for repair). There is a zero lead-time for outside procurements. An optimal policy for this model is no longer a simple critical number policy, but a complex function of the vector of stock issued to meet prior demands. The authors develop a simple critical number approximation and provide numerical comparisons which indicate its effectiveness over a range of demand and cost parameters.

Haber and Sitgreaves [94] consider a model where items fail during some fixed time T_1, and are then replaced by repair or external procurement in a subsequent period T_2. Based on assuming given costs of overage and underage and probability distribution for failure and repairs, a simple Newsboy solution is developed to determine the optimal level of outside procurements.

6. Spares provisioning using queueing models

The application of Palm's theorem to the METRIC-based inventory models requires the assumption that the mean repair time for an item entering service is constant and is independent of the state of the system. However, it is clear that the time required to repair will strongly depend upon the number of items which are queued up at the repair station. Another, but perhaps less serious, shortcoming of these inventory models, is that the failure rate (demand rate) is also assumed to be constant and independent of the state of the system. However, the actual failure rate at any point in time depends upon the number of units which are operating. In systems where the total number of operational units is small, this effect could be significant.

One approach for dealing with both of these phenomena is the machine repair model. Suppose M machines which operate continuously are supported by S spares. When a failure occurs, the item enters a repair facility and queues up for service. A spare immediately replaces the failed item if one is available. The repair facility is

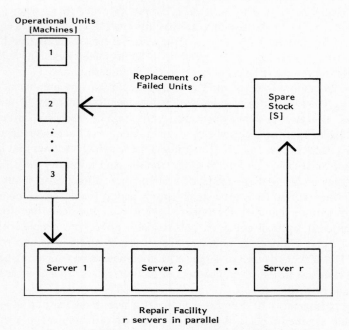

Fig. 6. Schematic of the machine repair queueing system.

assumed to consist of $r \geqslant 1$ servers acting in parallel and units are repaired on a first come first served basis. The system is illustrated in fig. 6.

In general, one assumes that each machine fails according to some specified distribution $F(\cdot)$ and machines are repaired according to another distribution $G(\cdot)$. However, explicit results for the general problem appear to be known only for the case where F and G are both exponential with respective parameters λ and μ, which we will henceforth assume.

The state of the system, say n, corresponds to the number of machines in the repair queue. If λ_n is the failure rate when the state of the system is n, then

$$\lambda_n = \begin{cases} M\lambda & \text{if } 0 \leqslant n < S, \\ (M-n+S)\lambda & \text{if } S \leqslant n < M+S. \end{cases}$$

Similarly, let μ_n be the rate at which units leave the repair facility when the system state is n. Then

$$\mu_n = \begin{cases} n\mu & \text{if } 0 \leqslant n < r, \\ r\mu & \text{if } r \leqslant n. \end{cases}$$

Explicit expressions for the stationary values of the state probabilities, say p_n, can be derived by analyzing the underlying birth-and-death process. These results are reported by Gross and Harris [91, page 123] for the model discussed here and by Barlow [12] for the more general case where λ_n and μ_n are arbitrary. Barlow also discusses some results for special versions of the problem when either the failure or service distributions are arbitrary.

The original application of the machine repair model to the problem of determining suitable levels of spares inventory appears to be due to Taylor and Jackson [230]. They use birth and death analysis to analyze the standard machine repair model, except they assume that when fewer than M machines are operational all machines cease to operate. Under this assumption, they derive the stationary distribution of the number of machines in the repair queue. They then consider the probability that a total breakdown in the system will occur as a function of the number of spare machines.

Mirasol [150] develops a model based on a cyclic queueing system. The stages correspond to the following five states that an item could be in:

(1) equipment operating,
(2) failures being transported to repair depot,
(3) failure waiting for repair,
(4) item in repair (the repair station consists of s parallel channels corresponding to s subunits in the main unit)
(5) repaired item being transported back to operating stock.

There is a probability distribution, $p_j, 1 \leqslant j \leqslant s$, which specifies the likelihood that a repair of type j is required. Under the assumption that all service and transportation times are independent and exponentially distributed, Mirasol derives the stationary distribution for the queue lengths at each location in the network. He then defines the "strategic unavailability", Ψ, as the product of the unavailability rate and the mean duration of the unavailability for each subunit j. An algorithm is developed to determine the minimum attainable value of ψ subject to a constraint on the available budget.

Gross et al. [90] consider using the basic machine repair model with spares to develop a multi-year optimization model to determine the optimal number of components to both purchase and repair, as well as the optimal number of service channels and the investment in a reliability growth program, subject to a constraint that the fill rate or availability be at least 90%.

Let P_n be the stationary probability that there are n units in repair. Following our notation above, the percentage of requests that can be filled from on hand spares at a random point in time is $\sum_{n=0}^{S-1} P_n$. However, as the authors point out, the availability should be defined in terms of the failure point probability, q_n, which is the stationary conditional probability that there are n units in repair given a failure is about to occur. Using Bayes' rule one obtains:

$$
q_n = \begin{cases}
Mp_n \Big/ \Big[M - \displaystyle\sum_{j=s}^{S+M} (j - S)\, p_j \Big], & 0 \leqslant n < S, \\[2em]
(M - n + S)\, p_n \Big/ \Big[M - \displaystyle\sum_{j=S}^{S+M} (j - S)\, p_j \Big], & S \leqslant n \leqslant S + M.
\end{cases}
$$

The fill rate constraint then becomes $\sum_{n=0}^{S-1} q_n \geqslant 0.90$. The optimization problem is an integer program with a single constraint for which a heuristic solution procedure is suggested.

An extension of the classical machine repair model to allow for more than a single stage in the repair phase is considered by Gross and Ince [88]. Their model is a special type of cyclic queueing system consisting of K stages in series with stage i having c_i parallel servers each of which has an exponentially distributed service time with rate μ_i. There are a total of exactly N identical customers in the system who are served on a first come, first served basis. The first stage corresponds to the working units which fail at a rate μ_1. Stages 2 through K correspond to different repair channels such as might be required for an item with submodules each of which must be inspected and, if required, repaired separately. Both exact and heuristic expressions are developed for the availability which is defined as above in terms of the failure point probabilities. One then determines the number of repair channels at each stage and the total number of customers (machines) in the system to achieve a desired availability level. Recently the authors have extended this analysis [89] to treat multiple types of customers (machines with varying expected repair times).

Lureau [141] also considers the use of machine repair models. His primary concern is to determine the waiting time of a unit, which is defined as the period of time elapsed since its failure until replacement by a spare unit (zero waiting time) or, if no spare units are currently available, by a repaired unit (positive waiting time). Models for both infinite source populations and infinitely many repair channels are considered.

Using numerical experimentation for a variety of test cases, he shows that the waiting time distribution depends only on the expected repair time. Using this empirical result, a streamlined algorithm is designed to select the optimal repair time and the optimal number of spares in order to minimize the long run expected average cost, which includes the cost of spares, the cost of providing repairs, and any convex function of the waiting time.

The queueing models clearly have a number of advantages over the inventory models. The most salient is that they do not require the usual assumption that there are infinitely many servers at the repair facility which is accurate only when utilization rates are relatively low. Also, they include the additional dimension that one can treat the number of service channels as a decision variable. However, they have a number of shortcomings as well. In particular, since interfailure times are assumed to be exponential, the variance to mean ratio of the number of failures in any unit time is assumed to be one. As we indicated previously, this is probably less than one would ordinarily encounter in practice. Another issue is whether or not the computations required in using a queueing model are too extensive to be implemented in a large scale multi-product system. An interesting study might be one which compares the performance of METRIC with a queueing approach using actual operational data.

Acknowledgement

The author is grateful to the editor and the referees for helpful suggestions regarding the revision of this paper. Special thanks go to Jack Muckstadt for a comprehensive review of the original draft.

TIMS Studies in the Management Sciences 16 (1981) 279–297

MULTI-ECHELON INVENTORY THEORY IN THE AIR FORCE LOGISTICS COMMAND

W. Steven DEMMY

Wright State University

and

Victor J. PRESUTTI

Air Force Logistics Command

This paper reviews several current applications of multi-echelon inventory theory in the Air Force Logistics Command. Application areas to be discussed include planning and budgeting, initial provisioning, replenishment, and distribution calculations. Methods used to resolve computational difficulties and other implementation issues are also discussed.

1. Introduction

The rapid developments in computer science and operations research techniques have spawned several technical revolutions in the past 30 years. Multi-echelon inventory theory is one of these areas. In 1950, only a few limited results from queueing theory were available to assist inventory managers. Today, computerized systems exist capable of computing jointly optimal inventory policies for thousands of items stocked at perhaps several hundred locations, considering assembly, subassembly relationships, and multi-echelon inventory/repair relationships. Several of these models have become major components of Air Force Logistics Command (AFLC) data systems. Application areas covered by these systems include planning and budgeting, initial provisioning, replenishment, and distribution.

This paper presents a review of those elements of multi-echelon inventory theory which have proven particularly useful in the AFLC. The paper consists of three major sections. In this section, we provide additional background on the nature and scope of the logistics systems which support Air Force commodities. In section 2, we review several mathematical models which have proven particularly useful in the management and control of AFLC reparable items. In section 3 we discuss some major application areas for these models, and several implementation issues, including techniques used to resolve the computational difficulties encountererd in systems involving several hundred thousand items.

1.1. An overview of AFLC logistics flows

A major mission of the AFLC is to provide supply, maintenance, and transportation support for the United States Air Force and other U.S. military agencies. To do this, the command provides logistics support for every major weapon system in the Air Force. These systems are operated from bases scattered throughout the world. This is a task of substantial size. It requires the management of several hundred thousand supply items, and expenditures for the procurement and maintenance of these items exceeds several billion dollars per year.

The techniques used to manage these inventories are tailored to fit the nature of each individual item. Basic commodity groupings include:

(1) End items – Those pieces of equipment such as aircraft, vehicles, Aerospace Ground Equipment (AGE), and automated test stations that retain their separate identity and value while in use.
(2) Recoverable spares – Assemblies such as navigational computers, pumps, and radio sets and generators that become part of a larger end item when in use, but which are subject to removal and repair. Approximately 170,000 items whose inventories are valued in excess of $10 billion fall into this category.
(3) Engines – Jet engines and other aerospace propulsion units are included in this class. Structurally, jet engines represent very expensive recoverable spares; however, because of the high resource impact of these items, separate management systems have been developed for specific classes of propulsion units to ensure adequate attention to these very important contributors to the Air Force mission.
(4) Consumable spares – Nonreparable parts, common hardware, and housekeeping materials that are lost or consumed when used. This category accounts for approximately 500,000 items, with inventories valued in excess of $2 billion.
(5) Petroleum – Those oils and fuels required to support the Air Force fleet of aircraft and other vehicles.
(6) Ammunition – This category includes bombs, incendiaries, and similar items utilized by the Air Force and its allies.
(7) General supplies – Clothing, commissary items, foods and medicines required for the support of personnel fall into this category.

The above is a simplified list of the many categories of items managed by the AFLC. All of these inventories are stocked at multiple locations and involve several levels of supply. Unfortunately, the inability of current theory to deal with large-scale, dynamic multi-echelon systems precludes application of multi-echelon models for most of these commodity classes. One important exception, however, is the area of reparable spares management.

1.2. Recoverable item management

Recoverable items represent an important subset of the total population of AFLC managed items. This class includes items which may be repaired upon failure and thus returned to a serviceable condition. Torque converters, fuel pumps, navigation computers, fire control systems, and landing gears are a few examples of items in this class. Typically, recoverable items have very high unit costs and low unit demand rates.

In general, recoverable items are supported by a two-echelon inventory/repair system such as that illustrated in fig. 1. When a weapon system is first added to the Air Force inventory, initial provisioning includes procurement of a number of serviceable spares. These spares would be dispersed to appropriate base locations to provide on-site support for operating forces. Usually, some serviceable spares are also maintained at a depot supply location. These depot stocks are used both to support depot repair activities, and to provide a backup source of supply for bases with unexpectedly high requirements.

When a recoverable item fails at base level, it is returned to base supply and a new serviceable unit is issued. If possible, the failed item is then repaired by the base maintenance organization and returned to base supply. Sometimes, however, the failed item must be returned to the depot where more sophisticated equipment and specialized skills are available. In this event, the base submits a requisition to the depot supply organization to obtain a serviceable replacement for the failed item.

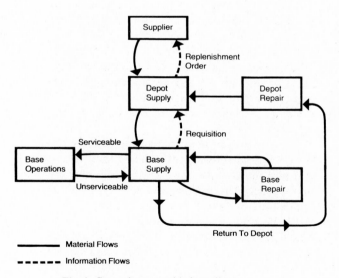

Fig. 1. General recoverable item flows.

As in most real systems, there are a number of items which do not fit the neat arrangement described above. At times, forward base locations will be supplied from another closely located base — resulting in a three-echelon supply system for this item. For other items, a manufacturer may provide both the source of procurement for new assets and the source of repair for failed items. When several hundred thousand items are involved, there are of course many other variations that can be observed. However, fig. 1 provides a good approximation to the logistics support system in existence for the majority of AFLC recoverable items.

2. Analytical models

A number of analytical models have been developed to assist AFLC in the efficient management of recoverable items. In this section, we discuss features of several analytical models which have proven particularly useful for recoverable item management.

2.1. The METRIC model

METRIC is an acronym for the "Multi-Echelon Technique for Recoverable Item Control". This model was originally developed by Sherbrooke [210] as a tool for managing the Air Force inventories.

The model provides a methodology for computing optimal stock levels in a two-echelon inventory/repair system consisting of a depot and several bases. Each location in this system may possess a supply of serviceable spares and a repair capability for returning unserviceable assets to a serviceable condition; however, specific capabilities may vary among locations. Demand in this system is assumed to follow a compound Poisson process. For purposes of visualization, a compound Poisson process may be thought of as a series of customers who arrive following a Poisson process, each of whom can demand an amount that is independently and identically distributed according to a "compounding" distribution. Until further notice, we consider one item stocked at each of J bases, each with known mean customer arrival rate $\lambda_j, j = 1, 2, .., J$.

When a customer arrives at a base to place one or several demands, he turns in an equal number of reparable units. It is assumed that these units can be repaired at base level with probability r_j, while $(1 - r_j)$ is the probability they must be shipped to the depot for repair. Under these assumptions, the customers from base j who arrive at the depot are described by a Poisson process whose mean is $(1 - r_j)$ times the mean of the Poisson customer arrival process at base j. Therefore, the total demand at the depot is compound Poisson, with mean customer arrival rate $\lambda = \Sigma \lambda_j(1 - r_j)$. Letting f_j be the mean demand per customer at base j, the mean depot demand rate for units is $\theta = \Sigma \lambda_j f_j(1 - r) = \Sigma \theta_j(1 - r)$, where θ_j is the mean unit demand rate at base j.

In general, the distribution of demands placed upon the depot is a complicated combination of the base compounding distributions. However, if demand at each base obeys a logarithmic Poisson [1] process with the same variance to mean ratio, the depot demand process is also logarithmic Poisson, with the same variance to mean ratio (see Sherbrooke).

Let $S_j, j = 1, 2, ..., J$, denote the stock level at base j, and let S_0 denote the depot stock level. We assume that each base and the depot follow a continuous review, one-for-one $(S_j - 1, S_j)$ replacement policy. In this case, the system will be managed so that at each base, inventory position (the sum of stock on hand plus on order plus in repair minus backorders) will always equal the S_j. The same rule also applies for the depot stock level S_0.

Ultimately, we wish to compute values for S_j that will minimize expected base-level backorders summed over all bases. To do this, we apply a fundamental result developed by Feeney and Sherbrooke [23]. Specifically, assume that demand at base j obeys a compound Poisson process with mean customer arrival rate λ_j, and suppose that the repair/resupply time t obeys an arbitrary distribution $g(t)$ with mean T_j. Assume that when a customer arrives, a resupply time is drawn from $g(t)$ that is applicable to all demands placed by that customer, and that excess demand is backordered. Then the expected backorders at a random point in time at base j is:

$$BO_j(S_j) = \sum_{x=S_j+1} (x - S_j) p(x \mid \lambda_j T_j) \tag{1}$$

where $p(x \mid \lambda_j T_j)$ is the compound Poisson probability with mean customer arrival rate $\lambda_j T_j$. In the special case of the logarithmic Poisson process, the probability that x customer demands are in the repair/resupply process is negative-binomial; specifically:

$$p(x \mid \lambda_j T_j) = \frac{(k+x-1)!}{(k-1)!x!} \frac{(q-1)^x}{q^{x+k}}, \qquad \begin{aligned} &x = 0, 1, 2, ..., \\ &q > 1, k > 0, \end{aligned} \tag{2}$$

where q is the variance to mean ratio of $p(x \mid \lambda_j T_j)$. The mean μ_j of this distribution equals $\lambda_j T_j f$, where the parameter k is given by

$$k = \mu_j/(q-1) = \lambda_j T_j f/(q-1).$$

The average resupply time T_j for a demand at base j may be computed as fol-

---

[1] A logarithmic Poisson process is a compound Poisson process in which the probability h_x that a given customer demands x units is given by $h_x = (x \cdot \ln \cdot q)^{-1} (p/q)^x$ for $x = 1, 2, 3 ...$ and $q = p + 1 > 1$, where q is a parameter of the distribution.

lows. Let

A_j = base repair cycle time — the average time required to repair an item at base level,

D = depot repair cycle time — the average time required to return an item to the depot, repair it, and to place the item into depot serviceable stock,

O_j = the order and ship time — the average time required for a requisition to be transmitted from a base to the depot, and to transport a requested serviceable unit back to the requesting base; this term includes no allowance for possible delays that might be encountered at the depot due to temporary stockouts of the item, and

$\delta(S_0)$ = average depot delay — the average delay incurred in filling a requisition at the depot due to temporary stockouts of serviceable units; the average delay is expressed as a fraction of the depot repair cycle time D, and S_0 denotes the total stock level assigned to the depot.

In this case, the average resupply time T_j at base j is given by

$$T_j = r_j A_j + (1 - r_j)(O_j + \delta(S_0)D). \tag{3}$$

The average depot delay $\delta(S_0)$ may be derived as follows. If depot stock were infinite, a requisition would experience no delays in being filled since stock would always be available. On the other hand, if no stock were allocated to the depot, an average delay of D would be incurred — that is, the delay would equal the amount of time required to transport the unserviceable asset to the depot, repair it, and to return the unit to serviceable stock. For positive depot stock level, the delay is between zero and D. To compute the average delay, it is necessary to compute the expected number of depot backorders.

As noted above, unserviceable assets arrive at the depot according to a compound Poisson process with customer arrival rate λ. Since it takes an average of D time units for an arrival to complete the repair process, the probability distribution of the number of units in the depot repair cycle is compound Poisson with mean λD. Hence, the expected number of units backordered at the depot is

$$BO(S_0|\lambda D) = \sum_{x=S_0+1} (x - S_0)p(x|\lambda D). \tag{4}$$

This expression represents the expected number of units on which delay is being incurred at a random point in time. The expected depot delay per unit demand is given by

$$\delta(S_0) \cdot D = \frac{BO(S_0|\lambda D)}{\theta}, \tag{5}$$

where $\theta = \lambda Df$ is the depot demand rate in units.

2.2. METRIC applications

METRIC has proven useful in three basic areas: (1) evaluation of the support effectiveness associated with a given set of stock levels, (2) distribution of a given number of assets among several locations, and (3) calculation of optimal stock levels consistent with a given investment constraint. Let us now consider each of these areas in more detail:

2.2.1. Evaluation

METRIC may be used to estimate the expected backorder levels associated with a given set of base stock levels $S = (S_0, S_1, S_2, ..., S_J)$. This may be done by first using equations (3), (4), and (5) to evaluate the average base resupply time associated with the given depot stock level S_0, and then computing expected base backorders using equations (1) and (2).

2.2.2. Distribution

METRIC may be used to compute the optimal distribution of a given number of assets among several stocking locations. Specifically, suppose we have N assets and that we wish to allocate these assets in order to minimize expected base backorders summed over all stocking locations J, $BS(N)$. Mathematically, the problem is to find a set of levels S which minimize $BS(N)$,

$$BS(N) = \sum_{j=1}^{J} BO_j (S_j | \lambda_j T_j) , \tag{6}$$

subject to

$$\sum_{j=0}^{J} S_j = N . \tag{7}$$

This problem is equivalent to the two-stage dynamic programming problem:

$$\min_{0 \leqslant S_0 \leqslant N} \left[\min_{S_1, S_2, ..., S_J} \sum_{j=1}^{J} BO_j(S_j | \lambda_j T_j) \right] , \tag{8}$$

subject to

$$\sum_{j=1}^{J} S_j = N - S_0 .$$

When S_0 is fixed, $BO_j(S_j | \lambda_j T_j)$ is a convex function of S_j. Hence, the summation inside the brackets is the sum of convex functions. Thus, the inner minimization may be achieved using a marginal analysis procedure. With this procedure, we first set all $S_j = 0$ for $j = 1, 2, ..., J$ and then allocate stock one unit at a time to the base with the greatest marginal backorder reduction potential, until

$$\sum_{j=1}^{J} S_j = N - S_0 . \tag{9}$$

The optimal distribution is then obtained by repeating this process for all possible values of S_0, $S_0 = 0, 1, ..., N$.

Sherbrooke [210] notes that the optimal system backorder function $BS(N)$ is not necessarily a convex function of system stock N, although the individual base-level functions $BO_j(S_j | \lambda_j T_j)$ are convex.

2.2.3. Budget allocation

Suppose we have a budget B for the procurement of spares in a multi-item system. Further, suppose we wish to allocate this budget in order to minimize the total base backorders summed over all items. Let us add a subscript i to the symbols defined above to denote values for item i. The budget allocation problem is then

$$\min \sum_{i=1}^{I} \sum_{j=1}^{J} BO_{ij}(S_{ij} | \lambda_{ij} T_{ij}) , \tag{10}$$

subject to

$$\sum_{i=1}^{I} c_i \sum_{j=0}^{J} S_{ij} \leq B .$$

This problem may be solved using a marginal analysis procedure which first sets the planned buy quantity, N_i, to zero for each item i. The next investment is then allocated to that item which produces the greatest decrease in expected backorders per dollar invested; that is, the item with the greatest value of V_i,

$$V_i = \frac{BS_i(N_i) - BS(N_i + 1)}{c_i} .$$

The allocation procedure stops when the budget limit B has been reached.

Before performing the marginal analysis procedure, however, the system backorder function $BS_i(N_i)$ must be replaced by its convex supportant. Sherbrooke

[210] shows that after this is done, the above marginal analysis procedure leads to an optimum solution to the original problem (10).

2.3. Fox and Landi optimization

Fox and Landi [78] observed that use of Lagrangian procedures could produce significant computational savings in solving the budget allocation problem (10). Specifically, let ϕ denote a Lagrange multiplier associated with the budget limitation B. Then the Lagrangian version of (10) is

$$\min_{S_{ij}} \sum_{i=1}^{I} \sum_{j=1}^{J} BO_{ij}(S_{ij}|\lambda_{ij}T_{ij}) - \phi c_i \sum_{j=0}^{J} S_{ij} , \tag{11}$$

which separates into I independent single-item optimization problems. Dropping the item subscript i, each of these sub-problems may be written as

$$\min_{S_0} \sum_{j=1}^{J} \min_{S_j} [BO(S_j|\lambda_j T_j) - \phi c_j S_j] - \phi c S_0 . \tag{12}$$

For a given depot stock level S_0, the base backorder function $BO_j(S_j|\lambda_j T_j)$ is convex with respect to the base stock level S_j. Hence, for a given depot stock S_0, the optimum base level is obtained by simply finding the smallest non-negative integer S_j satisfying

$$BO(S_j + 1|\lambda_j T_j) - BO(S_j|\lambda_j T_j) \geqslant \phi c_j . \tag{13}$$

To determine the Lagrange multiplier associated with a given budget B, Fox and Landi suggest that a binary search procedure be used. They observed that suitable bounds on the optimum value of ϕ are usually available from experience with previous runs. In experiments using such bounds, they found that at most six bisections were required to obtain optimal budget allocations that were within one-half of 1% of the original budget B.

2.4. MOD-METRIC

Many AFLC reparable items contain subassemblies or other components which are also reparable. In this case, repair of a failed item is usually accomplished by removal and replacement of the failed component of this item. The failed component is then repaired either at the base or depot level depending upon the complexity of repair. Many reparable items may be removed and replaced on the flight line. The term line replaceable unit (LRU) is used for this class of items; the term

shop replaceable unit (SRU) is used to describe components or subassemblies of an
LRU that are removed and replaced in the base or depot repair shops.

At best, a backorder for a LRU will result in an aircraft that is not fully
equipped to perform its assigned missions, the worst situation corresponds to a
grounded aircraft. On the other hand, backorders for SRUs result in delays in
repairing the associated LRU. If delays due to SRU backorders are long enough,
LRU backorders and inoperable aircraft will eventually result; however, this effect
is usually not immediate. Clearly, aircraft availability is more immediately affected
by LRU backorders than by SUR backorders.

Several authors, including Sherbrooke [209], Demmy [53], Fawcett [71] and
Porteous and Landsdowne [179] have developed models which expand the basic
METRIC model to consider these relationships. However, Muchstadt's MOD-
METRIC model [151] has had the most influence on Air Force applications.

In MOD-METRIC, it is assumed that the average base repair time B_j for a specific
LRU at base j is given by

$$B_j = R_j + \Delta_j,$$ (14)

where R_j = average repair time at base j if all required SRUs available, and Δ_j = the
average delay in LRU repair time due to shortage of required SRUs.

The average LRU delay, Δ_j, may be computed in a manner very similar to the
computation of depot delays. To see this, consider a family of items consisting of a
single LRU and its associated set of SRUs. Let the subscript i, $i = 1, 2, 3, ..., I$
denote the ith component (SRU) and let $i = 0$ denote the LRU. Further, assume that
repair of a given LRU requires the removal and replacement of at most one SRU. In
this case, the expected delay in the LRU base repair time due to a shortage of SRU
i is given by

$$\Delta_{ii} = \frac{\displaystyle\sum_{x_{ij} > s_{ij}} (x_{ij} - s_{ij}) p(x_{ij} | \lambda_{ij} T_{ij})}{\lambda_{ij}},$$ (15)

where the symbols x_{ij}, S_{ij}, and T_{ij} are defined as in the METRIC model, with
obvious adjustments for the item subscript i. Let λ_j denote the total LRU failure
rate at base j and let r_j denote the probability that a failed LRU is repaired at base
j. Then

$$r_j \lambda_j = \sum_{i=1}^{I} \lambda_{ij},$$ (16)

and the ratio $\lambda_{ij}/r_j \lambda_j$ denotes the probability that a given LRU failure at base j will
require replacement of SRU i. The expected delay in repairing a failed LRU at base

j is then

$$\Delta_j = \frac{1}{r_j \lambda_j} \sum_{i=1}^{I} \lambda_{ij} \Delta_{ij} , \tag{17}$$

and the average resupply time for a failed LRU at base j is

$$T_j = r_j (R_j + \Delta_j) + (1 - r_j)(O_j + \delta(S_0) \cdot D), \tag{18}$$

where S_0 is the depot stock level for the LRU. The expected backorders for the LRU at base j may be computed using (18) in a standard METRIC backorder calculation.

2.5. MOD-METRIC budget association

Suppose we have a budget B for procurement of LRU and SRU spares. How should this budget be allocated? Muckstadt suggested a calculation procedure with the following steps:

Step 0. First partition the total budget B into two components, B_1 and B_2.

Step 1. Allocate the budget B_1 among the SRUs so as to minimize the expected LRU repair delays summed over all bases. Mathematically, the problem is to minimize Z,

$$Z = \Sigma_j r_j \lambda_j \Delta_j$$

subject to the budget constraint B_1. This problem may be solved using the METRIC budget allocation procedure.

Step 2. Given the results from step 1, compute the average resupply time T_j for the LRU at each base j. Then allocate the remaining budget B_2 so as to minimize expected LRU base-level backorders. The METRIC budget allocation procedure may again be used to solve the problem.

Step 3. Steps 2 and 3 provide a set of proposed stock levels based upon a given partitioning of the total budget among the LRUs and the SRUs. These two steps are than repeated several times using new values for B_1 and B_2 to establish the best partitioning of the total budget.

This algorithm does not guarantee an optimal solution to the problem of minimizing expected base-level LRU backorders. However, we have found that budget allocations based upon MOD-METRIC consistently result in lower levels of LRU backorders than is produced by the original METRIC budget allocation procedure. It has been conjectured that MOD-METRIC will always produce allocations that dominate the LRU backorder curves produced by METRIC solutions; however, this conjecture has not been proven.

2.6. The LMI Procurement Model

The LMI Procurement Model [128] was developed by the Logistics Management Institute (LMI) as a means of computing optimal procurement programs by relating the expected number of operational aircraft to alternate Air Force stocking policies. In essence, this model combines a classical series-reliability model for equipment availability with the standard METRIC assumptions describing single-item, two-echelon material flows.

The LMI Procurement Model may be developed as follows. Let

M = quantity of aircraft to be supported,
i = the index of a particular component whose failure makes the aircraft unable to perform its assigned mission, where $i = 1, 2, ..., I$,
c_i = unit cost for item i,
QPA_i = quantity per application – the quantity of component i on one operational aircraft; we assume that the failure of any one of these components will cause the aircraft to be unavailable,
N_i = quantity of spares for component i to be procured, and
$BO_i(N_i)$ = the expected quantity of base-level backorders on component i when N_i assets are procured and then positioned at bases using an optimum METRIC distribution.

Now let q_i denote the probability that a randomly selected aircraft at a randomly determined point in time does not have any components of type i missing. Assuming that all bases are identical, with equal numbers of aircraft and identical flying programs, we may estimate q_i as:

$$q_i(N_i) = \left[1 - \frac{BO_i(N_i)}{M\,QPA_i}\right]^{QPA_i} \tag{19}$$

This expression results from the following arguments. If all M aircraft are to be operational, the required total number of units of component i is $M \cdot QPA_i$. Recall that $BO_i(N_i)$ denotes the expected number of "holes" in aircraft due to backorders of component i, where N_i is the number of spares procured. Hence, $BO_i(N_i)/(M \cdot QPA_i)$ is the probability that a particular "hole" for item i is empty due to a backorder for that item. Thus, one minus this value is the probability that a given unit of component i is not causing the aircraft to be inoperable. Finally, since each aircraft contains QPA_i units of component i, we must raise the probability that each component i unit is operational to the QPA_i power to determine the probability that all QPA_i units are operational simultaneously.

Once the component availabilities, q_i, are known, we may determine Q, the probability that a randomly selected aircraft is operational. This is given by:

$$Q = \prod_{i=1}^{I} q_i(N_i) \tag{20}$$

that is, the probability that a randomly selected aircraft is operational equals the probability that none of its components is in a backorder status. The expected number of operational aircraft in a fleet of M aircraft is $M \cdot Q$. Hence, the expected number of operational aircraft, ENOA, is given by

$$\text{ENOA} = M \cdot \prod_{i=1}^{I} q_i(N_i) . \tag{21}$$

2.6.1. Optimization

Suppose we wish to establish procurement quantities N_i which maximize the expected number of operational aircraft subject to a budget constraint B, that is, we wish to find values for N_i to solve

$$\max \text{ENOA} = M \cdot \prod_{i=1}^{I} q_i(N_i) , \tag{22}$$

subject to

$$\sum_{i=1}^{I} c_i N_i \leqslant B . \tag{23}$$

Taking logarithms in (22),

$$\ln (\text{ENOA}) = \ln M + \sum_{i=1}^{I} \ln q_i(N_i) , \tag{24}$$

which may be written

$$\ln (\text{ENOA}) = \ln M + \sum_{i=1}^{I} \text{QPA}_i \cdot \ln \left[1 - \frac{BO_i(N_i)}{M \cdot \text{QPA}_i} \right] . \tag{25}$$

Suppose $BO_i(N_i)$ is replaced by its convex supportant in (25). The resulting function is a discretely convex function of N_i. Hence, (25) may be optimized by a marginal analysis procedure that first sets N_i equal to zero for all items i. We then identify the specific item which produces the greatest marginal increase in (25); that is, we identify the item with the greatest value of $\Delta_i(N_i)$,

$$\Delta_i(N_i) = \frac{\ln q_i(N_i) - \ln q_i(N_i - 1)}{c_i} . \tag{26}$$

We then increase N_i by one unit. This process is repeated until the budget limit B is met or exceeded.

To implement the LMI marginal analysis procedure, the efficient utility sort routines available on large-scale computers is employed. To do this, the following steps are used:

(1) Set $i = 1$.
(2) Set N = number of assets of type i currently in the system.
(3) Set $N = N + 1$ and compute $\Delta_i(N)$; LMI refers to this as a "sort value". Write i, N, C_i, $\Delta_i(N)$, and other bookkeeping values to an external file (e.g., magnetic tape or disc).
(4) If N has reached a given upper bound, go to step 5; otherwise, go to step 3.
(5) If all items have been processed, go to step 6; otherwise, increase i by one and go to step 3.
(6) Sort the file built in step 3 into decreasing order by $\Delta_i(N)$. The resulting file is called a "shopping list". Table 1 illustrates a hypothetical shopping list for B-52 aircraft.

The shopping list produced in step 6 may be used to produce optimal procurement plans and corresponding budgets for all possible funding limits. Every possible number of spare units for every item will have a unique position in the shopping list and the list will be ordered so that the first k units (involving many different items) found in the list represent an optimum procurement plan for the amount of money they will cost. In other words, as one procures units in the order of the list, he can be assured that each step has reduced the expected number of unavailable aircraft by the maximum amount possible given the amount of money spent up to that

Table 1
A hypothetical shopping list for B-52 aircraft

Unit and component	ENOA reduction	Cumulative ENOA reduction	Unit cost	Cumulative cost	Sort values [a]
6th A[b]	0.03108	0.03108	1,598	1,598	0.403172×10^{-7}
1st B	0.04147	0.07255	2,300	3,898	0.400377×10^{-7}
2nd C[b]	0.18749	0.26004	10,400	14,298	0.400198×10^{-7}
2nd B	0.03532	0.29536	2,300	16,598	0.377182×10^{-7}
1st D	0.20969	0.50505	13,800	30,398	0.330429×10^{-7}
7th A	0.02333	0.52838	1,598	31,996	0.316683×10^{-7}
2nd E	0.00276	0.53114	202	32,198	0.310552×10^{-7}

[a] The sort criterion guarantees that the procurement of two As, two Bs, one C, and one D will maximize ENOA reductions given $31,996.
[b] Without additional procurement, five A spares and one C spare will be available.

point. For example, table 1 indicates that if $ 31,996 is to be spent, the optimum procurement plan is to purchase two units of item A, two units of item B, and one unit each of items C and D.

2.7. Procurement-Repair Model

A fundamental assumption underlying all of the models discussed above is that sufficient funds, facilities, and manpower are available to begin repair activities as soon as an item fails. In today's austere funding environment, this assumption is often violated. For example, if there is not sufficient funding of depot repair activities, not all of the assets to be repaired at the depot level can be repaired in the current fiscal period.

To deal with this situation, the LMI developed the Procurement-Repair Model. In this model, reparable items are assumed to follow the flow patterns illustrated in fig. 2. This flow pattern is identical to the METRIC flow patterns discussed above, with one important exception. In this model, we have introduced a "Holding Pool". The Holding Pool represents unserviceable assets which have been intentionally withdrawn from the normal repair/resupply system because of the lack of sufficient repair funds. Individual assets which are placed in this pool are referred to as "dormant spares", since these assets may be returned to a serviceable condition at some future time should additional repair funds become available.

To determine optimal procurement plans for this system, LMI utilizes a computation procedure which follows these basic steps. First, it is assumed that all items projected to fail during the current fund-constrained fiscal period are placed

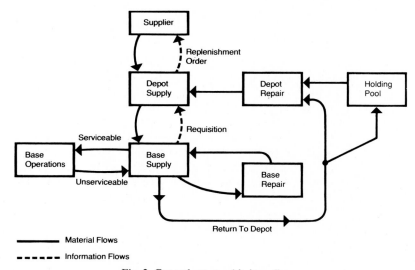

Fig. 2. General recoverable item flow.

into the Holding Pool. The assets placed in this pool represent the total number of assets expected to be removed from the logistics support system if no repair is to take place. Second, the LMI optimization algorithm is applied. In this step, the unit cost c_i used in computing the sort value is initially set equal to the repair cost. This value for c_i is used until all the assets in the holding pool for item i are repaired. Each additional asset to be added to the logistic support system must then be procured from an outside vendor. Consequently, c_i is set equal to the unit procurement cost for all additional assets to be added to the repair/resupply system. Finally, the shopping list produced by the optimization algorithm is used to develop a joint procurement and repair plan.

The above optimization algorithm assumes that both repair and procurement dollars come from the same pot of money, and answers produced by the above optimization procedure are only optimum under this assumption. In reality, however, procurement funds and repair funds are associated with different line items in the Congressional Budget. Consequently, the problem faced by AFLC managers is how to optimize weapon system performance subject to distinct constraints on available funds: one constraint for procurement funds and another constraint for repair funds. LMI is currently working to extend its computational algorithms to deal with this situation.

The LMI has also made several other important extensions to their calculation model. Major extensions include methods to handle multiple weapon systems, common items, and assembly/subassembly relationships. The reader is referred to references [128], [129], [169] and [226] for details.

3. Applications

3.1. Initial provisioning

The Air Force has two techniques in use for initial provisioning. The first is described in AFLC Regulation 57–27. It is a deterministic technique that allows for no variability of demand. That is, enough stock is purchased to cover the expected resupply times at the expected demand rate. The allocation of the total stock computed by the "57–27" technique to individual bases is negotiated by AFLC's item and system managers (IMs and SMs) and the command owning the bases/weapon systems in question. The expected demands at the base during the expected resupply time for that base (made up of a combination of the order and ship time and the base repair cycle time) serves as a guide during negotiation. In theory, the "57–27" technique is used for initial provisioning unless otherwise stated. In current practice, it is used only for provisioning less than complete weapon systems, for example a modification to an existing aircraft.

MOD-METRIC is the other technique used in provisioning new weapon systems. Actually the IM can override the MOD-METRIC computation (or the "57–27" computation) by manually prepared inputs of stock levels provided he has information not available to the model. However, the total requirement from MOD-METRIC is usually accepted as the buy quantity by the IM. MOD-METRIC also specifies now to distribute stock among the bases (i.e., the stock levels at the depot and each base are specified). Here again, the stock level at the bases is negotiated by the IMs and SMs and the command which owns the bases/weapon systems in question. The MOD-METRIC base stock levels serve as guides during this negotiation.

3.2. Replenishment spares

For follow-on buys of recoverable item spares, the Air Force uses a computation based on Sherbrooke's METRIC model to determine worldwide requirements. This computation is known as the Variable Safety Level Computation, or VSL.

In VSL, it is assumed that all bases are identical, each with the same demand rates, repair times, and base repair fractions. Hence, in the Fox and Landi Lagrangian problem, the optimal stock level for one base will be the optimal stock level for every base. Let the symbol S_b denote the stock level for this "average" base. Since there are J bases, the total expected base backorders in this system will be $J \cdot BO(S_b|\lambda_b T_b)$ and the total spares investment is given by $c(JS_b + S_0)$, where c denotes the cost of a single unit, and λ_b and T_b denote the failure rate and resupply time for the average base.

Now let L_0 and U_0 denote lower and upper bounds, respectively, on the depot stock level S_0 and let L_b and U_b denote similar bounds for the base stock level. The VSL computation then solves the Lagrangian problem

$$\min_{L_0 \leqslant S_0 \leqslant U_0} \left\{ \min_{L_b \leqslant S_b \leqslant U_b} J\, BO(S_b|\lambda_b T_b) - \phi J c S_b] - \phi c S_0 \right\} \qquad (27)$$

for the optimum values of S_0 and S_b.

For a given value of S_0 the optimal value for S_b is either the greatest non-negative integer satisfying

$$BO(S_b + 1|\lambda_b T_b) - BO(S_b|\lambda_b T_b) \geqslant \phi c \qquad (28)$$

or the appropriate upper or lower bound. The constrained optimal solution is then found by repeating this computation for all possible values of S_0 lying within the bounds L_0 and U_0.

The Lagrange multiplier, ϕ, is a management input to the VSL computation. Its value is established through experience with previous runs and through knowledge obtained from the budgeting computation to be discussed in the next section.

At present, the lower bound on base stock L_b is set equal to the expected number of demands during the average base resupply time, and the lower limit for depot spares, L_0 is set equal to the expected number of assets that are either in transit to or in depot repair. The upper limits, U_0 and U_b, are set so that no additional assets are allocated after system base backorders are reduced below a given threshold value.

The upper bounds used in VSL were adopted primarily to improve the computational performance of the algorithm. However, the lower limits represent a significant philosophical difference between the METRIC and VSL models.

In METRIC, zero is the lower bound on base and depot stocks. In VSL, however, the lower limit is set so that every item will have enough stock at both the base and depot to take care of the expected demands during the resupply time. Thus, while METRIC uses marginal analysis to decide whether or not to stock each unit of an item, VSL first sets an item's stock level equal to the expected amount in the "pipeline." Marginal analysis is then used to determine how much additional stock will be allocated to each item. Management insisted on this constraint because of METRIC's built-in bias against stocking high-cost items.

Another important difference between VSL and METRIC is in the modification of the unit price. In VSL, a modified unit price C' is obtained by multiplying the original price C by a discount factor. This discount equals (1 − fraction of base demands resupplied from the depot). In no case, however, is this factor allowed to be less than 0.10. The modified price then replaces c in the optimization. Thus, for an item which has a high percent of the failures sent back to the depot for processing, the modified unit price will be only a small fraction of the actual unit price. On the other hand, for items where only a small percent of failures are sent back to the depot, the modified unit price will be close to the actual unit price. This price modification tends to produce higher base stock levels for items with a small base processing rate. This modification was adopted because it was observed that high cost recoverable SRUs were not being stocked at the bases in sufficient quantities. It was also noticed that these high cost items tended to have a small base processing rate. Consequently, the technique described above was used to "reduce" the cost of these items so that more units of them would be stocked.

3.3. Budgeting

The VSL computation is also utilized in a budgeting mode. In this case, cost-effectiveness curves are constructed by solving the Langrangian problems several times for several different values of the Lagrange multiplier.

These curves estimate the impact of alternate funding levels upon expected base backorders. Such curves are one of the important information items reviewed during the congressional budget approval process.

3.4. Distribution

As discussed in section 2, METRIC can be used to determine optimal stock levels for each base in a multi-base system. Unfortunately, substantial data processing problems must be resolved before such a centralized calculation can be implemented in a system as large and complex as the Air Force supply system. Work to develop such a system is now under way. In the meantime, individual base stock levels are set by a decentralized calculation made at each Air Force base. This calculation sets the stock level for a given base equal to the expected demands in the base resupply time plus one standard deviation. If demands are normally distributed, such levels provide a theoretical fill rate of 85%.

3.5. "What If" computations

In addition to the routinely used computations discussed above, several specialized versions of the VSL computation have been developed to support special studies. For example, "What If" models have been used to study the funding and effectiveness impacts of changing the mix of transportation modes used to move varying classes of Air Force commodities, and to study the effect of establishing an additional aerial port linking the United States with Europe and the Pacific. The impact of changing flying hour programs upon recoverable item requirements has also been studied using this model.

4. Conclusions

Multi-echelon inventory theory has made important contributions to the efficient management of Air Force recoverable items. However, much more work is needed to provide practical answers for the management of all classes of Air Force commodities.

TIMS Studies in the Management Sciences 16 (1981) 299–330
© North-Holland Publishing Company

EXPERIENCES WITH A MULTI-INDENTURED, MULTI-ECHELON INVENTORY MODEL

Andrew J. CLARK

CACI, Inc.

Personal experiences with the development and testing of a multi-indentured, multi-echelon inventory model are related. The model, based on previous work (METRIC, MOD-METRIC), is designed to maximize operational availability of end equipments subject to budget constraints on spares stockage. Events leading to the initial formulation and development of the model in the Navy logistics support environment are given. Then the model itself is described in terms of its structure and solution procedure, avoiding technical details and proofs as much as possible. Finally, a chronology of subsequent model development and evaluation is given in the context of shifting and sometimes conflicting criteria among diverse Navy organizations. Major problems, successes, and setbacks in this on-going program are discussed with the hope that this experience will provide some insight in filling the gap between theory and application, a perennial problem in operations research.

1. Introduction

Of all the specialized topics of operations research, inventory theory has perhaps the greatest opportunities for practical application on the one hand and the most extensive available theory on the other. The military services have sponsored, directly or indirectly, most of the research and development in this field over the past 25 years at a cost of many millions of dollars, a justifiable expenditure considering the billions of dollars' worth of inventories involved. Elementary results of inventory theory have achieved fairly widespread implementation. More advanced techniques are confined to particular applications of rather narrow scope. However, large segments of military inventories are still being managed by policies which, even though computerized, have no theoretical foundation whatsoever.

Part of the implementation problem in the services is the number of different inventory models that have been proposed. Another part is the set of barriers, accruing in part from the sheer size of the bureaucracies involved, that have been erected between the proposals and their use in actually controlling inventories. Such barriers are warranted in view of the huge implementation costs for applications of other than very narrow scope. Accordingly, it is understandable that any new technique should undergo the acid test of critical scrutiny by managers who are unconcerned about the wonderful theory involved as long as it is understandable, really works in the real world, and has a demonstrated payoff. It should also be realized that the technique must achieve some threshold of either acceptance or neutrality on the part of the many diverse organizations, each with its special interests, directly or indirectly affected by the proposal.

How does an inventory model actually progress from theory to practice in the military services? I doubt if anyone has all the answers to this question, particularly since each implementation is unique. To shed light on this subject, I would like to relate some of my experiences over the past two years in just such an effort for the Navy. This project is currently in mid-course, and its outcome is uncertain; yet events leading to the birth of the model and starting it down the road toward possible implementation may be instructive, at least to the extent of how to avoid infant mortality, which has been the fate of other efforts of this kind.

The model itself is a lineal descendent of a series of multi-echelon models developed over the past 20 years. The objective function is new and the solution procedure is different, but the structure of the model is a generalization of the well-known METRIC [210] and MOD-METRIC [151] models. Since the primary objective in this paper is to provide insight into the processes involved in implementing this kind of model, the model itself is described in simple terms and I only hint at its theoretical foundation, relying instead upon that of its illustrious antecedents.

In the next two sections, the background leading to the development of the inventory model is established. Then the model itself is described and also the procedure for calculating levels according to an equipment availability objective function. The remainder of the paper gives a chronology of subsequent model development and evaluation within the context of shifting and sometimes conflicting criteria among diverse Navy organizations.

2. Prologue

A perpetual problem in providing logistics support for weapon systems is one of accountability for investments in logistics resources. With respect to inventories, managers and budgeteers have complained for years about the lack of operationally significant performance measures of spares investments. The basic question is: what impact does an increase or decrease in inventory budgets have upon keeping ships sailing and airplanes flying? Traditional measures, such as fill rates, expected shortage days, etc., are indices of supply behavior and do not directly relate to how well equipments are supported by inventories used in maintenance functions; furthermore, even as descriptors of supply performance, issues of interpretation, consistency and adequacy arise [22]. In general, ways of determining inventory investment required to achieve specified system operational availability goals have not been available for practical application. The notion of a shortage cost — the cost consequence of an unfilled demand — is designed to bridge this gap in classical inventory theory, but has proven to be an unusable concept in practice.

In the Navy, one result of this accountability gap has been a gradual reduction in spares budgets relative to the systems being supported. It is understandable that budgeters are inclined to reduce investments if direct correlation to performance degradation of weapon systems cannot be demonstrated. Yet there undoubtedly has been an effect. Evidence shows that Navy systems, particularly older ships, have gradually deteriorated recently due, in part, to lack of readily available spares.

Concerned over this trend, the Chief of Naval Operations (CNO) issued a study directive in August, 1971 to "define, develop and propose an automated model by which supply support dollar outlays may be related to fleet capability" [27]. In view of later developments, it is interesting to note that the study directive continued: "It is anticipated that this study will result in a new OPNAV directive for the management of secondary items . . .". A CNO task force, referred to as the S⁴ (Ship Supply Support Study) project, consisting of representatives from all major Navy logistics support commands was established in response to this directive.

In the ensuing effort on this project, the general scope of the problem was established, and a model was constructed to simulate the operation of the supply support system in response to fleet demands. In particular, a model was designed to measure supply response times as functions of stockage availability, repair turn-around times, and other factors. The model was used in several analyses of fleet operations, using histories of observed demands, with results given in working papers and a final report [212]. In general, however, the model and associated analyses did not become the predictive tool originally contemplated in the study directive.

In April, 1975, CNO issued another study directive "to identify or develop quantitative relationships between expenditures for material support and fleet readiness and to demonstrate how the relationship can be used to forecast the consequences, in terms of fleet readiness, of changes in the funding levels of major support programs" [28]. Performance responsibility for this study was directed to the Center for Naval Analyses (CNA).

In this study, several analyses were conducted on various aspects of the problem. In one set of tasks, standard aggregate measures of ship and aircraft readiness were analyzed to determine if long-term trends existed. A similar trend analysis was made for several categories of fund expenditures in the operation and support of the systems. Statistical methods were then applied to identify specific expenditure—readiness relationships.

In another part of the CNA study, an analytic definition of equipment operational availability was established. Symbolized by "A_0", this definition became a standard for later work in this area including, in particular, the inventory model described below. A model was also developed for Mean Supply Response Time (MSRT), one of the ingredients in the A_0 definition. This model was then evaluated with data collected from the Navy inventory management system. The model and other results of the CNA study were presented in a series of memoranda and reports [135]. As in the S⁴ study, however, no viable technique relating material support to fleet readiness for everyday Navy use materialized.

Although these studies provided some of the analytic structure of the inventory model given below their main importance was in establishing a climate of acceptability for the model. The interest at high levels in the Navy was in techniques for determining inventory requirements, equipment availability, and mission readiness goals. As described in the next section, this interest motivated the design of the model to a large extent.

3. Genesis

In December, 1973, a special project organization, PMS-306, reporting to the Deputy Chief of Naval Operations, Logistics (OP-04), was established to implement a maintenance and support program on an interim basis for several new classes of ships. This program, originating in a previous Chief of Naval Material (CNM) study, was concerned with support of ships with imposed constraints on shipboard manning, ship displacement, and follow-up cost. Referred to as "LO-MIX" ships, the ship classes involved were a new class of frigate (FFG-7), a hydrofoil patrol ship (PHM), and a light, "cheap" aircraft carrier (later cancelled). PMS-306 was formally chartered in January, 1975 to support the LO-MIX program.

An analogous program was established by Vice Chief of Naval Operations direction in August, 1974 to re-engineer and improve maintenance systems and practices for 74 ships of the DD-1052, DDG-37, CG-16, and CG-26 classes. These are destroyers and other ships with severe limitations on shipboard manning and maintenance capabilities. This program was expanded on August, 1976 to include 23 ships of the DDG-2 class.

In April, 1977, PMS-306 was rechartered within the Naval Sea Systems Command to include both of these programs under the name, "Ship Support Improvement Project (SSIP)". This project was established in response to CNO Objective No. 3 (Improvement of Material Condition in the Fleet) as the main, long-term initiative associated with this objective. The new direction for PMS-306 was expanded in scope to the degree necessary to achieve a total, effective, integrated ship maintenance strategy for the Navy.

Almost from its inception, PMS-306 obtained contract support in accomplishing portions of its objectives. It was in this connection that I became involved in the project. Under previous Navy sponsorship, I had developed a model [37] named the "Logistic Support Economic Evaluation (LSEE)" model, which was designed for use in a broad spectrum of logistics support analyses and studies. The capabilities of LSEE were expanded and used (and are still being used) in support of PMS-306 to estimate inventory budget requirements for FFG-7 class ships.

The LSEE model calculates support resource requirements and their costs over time according to the phase-in schedule and worldwide distribution of one or more equipments. In the model, expected quarterly failures of the equipments and included parts are calculated from failure factors and the way in which items are interrelated in a top-down breakdown of parts within the equipment. According to these failures, and using input descriptions of the supporting supply and maintenance activities and their interrelationships, material flow through the system for stock replenishment and repair process is calculated by a set of routines referred to as the Material Flow Model. Included, in particular, are expected demands upon inventory, and expected losses due to discard of shipment elsewhere for repair. Using these demand and loss rates, inventory levels at all stockage locations are calculated according to designated inventory policies. Support resources (manpower, support equipment, etc.) needed to satisfy the calculated maintenance work loads are determined for each location. Finally, costs associated with the inventory levels and maintenance support resources, as well as transportation and other costs, are determined and summarized.

In its PMS-306 application, only those portions of the LSEE model involving demand and loss-rate calculations, inventory level determination, and inventory cost summaries are used. Applying current Navy wholesale system stockage policies, inventory levels are calculated according to the phase-in schedule of ships involved. Estimated budgets are then derived by summarizing inventory investment and replacement requirements by fiscal year.

In late 1976, a situation arose in which the budget requirements derived by LSEE from current Navy stockage policies exceeded the amount of funds expected to be available. A request was made to devise a procedure for "backing off" from the calculated investments. Due to the influence of the prior CNO and CNA studies on operational availability, a criterion was given to reduce stock levels in such a way as to result in least degradation of the operational availability of installed equipments.

In February, 1977, I started to analyze this particular problem. I was to reach three general conclusions:

(1) The problem required consideration of all echelons of the support system. Even though the budgets involved were for wholesale system stocks, shipboard stock levels could not be ignored. Reductions in wholesale stocks for items with high shipboard levels would have less impact on equipment availability than for items with lower shipboard levels. Thus, the problem was multi-echelon in scope.

(2) The problem required consideration of how parts are interrelated in the parts breakdown of the equipment. Reductions in stock levels for higher assemblies in the equipment would have a more immediate effect upon equipment availability than for lower level assemblies and parts. Thus, the problem was multi-indentured in scope.

(3) If a procedure could be developed to reduce levels with least impact upon operational availability, then it was likely the same method could be used to increase levels so as to maximize operational availability per unit of additional investment. If applied with zero stock levels to start with, the procedure would be a general multi-indentured, multi-echelon inventory model with an objective

function based upon the operational availability of end-equipments.

Having reached these conclusions, I then sought to relate them to available theory on the subject. The METRIC model, developed by Sherbrooke [210], and the follow-up MOD-METRIC model by Muckstadt [151], were of particular relevance and interest. Since I was thoroughly familiar with these models and had more or less followed the progress of their implementation in the Air Force, I was quickly able to identify a way to change the structure to accommodate an operational availability objective function as defined by the CNA study. Also, due to my recent work on another model (a level-of-repair model developed for the Naval Air Systems Command), a solution procedure based on dynamic programming appeared to offer advantages over previous solution methods.

Collecting these notions together, none of which were really formalized, I gave a briefing in March, 1977 to PMS-306 management in which I summarized the available theory and outlined the approach I had in mind. I pointed out that the LSEE model already had the necessary environmental representation in terms of the parts breakdown relationships, support system hierarchy, and calculations of demand, loss, and other factors needed by the proposed model. In summary, I recommended that the multi-indentured, multi-echelon operational availability inventory model be developed as an enhancement to LSEE, not only to satisfy the budget reduction requirement but also to respond generally to previous CNO and CNM interest in relating supply support to fleet readiness.

PMS-306 reception of this recommendation was positive, and arrangements were made to start the project. Without further detailed analysis, I began designing and programming the inventory model in the form of additional routines to the LSEE model. Several months after the model was programmed and operating, I documented the structure of the model and its solution procedure in mathematical terms. This model, referred to as the Optimal A_0 Inventory Model, is summarized in the next two sections.

4. The model

The basic concept of the Optimal A_0 Inventory Model is relatively easy to grasp. First of all, it is a multi-indenture model, meaning that the parts breakdown of an equipment, as illustrated in fig. 1(a), should be kept in mind. Second, it is a multi-echelon model, and therefore a hierarchical maintenance supply support system, as illustrated in fig. 1(b), should be considered, where each defined location may have both repair and stockage capabilities. Finally, an $(S - 1, S)$ ordering rule is used for all items and locations: whenever a unit is lost from stock, a replacement unit is ordered from the next higher location in the support system (the manufacturer "orders" by fabricating replacement units from an unlimited supply of raw materials). As part of the ordering rule, it is assumed that each demand for an item that can be repaired is accompanied by the return of a failed unit: a one-for-one exchange of a good unit for a bad one.

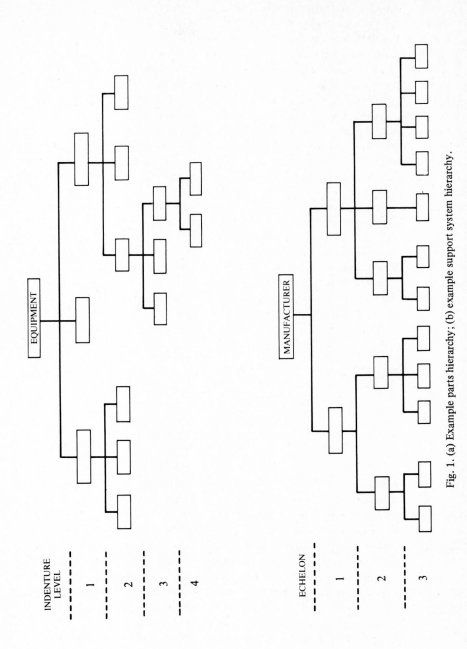

Fig. 1. (a) Example parts hierarchy; (b) example support system hierarchy.

Consider now an arbitrary reparable item at a given supply/repair location. A customer arrives with a failed unit of the item and asks for a good unit in exchange. If a good unit is available from stock, the customer goes away happy, and the failed unit goes to the repair shop to be fixed. On the other hand, if no spares are in stock and no receipts are expected from repair or a higher supply source, the customer must wait until his failed unit gets repaired (assuming this is faster than getting a new unit from the higher supply sources). The repair takes a certain length of time, the *repair cycle,* providing that parts needed for the repair are available from stock. If one or more needed parts is not available, however, an *extra repair time* is required to order and receive the parts (or to receive previously ordered parts that are on their way). Thus, the total repair time is given by the repair cycle, which is based upon complete parts availability, plus an increment if there are shortages of needed repair parts.

There is another factor to be considered: when the failed unit enters the repair shop, there is some chance that it is beyond the shop's repair capability due to lack of expertise, special tools, or other resources. In this case, the unit is sent to the next higher level repair facility in the support system and a good unit is requested in exchange. If a unit is available from stock at the higher location, a certain length of time, the *resupply time,* is involved in the transaction. If not available, an *extra resupply time* is incurred while the higher location awaits receipt of a good unit from repair or from a still higher supply source.

The original customer wait time can now be summarized as follows:

$$
\begin{matrix} \text{Customer} \\ \text{wait time} \end{matrix} = \begin{bmatrix} \text{Loss} \\ \text{probab.} \end{bmatrix} \begin{bmatrix} \text{Resupply} & \text{Extra} \\ \text{time} & + \text{resupply} \\ & \text{time} \end{bmatrix}
$$

$$
+ \begin{bmatrix} 1 - \dfrac{\text{Loss}}{\text{probab.}} \end{bmatrix} \begin{bmatrix} \text{Repair} & \text{Extra} \\ \text{cycle} & + \text{repair} \\ & \text{time} \end{bmatrix}
$$

where the loss probability is the probability that a failed unit cannot be repaired at the repair shop and instead is discarded or sent elsewhere for repair.

The customer wait time given by this formula applies only if a replacement unit is not available from stock. The chance of this occurring will depend upon how many spares of the item are stocked at the given location. Thus, the *expected* wait time will depend upon the initial stock level and the chance of there being no stock on hand when demanded. This expectancy is defined as the *mean supply response time* (MSRT) for a given item at a given location. A specific formula for calculating the MSRT for a particular stock level will be given below.

The MSRT also depends upon the stock status of lower parts in the parts hierarchy and upon the stock of the item at higher locations in the support hierarchy. The term *extra resupply time* is nothing more than the MSRT of the item at the higher location. Similarly, the extra repair cycle time can be derived from MSRTs of parts within the given item.

Now let us turn attention to the end-equipment itself, the top item in the parts breakdown, and a location at the bottom of the support system hierarchy which actually operates the equipment. By a recursive procedure an MSRT for this item and location can be calculated which will depend upon the stock levels for all lower level parts and all stockage locations. Since the MSRT is defined on a per-failure basis, the calculated MSRT can be interpreted as the expected length of time the equipment is unavailable for use upon failure due to spares shortages.

In addition, the equipment can be down for lengths of time that are unrelated to supply availability, for example, time required to diagnose and isolate the failures, remove and replace defective parts, and check-out the equipment afterwards for satisfactory performance. The average time required to perform these repair functions is referred to as the *mean time to repair* (MTTR).

The expected operational availability of the equipment can now be calculated from the following formula:

$$\frac{\text{Operational}}{\text{availability}} = A_0 = \frac{\text{Up time}}{\text{Up time} + \text{Down time}} = \frac{\text{MTBF}}{\text{MTBF} + \text{MTTR} + \text{MSRT}}$$

where:

$$MTBF = \text{mean time between failures,}$$
$$MTTR = \text{mean time to repair, and}$$
$$MSRT = \text{mean supply response time.}$$

The derivation of this formula is apparent from the schematic:

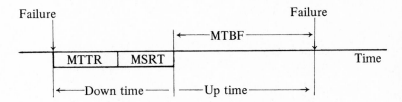

Thus A_0 is the average fraction of time that the equipment is in an operable condition: A_0 may also be interpreted as the probability that the equipment is in an operable condition at a random point in time. Note that this definition assumes that the equipment is "down" upon failure even though, in fact, it may still be operative but with possibly degraded performance.

The description of the Optimal A_0 Inventory Model given above can be formalized in mathematical terms by a set of interrelated equations. Consider an arbitrary item i in the parts breakdown of the equipment and an arbitrary location

u in the support system. Assume that all factors involving time use days as a common time unit. The model is then formally defined by the six following equations:

$$M_{iu} = D_{iu} + \tau_{iu} , \tag{1}$$

where:

M_{iu} = mean time to return a failed unit of item i at location u to a serviceable condition,

D_{iu} = mean supply response time (MSRT for item i at location u), and

τ_{iu} = mean time to repair (MTTR) for item i at location u when all needed repair parts are available,

= 0 if location u does not operate the equipment.

Equation (1) is subject to different interpretations according to whether location u operates the equipment (u is a user site). The term, τ_{iu}, defined only for user sites, represents the time to remove a failed unit from the equipment and replace it with a serviceable spare, assuming that the spare is immediately available. In general, the term τ_{iu} captures all the time that equipment is inoperable due to causes other than supply availability. It also includes any time required to identify item i as the cause of the equipment failure, assuming that the problem has already been isolated down to the next higher assembly of the item. In addition, this term can include any time required to locate and retrieve the spare unit from stock bins at the location. For both user and higher-level support facilities, the term D_{iu} represents the average time required to satisfy a demand upon inventory at that location. This depends upon how much stock of the item is carried at the location:

$$D_{iu} = 1/\lambda_{iu} \, \Sigma_{x > S_{iu}} \, (x - S_{iu}) p(x; \lambda_{iu} T_{iu}) , \tag{2}$$

where:

S_{iu} = stock level of item i at location u,

λ_{iu} = expected number of demands per time unit upon inventory for item i at location u,

$p(x; \lambda_{iu} T_{iu})$ = probability of x units of stock reduction for item i at location u, and

T_{iu} = mean stock replenishment time (time to replace an inventory loss through repair or procurement for item i at location u).

The summation term in equation (2) represents the backorder function. This function captures the concept that demand is uncertain .and that shortages will occur at some probability according to the stock level, S_{iu}. It gives the expected number of units short (demand exceeding supply) at any time for a given stock level S_{iu}. For the kind of order policy we assume, it also gives the expected number of shortage days per day (see [95], page 20). Dividing by the expected number of demands per day gives the average length of time a customer must wait for satisfaction of a demand upon inventory. If the stock level, S_{iu}, is zero, then $D_{iu} = T_{iu}$, meaning the customer must wait the full time required to obtain an item from repair or resupply each time he places a demand upon the inventory:

$$T_{iu} = \gamma_{iu}(L_{iu} + L'_{iu}) + (1 - \gamma_{iu})(R_{iu} + R'_{iu}) , \qquad (3)$$

where:

γ_{iu} = probability that a demand for item i at location u results in a loss (discard or sent elsewhere for repair) which must be replaced through resupply,

L_{iu} = average resupply time assuming stock is available at the resupply source,

L'_{iu} = average additional resupply time due to expected shortages at the resupply source,

R_{iu} = average repair cycle assuming availability of spares for items within i at the next lower indenture of the parts breakdown, and

R'_{iu} = average additional repair cycle due to expected shortages of spares for items within i at the next lower indenture.

It can be seen that equation (3) is the same as the customer wait-time formula given in the preliminary description of the model. It contains the terms R'_{iu} and L'_{iu}, which represent the average stock replenishment time for a given item dependence upon time delays caused by parts shortages within the item and at higher support facilities. The loss factor, γ_{iu}, specifies the degree to which resupply time versus repair time contributes to total mean replenishment time. For a totally consumable item $\gamma_{iu} = 1$, and the only consideration is the time it takes to obtain resupply from a higher source. For a totally reparable item (at the given location, u), $\gamma_{iu} = 0$, and the repair time accounts for all of the stock replenishment time. By assignment of this factor, both consumable and reparable items in any mix can be considered by the model

$$L'_{iu} = D_{iv} , \qquad (4)$$

where v = the higher level support facility providing resupply of item i to location u.

In this equation (4), $L'_{iu} = 0$ for the facility (manufacturer) at the top of the support hierarchy since it has no resupply source. L'_{iu} is also zero for all locations immediately below the top facility since an infinite supply is assumed there which causes D_{iv} to be zero. This equation gives the connection between activities in the multi-echelon support system. It states that the extra resupply time at a particular location u is given by the mean time to respond to a demand placed upon its resupply source, v. As shown by equation (2), this will depend upon the stock status and other factors at location v.

$$R'_{iu} = \Sigma_{j \in i}\, \lambda_{ju} M_{ju}/\Sigma_{j \in i}\, \lambda_{ju} \tag{5}$$

where j = items within i at the next lower indenture level of the parts breakdown.

If item i has no lower level parts, $R'_{iu} = 0$. Equation (5) states that the extra repair time for item i at location u due to shortages of lower level parts is given by the weighted average of the mean time required to return the parts to a serviceable condition through replacement or further repair. The weighting factor, λ_{ju}, is the demand rate for item j. This equation gives the connection among items in the parts breakdown, and reflects the fact that response to a demand upon inventory for a given item i depends upon the stock status and other factors pertaining to lower level parts within i.

$$A_{eu} = 1/(1 + \lambda_{eu} M_{eu}), \tag{6}$$

where A_{eu} = fraction of the time equipment e is available for use at location u.

Equation (6), defined only for the item e (end-equipment) at the top of the parts breakdown and for locations u that operate the equipment, is equivalent to the formula for operational availability, A_0, given in the preliminary description of the model. [The previous formula is easily obtained by setting $\lambda_{eu} = 1/(\text{MTBF})_{eu}$ and using equation (1) for M_{eu}.] The substitution of equation (1) for M_{eu} and subsequent recursive substitutions in all of the equations given above, demonstrate the dependence of the operational availability of the equipment upon the stock status and other factors pertaining to all included items and all support locations.

The various factors given in equations (1) – (6) are listed in table 1. Since the factors apply to each item and location (unless otherwise noted), subscripts have

Table 1
Factors used in the Optimal A_0 Inventory Model

Factor	Symbol	Source	Comments
Mean recovery time	M	Eq. (1)	
Mean supply response time (MSRT)	D	Eq. (2)	
Mean time to repair (MTTR)	τ	Input	Defined only for user sites
Stock level	S		Given by solution
Demand rate	λ	Input	
Mean stock replenishment time	T	Eq. (3)	
Loss factor	γ	Input	= 1 for consumable items
Average resupply time	L	Input	
Additional resupply time	L'	Eq. (4)	= 0 for top support sites
Average repair cycle	R	Input	
Additional repair cycle	R'	Eq. (5)	= 0 for lowest level parts
Operational availability	A	Eq. (6)	Defined only for equipments at user sites

been omitted. Each factor is either provided as an input parameter or computed by the indicated equation. The demand rate, λ, requires a further discussion. Even though this factor is indicated as being given for each item and location, demand rate values are actually interdependent among both items and locations. Consider a given item and various locations that stock or use the item. Under the assumed ordering policy, some fraction (given by the loss factor γ) of demands upon inventory at the lowest (user) sites are passed up as demands upon inventories at the next higher support facilities. Similarly, some fraction of these demands are passed up to still higher-level support locations, and so on. The various fractions depend upon the repair characteristics of the item and the capabilities of the respective maintenance shops. For a consumable item, the loss factor γ is set to 1 for all locations, and a demand at a user site becomes a stock replenishment demand at each higher-level support facility. For reparable items, the loss factor is less than 1, and only units that a given facility cannot repair become demands upon higher-level locations. For some reparable items, the user sites may have no repair capability at all, so the loss factor is set to 1 for these sites and at some lesser value at higher maintenance locations according to the amount of repair accomplished there.

In general, demands and corresponding stock requirements at any location occur to support repair operations at the location and to provide stock replenishment of lower-level activities. The demand rates are interdependent according to parts breakdown and support system relationships. Although it is possible to measure independently the demand rates and loss factors from observed data and to use these values in the model, it is more practical (particularly for new equipments where demand experience is not available) to calculate them from another set of parameters applied in conjunction with the parts breakdown and support system relationships. This function is accomplished by the Material Flow Model.

Before passing on to the next subject, a parenthetical note is in order. The six equations given above define the structure of the model. Justification for this formulation rests upon a number of key assumptions and the results of previous research. Using inventory theory jargon, the main assumptions of the formulation are: excess demand is backlogged; continuous review $(S - 1, S)$ ordering policies are used at all locations; demand distributions are stationary and satisfy Palm's theorm; no lateral resupply; and the parts hierarchy structure is an arborescence.

The formulation of the model is a generalization of early work initiated by Rosenman and Hoekstra [193], Hoekstra *et al.* [101], and Sherbrooke [210]. Subsequent development and applications were accomplished by Muckstadt [151], [154], [155], Logistics Management Institute [138], Slay and O'Malley [225], and Fitzgerald [76]. Of these assumptions the $(S - 1, S)$ ordering policy is the most restrictive. In particular, it is not realistic for consumables which are subject to economic order quantity (EOQ) considerations. Modifications of the model for a general (s, S)-type ordering policy are suggested in [36].

The stationarity assumption of the model is also subject to question in terms of practical application. In the real world, a host of dynamic factors are present: reliability growth, maintenance learning, changes in applicable spare parts due to equipment modification, etc. Such concerns, however, are largely alleviated by the usual practice of periodic recomputation. However, if the model is used to determine budget requirements over a 4–5-year time horizon, the dynamic changes cannot be ignored. In such applications, the stationarity assumption of the model must be recognized as a significant limitation.

5. The solution

The model formulation given by equations (1)–(6) establishes structural relationships among stock levels for all items and locations and relates them to a measure for end-equipment operational availability. The remaining problem is to find values for the stock levels such that particular availability goals are met. According to Navy objectives, this problem is stated as follows:

Find values for stock levels for all items and locations within the structure given by equations (1)–(6) such that the equipment operational availability is maximized for a given total investment in spares.

As it turns out, the procedure for solving this problem also solves the following:

Under the same conditions, find values for stock levels such that a given equipment operational availability is achieved at least cost for spares.

As a preliminary step towards solving these problems, consider using the model structure so far defined as a way to measure expected A_0. Suppose that values for the stock levels, S_{iu}, are given for all items i and locations u in the support system, and that all other input factors identified in table 1 are given. Then, it is possible to use equations (1)–(6) to derive an expected equipment operational availability. This is done by the following recursive calculation referred to in the A_0 evaluation procedure:

(1) Start the procedure by considering items at the bottom of the parts breakdown and locations (depots) at the top of the support system hierarchy. For these items and locations, the extra repair cycle, R'_{iu}, and extra resupply time, L'_{iu}, are both zero. Use equations (3), (2) and (1), in that order, to derive $M_{iu} = D_{iu}$, the mean supply response time, for each such item and location.

(2) For the same locations (at the top of the support system), use equation (5) to calculate the extra repair cycle, R'_{iu}, for all immediate next higher assemblies of the items considered in step 1. Since the extra resupply time, L'_{iu}, is still zero for these assemblies, equations (3), (2) and (1) can again be applied to derive D_{iu} for all of the assemblies.

(3) Repeat step 2, keeping the locations the same but moving up another indenture

level of the parts hierarchy. Continue the recursion until the top of the parts hierarchy (the end-equipment) is reached. At this point, values for mean supply response time, D_{iu}, will have been determined for all items i and all locations u at the top of the support system hierarchy.

(4) Now consider locations at the next lower level in the support system hierarchy. The extra resupply times, L'_{iu}, for all items at such locations are now given by equation (4). Reapply steps 1 through 3 for these locations, starting with items at the bottom of the parts hierarchy and continuing up the hierarchy until the end-equipment is reached.

(5) Reapply step 4, but for locations at still another next lower level. Continue until locations at the bottom of the support system hierarchy (user sites) are reached, with values of M_{iu} being obtained for all items (including e, the end-equipment) and user sites (note that the term τ_{iu} in equation (1) can now be nonzero for these locations).

(6) Use the value for M_{eu}, calculated by step 5, in equation (6) to derive the answer, the expected operational availability of the end-equipment.

This procedure can be applied to determine the consequences, in terms of expected operational availability of the equipment at user sites, for any given set of stock levels including, in particular, levels calculated by currently used inventory policies. A cost-effectiveness measure for the given stock levels can be easily determined. The cost is found by adding up the inventory investment (unit price times stock level) for all items and locations. The effectiveness is the expected operational availability value calculated by the above procedure. This cost-effectiveness measure can be plotted as shown in fig. 2, where each point gives the cost and A_0 effectiveness of a particular given set of stock levels.

Suppose that cost-effectiveness points are plotted for all possible sets of stock levels. There will be a very large number of such points, one for each combination of item, location, and attainable stock level. If plotted they will all lie below some curve such as the one shown in fig. 2. For any investment in spares, this curve gives a bound on the highest equipment operational availability that is obtainable from spares stockage or, conversely, the least investment in spares that will yield a given operational availability. It should be noted that only a relatively few points on the curve are actually attainable due to the fact that stock levels are confined to integer values.

The most efficient curve of equipment operational availability as a function of spares investment has several general characteristics. First, there will always be some value of operational availability for a zero investment in spares (stock levels are zero for all items and locations) since the probability of zero demand upon inventory is always non-zero. Second, the curve usually rises very rapidly at the start, since a small investment in spares will buy stockout protection with a variety of cheap items; the curve starts to flatten out as more expensive items are stocked. Finally, as the spares investment gets very large, the curve asymptotically approaches some value less than one.

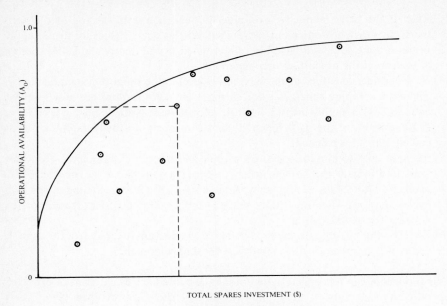

Fig. 2. A cost-effectiveness curve.

The problem of finding stock levels according to the given criteria can now be visualized as one of finding sets of stock levels that yield the most efficient cost-effectiveness curve. This is actually a very difficult computational problem. The method used is only an approximation, but a fairly good one in practical applications. It is based upon the notion of assuming the stock level is set at some value for each item and location, and then finding the particular item and location for which an additional unit of stock will give the largest increase in A_0 per investment dollar. If stock level values are set to zero for all items and locations to start with, then repeated application of the procedure will construct a close approximation to the cost-effectiveness curve depicted in fig. 2.

To solve the general problem, then, the following subproblem is formulated:

Assume the stock level is set at some value for each item and location. For an arbitrary item i and location u, find the item i^* (which may be item i) and location u^* (which can be location u) for which a one-unit increase in stock will yield the largest decrease in D_{iu}, the mean supply response time, per dollar.

If applied to item e, the end-equipment, and user site u, equation (6) shows that this is equivalent to maximizing the increase in operational availability, A_{eu}, resulting from a one-unit increase in stock for some subordinate item at some location.

A procedure for solving this subproblem will now be given. For an arbitrary item i and location u, an inspection of equations (2) and (3) shows that there are three possible ways to reduce D_{iu}, the mean supply response time:

(1) The stock level, S_{iu}, for the given item and location can be increased by one
unit.
(2) The extra resupply time, L'_{iu}, can be reduced by increasing the stock level of
item i, or one of its subordinate items, at the resupply source for location u
or some higher supply facility. Call the least of such reduced values, L'^*_{iu}, and let
i' and u' represent, respectively, the item and location that yield L'^*_{iu}.
(3) The extra repair time, R'_{iu}, can be reduced by increasing the stock level of some
item subordinate to i in the parts breakdown at location u or some higher
supply source for u. Call the least of such reduced values R'^*_{iu}, and let i'' and u''
represent, respectively, the item and location that yield R'^*_{iu}.

First, for the given stock levels, D_{iu} can be calculated by the A_0 evaluation
procedure previously described, which also gives values for the extra delay times,
L'_{iu} and R'_{iu}, used in equation (3). Then, to determine reductions in D_{iu} for alternative 1, equation (2) can be used by substituting $S_{iu} + 1$ for S_{iu}. For alternative 2,
suppose we *know* the value of L'^*_{iu} (and corresponding item i' and location u').
Then, the reduction in D_{iu} can be calculated using equations (2) and (3) by substituting L'^*_{iu} for L'_{iu} and leaving all other terms the same. Similarly, for alternative 3,
suppose we *know* the value of R'^*_{iu} (and corresponding item i'' and location u''). The
associated reduction D_{iu} is then determined from equations (2) and (3) by substituting R'^*_{iu} for R'_{iu} and leaving all other terms the same. For each of the three
alternatives, the net reduction in D_{iu} per dollar is calculated by dividing the respective reductions by the unit price of the item involved (i, i' or i''). The alternative
which gives the largest net reduction per dollar is then chosen and the solution of
the subproblem is given by (i^*, u^*), the item–location pair (i, u), (i', u') or (i'', u'')
that corresponds to the chosen alternative.

The question arises: how can values for L'^*_{iu} and R'^*_{iu} be found? Equation (2)
states that L'^*_{iu} is equal to the solution of the subproblem for item i at location v,
the supply force for location u. Using equation (5), R'^*_{iu} can be easily calculated
from subproblem solutions for items j within i (at the next lower indenture) at
location u. The particular subproblem solution is accepted for the item j' which
yields the largest decrease in R'_{iu} per dollar according to this equation, with values
for M_{ju} being left unchanged for subordinate items other than j'. Thus, to solve the
subproblem for a particular item i and location u, we first solve it for item i and
the next higher support location and also for all next lower items j at location u.
This recursively defines a set of interconnected subproblems that goes up the
part hierarchy structure from location u and down the parts breakdown from item
i.

According to this recursion, the subproblem for item i and location u is solved
by the same methodology as used in the A_0 evaluation procedure previously
described. First considered are items at the bottom of the parts breakdown and the

locations at the top of the support system hierarchy where the extra resupply time and extra repair cycle are both zero. For such items and locations, only the first of the three decision alternatives is available, and the subproblem solution, in each case, is to increase the stock level of the item and location. With these results, the subproblem can then be solved for next higher assemblies at the same locations and also for the same items at next lower-level support sites. These solutions, in turn, are used for the next higher-level assemblies and next lower-level locations; the recursion continues until the given item i and location u are reached. For the end-equipment e at user site u, the recursion must be applied throughout the entire parts breakdown and support system hierarchy.

To use this procedure to construct the cost-effectiveness curve, all stock levels are set to zero at the start. The subproblem is then applied for the end-equipment and user sites to find the first unit of stock to be procured, the one giving the highest payoff in equipment A_0 per dollar over all user sites. The stock level for the selected item and location is increased by one unit and the subproblem is solved again for the end-equipment to find the next unit to be added to stock. Again, the associated stock level is increased. The procedure is continued unit by unit, and at each step a new point on the cost-effectiveness curve is established, with the A_0 value being the new operational availability given by equation (6) and the cost being the previous cumulative cost plus the unit price of the selected item. If the full cost-effectiveness curve is to be developed, the procedure terminates when no further increase in A_0 occurs; this is equivalent to zero values for D_{iu}, the mean supply response time, being attained for all items and locations. Alternatively, the process can be terminated when either a given A_0 or a spares investment goal is reached.

6. First success

Although the initial programming of the inventory model was accomplished in a relatively few days, checkout extended throughout April and May, 1977. For this purpose I extracted data for an equipment on the FFG class of ships consisting of 29 items organized in the parts breakdown shown in fig. 3. I assumed that the equipment itself was not subject to stockage and the six assemblies making up the equipment were reparable aboard the ship. The items at the bottom of the breakdown were all reparable but at depot level only. (They could be removed and replaced on the ship, with failed units being sent to the depot for repair.) The support system was assumed to be one ship and one depot.

On June 10, 1977, I was attending an informal conference with PMS-306 staff members. During coffee break, I retrieved the latest run from our terminal and was happy to see that the model had run all the way through for the first time. I could tell at a glance that the results were reasonable. Since the computation time was surprisingly short (1.25 CPU sec), I knew for the first time that the solution algo-

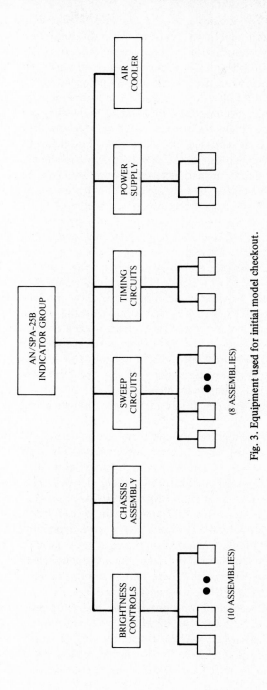

Fig. 3. Equipment used for initial model checkout.

rithm was practical. Returning to the conference, I announced something to the effect that "I have just obtained the first successful run of a general multi-indentured, multi-echelon model with an A_0 objective function." After a few minutes of explanation of the output, the discussion passed on to other subjects.

At the conference were two people vitally interested in the subject. They had been principals in the CNO-directed studies on fleet readiness issues and had the technical background to understand the model. These two highly qualified professionals became increasingly enthusiastic over the next several days with the potential of the model. They arranged for me to give a briefing to PMS-306 on June 15, 1977. In this briefing, I outlined the structure of the model and its solution procedure. A variety of significant and penetrating questions were raised, yet the general response was very favorable. It was agreed to test the model further with two relatively small equipments, a sea water pump and a portion of the UYK-7 computer (a general-purpose computer widely used for many shipboard functions). In retrospect, acceptance of the model at this point was a critical event with respect to possible implementation: a direction was established which was eventually to cause more funding for evaluation and improvement of the model, and for testing it in realistic situations.

The next few months were spent in collecting data on the two equipments and refining certain model routines. The first equipment, the sea water pump, consisted of a mix of 34 reparable and consumable items broken down into three indenture levels. The second equipment, the UYK-7 computer, consisted of 280 reparable and consumable items also broken down into three indenture levels. For both examples, a two-echelon support system consisting of 1 ship and 1 depot was assumed. Failure rates, unit costs, and other item characteristics were obtained from Navy files. Nominal values were assigned for resupply times, repair cycles, and other parameters.

The cost-effectiveness curves for the pump are given in fig. 4. Reading from the left, the first curve gives the expected operational availability of the pump as a function of total spares investment, with levels at both support echelons being calculated by the Optimal A_0 Inventory Model. The second curve was similarly derived but with shipboard levels being determined and fixed by current Navy policy, and depot stocks being calculated by the model. The third curve assumes depot stocks are determined by current policy with shipboard stocks being "optimally" determined. Finally, the point on the right gives the expected A_0 and investment for current Navy policies at both the ship and depot echelons.

Computational experience for these two examples was encouraging. The small pump case ran in 2.76 CPU sec to generate the optimal cost-effectiveness curve of which 1.13 CPU sec were used for input, output, and setup processes. The 280-item computer case ran in 9.55 CPU sec of which 6.90 sec were used for input, output, and setup. Both examples, as well as all applications discussed below, were run on an IBM 370-165 computer. However, in considering the run times for these early applications, it must be noted that the equipment indenturings were shallow (three

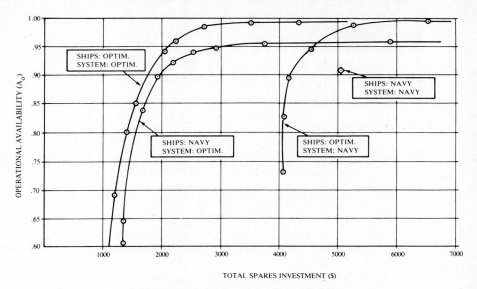

Fig. 4. Cost-effectiveness curve for the sea water pump.

levels) and the support system consisted of only two locations.

Final runs on the two examples were made in October, 1977 and the results were presented in a briefing for PMS-306 management on October 25, 1977. Reception was very favorable. The chart given in fig. 4, showing comparative cost-effectiveness results for the pump, and the similar results for the other example, attracted particular interest and received a fairly wide distribution afterwards. Those attending the briefing were experienced professionals in Navy logistics and had seen other glowing promises like those implicit in the charts (e.g., the new policy achieves the same A_0 as current policies at 40% of the cost). The general consensus, however, was that even after applying the most restrictive set of caveats, a potential existed for significant benefits. Some attendees could also discern in the model a first step towards an analytic solution of the long-outstanding problem of relating material support to fleet readiness.

In this meeting, the general subject of model validation was also covered. The main issues were how well does the model predict equipment availabilities as actually experienced in the field, and can the model in fact achieve the indicated improvements over current policies. Methods and data sources for resolving these issues were discussed. Citing several previous experiences with field tests and retrospective simulation, I indicated some of the problems involved including, in particular, the considerable time and expense required, distortions of results because of questionable and incomplete data, and the frequent domination of results by abnormal or nonrepresentative events and circumstances encountered in such exercises. I expressed the opinion that it was more important, at that time, to assess the computational characteristics of the model including its ability to cope with available data and real-world situations. It was thereupon decided to defer validation efforts until this assessment was made. Rather accidentally, however, one validation of sorts was in fact accomplished, as will be mentioned below.

7. Building momentum

In the October, 1977 briefing, "next steps" in the continued development and testing of the model were also recommended. Included were further evaluations with large and more complex equipments. By this time, however, a significant portion of the overall PMS-306 program had been contracted to another consulting firm. Since the model fell within the scope of its work, it was arranged that further efforts on the model would be under its contractual auspices on a multi-year funding basis. According to this arrangement, model improvements and evaluations continued through the rest of 1977 and all of 1978. The next equipment selected for testing was the steering system of the DD-1052 class of destroyers. Data was obtained from Navy files for 243 reparable and consumable items of the system, broken down into four indenture levels as shown in fig. 5. A two-echelon support system, consisting of 10 ships and a depot was assumed. As indicated in fig. 5, repair of higher assemblies was accomplished at ship or depot level. Again, nominal values were assigned for resupply times, repair cycles and other factors.

Results, in the form of a set of cost-effectiveness curves similar to those for the first examples, are shown in fig. 6. These results reinforced those of the previous cases in terms of demonstrating a potential for significant benefits. Computation time was still good — 26.39 CPU sec for the "optimal" case. In addition, a limited number of sensitivity analyses were conducted on key input parameters. As a follow-up, the boiler system of the DD-1052 class of ships was selected for further model evaluation. The system, consisting of 426 items, presented new problems to be overcome. The most important was the fact that many item failures would have little or no effect upon the operational availability of the boiler system. Although various degrees of performance degradation could occur, the boiler would not be completely inoperable, as assumed by the A_0 definition of the model. An analysis of this problem was conducted which included a classification of all items according to their failure effects upon system availability. More extensive sensitivity analyses of this system were also conducted [19].

During this time period, other model applications were also undertaken. One of the attendees at the November, 1977 briefing was a representative of the Naval Supply Systems Command (NAVSUP). This organization is responsible for directing the analyses and implementation of new inventory management policies and techniques in the Navy. Due to previous experiences with a model of similar characteristics implemented at the Aviation Supply Office in Philadelphia, this

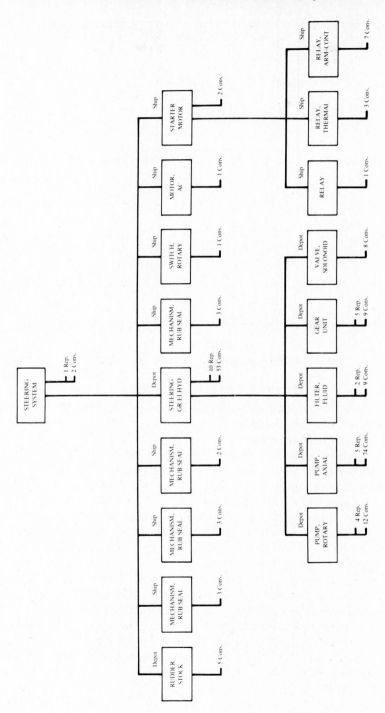

Fig. 5. Parts breakdown of the steering system.

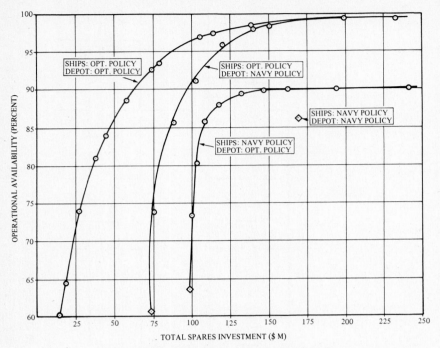

Fig. 6. Cost-effectiveness curves for the steering system.

NAVSUP representative was particularly interested in the Optimal A_0 Inventory Model. With his support, arrangements were made to apply the model to a new weapon system currently under procurement.

The new weapon was a very rapid firing gun, known as the PHALANX system, to be mounted on a large number of ships. This system presented additional complexities to be handled by the model. First, deliveries of the gun had been scheduled for installation over several years. Second, the ships involved can receive 1, 2 or 3 guns, thereby defining three classes of users with different sets of ship-board stocks. The main interest in applying the model was to provide estimates of multi-year funding requirements for spares in order to achieve a 90% operational availability goal.

Since LSEE, the larger model containing the Optimal A_0 Inventory Model, was already designed to consider such scenarios, little difficulty was encountered in applying the model to this problem. Levels were calculated on a snapshot basis at the end of each fiscal year according to the number of ships and gun installations in place at that time. Shipboard stock levels were computed for the first increment of ships in the three user classes and then applied to subsequent ships according to the phase-in schedule. System stock levels were carried over from year to year and augmented according to the additional number of ships to be supported. Each time, the solution algorithms of the model incremented stock levels until the 90% availability goal was reached. All in all, this model application went smoothly, in severe contrast to the next case that was encountered.

8. The trap

To further demonstrate the capabilities of the model, NAVSUP also arranged for a small project to apply the model to an important Navy equipment of considerable topical interest to several influential logistics management organizations. This equipment is the Fleet Satellite Communications System (FLTSATCOM) which is installed on a large number of ships for general communications purposes via satellite.

My colleague in the model applications was familiar with this system and the community of interest. He indicated that we were not ready for such a complex case and advised not accepting it because of the large number of items involved, data collection problems, and technical and other difficulties likely to occur. However, I viewed this as yet another challenge to the model's capabilities and was willing to get involved. It turned out that my colleague was correct about this project: the first data collection effort was abortive. When set up for a model run, it turned out that data for large portions of the equipment breakdown was missing, particularly for parts used only for repair of assemblies at depot-level facilities. However, data for the full equipment breakdown was soon obtained from other Navy files. Upon inspection of the raw data it became apparent that further processing and refinement were needed. Due to the number of items involved, I decided to program additional routines (referred to hereafter as the *Item Editor*) designed to check the consistency of several data elements that are interrelated in the parts breakdown. For example, the unit cost times the number of unit appearances was calculated and summed over all next-lower parts of an assembly and compared with the unit cost for the assembly as a whole. If order of magnitude differences occurred, as occasionally happened, the assembly was flagged on an output report as having missing items or containing errors in pricing data. Similar checks were included for expected failure rates. The editing that produced the largest problems, however, concerned Navy codes assigned to each item, (a) to designate the lowest maintenance echelon authorized to remove and replace the item and (b) to discard upon removal or else to designate the lowest maintenance level authorized to have complete repair capability for the item. These "level-of-repair" codes caused trouble in two ways. First, the Material Flow Model in LSEE was designed to operate with a simpler coding scheme and had to be revised to accommodate the Navy codes. Second, the edit process uncovered apparent inconsistencies in the codings that had to be resolved. For example, there were assemblies coded for discard upon failure but with repair parts listed beneath them in the parts breakdown. In another example, an assembly had all of its included parts authorized for removal and replacement at shipboard level but with the depot being given as the lowest level for complete repair. In general, these problems came from practices which assigned the maintenance codes on an individual item basis without full consideration of the parts-indenturing relationships within the equipment.

The full set of data for the FLTSATCOM system also brought another major problem. Altogether, there were 2,569 parts in the breakdown but only 1,530 unique items. There were 370 "common" items that appeared in more than one place in the parts breakdown. Some of these common items, such as resistors and condensers, appeared in dozens of places, but the average over all common items was about three appearances each.

Although the LSEE model was designed to handle such common items in terms of input processing, demand rate calculations, and other functions, the volume of items involved was now so large that a special pre-processor had to be constructed to set up the data in the form required by LSEE. Furthermore, a "quick fix" in the Optimal A_0 Inventory Model had to be made to accommodate common items which had not been considered in the original model design. Later, a more thorough investigation of common item problems in this kind of model was accomplished [35].

Several other problems of lesser difficulty were also encountered. Although most of the items had relatively low failure rates, a few were high enough to require several thousand units of stock at the depot level. To avoid excessive computation time, a minimum amount of stock was prepositioned at the depot for the six or so items involved, with additional amounts then being calculated by the model. Several program bugs were uncovered as caused by special features of the equipment and support system not previously exercised including, in particular, more indenture levels in the parts breakdown and more locations in the support system. The sheer size of the system, several times that of previous exercises, caused problems, especially with regard to computer turnaround time.

The FLTSATCOM system finally was broken down into five indenture levels, as indicated in fig. 7. The diagram also shows the mix of reparable and consumable items within the equipment, and locations of repair for lower-level assemblies. The five major components making up the system were assumed not to be subject to sparing in the support system. The support system consisted of 139 ships, each with one unit of the equipment, and one depot-level stockage and repair facility.

Results of the computation are given in fig. 8, with two points being given for current policies according to items being coded vital or nonvital, a factor considered in the Navy's shipboard stockage formulas. Computation time required for the optimal case was 8.5 min; the amount of core required was 920k bytes. This performance indicated that the FLTSATCOM system was about as large an equipment as could realistically be handled by the model in its current form and on the given computer.

Our report describing the system and giving results of the model was distributed

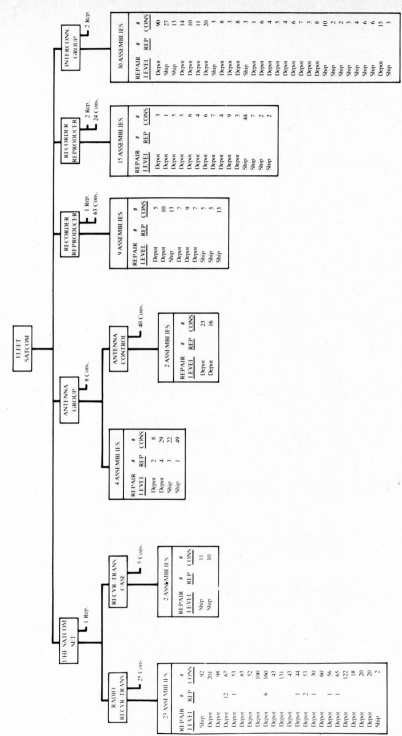

Fig. 7. Parts breakdown of the FLTSATCOM system.

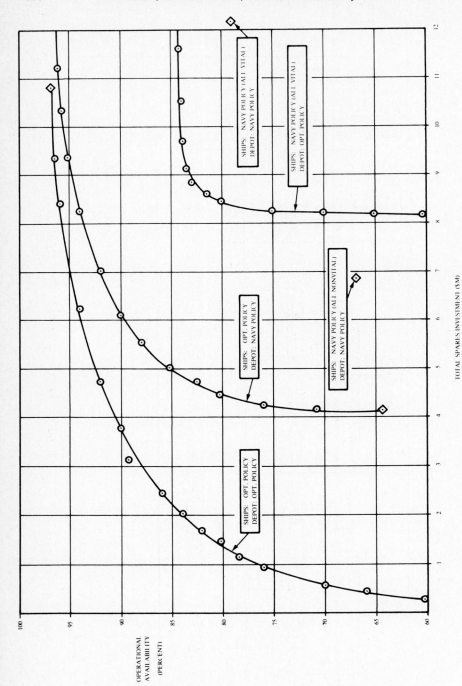

Fig. 8. Cost-effectiveness curves for the FLTSATCOM system.

by NAVSUP to several interested Navy organizations for review and comment. The most significant response was from OP-41, the Material Division of the Deputy Chief of Naval Operations for Logistics. This organization is responsible for making and establishing policies for supply management in the Navy, and its reaction was therefore of great interest.

The OP-41 critique of the model, as applied against the FLTSATCOM system, was received in October, 1978. The main interest of OP-41 was in shipboard stocks and comparative differences between levels calculated by the model and those given by the current shipboard stockage policy. Also, OP-41 had conducted a previous analysis of the FLTSATCOM system and had accumulated a history of observed failures and equipment downtimes against which the model results could be evaluated [171].

Aside from a variety of observations concerning particular items which involved data errors and, in some cases, apparent misunderstandings of the model's operation, the main thrust of the critique concerned the range of items stocked by the A_0 model versus that of the current policy. Of the 672 item candidates for shipboard stock, the Navy policy stocked 66 (9.8% of range), whereas the A_0 model would stock 426 items (63.4% of range). According to observed demands, only about 1% of the items stocked by the A_0 model would experience movement, whereas 3% of items stocked by current policy had one or more demands. It should be noted that the FLTSATCOM was an exceptionally reliable equipment according to observed demand, and uptime performance exceeds that of most other Navy electronic equipments. In fact, there were only 105 demands by 149 ships in 108 operating years. Due to its increased range, the A_0 model would have satisfied 90 of these demands (86%) in contrast with 57 (54%) for the policy actually used.

In the 1971—72 time frame, the General Accounting Office (GAO) conducted an audit and found that only 10—15% of parts on ships' allowances showed demands in a four-year period. Based on the GAO audit, the Office of the Secretary of Defense (OSD) provided budget guidance to the Navy, and CNO reduced the shipboard allowance criteria to severely restrict the range of items stocked. In its critique of the A_0 model, OP-41 cited this history and pointed out that the stock "movement" rates (percent of items stocked that have one or more demands during a given experience period) for both policies were much lower than the 10—15% rate for which GAO had criticized the Navy, but that the movement rate for the current Navy policy with greatly reduced range was three times that of the A_0 model. *Though the A_0 model stockages were cheaper for a given A_0 (the model stocks a wide range of inexpensive items) and satisfied more demands, it was felt that the increased range and low movement rate would jeopardize fundings in view of pressure generated from the GAO audit.*

From this critique, it is clear that OP-41 was faced with two conflicting stockage criteria for shipboard stocks. One criterion, implicitly set by GAO, was to increase the movement rate according to "good business practices". The other, set by CNO in its previous study directives and other policy statements, was to maximize expected operational availability of equipments and fleet readiness for a given investment. This criterion could only be obtained through increased range with concomitant reductions in movement rates. Despite this conflict, OP-41 did not raise significant barriers to continued research and development work on the A_0 model. However, a possible obstacle was raised, against eventual implementation. Convincing evidence would have to be developed to counter the arguments of OP-41 before any large-scale implementation of the model could be contemplated.

9. A New Path

In November, 1978 it was decided to restructure and reprogram the LSEE model and include the Optimal A_0 Inventory Model into a so-called "production" version (not to be confused with a version designed for actual implementation in the Navy inventory management system). The reason for this effort was that the existing models had been more or less patched together in a "bread-board" fashion, and consequently, could only handle a few equipments at a time. The objective of the new version is to provide a capability to generate A_0 cost-effectiveness curves and associated stock levels for thousands of equipments and ship systems in an efficient manner. Also, and perhaps more important, redesign would give us an opportunity to include additional features and capabilities suggested by the previous studies and reviews. In addition, I anticipate significant reductions in computer resource requirements due to more efficient programming. Furthermore, since the new model is being designed to facilitate the extraction of needed data directly from Navy files, much of the tedious manual work previously required for data preparation can be avoided. The new model will also provide a foundation for the final step: relating supply investments to fleet readiness, the original CNO goal. Heretofore, only individual equipments have been treated with respect to relating supply investment to operational readiness. Now whole ships and fleets of ships may be considered.

Anticipating this need, a technique referred to as the "A_0 Allocation Model" has been formulated [33]. The objective of this model is to allocate goals for overall ship availability for mission requirements to corresponding availability targets for individual equipments in a most cost-effective way. The model formulation considers the multiple missions normally assigned to ships, each with a particular set of equipments that must be operational. Also, reliability interdependencies of equipments are considered, such as cases where operation of certain equipments requires the simultaneous operation of other equipments or situations where various kinds of redundancies are present in multiple installations of an equipment or equipments of overlapping functions. Once overall availability goals for ship performance against mission requirements are allocated to individual equipments by this model, spares and corresponding investments needed to achieve the equipment availability targets can be derived by the Optimal A_0 Inventory Model. Although further development of the A_0 Allocation Model is not included in our current program, the production version of the A_0 Inventory Model is being designed to accommodate this larger objective at a later time.

10. Epilogue

Two years have now passed since the inception of the Optimal A_0 Inventory Model. It is nowhere near the point of actually being used to control inventories. If it seems strange that implementation should take so long, it must be remembered that any multi-indentured, multi-echelon inventory model is, by definition, relatively complicated, encompasing the functional responsibilities of many separate organizations. Previous experience in the military services with similar models indicates that 4–5 years are required to achieve even limited implementation.

Our general strategy is to make the model available to managers of new equipment procurements who have overall responsibility for determining initial logistics support requirements. At least, the model can be used for budget estimate purposes and a variety of support performance analyses. At best, initial stockages can be procured in accordance with stock levels determined by the model. As familiarity with the model and its capabilities increases, it may be accepted for use in support of established equipments as well as new ones.

Use of the model is also anticipated in the manner originally contemplated by the CNO study directives for relating supply support to fleet readiness. If development continues as planned, a tool should become available for general practical use in determining and defending budget requests for supply support that are commensurate with equipment availability and readiness goals. This should provide a way to demonstrate that stockages of technical spares in the services should not be made to conform with so-called "good business practices" concerning movement, or stock-turnover rates, or other such performance measures. It is easy to see that the Optimal A_0 Inventory Model can achieve any movement rate desired merely by controlling the range of stockage candidates. At the extreme, only the equipment itself can be considered as a stockage candidate, thereby achieving a 100% movement rate. By limiting stockages to higher level assemblies within the equipment, lesser but still high movement rates will occur. Continuing down the parts breakdown in terms of inclusion as stockage candidates, keeping in mind repair capabilities and inventory management constraints, we should be able to use the model to plot stockage investment as a function of range or movement rate for a given equipment availability target. In this way, it should be possible to determine some kind of an "optimal" movement rate.

Turning to the question originally raised as to how advanced inventory models can be implemented, I cannot provide any comprehensive answer on the basis of my experiences with this project. Yet, I think the history of the project points out some of the important ingredients of a successful implementation program, at least to the extent of getting it off the ground.

First, and most important, there must be a manager with funding resources who is chartered to take innovative actions against significant problems in this area and who is willing to invest in research on new techniques. The PMS-306 Project Manager has admirably filled this role in the current project. In addition, such a manager must be supported by technical expertise to judge the worthiness and viability of the proposed inventory model. Specialists on the PMS-306 staff have provided this capability in the current project. Without their extensive experience, interest and support, the project could not even have been initiated. They have provided invaluable assistance in establishing the overall direction of the project.

Second, the development team should include someone who is intimately familiar with the environment in which the model is to be used and who can maintain continual liaison with the organizations and managers who are involved and affected. I have been fortunate in having associates on the current project who have fulfilled this role as well as providing significant contributions to the model development.

Third, the general attitude of the development team is important. There must be a willingness to do everything that must be done, including tedious data preparation, endless struggles in getting computer programs to work properly, preparing reports and briefing materials, and all other necessary tasks. Problems must be faced as they occur and solutions found, compromising theoretical niceties as may be required. Above all, there must be a complete responsiveness to customer needs and interests.

For me, forthcoming events in the continued development and use of the Optimal A_0 Inventory Model will be of great interest. The model was explicitly designed for practical use and implementation rather than as a theoretical exercise. The extent to which this goal is reached remains to be seen.

TIMS Studies in the Management Sciences 16 (1981) 331–352
© North-Holland Publishing Company

POLICY STRUCTURE IN MULTI-STATE PRODUCTION/INVENTORY PROBLEMS: AN APPLICATION OF CONVEX ANALYSIS

Uday S. KARMARKAR

University of Rochester

Certain production and inventory models with stochastic demand have a common mathematical formulation which can be exploited by analyzing the common formulation to draw conclusions that then apply to any specific examples. In examining multi-location inventory problems with this form, it is shown, using convex analysis, that the optimal policy has a certain structure which can be characterized constructively. The application of these and other results to specific problems is discussed. Examples drawn from the literature include reparable inventory, multi-process production, and multi-location inventory problems.

1. Introduction

Consider the following formulation of the one-period, n-location distribution problem (Karmarkar and Patel [115]):

$$\inf \sum_{i=1}^{n} C_i Z_i + \sum\sum_{j \neq i} c_{ij} z_{ij} + \sum_{i=1}^{n} l_i(y_i),$$

$$\text{s.t. } Z_i - \sum_{j \neq i} z_{ij} + \sum_{j \neq i} z_{ji} = y_i - x_i, \qquad \text{for } i = 1, 2, ..., n,$$

$$Z_i, z_{ij} \geq 0, \qquad i, j, = 1, 2, ..., n,$$

where:

x_i = initial stock at location i,

y_i = target stock at location i,

Z_i = exogenous supply to location i at cost of \$ C_i/unit,

z_{ij} = transfer from i to j at \$ c_{ij}/unit, and

$l_i(y_i)$ = the (convex) expected costs of holding inventory and shortage at the ith location given a stock level y_i (see section 2 on the Newsboy problem).

This model was analyzed in [115] to show that optimal policies have a certain structure. It was shown in [112] that the same type of policy structure is obtained in a more general formulation:

$$v(x) = \inf c \cdot z + L(y),$$

$$\text{s.t. } Az = y - x, \qquad z \geq 0.$$

Here the n-vector x can be thought of as the initial state of a system; the state can be altered by activities in the m-vector z, so as to move to a new state $y = x + Az$. The matrix $A(n \times m)$ indicates how the activities z act to change the state. The cost of undertaking activities in z is given by the cost vector c. Finally, choosing state y results in certain (expected) costs, given by the function $L(y)$, which is assumed to be closed (lower semicontinuous) and convex.

In the multi-period case of the multi-location inventory model described, above, with backorders, the initial stock in any period is the "target" stock in the previous period less the demand observed in that period: $x_i^{t-1} = y_i^t - \tilde{d}_i^t$, where $\tilde{d}_i^t$ is the (random) demand at location i in period t. The initial stock in period t is thus a random variable conditioned on previous decisions and demands. More generally, the initial stock x may be some random function of the previous period's target stock y and demand $\tilde{d}$; i.e., $x = w(y, \tilde{d})$. Given such a transition law we can write each period of a multi-period problem as

$$v^t(x) = \inf_{y,z} \{c^t \cdot z + L^t(y) + \rho E v^{t-1}(w(y, \tilde{d}^t))\},$$

$$\text{s.t. } A^t z = y - x, \qquad z \geq 0.$$

The convention of numbering periods backwards is being used here. This problem has been studied by Karmarkar [114]. It will be seen that the analysis described later in the paper depends heavily on convexity of the objective function — in particular on convexity of $L(\cdot)$ and the perturbation functions $v^t(\cdot)$. For certain choices of the transition law, $w(\cdot)$, these convexity properties are preserved, and the multi-period problem (MP) has essentially the same form in each period as the problem (P). For example, in the n-location inventory problem above, the transition law arising from the case of backordering preserves convexity (a sufficient condition is given in P.5 in section 5). Thus the optimal policy has the same qualitative form. More specific results are derived in [114] for the multi-location inventory case.

This general model, while including the multi-location inventory problem, also encompasses many other formulations of stochastic multi-variate (multi-facility) production and inventory problems. Thus, results from the analysis of the general formulation carry over to the particular cases. Small (two-dimensional) problems, particularly in the one-period case, can often be analyzed completely and the optimal policy characterized for all starting conditions. The duality and optimality analyses transfer directly to particular cases and will indicate conditions for the problem to have a well-behaved solution. The results on the form of the optimal policy hold for single and multi-period problems although details of the form usually have to be analyzed for each case.

Finally, the infinite horizon stationary problem has been studied for the multi-location inventory case by Karmarkar [113] and in an investment-consumption setting by Abrams and Karmarkar [2]. These results can be used to establish the existence of optimal or ϵ-optimal stationary policies of the same form as the one-period and multi-period models. In some cases, more detailed results on the parameters of the policy can be obtained.

2. A preview of the analysis

The methodology used to investigate the problem formulated in (P) is a direct application of convex analysis (Rockafellar [189]). The approach produces primarily qualitative results: Firstly, the analysis of the general problem provides the appropriate duality and optimality framework for this class of problems. Secondly, the analysis leads to a characterization of optimal policy structure that is constructive and geometrically intuitive. Computationally, the approach does suggest some numerical procedures, especially for the one-period case. For example, a five-location one-period inventory problem is solved efficiently in Karmarkar and Patel [115]. However, the multi-period problem seems hard to solve in general. What the qualitative characterization of the optimal policy structure can do is to give clues on how the problem may be solved or at least approximated.

The well known "Newsboy" problem provides a convenient illustration of the kind of results that can be expected in terms of policy structure. The major ideas of the general analysis are captured in this problem. We shall examine the Newsboy problem with disposal; it can be written as follows:

$$v(x) = \min c^+ z^+ + c^- z^- + l(y),$$

$$\text{s.t. } z^+ - z^- = y - x,$$

$$z^+, z^- \geq 0.$$

where

$$l(y) = h \int_0^y (y - D) \, dF(D) + p \int_y^\infty (D - y) \, dF(D),$$

h = unit cost of holding or excess stocks (\$/unit) ,
p = unit cost of shortage (\$/unit) ,
D = (random) demand ,
$F(D)$ = c.d.f. of demand,
y = quantity stocked to meet demand,
x = initial stock available,
z^+ = quantity ordered (stock increase),
z^- = quantity disposed of (stock decrease),
c^+ = variable cost of ordering (\$/unit), and
c^- = variable cost of disposal (\$/unit).

It is well known that $l(y)$ is a convex function and that the optimal policy can be stated in terms of the stock levels y^* and y_*, such that

$$\left. \frac{dl}{dy} \right|_{y=y_*} = c^- ,$$

$$\left. \frac{dl}{dy} \right|_{y=y_*} = -c^+ .$$

The optimal policy is:

do nothing for $y_* \leqslant x \leqslant y^*$,

order $(y_* - x)$ if $x < y_*$

dispose of $(x - y^*)$ if $x > y^*$.

This policy structure is shown in fig. 1(A). It is natural to think of the policy in terms of the two critical numbers, y_* and y^*. However, a more "correct" view that generalizes to larger problems sees the structure as a "do-nothing" region of no transactions (RNT), with cones attached to the boundary points such that it is always optimal to move to the vertices of these cones. We also see that the optimal value function $v(x)$ is convex, equal to $l(\cdot)$ in the RNT and is (piecewise) linear on the cones attached to the RNT with slopes $-c^+$ and c^-. Finally note that we can write the problem as

$$v(x) = \min C(y - x) + l(y) ,$$

where the function C, shown in fig. 1(B), is given by

$$C(u) = \begin{cases} c^+ u, & u \geqslant 0 , \\ -c^- u, & u > 0 . \end{cases}$$

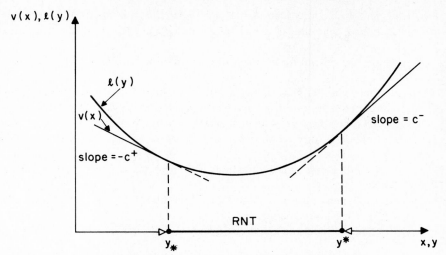

Fig. 1(A). "Newsboy" problem: $l(y)$, $v(x)$ and optimal policy.

This is a piecewise linear, positive homogeneous function, which captures the costs of changing the state (stock level) in the problem. Note that the RNT is that set of stock levels, y, where the slope of $l(y)$ (i.e., the marginal benefit from changing stock levels) lies between $-c^+$ and c^- (does not justify the cost of changing the stock level).

All these ideas generalize to the problem (P): The essential ingredients are a convex loss function, $l(\cdot)$, and a linear transfer/transaction structure with proportional costs.

The Newsboy problem rarely appears in a realistic context in its pristine form. Rather its analysis serves to provide intuition about good stocking policies and about concepts like safety stocks. The problem can also appear as a subproblem in

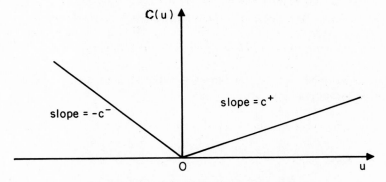

Fig. 1(B). Ordering and disposal cost function.

more realistic formulations such as the (s, S) and (Q, r) models. In the same way, it may be hoped that similar useful intuitions will appear with regard to other problems.

To reiterate, the general formulation and analysis discussed here will:

(1) Provide a unifying framework for a variety of different stochastic, multivariate, production-inventory problems that have appeared in the literature.
(2) Suggest a way to formulate and analyze new research problems.
(3) List some basic duality, optimality, and existence results that apply to these problems.
(4) Provide a constructive characterization of the optimal policy in such problems; and thereby possibly
(5) Lead to some new intuitions about "good" realistic policies for these problems; and finally at least on occasion
(6) Suggest computational tools that could be useful in certain cases.

In the next section we describe some problems that are encompassed by the formulation (P). Section 4 describes how the results for the general problem can be applied to one-period versions of some of the problems; the multi-period and infinite horizon cases are discussed briefly. In each case the results are cited without proof. Some of the examples below are drawn from the recent literature; others are designed to show how certain variations on standard problems can be fitted within the scheme of (P).

3. Examples

In the following formulations, the time superscript will be dropped for convenience, except when indicating how the transition to the succeeding period is made. The first two examples are intended to show how variations on standard problems can be accommodated in the given format. One-location examples are used for simplicity; the extension to multi-location cases is straightforward.

3.1. One-location inventory problem with constrained supply

This can be imbedded in a two-location redistribution problem with demand occurring at location 1 only:

$$\min c_{21}z_{21} + l_1(y_1) + l_2(y_2),$$

$$\text{s.t.} \, z_{21} = y_1 - x_1,$$

$$-z_{21} = y_2 - x_2,$$

$$y_1, y_2, z_{21} \geqslant 0 \,,$$

where:

z_{21} = the order quantity,

$l_1(y_1)$ = the expected shortage and holding costs at the location, and

$l_2(y_2)$ = a dummy loss function which is identically zero over its domain.

The transition law from one period to the next is depletion at location 1, while location 2 always moves to Q. The solution can be obtained for all values of $x = (x_1, x_2)$; to get the solution to the original problem we simply examine the cases for which $x_2 = Q$, the available supply quantity.

3.2. One-location problem with variable ordering costs

In a one-location problem, suppose that up to Q units can be ordered at a cost c_2 while any units ordered in excess of Q cost c_1 with $c_1 > c_2$. The problem is formulated in a manner analogous to example 1, with a dummy location 2 serving to represent orders of Q or less:

$$\min c_1 z_1 + c_2 z_{21} + l_1(y_1) + l_2(y_2) \,,$$

$$\text{s.t. } z_1 + z_{21} = y_1 - x_1 \,,$$

$$-z_{21} = y_2 - x_2 \,,$$

$$y_2, z_1, z_{21} \geqslant 0 \,.$$

Here $l_1(y_1)$ and $l_2(y_2)$ are as in the previous example; z_{21} represents orders of Q or less and Z_1 represents the excess ordered over Q. The solution is examined for the special cases where $x_2 = Q$. The transition law is the same as the previous example.

The next three examples are drawn from the literature on stochastic production-inventory problems.

3.3. Reparable inventory (Simpson [217])

In this problem, an inventory of unrepaired but reparable items is maintained in addition to the stock of serviceable items that can be used immediately. The reparables can be made serviceable at some cost, or may be junked. Serviceable units can also be purchased directly. In each period there is some demand for serviceable units and some items are returned into the reparable stock; in general, the demand and returns are correlated. The one-period problem can be formulated as follows:

$$v(x) = \min c_1 z_1 + c_2 z_2 + l_1(y_1) + l_2(y_2) \,,$$

$$\text{s.t. } z_1 + z_2 = y_1 - x_1 \, ,$$

$$-z_2 - z_3 = y_2 - x_2 \, ,$$

$$z_i, y_i \geqslant 0 \, ,$$

where:

z_1 = serviceable units purchased,
z_2 = units repaired,
z_3 = unrepaired units junked,
x_1, y_1 = initial and target stocks of serviceables,
x_2, y_2 = initial and target stocks of reparables,
$l_1(y_1)$ = expected shortage (backorder) and holding costs of serviceables, and
$l_2(y_2)$ = $k_2 \cdot y_2$ = costs of holding reparables.

The transition law is given by

$$x_1^{t-1} = y_1^t - \tilde{d}_1^t \, ,$$

$$x_2^{t-1} = y_2^t + \tilde{d}_2^t \, ,$$

where $\tilde{d}_1$ = demand for serviceables, and $\tilde{d}_2$ = return of reparables.

In the multi-period case, the objective function in period t has the added term $\rho E v^{t-1}(y_1 - \tilde{d}_1, y_2 + \tilde{d}_2)$, where the expectation is with respect to the joint probability and v^{t-1} is the value (perturbation) function in the subsequent period.

3.4. Multi-product, multi-process production (Deuermeyer and Pierskalla [55])

There are two products (1 and 2) and two processes (A and B) such that process A results in both products while process B results only in product 2. The one-period problem, assuming backlogging, is formulated as

$$v(x) = \min c_A z_A + c_B z_B + l_1(y_1) + l_2(y_2) \, ,$$

$$\text{s.t.} \quad a_{1A} z_A = y_1 - x_1 \, ,$$

$$a_{2A} z_A + a_{2B} z_B = y_2 - x_2 \, ,$$

$$z_A, z_B \geqslant 0 \, .$$

Here:

z_A, z_B = production levels of processes A and B,
a_{1A}, a_{2A}, a_{2B} = production rates of 1 and 2 from processes A and B,
$l_i(y_i)$ = expected holding and backorder costs for product i, and

x_i, y_i = initial and target stock levels for product i.

The transition between periods involves depletion of inventories exactly as in the multi-location inventory problem. In the multi-period case, the term $\rho E v^{t-1}(y - \tilde{d})$ is added in the objective function as in (MP) and the preceding example.

3.5. Stochastic production smoothing problem (Beckman [13], Sobel [227])

This is a single commodity problem in which costs are incurred for changing production levels from period to period. Let x_1 = starting inventory in period t, x_2 = last period's production level. The production level in the current period is y_2 and z_1, z_2 represent, respectively, the increase or decrease from the previous period with c_1 and c_2 the costs of changing production levels. The one-period problem can be stated as

$$v(x) = \min c_1 z_1 + c_2 z_2 + L(y_1, y_2),$$

$$\text{s.t.} \qquad 0 = y_1 - x_1,$$

$$z_1 - z_2 = y_2 - x_2,$$

$$y_2, z_1, z_2 \geqslant 0.$$

Here

$$L(y_1, y_2) = C y_2 + E g(y_1 + y_2, \tilde{d}),$$

C is a variable cost of production and the function g represents shortage and holding costs given total available stock and demand d. There may be an additional term in L representing the salvage value of units in excess and the costs of stopping production. The transition to the next period is represented by

$$x_1^{t-1} = y_1^t + y_2^t - \tilde{d}^t$$

$$x_2^{t-1} = y_2^t.$$

The multi-period problem can be formulated as in (MP) or the examples above.

3.6. Other examples

The formulation given here also encompasses or is related to several other production and inventory problems such as the multi-product production problem of Evans [68], the stochastic transportation model of Elmaghraby [61], the multi-product inventory model of Veinott [235], the purchase and redistribution, multi-location models of Das [50] and Showers [213] and the multi-echelon models of Bessler and Veinott [15], Ignall and Veinott [106], and Iglehart and Lalchandani [105]. The model is also related to problems in other areas such as cash management (Eppen and Fama [64]), multi-asset investment-consumption (Abrams and Karmarkar [1]), and economic growth (Brock and Mirman [23]).

4. Analysis of the one-period problem

The one-period problem is important because its analysis is usually straightforward and provides clues for the analysis of multi-period problems. Since the multi-period problem can be written, via dynamic programming, as a sequence of one-period problems, some of the results carry over. We will discuss here a few of the more intuitive results from the analysis of the general problem; a detailed account is given by Karmarkar [112,114] and Abrams and Karmarkar [1].

Given the problem in the form

(P) $v(x) = \inf cz + L(y)$,

s.t. $Az = y - x$,

$z \geqslant 0$.

we can rewrite it in "unconstrained" form as

(UP) $\phi(x) = \inf_{y} C(y - x) + L(y)$,

where C is the perturbation function of the linear problem (LP):

(LP) $C(u) = \inf\{cz \mid Az = u, z \geqslant 0\}$.

                $= \sup\{\pi u \mid \pi A \leqslant c\}$.

Define the problem:

(CP) $-Lv(-\pi) = \inf_{y}\{\pi y + L(y)\}$.

Here L^* is the convex conjugate function of L. The problem can be thought of as determining the optimal target vector y given a marginal cost π of changing the state. In one-period problems, L^* can often be written in closed form (Karmarkar [114]). The dual to the original problem can be written in terms of L^* by direct application of Fenchel's Duality Theorem (Rockafellar [189])

(D) $\qquad d(x) = \sup\limits_{\pi} -L^*(-\pi) - \pi x,$

$\qquad$ s.t. $\pi A \leqslant c$.

We can also think of CP as determining the point at which L has the (sub)gradient-π. A *subgradient* of a convex function $f(y)$ at a point $\bar{y}$ in its effective domain, is any vector λ such that for any other y, $f(y) \geqslant f(\bar{y}) + \lambda(y - \bar{y})$. There may in general be more than one subgradient to a convex function at a point; differentiability corresponds to there being a unique subgradient. Define the set D as all vectors π for which CP is bounded. The set $-D$ is the effective domain of L^*. Also define D' as the set of π satisfying $\pi A \leqslant c$. The following condition (Rockafellar [189]) indicates when the problem (P) is well behaved; here int D indicates the interior of the set D.

Proposition 1. Suppose that

$\qquad$ int $D \cap$ int $D' \neq \phi,$

then (i) there is no duality gap; $d(x) = v(x)$; (ii) the optimum in (P) is attained.

$\qquad$ This condition roughly means that the sets D and D' should overlap sufficiently. For example it is not satisfied if the sets (in two dimensions, say) only touch at a point or along a line. The condition can be weakened to read

$\qquad$ r.i. $D \cap$ r.i $D' \neq \phi$

where r.i. D denotes the relative interior of the set D. The *relative interior* of a set is the interior relative to the affine hull of the set. The *affine hull* in turn, is the set produced by taking all linear (not convex) combinations $\lambda x + (1 - \lambda)y, \lambda \geqslant 0$ of any two x and y in the set. (See Rockafellar [189] for a complete exposition.) Interestingly, while the condition in P.1 suffices for most of the examples given, the weaker form is needed in example 5. Hereafter assume that this condition is satisfied. Note that the condition does not depend on the starting state x. When the problem has a solution it can be characterized as follows.

Proposition 2. (π^0, y^0) solve (P) and (D) if π^0 solves the (LP) dual for $u = y^0 - x$ and y^0 solves (CP) for $\pi = \pi^0$.

This result can be used to characterize the form of the optimal policy to the problem (P). First define the normal cone to D', the dual feasible region in the (LP) at any $\bar{\pi}$,

$\qquad K(\bar{\pi}) = \{u \,|\, \bar{\pi}u \geqslant \pi u \text{ for any } \pi \in D'\}$.

Thus $K(\pi)$ consists of those vectors u for which $\bar{\pi}$ is optimal in the dual of (LP). Now the optimal policy can be constructively characterized. We can think of the optimal policy as consisting of a region of no transactions (RNT) such that it is optimal to do nothing when x is in RNT; furthermore, each point in the RNT is the vertex of a cone such that for any starting position in the cone it is optimal to move to the vertex. The RNT and the associated cones are described in the next proposition.

Proposition 3. For any π^0 in $D' \cap D$, solve (CP) for $\pi = \pi^0$. If a solution y^0 is obtained then y^0 is in the RNT. In fact, the RNT is the union of all such y^0. Furthermore, each such y^0 is also optimal for any x such that $(y^0 - x) \in K(\pi^0)$.

Some facts about the perturbation function or value function $v(x)$ are summarized next.

Proposition 4.
(i) $v(x)$ is a closed convex function.
(ii) If π^0 is optimal in (D) then $-\pi^0$ is a (sub)gradient of v at x.
(iii) If (π^0, y^0) are optimal in P for some x, then v is linear on $\{x | x = y^0 - k, k \in K(\pi^0)\}$ with (sub)gradient $-\pi^0$.
(iv) If L is differentiable everywhere then v is differentiable. If L is differentiable at $y^0 \in$ RNT, then v is differentiable at all x for which y^0 is optimal.

It can be shown that if L is differentiable everywhere, then v is too (Karmarkar [114]). In this case in parts (ii) and (iii) above $-\pi^0$ is the gradient of v.

We now discuss the application of these results to some of the examples described in §3.

Example 2 (one-location problem, variable ordering costs)
    The dual to (LP) can be written as

$$C(y_1 - x_1) = \max \pi_1 (y_1 - x_1) + \pi_2 (y_2 - x_2),$$

$$\text{s.t. } \pi_1 \leqslant c_1,$$

$$\pi_1 - \pi_2 \leqslant c_2.$$

The feasible region can be plotted as in fig. 2 for $c_1 > c_2$. The problem CP decouples as

(CP_1) $-l_1^*(-\pi_1) = \inf\limits_{y_1} \{\pi_1 y_1 + l_1(y_1)\}$,

(CP_2) $-l_2^*(-\pi_2) = \inf\limits_{y_2 \geqslant 0} \{\pi_2 y_2 + l_2(y_2)\} = \inf\limits_{y_2 \geqslant 0} \pi_2 y_2$.

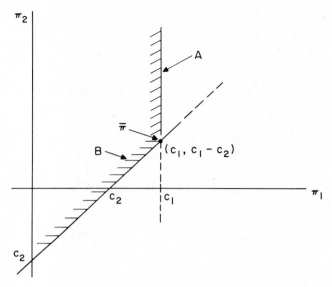

Fig. 2. LP dual region for example 2.

The set D is thus the product of sets D_1 and D_2, where $D_1 = \{\pi_1 | -h \leqslant \pi_1 \leqslant p\}$ with h the cost of holding stock, p the cost of shortage and $D_2 = \{\pi_2 | \pi_2 \geqslant 0\}$.

We can see that for proposition 1 to apply, it is sufficient that $0 < c_1 < p$. We can now use proposition 3 to generate the optimal policy for all starting stock levels. As an example consider the point $\bar{\pi} = (c_1, c_1, -c_2)$ in $D \cap D'$. Using this in CP_1 and CP_2, we get $y_1^* (c_1)$ as the solution to $F(y_1) = [(p - c_1)/(h + p)]$ in the usual way, state space (fig. 3). To determine all the starting states for which this is optimal, we determine $K(\bar{\pi})$, the normal cone to D' at $\bar{\pi}$. We can see from fig. 2 that $K(\bar{\pi})$ is the cone bounded by the rays generated by the normals to the two linear dual constraints: $(1, 0)$ and $(1, -1)$. Since $\bar{y} - x$ must be in $K(\bar{\pi})$, x must be in the set $\bar{y} - K(\bar{\pi})$. This is shown in fig. 3, which represents starting states (x_1, x_2) as well as optimal states (y_1, y_2).

Applying the same procedure to the line segment B produces the line B' in fig. 3, with the normal cone being generated by $(1, -1)$ only. The line segment A maps entirely into the point $\bar{y}$. Finally, whenever $\pi_2 = 0$, the set of optimal y_2 is simply all the nonnegative y_2. The complete policy is shown in fig. 3; when the lower cost c_2 is only available for Q units, we examine the special case of starting stock $x_1 = Q$ to get the optimal policy as follows. The optimal policy has four regions:

(1) If $x_1 \leqslant y_1^*(c_1) - Q$, order Q units at price c_2 and $(y_1^* - x_1 + Q)$ at c_1.
(2) If $y_1^*(c_1) - Q \leqslant x_1 \leqslant y_1^*(c_2) - Q$, order Q units at price c_2.
(3) If $y_1^*(c_2) - Q \leqslant x_1 \leqslant y_1^*(c_2)$ order up to $y_1^*(c_2)$ at price c_2.
(4) If $x_1 \geqslant y_1^*(c_2)$, do nothing.

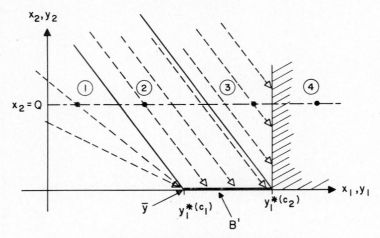

Fig. 3. Optimal policy for example 2.

These four regions are shown in fig. 3, where the dashed lines show how the stock levels are changed. That is, in each region from any point lying on one of the lines, it is optimal to move to the point shown by the arrowhead. The line segment B', together with the shaded region, constitutes the RNT.

Example 3 (reparable inventory)
    The LP dual is written

$$\max \pi_1(y_1 - x_1) + \pi_2(y_2 - x_2),$$

$$\text{s.t. } \pi_1 \geqslant c_1,$$

$$\pi_1 - \pi_2 \leqslant c_2,$$

$$\pi_2 \geqslant 0.$$

The feasible region is sketched in fig. 4 for $c_1 > c_2$.
    Again for the one-period problem, (CP) decouples to

(CP$_1$) $-l_1^*(y_1) = \inf_{y_1 \geqslant 0} \pi_1 y_1 + l_1(y_1),$

(CP$_2$) $-l_2^*(y_2) = \inf_{y_2 \geqslant 0} \pi_1 y_2 + h_2 y_2.$

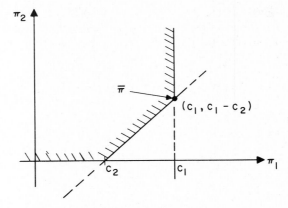

Fig. 4. LP dual region for example 3.

These problems are bounded for $\pi_1 \geqslant -h_1$, the holding cost for serviceables and $\pi_2 \geqslant h_2$ the holding cost for reparables. Furthermore, if reparables are to be held at all, $\pi_1 < p_1$, the shortage of reparables.

Considering $\bar{\pi} = (c_1, c_1 - c_2), p_1 > c_1 > h_1$, we can solve (CP$_1$) and to get $y_1^*(C_1)$ while $y_2^* = 0$. $K(\bar{\pi})$ is bounded by the rays generated by $(1, 0)$ and $(1, -1)$ as in the previous example. Continuing this process for π which are dual feasible, we get the policy shown in fig. 5. Once more, the dashed lines show the directions in which

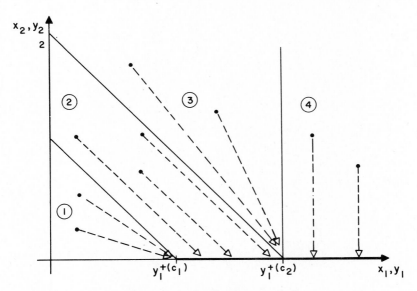

Fig. 5. Optimal policy for example 3.

stock levels must be changed. For example, in region 1, it is optimal to move to $y_1^*(c_1)$ by repairing all reparables and ordering additional serviceable stock. Region 2 represents repairing all reparables and no ordering. Region 4 is disposal of all reparables. The RNT is the x_1, y_1 axis to the right of $y_1^*(c_1)$.

Note that in the one-period case, it is never worth holding reparables. However, this changes in the multi-period case due to the future usefulness of reparables.

Example 4 (multi-product, multi-process)

The LP dual feasible region is given by

$$a_{1A}\pi_1 + a_{2A}\pi_2 \leqslant c_A ,$$
$$a_{2B}\pi_2 \leqslant c_B .$$

This is illustrated in fig. 6. For the point

$$\bar{\pi} = \left(\frac{c_A - a_{2A}(c_B/a_{2B})}{a_{1A}} , \frac{c_B}{a_{2B}} \right)$$

to have some significance, we assume that its first component satisfies $-h_1 < \bar{\pi}_1 < p_1$ and its second satisfies $-h_2 < \bar{\pi}_2 < p_2$, where h_i and p_i are, respectively, costs of holding and shortage for the two products. Following the procedure described above yields the picture of the optimal policy displayed in [55].

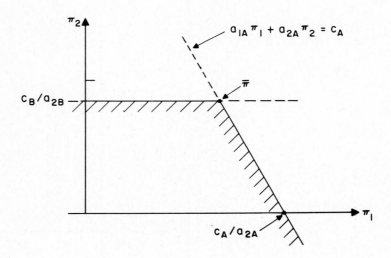

Fig. 6. LP dual region for example 4.

Example 5

The LP dual is

$$\max \pi_1(y_1 - x_1) + \pi_2(y_2 - x_2),$$

$$\text{s.t. } \pi_2 \leqslant c_1,$$

$$-\pi_2 \leqslant c_2.$$

The problem (CP) does not decouple in this case.

$$\text{(CP)} \qquad -L^*(-\pi) = \inf_{y_1, y_2 \geqslant 0} \{\pi_1 y_1 + (\pi_2 + C)y_2 + Eg(y_1 + y_2, \tilde{d})\}.$$

If we take g to be the usual piecewise linear excess and shortage cost function, we have

$$\nabla L = ((h + p)F(y_1 + y_2) - p, \ C + (h + p)F(y_1 + y_2) - p).$$

Boundedness in (CP) thus requires that $-h \leqslant \pi_1 \leqslant p$ and $-C - h \leqslant \pi_2 \leqslant p - C$. The feasible region for the dual is shown in fig. 7. The components of ∇L are not inde-

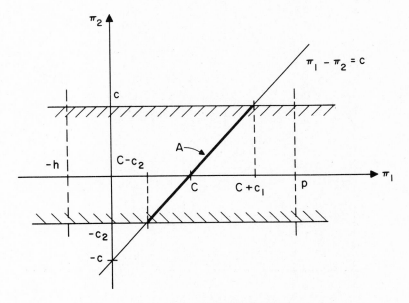

Fig. 7. Dual region for example 5.

pendent but bear the relation $(\nabla L)_1 - (\nabla L)_2 = -C$. Thus to satisfy the first-order conditions for (CP) we must have $\pi_1 - \pi_2 = C$. This line is depicted on fig. 7 where it has been assumed that $C + c_1 < p$ (which seems reasonable). We are thus interested only in the line segment A in fig. 7. For π on this line, we have the solution to (CP) as

$$F(y_1^* + y_2^*) = \left(\frac{p - \pi_1}{h + p}\right) = \left(\frac{p - \pi_2 - C}{h + p}\right).$$

Let

$$F(L) = \frac{p - C - c_1}{h + p}$$

and

$$F(U) = \frac{p - C + c_2}{h + p} \ .$$

Then the optimal policy is sketched in fig. 8. Here the RNT is the shaded region between the parallel lines. Above the region it is optimal to move "down" cor-

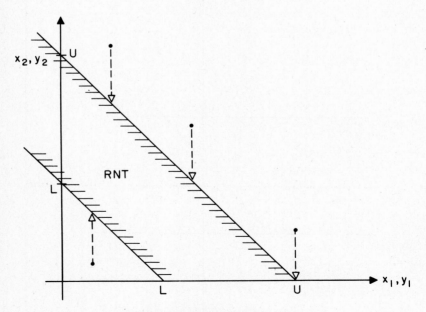

Fig. 8. Optimal policy for example 5.

responding to a reduction in the production rate from x_2 to y_2. Below the region it is optimal to increase the production rate.

5. Multi-period and infinite horizon problems

Each period of the multi-period version of (P) can be written as (MP_t)

$$v^t(x) = \inf C^t(y - x) + L^t(y) + \rho Ev^{t-1}(w(y))$$

where $w(y)$ is the stochastic transition made between periods conditional on y. This problem is of the same form as CP if the last term can be shown to be convex. The following sufficient condition applies for all the examples we have described, and for many others.

Proposition 5. Suppose that the transition law w has the form $w(y) = \tilde{T}y + \tilde{a}$, where $\tilde{T}$ is a random matrix (i.e., its elements are random variables) and $\tilde{a}$ a random vector. Then $\rho Ev(w(y))$ is a convex function of y for convex v.

The multiplicative term allows the inclusion of random multiplicative losses or gains, or of random transfers between levels. The additive term, apart from depletion due to demand, can also incorporate the stochastic supply instance where there are random additions to inventory or production as in (say) agricultural supply. The structure also accommodates the case where the output of a production process is not deterministic.

By the usual induction argument it can be seen that

Proposition 6. (MP_t) is of the same form as (P), (UP) by writing $\overline{L}(y) = L^t(y) + \rho Ev^{t-1}(w(y))$. Then the results of propositions 1–4 apply to each period of the multiperiod problem.

Thus qualitatively, the optimal policy in the multi-period problem has the same form as for the one-period case. However, there may be considerable differences in the specific details in some cases. For examples 1, 2, and 4 the multi-period policy is visually very similar to the one-period problem, but there are significant differences in other cases. The multi-period problem is in general more difficult to analyze because the subproblem CP has a more complex form and does not decouple as in some of the examples above. It is thus more difficult to establish existence results of the type in proposition 1. Furthermore, computation of optimal policies seems to become prohibitively difficult although there is reason to believe that one period approximations are effective.

In the infinite horizon stationary case, certain assumptions are required in addition to the convexity property described above, to make sure that the problem is bounded. The key assumptions can be stated as follows. There exists a function $p(x) \geqslant 1$ such that:

(A1) $\inf_{y} C(y - x) + L(y) \geqslant \underline{M}p(x)$

            for some $|\underline{M}| < \infty$.

(A2) There exists a decision rule $Y(x)$ selecting y as a function of x such that

$$C(Y(x) - x) + L(Y(x)) \leqslant \overline{M}p(x), \text{ for some } |\overline{M}| < \infty.$$

(A3) $Ep(w(y)) \leqslant \alpha p(x)$ for any feasible y given x, $\alpha > 0$, $\rho\alpha < 1$.

    In inventory examples where $L(y)$ represents the expected cost of holding and shortage, the function p can usually be chosen as $\max\{1, \Sigma_i(\beta_i x_i^+ + \beta_i x_i^-)\}$. Where $\beta_i = \max\{|h_i|, |p_i|\}$, p_i and h_i are shortage and holding cost respectively, $x_i^+ = \max\{0, x_i\}$, $x_i^- = \max\{0, -x_i\}$.

    A policy that satisfies (A2) for the multi-location case is the "do-nothing" policy $Y(x) = x$; this seems likely to work for other problems. The third assumption (A3) is essentially a limitation on the probability distribution of the transition law. It is conjectured that in many cases (for p of the form above) a finite mean and discount factor less than one will suffice to establish (A3). However, the author has not as yet studied the application of these methods to examples other than the multi-location case.

    It is shown in [113] that given assumptions of the type above, the stationary infinite horizon version of (P) has ϵ-optimal stationary policy of the same qualitative form as in the one-period multi-period cases. If, in addition, it can be shown that the optimum is attained in each period, then an optimal stationary policy exists. However, the conditions necessary to establish the latter requirement have not as yet been established.

6. A multi-level, multi-product production example with stochastic supply

    In this section we present an illustration of the kind of multi-level problem to which the methods in this paper might be applied. As far as this author knows, this kind of problem has not been extensively investigated in the literature. Consider a raw material that can be processed first into saleable intermediate products and then further into finished products. There are thus three levels of inventory separated by two production stages. An example might be a metal that is first processed to produce billets or ingots with their own markets, and then into products such as bar, rod or sheet stock. (Additional levels of processing and fabrication could also be accommodated by the model.)

Suppose that in each period the incremental supply of raw material available is a random variable. Furthermore, some stocks of intermediate and finished products are available at the start of each period, and there is some (random) demand for the products in each variable. In each period a decision is made on the amounts of intermediate and finished products to be produced. Production costs and the costs of holding inventory or backordering are all assumed to be proportional.

Leaving out time period indices, let:

$\tilde{S}$ = supply of incremental raw material available at the end of the period,
X = initial inventory of raw material,
Y = inventory of raw material after allocation,
z_j = amount of intermediate product j to be produced,
a_j = units of raw material required per unit of j,
C_j = processing cost per unit of product j,
x_{1j} = initial inventory of intermediate product j,
y_{1j} = inventory of j after allocation to second processing stage,
z_k = amount of final product k to be produced,
x_{2k} = initial inventory of k,
y_{2k} = inventory of k after production; $y_{2k} = x_{2k} + z_k$,
b_{jk} = amount of j required per unit of k produced,
c_k = cost per unit of k produced,
$\tilde{d}_{1j}$ = demand for intermediate product j,
$\tilde{d}_{2k}$ = demand for final product k,
$l_{1j}(y_{1j})$ = expected costs of inventory holding and backordering for intermediate product j, given a stock level y_{1j},
$l_{2k}(y_{2k})$ = expected costs of inventory holding and backordering for intermediate product j, for final product k, and
H = cost of holding raw material inventory.

The transition law for the multi-period case (with periods indexed in reverse order) is

$$X^{t-1} = Y^t + \tilde{S}^t,$$
$$x_{1j}^{t-1} = y_{1j}^t - \tilde{d}_{1j}^t,$$
$$x_{2k}^{t-1} = y_{2k}^t - \tilde{d}_{2k}^t,$$

In larger problems such as this one, since more than two dimensions are involved it is not convenient to sketch the LP dual and to thereby get a quick idea of the nature of the optimal policy. In general, while the methods described earlier will go a long way towards assisting the analysis, a great deal of specific analysis may be required for each case. In this particular problem, for example, one might be interested in investigating the conditions under which it is better to stock intermedaite products rather than finished products. In fact there is a close analogy between this problem and the problem of stock positioning in inventory systems.

7. Summary

A model has been presented that provides a unified basis for the study of many different stochastic multi-state production and inventory problems. The applicability of this model to several formulations from the literature is illustrated in the context of one-period problems. The multi-period and infinite horizon problems are discussed very briefly.

TIMS Studies in the Management Sciences 16 (1981) 353--378
© North-Holland Publishing Company

ANALYSIS OF ORDERING AND ALLOCATION POLICIES FOR MULTI-ECHELON, AGE-DIFFERENTIATED INVENTORY SYSTEMS *

Morris A. COHEN, William P. PIERSKALLA

University of Pennsylvania

and

Hsiang-chun YEN

Bell Laboratories

This paper considers the problem of determining optimal order and allocation policies for a multi-echelon inventory system in which the product is differentiated by its age. The cost structure includes standard inventory costs as well as a penalty cost for using the product beyond a certain age. Two age-allocation policies are considered: one where the quantity of product of a given age shipped from the central depot to the warehouse is proportional to each warehouse's order; and one where the quantity is based on a fixed fraction, with the possibility of re-allocation of excess supply. Optimal inventory levels at the central depot and at each satellite location are considered for both cases. In addition, conditions for the equivalence of the allocation policies are derived. Potential applications of the models' results include central and regional blood banks, food and chemical product distribution networks, and age-differentiated military logistic systems.

1. Introduction

A large and important fraction of inventory investment for many firms is to be found in multi-echelon distribution systems containing products differentiated by their age. Age-differentiated products occupy an intermediate position between pure services, which are not storable, and most manufactured items which have a virtually indefinite lifetime. Examples of age-differentiated products include food, blood, pharmaceuticals, photographic film, chemicals, and certain military ordnance. In some cases such products are perishable if they cannot be used to meet demand after reaching a specified maximum age (e.g., 21 days for whole blood).

* This project was partially supported by Grant Number HS 02634 from the National Center for Health Services Research, OASH and Grant Number ENG 77-07463 from the National Science Foundation.

Inventory policy for multi-echelon, age-differentiated distribution systems must consider both the quantity of stock to be stored at each location and the age distribution of shipments between locations. Order policy determines target stocking levels and age-allocation policy determines rules for specifying the age composition of shipments. In this paper we will be concerned with the interaction between these two classes of inventory control policies.

The problem explicitly considered here is a single, age-differentiated product system consisting of a central depot and a number of satellite warehouses all operating in an environment of stochastic demand. Target inventory stocking levels at the central depot and at the warehouses are set in a manner which minimizes the sum of discounted, expected over-age, shortage, and holding costs over an infinite horizon. A general stationary cost model for this system is developed in which these stocking levels are decision variables. The model assumes zero lead time. The inclusion of an over-age cost serves to approximate the finite lifetime, perishable inventory problem.

Inventory at each warehouse is reviewed each period, and orders are sent to the central depot to bring the warehouse inventories up to their critical (target) level. Both the depot and the warehouse operate under stationary critical-number ordering policies. It is also assumed that the central depot has access to an unlimited supply of fresh stock to meet these warehouse orders, and hence all warehouse orders are filled in the period they are placed. Backlogging can occur at the warehouses and excess warehouse demand at the depot is satisfied at a cost premium from the supply pool. These ordering assumptions are consistent with the operation of multi-echelon systems in which the central depot's role is to ensure that the warehouses can provide a high level of service. Our experience with central blood bank systems (see Cohen et al. [47]) indicates that such ordering procedures are often used.

Given stochastic demand and the age-differentiation of the product, it is necessary to consider the manner in which stock of various ages is allocated to the warehouses from the central depot. Stock is issued at both the depot and the warehouses according to the FIFO (first in, first out) issuing discipline, which is desirable in age-differentiated product systems (see Pierskalla and Roach [175]). This rule allocates the oldest stock first and determines an issuing quantity of central depot stock of each age to meet the total warehouse demand (summed over all warehouses). It is then necessary to divide the central depot issue quantity of each age among the warehouses. Although it is possible to define an optimal allocation policy, we restrict our attention to specific allocation rules which have desirable managerial properties. Two particular cases of such age-allocation policies are analyzed:

(1) A random fraction of the quantity of central depot stock of each age issued to meet total warehouse demand is allocated to each warehouse. This fraction is determined by the ratio of each warehouse's current demand (order quantity)

to total demand (summed over all warehouses) for the system.

(2) A fixed fraction of the quantity of central depot stock of each age issued to meet total warehouse demand is initially allocated to each warehouse. In the event that a warehouse's allocation exceeds its total request from the depot, the excess is redistributed to another warehouse whose request exceeds its initial allocation.

The first age-allocation policy represents an equitable distribution of the product since each warehouse receives stock of each age category in direct proportion to its demand. By fixing the proportion initially allocated, the second policy establishes a priority rule for each warehouse. For example, if a warehouse's allocation fraction is zero, it only receives product after *all* other warehouses in the system are serviced by the FIFO issuing doctrine. Consequently, such a warehouse would receive a higher proportion of younger stock in its shipment, since oldest stock is issued first by FIFO and the central depot receives only fresh stock. Conversely, the warehouse whose fraction is one will have its order filled by the older stock first, and will receive fresh stock only if the entire supply at the central depot is less than that warehouse's order quantity. In a central blood bank system, where the warehouses are hospital blood banks, we often observe that hospitals doing specialized procedures (e.g., open heart surgery) receive a higher priority for fresh blood. Similarly, in a retail distribution system, it is conceivable that market areas served by certain warehouses may have higher priority for younger stock due to differences in profitability and corporate marketing strategy.

As noted above, the cost structure for this model consists of shortage, holding, and over-age, costs. Order costs were not included since order policy is restricted to the critical-number class wherein the expected quantity ordered per period is a constant (equal to mean demand).

Several approaches have been used to analyze single-echelon perishable inventories in which a penalty is paid for over-age units where such units are discarded from the inventory. In this paper a penalty cost for holding over-age stock is used but such units are not removed from the inventory. By setting the penalty cost sufficiently high, we can ensure that the expected quantity of over-age stock consumed can be made arbitrarily small, and thereby ensure that this approach provides a reasonable approximation to the multi-echelon perishable problem. Moreover, the complexity of the problem is reduced, since perishability need not be considered explicitly in the system transfer equations.

In the next section we relate this model to previous work in perishable and multi-echelon inventories. Section 3 presents the model notation and assumptions in detail. Section 4 contains the derivation of expected costs for both allocation policies. For the case of the random-fraction allocation policy a general condition to ensure convexity of expected costs is derived. This condition is somewhat unintuitive, but is shown to be always satisfied for the case where product lifetime is two or three periods and where critical inventory levels are set to equalize the probability of shortage at each warehouse or where each warehouse has the same critical inventory level. We consider the special case where the central depot target inventory level is either fixed or determined independently of the warehouse stocking and allocation decisions. Such a case allows us to focus on the differences between the two allocation policies. In this case, convexity of expected costs is demonstrated for both allocation policies. Comparison of optimal warehouse ordering policies between the two allocation systems is carried out for this case in section 5. It is shown that it is possible to compute a fixed-fraction allocation rule which yields an optimal order policy identical to the optimal order policy under the random-fraction allocation rule. This result is of importance because it demonstrates the existence of an *a priori* priorization of warehouses which can achieve equitable (random fraction) age allocation. The paper concludes with a discussion of the key results and areas for further research.

2. Literature review

There has been considerable progress in both the areas of multi-echelon inventory and perishable product inventory systems.

Clark and Scarf [39] were the first to formulate and characterize the form of the optimal policy in a multi-period, multi-echelon inventory model subject to stochastic demands. Gross [87] considered the transshipment decision in a wheel system with stochastic demands. Zangwill [254] studied a deterministic demand model structured as an arbitrary acyclic network where the output of any facility cannot return to the facility either directly or indirectly. Tan [229] considered optimal allocation policies of a multi-echelon inventory system where the warehouse can allocate stock to the satellite facilities in each period, but can reorder from an exogenous source only after a fixed number of periods. The optimal quantity to be shipped from a warehouse to each satellite facility in each period is determined by the system configuration in the period.

Veinott [235] developed a general single-facility inventory model. Optimal ordering policies are given for a multi-product, dynamic, non-stationary inventory model, which takes the form of a single critical-number for each period and for each product. Besseler and Veinott [15] later interpreted the stocks of different products as the stocks of a common product carried at different facilities in a multi-echelon system, and hence optimal ordering policies at all facilities are also of the single critical-number type in each period.

Early work on perishable inventory models was concerned with issuing policy. Analysis focused on LIFO (last in, first out) and FIFO (first in, first out) policies. Models have been developed where the field life of the perishable product is deterministic (Eilon, [54]) or random (Pierskalla, [174]), and where there is either a single demand source withdrawing items from the stockpile (Lieberman, [136]; Pierskalla, [174]), or multiple demand sources (Eilon, [60]). FIFO issuing policies are typically optimal under reasonable cost function conditions. Pierskalla and Roach [175] showed that FIFO was optimal for a perishable product model of a hospital or central blood bank where the utility of the product is non-increasing with age. They showed, in particular, that FIFO is optimal for three objective functions: maximize the utility of the product consumed; minimize the stock-out probability; and minimize the quantity of stock outdated.

More recently there has been significant progress in developing mathematical models of single-echelon perishable inventory systems where the objective is to develop optimal order policies: Nahmias and Pierskalla [165,166] Nahmias [164, 163], Fries [82], and Cohen [41]. Nahmias and Pierskalla [165] developed a model in which the amount to be outdated was expressed recursively in terms of previous outdates and demands. The cost function, including shortages and outdates, was then formulated as a dynamic program. The optimal ordering policy is shown to be dependent on the age distribution of the inventory, and is thus non-stationary. Since the optimal solution to the dynamic program is difficult to compute, approximations on the optimal ordering policies have been studied and evaluated in Nahmias [164,163] and Chazan and Gal [26].

Fries [82], independently of Nahmias and Pierskalla [165], also formulated the problem as a dynamic program. These two models differ in the way that outdates are counted in the objective function. The model of Nahmias and Pierskalla [165] counts the quantity of stock which outdates in the current period, whereas Fries [82] counts the quantity of the current order to be outdated in the $m - 1$st period in the future (where the product lifetime is m). The Fries approach led to the dependence of the optimal ordering policy on the length of the planning horizon relative to the life of the product. However, the optimal ordering policy is still dependent on the age distribution of the inventory. (Nahmias [161] compared the two approaches directly.) Both Fries and Nahmias and Pierskalla also noted that as the life of the product m approaches infinity the single critical-number policy becomes optimal.

Since the optimal ordering policy in the dynamic program is difficult to compute even for moderate m, several authors have examined an ordering policy which is easy to implement, namely the stationary single critical-number policy (Van Zyl [232], Cohen [41], Nahmias [163]). Cohen [41] demonstrated the existence of an invariant distribution of the disposition process and developed closed-form solutions for this disposition process for the two-period lifetime case. Numerical procedures were also developed for longer product lifetimes. Chazan and Gal [26] demonstrated that expected outdates for the stationary critical-number policy were convex, and developed bounds for the determination of optimal policy for an arbitrary product lifetime. In a recent paper Cohen and Pekelman [44] examined the stochastic process of inventory systems governed by LIFO issuing.

The analysis of multi-echelon, age-differentiated systems is not nearly as well developed as is the work on single-echelon perishable systems. The model of this paper and a number of its results (theorem 1 and its corollaries) were developed by

Yen [245] in his doctoral dissertation. Prastacos [183,181] considered the allocation problem in a perishable product, two-echelon system in which inputs are
random and not controlled. The perishability process was reduced to a two-period
lifetime process by considering only fresh and old-age categories for the product.
Recently Prastacos [182] considered the same problem where LIFO issuing is in
force. Except for Yen's thesis [245], this paper, and Veinott's dissertation [234],
which considered similar problems where demand is deterministic, we know of no
results where ordering decisions, allocation, and product age differentiation are
considered together.

There is also a large literature on the blood inventory management problem.
Although these analyses have occasionally considered multi-echelon systems, they
have, for the most part, been carried out as simulation studies. See Cohen and
Pierskalla [46] for a recent example of this approach.

3. A two-echelon, age-differentiated model

3.1. Notation and model structure

A two-echelon, two-warehouse, age-differentiated inventory system is shown in
fig. 1. A facility, labeled as facility 0, supplies two other facilities, labeled facility 1
and facility 2, respectively. Facilities 1 and 2 are subject to non-negative, independent stochastic demand from external users in each time period. Facility 0 does not
have any external users; however, it has internal users in the sense that orders from
facilities 1 and 2 have to be satisfied. Let D_{ij} be the demand at facility j in period i
with finite expectation and with the distribution function $F_{ij}(\cdot)$. Let $D_i = (D_{ij})$.

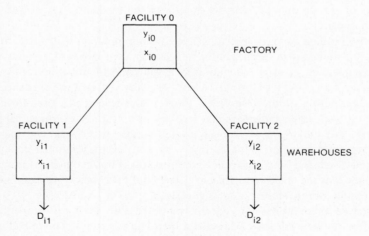

Figure 1

The generalization of this model to a wheel structure with an arbitrary number of destination facilities is notationally complicated but conceptually straightforward. An order for stock may be placed at the beginning of each period and delivery is immediate. Let y_{ijn} denote the quantity of inventory on hand of age n after orders have been placed in period i at facility j but before demands. Let $y_{ij} = (y_{ijn})$ be the vector of such inventories and let $y_{ij}^k = \Sigma_{n=k}^{\infty} y_{ijn}$ denote all inventory on hand which is of age older than or equal to k at facility j in period i after ordering but before demands and denote by y_i^k the vector (y_{ij}^k). Consequently, y_{ij}^1 will be the total inventory available for meeting demand in period i at facility j. Let $y_i = (y_{ijk})$ be the matrix which represents the system inventory configuration of all ages at all facilities in period i. Since $y_{ijk} = y_{ij}^k - y_{ij}^{k+1}$, once the matrix (y_{ij}^k) is known, y_{ijk} can be calculated and vice versa. Hence, (y_{ij}^k) shall also be referred to as the inventory configuration of all ages at all facilities in period i.

After D_i is removed from y_i^1, the remainder is carried over to the next period and its age increased by 1. In the beginning of period i before ordering and after the ages are updated there will be a vector $x_{ij} = (x_{ijn})$ of initial inventories on hand of age n at facility j. Let $x_{ij}^k = \Sigma_{n=k}^{\infty} x_{ijn}$ denote the amount of inventory on hand which is of age k or older at the beginning of period i at facility j. Since no inventory can be of age 1, define x_{ij}^1 as the backlogged demand from period $i - 1$. The total system inventory configuration of all ages at all facilities before ordering in period i will be denoted by the matrix $x_i = (x_{ijk})$.

There are specified rules by which demands are satisfied and orders are filled. It is assumed that there is an unlimited supply at an external source to fill orders from facility 0. After facility 0 has received its delivery in the period, the amount available there will be used to fill orders from facilities 1 and 2. In case there is insufficient stock at facility 0 to fill those orders, facilities 1 and 2 will still get what they ordered; the insufficient amount is assumed to be borrowed from an external source and to be returned in the next period. In this case the borrowed amount will be indicated by a negative inventory level at facility 0 and $y_{ij}^1 - x_{ij}^1$ will be the amount facility j ordered and received in period i for $j = 1$ and 2. Demands at facilities 1 and 2 are satisfied by their own stock and excess demands in the current period are backlogged there. The shortage incurred at facility j in period i, $v_{ij}(D - y)$, may be expressed as

$$v_{ij}(D - y) = (D_{ij} - y_{ij}^1)^+, \qquad j = 0, 1, 2, \tag{1}$$

where $a^+ = \max(a, 0)$.

It is assumed that the age of all incoming orders for facility 0 is 1. When demands arrive from facilities 1 and 2, the stock is then issued according to a FIFO policy, that is, the oldest stock will be issued first. This issued stock is placed in inventory at facility 1 or 2 waiting to be issued to its users on a FIFO basis. Because the FIFO issuing policy is used throughout the system, $x_{i+1,j}^{k+1}$ may be expressed as

$$x_{i+1,j}^{k+1} = (y_{ij}^k - D_{ij})^+, \qquad j = 0, 1, 2 \text{ and } k = 1, 2, ..., \tag{2}$$

$$x^1_{i+1,j} = y^1_{ij} - D_{ij} , \qquad j = 0, 1, 2 . \tag{3}$$

The argument of the function x^k_{ij} has been suppressed for ease of writing. The quantity of stock remaining against which a holding cost is charged is $h_{ij}(D - y) = (y^1_{ij} - D_{ij})^+$.

Once the units to be issued by facility 0 are determined by the FIFO issuing policy, it is necessary to decide how to allocate those units between facilities 1 and 2. Let $z^k_{ij}(y - x)$ be the amount of stock of age older than or equal to k allocated from facility 0 to facility j in period i, when the vector $y - x = (y^1_i - x^1_i)$ is ordered by the system. The sum of allocations of age k or older at facilities 1 and 2 must not be larger than the total amount age k or older at facility 0 or the total amount ordered. This may be expressed mathematically:

$$\sum_{j=1}^{2} z^k_{ij}(y - x) = \min\left(\sum_{j=1}^{2} (y^1_{ij} - x^1_{ij}), y^k_{i0}\right), \qquad \text{for } k > 1 \tag{4}$$

and

$$\sum_{j=1}^{2} z^1_{ij}(y - x) = \sum_{j=1}^{2} (y^1_{ij} - x^1_{ij}) . \tag{5}$$

To this point we have defined all relevant variables for the model. In the next subsection the various components of the objective function are introduced. The final subsection of section 3 explicitly defines the class of order policies and allocation policies to be considered in the paper.

3.2. Objective function

We assume three types of costs in a period i: shortage, holding and over-age. It follows from the stationary critical-number policy that the ordering quantity becomes the demand of the previous period and therefore its expected value is a constant. The shortage cost p_j allocates a penalty for the system to be out of stock and is charged against expected value of shortage $v_{ij}(D - y)$. The holding cost c_j is charged against the expected value of total stock remaining, $h_{ij}(D - y)$. The over-age cost q_j is the penalty paid for having over-aged stock. However, this over-age cost is charged against $x^m_{i+m-1,j}$ rather than x^m_{ij} because the decision variable associated with $x^m_{i+m-1,j}$ is y^1_{ij} which is the inventory after ordering in the current period. By assuming that $x^k_{0j} = 0$ for all j and k, x^k_{ij} may be expressed recursively in terms of demand and y^1_{ij}. These expressions follow from the definition of variables and FIFO. Their formal proof can be found in Yen [245].

$$y_{i0}^k = x_{i0}^k = \left(y_{i-k+1,0}^1 - \sum_{n=1}^{k-1} D_{i-n,0} \right)^+, \qquad \text{for } k > 1 \text{ and } i \geqslant k. \quad (6)$$

$$= 0 \qquad \text{if } i < k.$$

Equation (6) indicates that stock of age k or more at the central depot before or after ordering (for $k > 1$) is determined by the depletion of the sum of $k - 1$ consecutive demands. (Recall that incoming stock at facility 0 is of age 1 and hence inventory before and after ordering are equal for $k > 1$.)

It follows from (6) that the quantity of stock of age m or greater at the depot in period $i + m - 1$ is related to the depot target inventory level in period i by the following formula:

$$x_{i+m-1,0}^m = \left(y_{i0}^1 - \sum_{n=0}^{m-2} D_{i+n,0} \right)^+. \quad (7)$$

The corresponding formula for warehouse j is

$$x_{ij}^k = \left(y_{i-k+1,j}^1 + \sum_{n=1}^{k-2} z_{i-n,j}^{k-n} (y - x) - \sum_{n=1}^{k-1} D_{i-n,j} \right)^+,$$

$$\text{for } k > 1, i > k, \text{ and } j = 1, 2 \quad (8)$$

$$= 0 \qquad \text{if } i < k.$$

where it was necessary to include the shipments of quantities of various ages to the warehouse from the depot. Equation (8) is established in Yen [245] by an inductive argument. The following equation is a direct consequence of (8):

$$x_{i+m-1,j}^m = \left(y_{ij}^1 + \sum_{n=1}^{m-2} z_{i+n,j}^{n+1} (y - x) - \sum_{n=0}^{m-2} D_{i+n,j} \right)^+,$$

$$\text{for } j = 1, 2. \quad (9)$$

Equations (7) and (9) define the random variable for over-age stock at the depot and warehouses respectively. These equations will be used in our derivation of expected costs.

We have not yet specified, however, the allocation policy in the system. Therefore, the value of the objective function will vary from one age-allocation policy to another. Let α_{ij} be an age-allocation policy in period i which (initially) allocates an amount of age k or greater to warehouse j, defined by

$$z_{ij}^k(y - x) = \alpha_{ij} \min\left(\sum_{j=1}^{2} (y_{ij}^1 - x_{ij}^1), y_{i0}^k\right)$$

for $0 < \alpha_{ij} < 1$, $\alpha_{i1} + \alpha_{i2} = 1$ and $k = 2, ..., m$. Note the age-allocation policy is defined only up to m because we shall charge an over-age cost for units older than or equal to m. Let $\alpha_i = (\alpha_{i1}, \alpha_{i2})$, and $\alpha = (\alpha_i)_{i=1,2,...}$.

Given the system will be following the FIFO issuing policy, and allocation policy $(\alpha_i, \alpha_{i+1,...}, \alpha_{i+m-1})$ and an ordering policy $(y_i^1, ..., y_{i+m-1}^1)$ in the next m periods, a cost $W_i(\cdot)$ will be incurred in period i. $W_i(\cdot)$ can be expressed explicitly in terms of demands and inventory level after ordering by equations (1) and (9):

$$W_i(y_i^1, ..., y_{i+m-1}^1, D_i, ..., D_{i+m-1}, \alpha_i, ..., \alpha_{i+m-1})$$

$$= \sum_{j=0}^{2} (p_j v_{ij}(D - y) + c_j h_{ij}(D - y) + q_j x_{i+m-1,j}^m) .$$

Because of the lengthy notation in expressing the dependence of $x_{i+m-1,j}^m$ and $W_i(\cdot)$ on $(y_i^1, ..., y_{i+m-1}^1, D_i, ..., D_{i+m-1}, \alpha_i, ..., \alpha_{i+m-1})$, we shall suppress all of them and include only those relevent to the development of the various results as needed.

Let $G_i(\cdot)$ be the expected value of W_i, then

$$G_i(\cdot) = \sum_{j=0}^{2} E[p_j v_{ij}(D = y) + c_j h_{ij}(D - y) + q_j x_{i+m-1}^m] .$$

Our objective is to find an ordering policy $(y_1^1, y_2^1, ...)$ to minimize the sum of expected, discounted costs,

$$\min_{(y_1^1, y_2^1, ...)} G(y) = \sum_{i=1}^{\infty} r^i G_i(y_i^1, ..., y_{i+m-1}^1) \qquad (10)$$

where r is a discount factor with $0 < r < 1$ and $y_i^1 \in R_+^3$ for $i = 1, 2, ..,$ and where the allocation policy α is specified.

3.3. Order policy and allocation policy restrictions

Additional assumptions will be made before proceeding to analyze optimal ordering policy. We shall restrict the ordering policy to the stationary single critical-number policy, that is, the inventory on hand after ordering y_{ij}^1 does not depend on i. Consequently, in each period an amount exactly equal to the demand in the previous period will be ordered so as to reach the desirable inventory level. Note this is true only if all excess demand is backlogged and the demand is non-negative so that the inventory level before ordering is always less than or equal to the desired inventory level after ordering. Furthermore, the demand in period i for facility 0 is the sum of the ordering amounts (the demands) from facilities 1 and 2 in the *previous* period, so $D_{i0} = D_{i-1,1} + D_{i-1,2}$, and D_{i0} will consequently be the ordering amount for facility 0 in period $i + 1$. The demands $(D_{ij})_{i=1,2,...}$, are independent random variables having a common distribution $F_j(\cdot)$ with density $f_j(\cdot)$ for $j = 1, 2$.

With regard to the allocation policy, two cases are considered. In case I we assume that each facility will receive an allocation of all ages proportional to its ordering amount with respect to the total ordering amount from facilities 1 and 2. Specifically, for this case, in each period i, $\alpha_{ij} = D_{i-1,j}/D_{i0}$, and for case II α_{ij} is fixed for all i and j, where values may be chosen to reflect relative costs for each warehouse or a qualitative priority ranking of each warehouse. After initial allocation to each warehouse, under case II, surplus at warehouse j (if it exists) is re-allocated to warehouse $k \neq j$ (if there is a shortage at k).

We now define the two allocation policies explicitly. Let

$$S_0 = 0, S_n = \sum_{k=0}^{n-1} D_{i+k,0} \, ,$$

for any $n \leqslant m$ we define:

Allocation policy I

$$z_{i+n,j}^{n+1}(y - x) = \frac{D_{i+n-1,j}}{D_{i+n,0}} \min(D_{i+n,0} \, , (y_{i0}^1 - S_n)^+) \, . \tag{11}$$

Allocation policy II

$$z_{i+n,j}^{n+1}(y - x) = \min \{D_{i+n-1,j}, \alpha_{ij}A_{i+n} + [(1 - \alpha_{ij}) A_{i+n}$$

$$- (D_{i+n,0} - D_{i+n-1,j})]^+\} \, , \tag{12}$$

where

$$A_{i+n} = \min(D_{i+n,0}, (y_{i0}^1 - S_n)^+) \, .$$

In both cases I and II, we note that, while each warehouse receives its entire order (e.g., a total of $D_{i,0}$ is always shipped from facility 0 and hence $z_{ij}^1(y - x) = D_{i-1,j}$;

the demand of last period), the age composition of that order may vary due to the allocation policy.

It is important to note that all costs in period i (shortage, holding, over-age) are only a function of the critical inventory vector $y_i^1 = (y_{i0}^1, y_{i1}^1, y_{i2}^1)$ in period i. Moreover, since as noted above y_{ij}^1 does not depend on i, by the critical number policy, it is sufficient to consider minimization of $G_i(\cdot)$ for arbitrary i. Finally, since expected holding and shortage costs are convex, it will be sufficient to examine the convexity of $E[x_{i+m-1}^m]$ to ensure convexity of $G(y)$. This particular issue is addressed in the next section.

4. Optimal order policies

The following properties can be easily established (see Yen [245]), and are important for the determination of an optimal ordering policy.

Property 1
  $v_{ij}(D - y)$, $Ev_{ij}(D - y)$, $h_{ij}(D - y)$ and $Eh_{ij}(D - y)$ are convex functions of y_i^1 over R_+^3 for $j = 0, 1, 2$.
Property 2
  $x_{i+m-1,j}^m$ is a continuous function of y_i^1 for $j = 0, 1, 2$, for allocation policies I and II.

The following theorem, first derived in Yen [245], demonstrates that, for allocation policy I, it is possible to establish convexity of expected over-age stock in the system under certain conditions on the demand process (see appendix for all proofs). This condition cannot be easily demonstrated to be true for all values of (y_0^1, y_1^1, y_2^1).

Theorem 1.   For allocation policy I,

If
$$\sum_{j=2}^{2} \sum_{l=2}^{m-2} E\left[\frac{D_{ij}}{D_{i1} + D_{i2}} F_j^{M-l-1}(y_{ij}^1 - D_{i1} - D_{i1})\right] f_0^l(y_{i0}^1)$$

$$\geqslant \sum_{j=1}^{2} \sum_{l=2}^{m-2} E\left[\frac{D_{ij}}{D_{i1} + D_{i2}} F_0^{l-1}(y_{ij}^1 - D_{i1} - D_{i2})\right] F_j^{m-l}(y_{ij}^1)$$

then $\Sigma_{j=0}^{2} Ex_{i+m-1,j}^m$ is convex in y_i^1.

Corollary 1.   If $m = 2$ or 3, then $\Sigma_{j=0}^{2} Ex_{i+m-1,j}^m$ is convex in y_i^1.

Corollary 2.   If the events $D_{ij} \leqslant y_{ij}^1$ are equivalent (equal probability) for $j = 1, 2$, then $\Sigma_{j=0}^2 Ex_{i+m-1,j}^m$ is convex in y_i^1.

Corollary 3. If D_{ij} are independent and identically distributed and if $y_{i1}^1 = y_{i2}^1$, then $\Sigma_{j=0}^2 Ex_{i+m-1,j}^m$ is convex in y_i^1.

Lemma 1. If $\Sigma_{j=0}^2 Ex_{i+m-1,j}^m$ is convex, and if $q_1 = q_2$, then $G(\cdot)$ is convex.

Theorem 1, its corollaries and lemma 1 indicate that when over-age costs are the same for the warehouses, and when demands at the warehouses are independent and identically distributed, then the over-age quantity function is convex in the critical-number decision variables. Yen [245] also derived a general condition for the optimality of allocation policy I and showed that this condition is satisfied for the same special cases noted above which were needed to ensure convexity.

The following theorem establishes convexity of expected over-age stock for both allocation policies when the level of stock at the central facility is fixed. As noted previously, this case may occur if depot stock ordering is controlled at a higher level or is uncontrollable. The restriction allows us to focus on the differences between warehouse ordering policies under each age-allocation policy.

Theorem 2. If y_{i0}^1 is assumed to be fixed or determined independently of y_{i1}^1 and y_{i2}^1, then $Ex_{i+m-1,j}^m$ is convex for $j = 1, 2$ and for allocation policies I and II.

Given the convexity of $\Sigma_{j=0}^2 Ex_{i+m-1,j}^m$ in y_i^1, and since $Ev_{ij}(D-y)$ and $Eh_{ij}(D-y)$ are also convex in y_i^1 for all j, the mathematical program given by (10) is a convex program. Consequently, optimal policies exist (level sets for the expected cost function are bounded since over-age costs increase as y_i^1 increases and short-age costs increase as y_i^1 decreases to zero), and nonlinear programming codes can be used to obtain the optimal y's.

Analysis of the general case (where y_{i0}^1 is variable) for allocation policy II was also carried out and led to results similar to that of theorem 1. Again, unconditioned convexity cannot be easily established. For the special case where y_{i0}^1 is a constant, theorem 2 indicates that solution of the first-order condition equations for both cases I and II will yield unique optimal inventory levels for each warehouse. In the final section we examine the sensitivity of these optimal levels to parametric changes and we compare the relative magnitudes for each case under the assumption that y_{i0}^1 is fixed.

5. Comparison of optimal policies

From the proof of theorem 1 (see appendix equation A4) and the definition of $G_i(\cdot)$, we note that for the allocation policy I, optimal inventory level at warehouse j, after ordering, for the case where central depot stock is fixed, is the solution to the following equation:

$$q_j \left\{ F_j^{m-1}(y_{ij}^1)\{1 - F_0(y_{i0}^1)\} + F_j(y_{ij}^1)F_0^{m-1}(y_{i0}^1) \right.$$

$$\left. + \sum_{l=1}^{m-2} \int_0^{y_{i0}^1} \int_0^\infty \int_{\rho_j(y)}^\infty F_j^{m-l-1}(\beta_j(y))F_j(\mathrm{d}t_j)F_k(\mathrm{d}t_k)F_0^l(\mathrm{d}t_0) \right\}$$

$$+ (p_j + c_j)F_j(y_{ij}^1) = p_j . \tag{13}$$

By theorem 2, when y_{i0}^1 is fixed, (13) is also a sufficient condition for the optimal policy. Let y_I^* be the unique value of y_{ij}^1 which solves (13) (where I refers to allocation policy I).

The solution to the following equation yields the optimal inventory level for warehouse j under allocation policy II (for the case where depot stock is fixed):

$$q_j \left\{ F_j^{m-1}(y_{ij}^1)\{1 - F_0(y_{i0}^1)\} + F_j(y_{ij}^1)F_0^{m-1}(y_{i0}^1) \right.$$

$$+ \sum_{l=1}^{m-2} \left[\int_0^{y_{i0}^1} \int_{\gamma_k(y)}^\infty \int_{\gamma_j(y)}^\infty F_j^{m-l-1}(y_{ij}^1 + \gamma_j(y) - t_j)F_j(\mathrm{d}t_j) \right.$$

$$\times F_k(\mathrm{d}t_k)F_0^l(\mathrm{d}t_0) + \int_0^{y_{i0}^1} \int_0^{\gamma_k(y)} \int_{\rho_j(y)}^\infty F_j^{m-l-1}(y_{ij}^1 + \rho_j(y) - t_j)F_j(\mathrm{d}t_j)$$

$$\times F_k(\mathrm{d}t_k)F_0^l(\mathrm{d}t_0) + \int_0^{y_{i0}^1} \int_{\gamma_k(y)}^\infty \int_{\rho_j(y)}^{\gamma_j(y)} F_j^{m-l-1}(y_{ij}^1)F_j(\mathrm{d}t_j)$$

$$\left. \left. \times F_k(\mathrm{d}t_k)F_0^l(\mathrm{d}t_0) \right] \right\} + (p_j + c_j)F_j(y_{ij}^1)$$

$$= p_j . \tag{14}$$

where

$$j \neq k, j = 1, 2 ;$$

$$\gamma_j(y) = \alpha_{ij}(y_{i0}^1 - t_0) ,$$

$$\gamma_k(y) = \alpha_{ik}(y_{i0}^1 - t_0) ,$$

$$\rho_j(y) = y_{i0}^1 - t_0 - t_k .$$

Again by theorem 2, the value of y_{ij}^1, to be denoted by $y_{II}^*(\alpha_{ij})$ which solves (14) is the unique optimal solution for allocation policy II when y_{io}^1 is fixed. Note that we have explicitly included the dependence of the optimal inventory level under allocation policy II, on the value of α_{ij}, the initial allocation fraction for warehouse j.

It is important to note that the solution of (13) and (14) is feasible since we have reduced the optimization problem to one of minimization of a one-dimensional convex function.

In the following theorem we demonstrate the relationship between the optimal inventory levels associated with each allocation policy.

Theorem 3. Assume y_{io}^1 is fixed:

Let
$$y_{II}^*(0) = \lim_{\alpha_{ij} \to 0} y_{II}^*(\alpha_{ij})$$

and

$$y_{II}^*(1) = \lim_{\alpha_{ij} \to 1} y_{II}^*(\alpha_{ij}) \, ,$$

then

(i) $y_{II}^*(1) \leqslant y_I^* \leqslant y_{II}^*(0)$,
(ii) $y_{II}^*(\alpha_{ij})$ is continuous in α_{ij},
(iii) there exists an $\hat{\alpha}_{ij} \in [0,1]$ such that $y_I^* = y_{II}^*(\hat{\alpha}_{ij})$ and moreover $\hat{\alpha}_{ij}$ is the solution to the following equation:

$$\left[\sum_{l=1}^{m-2} \int_0^{y_{io}^1} \int_{\rho_j(y)}^{\infty} \int_0^{\infty} F_j^{m-l-1}(\beta_j(y_1^*)) \, F_j(dt_j) F_k(dt_k) F_0^l(dt_0) \right.$$

$$- \int_0^{y_{io}^1} \int_{\gamma_k(y)}^{\infty} \int_{\gamma_j(y)}^{\infty} F_j^{m-l-1}(y_1^* + \gamma_j(y) - t_j) F_j(dt_j) F_k(dt_k) F_0^l(dt_0)$$

$$- \int_0^{y_{io}^1} \int_0^{\gamma_k(y)} \int_{\rho_j(y)}^{\infty} F_j^{m-l-1}(y_1^* + \rho_j(y) - t_j) F_j(dt_j) F_k(dt_k) F_0^l(dt_0)$$

$$\left. - \int_0^{y_{io}^1} \int_{\gamma_k(y)}^{\infty} \int_{\rho_j(y)}^{\gamma_j(y)} F_j^{m-l-1}(y_1^*) F_j(dt_j) F_k(dt_k) F_0^l(dt_0) \right] = 0 \, , \quad (15)$$

where

$$\beta_j(y^*) = y_1^* + \frac{t_j}{t_j + t_k}\,(y_{i0}^1 - t_0) - t_j\;.$$

Equation (15) indicates that it is possible to compute an allocation fraction (and hence an *a priori* warehouse prioritization) which yields the same expected costs and optimal warehouse order policies as that of allocation policy I. As noted previously, allocation policy I is equitable and under certain conditions is also optimal. Allocation policy II, on the other hand, may be easier to implement in those situations where consistent (rather than random) allocation rules are important. The equivalence of these two allocation policies has important managerial implications. Further research needs to be undertaken to investigate the sensitivity of the optimal order policy $y_{\mathrm{II}}^*(\alpha_{ij})$ to changes in α_{ij} and to evaluate the magnitude of the difference between $y_{\mathrm{II}}^*(\alpha_{ij})$ and y_{I}^* as a function of α_{ij}.

6. Conclusions

This paper has examined a specific class of multi-echelon inventory systems where the product can be differentiated by age. The interaction between optimal order policies and age-allocation policies was examined for the case of stationary critical number ordering and both random and fixed-fraction allocation rules. The random allocation rule can be viewed as equitable, and the fixed-fraction rule allows for prioritization of each warehouse. A general condition for convexity of expected costs was developed for the random fraction allocation rule model. Since this condition was shown to be satisfied for a number of special cases, we conjecture that the condition may, indeed, not be needed. Proof of this conjecture remains for future research.

Consideration of the cases where the central depot stocking level was assumed to be fixed or determined independently of warehouse stocking levels led to the derivation of closed form results for optimal warehouse order policy for each age allocation rule. It was also possible to prove the existence of a fixed allocation fraction value which makes the two age-allocation systems equivalent. Further research is needed to explore the general validity of convexity and to apply one-dimensional search algorithms to solve the necessary condition equations associated with the fixed depot stock model. Investigation of the equivalence between the age-allocation policies should also be carried out. Analysis of the more general problem where perishability (finite lifetime) is treated directly rather than by means of an over-age cost in an age-differentiated model, remains as a challenging research problem in the context of multi-echelon systems.

Appendix

Proof of theorem 1

It is sufficient to show that the Hessian for $\Sigma_{j=0}^{2} Ex_{i+m-1,j}^{m}$ is positive semi-definite. Denote by $D_k Ex_{i+m-1,j}^{m}$ the partial derivative of $Ex_{i+m-1,j}^{m}$ with respect to y_{ik}^1 for $j, k = 0, 1, 2$. Let

$$S_0 = 0 \text{ and } S_n = \sum_{k=0}^{n-1} D_{i+k,0} .$$

Define

$$N(y) = \sup\{n: S_n < y_{i0}^1\} .$$

By conditioning $N(y)$, $Ex_{i+m-1,j}^{m}$ for $j = 1, 2$ can be expressed as

$$Ex_{i+m-1,j}^{m} = E\left\{\left(y_{ij}^1 - \sum_{n=0}^{m-2} D_{i+n,j}\right)^+ ; N(y) = 0\right\} + E\{y_{ij}^1 - D_{i+m-2,j}\}^+;$$

$$N(y) \geqslant m - 1\} + \sum_{l=1}^{m-2} E\left\{\left(y_{ij}^1 + \frac{D_{i+k-1,j}}{D_{i+k,0}} (y_{i0}^1 - S_l)\right.\right.$$

$$\left.\left. - \sum_{n=l-1}^{m-2} D_{i+n,j}\right)^+ ; N(y) = l\right\}. \tag{A1}$$

Because of the equivalence of the events $(N(y) = l)$ and $S_l < y_{i0}^1 \leqslant S_{l+1}$ for $l = 0, 1, ..., m$-2 and of $(N(y) \geqslant m - 1)$ and $(S_{m-1} < y_{i0}^1)$ and because of the independence of random variables $\Sigma_{n=0}^{m-2} D_{i+n,j}$ and D_{i0} and of $D_{i+m-2,j}$ and S_{m-1} for $j = 1, 2, (A1)$ can then be rewritten as

$$Ex_{i+m-1,j}^{m} = \int_0^{y_{ij}^1} (y_{ij}^1 - t_j) F_j^{m-1}(dt_j) \{1 - F_0(y_{i0}^1)\}$$

$$+ \int_0^{y_{ij}^1} (y_{ij}^1 - t_j) F_j(dt_j)\{F_0^{m-1}(y_{i0}^1)\}$$

$$+ \sum_{l=1}^{m-2} \int_0^{y_{i0}^1} \int_0^\infty \int_{\rho_j(v)}^\infty \int_0^{\beta_j(v)} \left\{ y_{ij}^1 + \frac{t_j}{t_j + t_k} (y_{i0}^1 - t_0) - t_j - u \right\}$$

$$\times F_j^{m-l-1}(du) F_j(dt_j) F_k(dt_k) F_0^l(dt_0), \tag{A2}$$

where $j \neq k$, $j = 1, 2$; $\rho_j(v) = y_{i0}^1 - t_0 - t_k$ and $\beta_j(v) = y_{ij}^1 + [t_j/(t_j + t_k)] (y_{i0}^1 - t_0) - t_j$.

Since the integrands in (A2) are continuous and differentiable between the limits of integration, the first-order partial derivatives can be calculated by the chain rule:

$$D_0 Ex_{i+m-1,j}^m = \int_0^{y_{ij}^1} (y_{ij}^1 - t_j) F_j^{m-1}(dt_j) \{-f_0(y_{i0}^1)\}$$

$$+ \int_0^{y_{ij}^1} (y_{ij}^1 - t_j) F_j(dt_j) \cdot \{f_0^{m-1}(y_{i0}^1)\}$$

$$+ \sum_{l=1}^{m-2} \int_0^\infty \int_0^\infty \int_0^{y_{ij}^1 - t_j} (y_{ij}^1 - t_j - u) F_j^{m-l-1}(du) F_j(dt_j) F_k(dt_k) f_0^l(y_{i0}^1)$$

$$- \sum_{l=1}^{m-2} \int_0^{y_{i0}^1} \int_0^\infty \int_0^{y_{ij}^1} (y_{ij}^1 - u) F_j^{m-l-1}(du) f_j(y_{i0}^1 - t_k - t_0)$$

$$\times F_k(dt_k) F_0^l(dt_0) + \sum_{l=1}^{m-2} \int_0^{y_{i0}^1} \int_0^\infty \int_{\rho_j(v)}^\infty \frac{t_j}{t_j + t_k} F_j^{m-l-1}(\beta_j(v))$$

$$\times F_j(dt_j) F_k(dt_k) F_0^l(dt_0). \tag{A3}$$

It is noteworthy that the first four terms can be cancelled out because the third and fourth terms are equivalent to

$$\sum_{l=1}^{m-2} \int_0^{y_{ij}^1} (y_{ij}^1 - t_j) F_j^{m-l-1}(dt_j) f_0^l(y_{i0}^1)$$

and

$$\sum_{l=1}^{m-2} \int_0^{y_{ij}^1} (y_{ij}^1 - u) F_j^{m-l-1}(\mathrm{d}u) f_0^{l+1}(y_{i0}^1),$$

respectively. The other first-order partial derivatives are calculated as follows:

$$D_j Ex_{i+m-1,j}^m = F_j^{m-1}(y_{ij}^1)\{1 - F_0(y_{i0}^1)\} + F_j(y_{ij}^1)F_0^{m-1}(y_{i0}^1)$$

$$+ \sum_{l=1}^{m-2} \int_0^{y_{i0}^1} \int_{\rho_j(y)}^\infty \int^\infty F_j^{m-l-1}(\beta_j(y)) F_j(\mathrm{d}t_j) F_k(\mathrm{d}t_k) F_0^l(\mathrm{d}t_0), \quad \text{(A4)}$$

$$D_k Ex_{i+m-1,j}^m = 0, \qquad \text{for } k \neq j \text{ and } j \neq 0,$$

$$D_0 Ex_{i+m-1,0}^m = F_0^{m-1}(y_{i0}^1),$$

and

$$D_k Ex_{i+m-1,0}^m = 0, \qquad \text{for } k = 1, 2.$$

The second-order partial derivatives can be calculated by taking partial derivatives from the first-order partial derivatives. Again by the chain rule,

$$D_0 D_0 Ex_{i+m-1,j}^m$$

$$= \sum_{l=1}^{m-2} \int_0^\infty \int_0^\infty \frac{t_j}{t_j + t_k} F_j^{m-l-1} (y_{ij}^1 - t_j) F_j(\mathrm{d}t_j) F_k(\mathrm{d}t_k) f_0^l(y_{i0}^1)$$

$$- \sum_{l=1}^{m-2} \int_0^{y_{i0}^1} \int_0^\infty \frac{t_j}{t_j + t_k} f_0^l(y_{i0}^1 - t_j - t_k) F_j(\mathrm{d}t_j) F_k(\mathrm{d}t_k) F_j^{m-l-1}(y_{ij}^1)$$

$$+ \sum_{l=1}^{m-2} \int_0^{y_{i0}^1} \int_{\rho_j(y)}^\infty \int^\infty \left(\frac{t_j}{t_j + t_k}\right)^2 f_j^{m-l-1}(\beta_j(y)) F_j(\mathrm{d}t_j) F_k(\mathrm{d}t_k) F_0^l(\mathrm{d}t_0),$$

$$\text{(A5)}$$

$$D_j D_0 E x_{i+m-1,j}^m = D_0 D_j E x_{i+m-1,j}^m$$

$$= \sum_{l=1}^{m-2} \int_0^{y_{i0}^1} \int_{\rho_j(y)}^\infty \int_{}^\infty \frac{t_j}{t_j + t_k} f_j^{m-l-1}(\beta_j(y)) F_j(\mathrm{d}t_j) F_k(\mathrm{d}t_k) F_0^l(\mathrm{d}t_0)$$

$$\text{(A6)}$$

$$D_j D_j E x_{i+m-1,j}^m = f_j^{m-1}(y_{ij}^1)\{1 - F_0(y_{i0}^1)\} + f_j(y_{ij}^1) F_0^m(y_{i0}^1)$$

$$+ \sum_{l=1}^{m-2} \int_0^{y_{i0}^1} \int_{\rho_j(y)}^\infty \int_{}^\infty f_j^{m-l-1}(\beta(y)) F_j(\mathrm{d}t_j) F_k(\mathrm{d}t_k) F_0^l(\mathrm{d}t_0), \quad \text{(A7)}$$

$$D_k D_j E x_{i+m-1,j}^m = 0, \qquad \text{for } k \neq j \text{ and } j = 1, 2, \quad \text{(A8)}$$

and

$$D_0 D_0 E x_{i+m-1,0}^m = f_0^{m-1}(y_{i0}^1). \quad \text{(A9)}$$

Now from the hypothesis and the following relationship:

$$\sum_{j=1}^{2} \int_0^{y_{i0}^1} \int_0^\infty \frac{t_j}{t_j + t_k} f_0^{m-2}(y_{i0}^1 - t_j - t_k) F_j(\mathrm{d}t_j) F_k(\mathrm{d}t_k) F_j(y_{ij}^1)$$

$$\leq \max_{j=1,2} \{F_j(y_{ij}^1)\}$$

$$\times \int_0^{y_{i0}^1} \int_0^\infty \sum_{j=1}^{2} \frac{t_j}{t_j + t_k} f_0^{m-2}(y_{i0}^1 - t_j - t_k) F_j(\mathrm{d}t_j) F_k(\mathrm{d}t_k)$$

$$= \max_{j=1,2} \{F_j(y_{ij}^1)\} \cdot f_0^{m-1}(y_{i0}^1) \leq f_0^{m-1}(y_{i0}^1),$$

we have

$$D_0 D_0 \sum_{j=0}^{2} E x_{i+m-1,j}^m \geq \sum_{l=1}^{m-2} \int_0^{y_{i0}^1} \int_{\rho_j(y)}^\infty \int_{}^\infty \left(\frac{t_j}{t_j + t_k}\right)^2 f_j^{m-l-1}(\beta_j(y))$$

$$\times F_j(\mathrm{d}t_j) F_k(\mathrm{d}t_k) F_0^l(\mathrm{d}t_0).$$

The Hessian is then positive semi-definite by the Schwartz inequality, that is,

$$\left[\sum_{l=1}^{m-2} \int_0^{y_{i0}^1} \int_0^\infty \int_{\rho_j(y)}^\infty \frac{t_j}{t_j + t_k} f_j^{m-l-1} (\beta_j(y) F_j(\mathrm{d}t_j) F_k(\mathrm{d}t_k) F_0^l(\mathrm{d}t_0) \right]^2$$

$$= \left[\int_0^{y_{i0}^1} \int_0^\infty \int_{\rho_j(y)}^\infty \left(\frac{t_j}{t_j + t_k} \right) \sum_{l=1}^{m-2} f_j^{m-l-1} (\beta_j(y)) f_j(t_j) f_k(t_k) \right.$$

$$\left. \times f_0^l(t_0) \, \mathrm{d}t_j \, \mathrm{d}t_k \, \mathrm{d}t_0 \right]^2$$

$$\leq \int_0^{y_{i0}^1} \int_0^\infty \int_{\rho_j(y)}^\infty \left(\frac{t_j}{t_j + t_k} \right)^2 \sum_{l=1}^{m-2} f_j^{m-l-1} (\beta_j(y)) f_j(t_j) f_k(t_k)$$

$$\times f_0^l(t_0) \, \mathrm{d}t_j \, \mathrm{d}t_k \, \mathrm{d}t_0$$

$$\int_0^{y_{i0}^1} \int_0^\infty \int_{\rho_j(y)}^\infty \sum_{l=1}^{m-2} f_j^{m-l-1}(\beta_j(y)) f_j(t_j) f_k(t_k) f_0^l(t_0) \, \mathrm{d}t_j \, \mathrm{d}t_k \, \mathrm{d}t_0$$

$$\leq \int_0^{y_{i0}^1} \int_0^\infty \int_{\rho_j(y)}^\infty \sum_{l=1}^{m-2} f_j^{m-l-1}(\beta_j(y)) f_j(t_j) f_k(t_k) f_0^l(t_0) \, \mathrm{d}t_0 \, \mathrm{d}t_k \, \mathrm{d}t_0 \qquad \text{QED}$$

Proof of corollary 1

When $m = 2$ or 3 the hypothesis of theorem 1 is satisfied. Furthermore, when $m = 2$, $Ex_{i+m-1,j}^m$ is reduced to $E(y_{ij}^1 - D_{ij})^+$ for $j = 0, 1, 2$, which is convex and represents the inventory on hand at the end of period i which will become age 2 at the beginning of period $i + 1$.

Proof of corollary 2

From the hypothesis we have $F_1^{m-l}(y_{i1}^1) = F_2^{m-l}(y_{i2}^1)$ for $l = 2, ..., m-2$. Since

$$E\left(\frac{D_{ij}}{D_{i1} + D_{i2}} F_j^{m-l-1} (y_{ij}^1 - D_{ij}) \right) = E\left(\frac{D_{ij}}{D_{i1} + D_{i2}} ; \sum_{n=0}^{m-l-1} D_{i+n,j} \leq y_{ij}^1 \right)$$

we have

$$\sum_{j=1}^2 E\left(\frac{D_{ij}}{D_{i1} D_{i2}} ; \sum_{n=0}^{m-l-1} D_{i+n,j} \leq y_{ij}^1 \right) = F_j^{m-l}(y_{ij}^1) .$$

Therefore the hypothesis in theorem 1 is satisfied because

$$\sum_{j=1}^2 \left[E\left(\frac{D_{ij}}{D_{i1} + D_{i2}} F_j^{m-l-1}(y_{ij}^1 - D_{i1}) \right) f_0^l(y_{i0}^1) \right.$$

$$\left. - E\left(\frac{D_{ij}}{D_{i1} + D_{i2}} f_0^{l-1}(y_{i0}^1 - D_{i1} - D_{i2}) \right) F_j^{m-l}(y_{ij}^1) \right]$$

$$= \sum_{j=1}^{2} [F_j^{m-l}(y_{ij}^1)f_0^l(y_{i0}^1) - f_0^l(y_{i0}^1)F_j^{m-l-1}(y_{ij}^1)]$$

$$= 0, \qquad \text{for } l = 2, ..., m - 2 .$$

Proof of corollary 3

Since the events $\{D_{ij} \leqslant y_{ij}^1\}$ are equivalent from the hypotheses, therefore the assertion is true from corollary 2.

Proof of lemma 1

Since the sum of convex functions is convex, consequently $G(\cdot)$ is convex in y_i^1.

Proof of theorem 2

Allocation policy I

By (A7) from the proof of theorem 1 we note that $D_j D_j Ex_{i+m-1,j}^m \geqslant 0$. By (A8) we note that $D_k D_j Ex_{i+m-1,j}^m = 0$ for $k \neq j$ and $j = 1, 2$. Convexity follows trivially.

Allocation policy II

By an argument similar to that in the proof of theorem 1 for case I, it can be demonstrated that

$$Ex_{i+m-1,j}^m = \int_0^{y_{ij}^1} (y_{ij}^1 - t_j)F_j^{m-1}(dt_j) \cdot \{1 - F_0(y_{i0}^1)\}$$

$$+ \int_0^{y_{ij}^1} (y_{ij}^1 - t_j) F_j(dt_j) \cdot \{F_0^{m-1}(y_{i0}^1)\}$$

$$+ \sum_{l=1}^{m-2} \left\{ \int_0^{y_{i0}^1} \int_{\gamma_k(y)}^{\infty} \int_{\gamma_j(y)}^{\infty} \int_0^{y_{ij}^1+\gamma_j(y)-t_j} [y_{ij}^1 + \gamma_j(y) - t_j - u] \right.$$

$$\times F_j^{m-l-1}(du) F_j(dt_j) F_k(dt_k) F_0^l(dt_0)$$

$$+ \int_0^{y_{i0}^1} \int_0^{\gamma_k(y)} \int_{\rho_j(y)}^{\infty} \int_0^{y_{ij}^1+\rho_j(y)-t_j} [y_{ij}^1 + \rho_j(y) - t_j - u]F_j^{m-l-1}(du)$$

$$\times F_j(\mathrm{d}t_j) F_k(\mathrm{d}t_k) F_0^l(\mathrm{d}t_0)$$

$$+ \int_0^{y_{i0}^1} \int_{\gamma_k(y)}^{\infty} \int_{\rho_j(y)}^{y_{ij}^1} [y_{ij}^1 - u] F_j^{m-l-1}(\mathrm{d}u) F_j(\mathrm{d}t_j) F_k(\mathrm{d}t_k) F_0^l(\mathrm{d}t_0) \Bigg\} \; ,$$

$$\text{(A10)}$$

where

$$\gamma_j(y) = \alpha_{ij}(y_{i0}^1 - t_0) \; ,$$

$$\gamma_k(y) = \alpha_{ik}(y_{i0}^1 - t_0) \; ; \qquad k \neq j \; ,$$

$$\rho_j(y) = y_{i0}^1 - t_0 - t_k \; .$$

The first-order partial derivative with respect to y_{ij}^1 is

$$D_j Ex_{i+m-1,j}^m = F_j^{m-1}(y_{ij}^1)\{1 - F_0(y_{i0}^1)\} + F_j(y_{ij}^1) F_0^{m-1}(y_{i0}^1)$$

$$+ \sum_{l=1}^{m-2} \Bigg\{ \int_0^{y_{i0}^1} \int_{\gamma_k(y)}^{\infty} \int_{\gamma_j(y)}^{\infty} F_j^{m-l-1}(y_{ij}^1 + \gamma_j(y) - t_j)$$

$$\times F_j(\mathrm{d}t_j) F_k(\mathrm{d}t_k) F_0^l(\mathrm{d}t_0)$$

$$+ \int_0^{y_{i0}^1} \int_0^{\gamma_k(y)} \int_{\rho_j(y)}^{\infty} F_j^{m-l-1}(y_{ij}^1 + \rho_j(y) - t_j) F_j(\mathrm{d}t_j) F_k(\mathrm{d}t_k) F_0^l(\mathrm{d}t_0)$$

$$+ \int_0^{y_{i0}^1} \int_{\gamma_k(y)}^{\infty} \int_{\rho_j(y)}^{\gamma_j(y)} F_j^{m-l-1}(y_{ij}^1) F_j(\mathrm{d}t_j) F_k(\mathrm{d}t_k) F_0^l(\mathrm{d}t_0) \Bigg\} \; ,$$

and

$$D_k Ex_{i+m-1,j}^m = 0 \; , \qquad k \neq j, j \neq 0 \; .$$

It follows then that

$$D_j D_j Ex_{i+m-1,j}^m = \sum_{l=1}^{m-2} \Bigg\{ \alpha_{ij} f_0^l(y_{i0}^1) F_j^{m-j}(y_{ij}^1)$$

$$+ (1 - \alpha_{ij}) \alpha_{ik} \int_0^{y_{i0}^1} f_k(\alpha_{ik} t_0) F_0^l(\mathrm{d}t_0) F_j^{m-l}(y_{ij}^1) \Bigg\} \geqq 0$$

and hence convexity is established.   QED

Proof of theorem 3

Let $\alpha_{ij} = 0$, which implies that $\alpha_{ik} = 1$, $\gamma_j(y) = 0$, $\rho_j(y) \leqslant \gamma_k(y)$. After eliminating common terms, we ignore the outer integral, with respect to t_0, in (13) and (14) and note that the three inner integrals in the summation in (14) become

$$\int_{\gamma_k(y)}^{\infty} \int_0^{\infty} F_j^{m-l-1}(y_{ij}^1 - t_j) F_j(\mathrm{d}t_j) F_k(\mathrm{d}t_k)$$

$$+ \int_0^{\gamma_k(y)} \int_{\rho_j(y)}^{\infty} F_j^{m-l-1}(y_{ij}^1 + \rho_j(y) - t_j) F_j(\mathrm{d}t_j) F_k(\mathrm{d}t_k)$$

$$- \int_{\gamma_k(y)}^{\infty} \int_0^{\rho_j(y)} F_j^{m-l-1}(y_{ij}^1) F_j(\mathrm{d}t_j) F_k(\mathrm{d}t_k) .$$

By decomposing the first integral above into two integrals, we get

$$\int_{\gamma_k(y)}^{\infty} \int_0^{\rho_j(y)} F_j^{m-l-1}(y_{ij}^1 - t_j) F_j(\mathrm{d}t_j) F_k(\mathrm{d}t_k)$$

$$+ \int_{\gamma_k(y)}^{\infty} \int_{\rho_j(y)}^{\infty} F_j^{m-l-1}(y_{ij}^1 - t_j) F_j(\mathrm{d}t_j) F_k(\mathrm{d}t_k)$$

$$+ \int_0^{\gamma_k(y)} \int_{\rho_j(y)}^{\infty} F_j^{m-l-1}(y_{ij}^1 + \rho_j(y) - t_j) F_j(\mathrm{d}t_j) F_k(\mathrm{d}t_k)$$

$$- \int_{\gamma_k(y)}^{\infty} \int_0^{\rho_j(y)} F_j^{m-l-1}(y_{ij}^1) F_j(\mathrm{d}t_j) F_k(\mathrm{d}t_k)$$

$$\leq \int_0^\infty \int_{\rho_j(y)}^\infty F_j^{m-l-1} \left(y_{ij}^1 + (\rho_j(y))^+ - t_j\right) F_j(\mathrm{d}t_j) F_k(\mathrm{d}t_k)$$

$$\leq \int_0^\infty \int_{\rho_j(y)}^\infty F_j^{m-l-1} \left(\beta_j(y)\right) F_j(\mathrm{d}t_j) F_k(\mathrm{d}t_k) ,$$

which is the inner integral in the summation in (13).

The final inequality follows from the monotonicity of $F_j(\cdot)$ and,

$$\beta_j(y) \geq y_{ij}^1 + (\rho_j(y))^+ - t_j$$

since

$$\frac{t_j}{t_j + t_k} (y_0 - t_0) \geq (y_0 - t_0 - t_k)^+$$

if and only if

$$y_0 - t_0 - t_k = \rho_j(y) \leq t_j ,$$

which is true by the region of integration.

Given the convexity of the expected over-age stock function for each allocation policy and the equality of the expected shortage function, the above relationship is sufficient to prove that $y_{II}^*(0) \geq y_I^*$.

We now let $\alpha_{ij} = 1$ and show by a similar argument that $y_{II}^*(0) \geq y_{II}^*(1)$. Looking at the three inner integrals with $\alpha_{ij} = 1$ we see that

$$\int_0^\infty \int_{\gamma_j(y)}^\infty F_j^{m-l-1} \left(y_{ij}^1 + \gamma_j(y) - t_j\right) F_j(\mathrm{d}t_j) F_k(\mathrm{d}t_k)$$

$$+ \int_0^\infty \int_{\rho_j(y)}^{\gamma_j(y)} F_j^{m-l-1} \left(y_{ij}^1\right) F_j(\mathrm{d}t_j) F_k(\mathrm{d}t_k)$$

$$\geq \int_0^\infty \int_{\rho_j(y)}^\infty F_j^{m-l-1} \left(y_{ij}^1 + \rho_j(y) - t_j\right) F_k(\mathrm{d}t_k)$$

and hence the lower bound for $\alpha_{ij} = 0$ is the upper bound for $\alpha_{ij} = 1$, which establishes that $y_{II}^*(0) \geq y_{II}^*(1)$.

Finally we note that

$$\int_0^\infty \int_{\gamma_j(y)}^\infty F_j^{m-l-1}(y_{ij}^1 + \gamma_j(y) - t_j) F_j(dt_j) F_k(dt_k)$$

$$+ \int_0^\infty \int_{\rho_j(y)}^{\gamma_j(y)} F_j^{m-l-1}(y_{ij}^1) F_j(dt_j) F_k(dt_k)$$

$$\geq \int_0^\infty \int_{\rho_j(y)}^\infty F_j^{m-l-1}(y_{ij}^1) F_j(dt_j) F_k(dt_k)$$

$$\geq \int_0^\infty \int_{\rho_j(y)}^\infty F_j^{m-l-1}(\beta_j(y)) F_j(dt_j) F_k(dt_k)$$

since

$$\frac{t_j}{t_j + t_k}(y_0 - t_0) \leq t_j$$

if and only if

$$y_0 - t_0 - t_k = \rho_j(y) \leq t_j,$$

which is true by the region of integration. Thus $y_{II}^*(1) \leq y_I^* \leq y_{II}^*(0)$.

We next observe that $y_{II}(\alpha_{ij})$ is continuous in α_{ij} since (14) is the sum of continuous functions of α_{ij}. Hence there exists an $\hat{\alpha}_{ij}$ such that $y_I^* = y_{II}^*(\hat{\alpha}_{ij})$ and moreover $\hat{\alpha}_{ij}$ is the root of (15).   QED

TIMS Studies in the Management Sciences 16 (1981) 379–390
© North-Holland Publishing Company

REFERENCES

[1] Abrams, R.A. and Karmarkar, U.S., "Optimal multiperiod investment consumption policies", *Econometrica,* Vol. 48, No. 2 (1980), pp. 333–353.

[2] Abrams, R.A. and Karmarkar, U.S., "Infinite horizon investment consumption policies", *Management Science,* Vol. 25, No. 10 (1979), pp. 1005–1013.

[3] Aggarwal, S.C., "A review of current inventory theory and its applications", *International Journal of Production Research,* Vol. 12, No. 4 (1974), pp. 443–482.

[4] Air Force Logistics Command Manual, "Requirements procedures for economic order quantity items", AFLCM 57-6, Headquarters, Air Force Logistics Command, Wright-Patterson Air Force Base, Ohio, 1973.

[5] Allen, S.G., "Redistribution of total stock over several user locations", *Naval Research Logistics Quarterly,* Vol. 5 (1958), pp. 337–345.

[6] Allen, S.G. "A redistribution model with set-up charge", *Management Science,* Vol. 8 (1961), pp. 99–108. (Also Chapter IX-36 in A.F. Veinott, Jr. (Ed.), *Mathematical Studies in Management Science,* Macmillan Co., New York, 1965, pp. 461–470.)

[7] Allen, S.G., "Computation for the redistribution model with set-up charge", *Management Science,* Vol. 8, No. 4 (1962), pp. 482–489.

[8] Allen, S.G. and d'Esopo, D.A., "An ordering policy for repairable stock items", *Operations Research,* Vol. 16, No. 3 (1968), pp. 669–675.

[9] Arrow, K.J., Harris, T. and Marschak, J., "Optimal inventory policy", *Econometrica,* Vol. 19 (1951), pp. 250–272.

[10] Arrow, K.J., Karlin, S. and Scarf, H.E. (Eds.), *Studies in the Mathematical Theory of Inventory and Production,* Stanford University Press, Stanford, California, 1958.

[11] Baker, K.R., Dixon, P., Magazine, M.J. and Silver, E.A., "An algorithm for the dynamic lot-size problem with time-varying production capacity constraints", Working Paper 117, Department of Management Sciences, University of Waterloo, 1978.

[12] Barlow, R.E., "Repairman problems", Chapter 2 in Arrow, K., Karlin, S. and Scarf, H. (Eds.), *Studies in Applied Probability and Management Science,* Stanford University Press, Stanford, California, 1962.

[13] Beckmann, M.J., "Production smoothing and inventory control", *Operations Research,* Vol. 9, No. 4 (1961), pp. 456–467.

[14] Bellman, R., *Dynamic Programming,* Princeton University Press, Princeton, New Jersey, 1957.

[15] Bessler, S. and Veinott, A.F., Jr., "Optimal policy for a dynamic multi-echelon inventory model", *Naval Research Logistics Quarterly,* Vol. 13, No. 4 (1966), pp. 355–390.

[16] Biggs, J.R., Goodman, S.H. and Hardy, S.T., "Lot sizing rules in a hierarchical multi-stage inventory system", *Production and Inventory Management,* First Quarter (1977), pp. 104–115.

[17] Blackburn, J. and Kunreuther, H., "Planning horizons for the lot-size model with backlogging", *Management Science,* Vol. 21, No. 3 (1974), pp. 215–255.

[18] Blackburn, J. and Millen, R.A., "Lot sizing in multi-level inventory systems", *Proceedings of 1978 AIDS Conference* (1978), p. 314.

[19] Blake, F., *Application of the Optimal Operational Availability (A_0) Inventory Model and Sensitivity Analysis,* CACI, Inc.-Federal, Arlington, Virginia, 1979.

[20] Boecker, B.J. and Fawcett, W.M., *Inventory Policy Model – Mod V, ERR-FW-1214*, General Dynamics, Fort Worth Division, Fort Worth, Texas, 1971.

[21] Bowman, E.H., "Production scheduling by the transportation method of linear programming", *Operations Research*, Vol. 3, No. 1 (1956), pp. 100–103.

[22] Brooks, R.B.S., Gillen, C.A. and Lu, J.Y., *Alternative Measures of Supply Performance*, the Rand Corporation, RM-6094-PR, 1969.

[23] Brock, W.A. and Mirman, L.A., "Optimal economic growth and uncertainty: the discounted case", *Journal of Economic Theory*, Vol. 4 (1972), pp. 479–513.

[24] Caie, J., Linden, J. and Maxwell, W.L., "Solution of a machine load planning problem", Technical Report No. 396, School of Operations Research and Industrial Engineering, Cornell University, 1978.

[25] Campbell, H.S. and Jones, T.L., Jr., *A Systems Approach to Base Stockage – Its Development and Test*, the Rand Corporation (1966) p. 3345.

[26] Chazan, D. and Gal, S., "A Markovian model for a central blood bank", *Management Science*, Vol. 23, No. 5 (1977), pp. 512–521.

[27] Chief of Naval Operations, *Study Directive for Ship Supply Support Study*, Ser. 397P96, Department of the Navy, Washington, D.C., 1971.

[28] Chief of Naval Operations, *Study Directive for the Material Support Study*, Ser. 96/59229, Department of the Navy, Washington, D.C., 1975.

[29] Cinlar, E., *Introduction to Stochastic Processes*, Prentice-Hall, Inc., New Jersey, 1975.

[30] Cinlar, E., "Markov renewal theory: a survey", *Management Science*, Vol. 21, No. 7 (1975), pp. 727–752.

[31] Cinlar, E., "Superposition of point processes", in Lewis, P.A. (Ed.), *Stochastic Point Processes: Statistical Analysis, Theory and Applications*, John Wiley and Sons, Inc., 1972.

[32] Clark, A.J., *A Dynamic, Single-item, Multi-echelon Inventory Model*, RM2297, the Rand Corporation, Santa Monica, California, 1958.

[33] Clark, A.J., A_0 *Allocation Model*, CACI, Inc.-Federal Arlington, Virginia, 1978.

[34] Clark, A.J., "An informal survey of multi-echelon inventory theory", *Naval Research Logistics Quarterly*, Vol. 19, No. 4 (1972), pp. 621–650.

[35] Clark, A.J. *Common Item Problems Involved in the Operation of the Optimal A_0 Inventory and Allocation Models*, CACI, Inc.-Federal, Arlington, Virginia, 1978.

[36] Clark, A.J., *Optimal Operational Availability Inventory Model*, R-7806, CACI, Inc.-Federal, Arlington, Virginia, 1978.

[37] Clark, A.J. *Logistics Support Economic Evaluation – An Introduction*, R7801, CACI, Inc.-Federal, Arlington, Virginia, 1978.

[38] Clark, A.J., "The use of simulation to evaluate a multi-echelon, dynamic inventory model", *Naval Research Logistics Quarterly*, Vol. 7, No. 4 (1960), pp. 429–445.

[39] Clark, A.J. and Scarf, H.E., "Optimal policies for a multi-echelon inventory problem", *Management Science*, Vol. 6, No. 4 (1960), pp. 475–490.

[40] Clark, A.J. and Scarf, H.E., "Approximate solutions to a simple multi-echelon inventory problem", Chapter 5 in Arrow, K.J., Karlin, S. and Scarf, H. (Eds), *Studies in Applied Probability and Management Science*, Stanford University Press, Stanford, California, 1962.

[41] Cohen, M.A., "Analysis of single critical number ordering policies for perishable inventories", *Operations Research*, Vol. 24, No. 4 (1976), pp. 726–741.

[42] Cohen, M.A., Nahmias, S. and Pierskalla, W.P., "A dynamic inventory system with recycling", *Naval Research Logistics Quarterly*, Vol. 27, No. 2 (1980), pp. 289–296.

[43] Cohen, M.A., Or, I., Pierskalla, W.P. and Yen, H., "Regionalization and regional management strategies for the blood banking system: an overview", *Proceedings of the Second National Symposium on the Logistics of Blood Transfusion Theory*, Southfield, Michigan, 1975.

[44] Cohen, M.A. and Pekelman, D., "LIFO inventory systems", *Management Science,* Vol. 24, No. 11 (1978), pp. 1150–1162.

[45] Cohen, M.A. and Pierskalla, W.P., "Management policies for a regional blood bank", *Transfusion,* Vol. 15, No. 1 (1975), pp. 58–67.

[46] Cohen, M.A. and Pierskalla, W.P., "Target inventory levels for a hospital blood bank or a decentralized regional blood banking system", *Transfusion,* Vol. 19, No. 4 (1979), pp. 444–454.

[47] Cohen, M.A., Purskalla, W.P., Sassetti, R.J. and Consolo, J., "An overview of a hierarchy of planning models for regional blood bank mangement", *Transfusion,* Vol. 19, No. 5 (1979), pp. 526–534.

[48] Crowston, W.B. and Wagner, M.H., "Dynamic lot size models for multi-stage assembly systems", *Management Science,* Vol. 20, No. 1 (1973), pp. 14–21.

[49] Crowston, W.B., Wagner, M.H. and Williams, J.F., "Economic lot size determination in multi-stage assembly systems", *Management Science,* Vol. 19, no. 5 (1973), pp. 517–526.

[50] Das, C., "Supply and redistribution rules for two-location inventory systems: one period analysis", *Management Science,* Vol. 21, No. 7 (1975), pp. 765–776.

[51] Das, C., "The $(S-1, S)$ inventory model under time limit on backorders", *Operations Research,* Vol. 25, No. 5 (1977), pp. 835–850.

[52] De Matteis, J.J. and Mendoza, G., "An economic lot-sizing technique, *IBM Systems Journal,* Vol. 7 (1968).

[53] Demmy, W.S., "Allocation of spares and repair resources to a multi-component system", Air Force Logistics Command Report 70–17, Wright Patterson Air Force Base, Ohio, 1970.

[54] Deuermeyer, B.L., "On continuous review (s, S) inventory systems, an application of regenerative stochastic processes", Paper No. 638, Krannert Graduate School of Management, Purdue University, 1977.

[55] Deuermeyer, B.L. and Pierskalla, W.P., "A by-product production system with an alternative", *Management Science,* Vol. 24, No. 13 (1978), pp. 373–383.

[56] Deuermeyer, B.L. and Schwarz, L.B., "A model for the analysis of system service level in warehouse-retailer distribution systems: the identical retailer case", Paper No. 716, Krannert Graduate School of Management, Purdue University, 1980.

[57] Ehrhardt, R., "The power approximation for computing (s, S) inventory policies", *Management Science,* Vol. 25, No. 8 (1979), pp. 777–786.

[58] Eilon, S., "A simpler proof of $L = \lambda W$", *Operations Research,* Vol. 17, No. 5 (1969), pp. 915–917.

[59] Eilon, S., "Obsolescence of commodities which are subject to deterioration in store", *Management Science,* Vol. 9, No. 4 (1963), pp. 623–642.

[60] Eilon, S., "Stock depletion for multi-channel outlets in maintenance work", *Proceedings of the 3rd Internaitonal Conference on Operational Research,* Oslo (1963), Dunod (Paris) and English Universities Press, Ltd., London, 1964, pp. 238–246.

[61] Elmaghraby, S.E., "Allocation under uncertainty when the demand has a continuous d.f.", *Management Science,* Vol. 6, No. 3 (1960), pp. 270–294.

[62] Elmagraby, S.E., "The economic lot scheduling problem (ELSP): review and extensions", *Management Science,* Vol. 24, No. 6 (1978), pp. 587–598.

[63] Eppen, G.D., "Note – effects of centralization on expected costs in a multi-location newsboy problem", *Management Science,* Vol. 25, No. 5 (1979), pp. 498–501.

[64] Eppen, G.D. and Fama, E.F., "Three asset cash balance and dynamic portfolio problems", *Management Science,* Vol. 17, No. 5 (1971), pp. 311–319.

[65] Eppen, G.D., Gould, F.J. and Pashigian, B.P., "Extensions of the planning horizon theorem in the dynamic lot size model", *Management Science,* Vol. 15, No. 5 (1969), pp. 268–277.

[66] Erlenkotter, D., "A dual-based procedure for uncapacitated facility location", *Operations Research,* Vol. 26, No. 6 (1978), pp. 992–1009.

[67] Evans, G.W., "A transporation and production model", *Naval Research Logistics Quarterly,* Vol. 5, No. 1 (1978), pp. 137–154.

[68] Evans, R.V., "Inventory control of a multiproduct system with a limited production resource", *Naval Research Logistics Quarterly,* Vol. 14, No. 2 (1967), pp. 173–184.

[69] Everett, H., "Generalized Lagrange multiplier method for solving problems of optimal allocation of resources", *Operations Research,* Vol. 11, No. 3 (1965), pp. 399–417.

[70] Fawcett, W.M. and Gilbert, R.D., *A Non-Steady Stochastic Representation of a Supply System for Aircraft Spares, ERR-FW-1349,* General Dynamics, Convair Division, 1972.

[71] Fawcett, W.M. and York, L.J., *Base-Depot Stockage Model, Research Report ERR-FW-621,* General Dynamics, Fort Worth Division, Fort Worth, Texas, 1967.

[72] Feller, W., *An Introduction to Probability Theory and Its Applications,* Vol. II, John Wiley and Sons, Inc., New York, 1971.

[73] Feeney, G.J. and Sherbrooke, C.C., "The $(s-1, s)$ inventory policy under compound Poisson demand", *Management Science,* Vol. 12, No. 5 (1966), pp. 391–411.

[74] Fishman, G.S., *Concepts and Methods in Discrete Event Digital Simulation,* Wiley and Sons, Inc., New York, 1973.

[75] Fishman, G.S., "Grouping observations in digital simulation", *Management Science,* Vol. 24, No. 5 (1978), pp. 510–521.

[76] Fitzgerald, J.W., *Three-Echelon LRU Search Algorithm,* Working Paper, Air Force Logistics Command, Wright-Patterson Air Force Base, Ohio, 1975.

[77] Florian, M. and Klein, M., "Deterministic production planning with concave costs and capacity constraints", *Management Science,* Vol. 18, No. 1 (1971), pp. 12–20.

[78] Fox, B.L. and Landi, D.M., *Optimization Problems with One Constraint,* The Rand Corporation, RM-5791, 1968.

[79] Fox, B.L. and Landi, D.M., "Searching for the multiplier in one constraint optimization problems", *Operations Research,* Vol. 18, No. 2 (1970), pp. 253–262.

[80] Fuller, W.A., *Introduction to Statistical Time Series,* John Wiley & Sons, Inc., New York, 1976.

[81] Furber, P.W., Working Paper, G-07-12, Eastman Kodak Company, Rochester, New York, 1967.

[82] Fries, B.E., "Optimal ordering policy for a perishable commodity with fixed lifetime", *Operations Research,* Vol. 23, No. 1 (1975), pp. 46–61.

[83] Galliher, H.P., Morse, P.M. and Simond, M., "Dynamics of two classes of continuous review inventory systems", *Operations Research,* Vol. 7, No. 3 (1959), pp. 362–384.

[84] General Dynamics Convair, Volume I. *The IOL Optimization Model,* U.S. Naval Weapon Systems Analysis Office, U.S. Marine Corps Air Station, Quantico, Virginia, WSAO-R-734, 1973.

[85] Geoffrion, A.M., "A guide to computer-assisted methods for distribution system planning", *Sloan Management Review,* Vol. 16 (1975), pp. 17–41.

[86] Graves, S.C., "Multistage lot-sizing: an iterative procedure", Technical Report No. 114, O.R. Center, Massachusetts Institute of Technology, 1979.

[87] Gross, D., "Centralized inventory control in multilocation supply systems", Chapter 3, *Multistage Inventory Models and Techniques,* Stanford University Press, Stanford, California, 1963.

[88] Gross, D. and Ince, J.F., "Spares provisioning for repairable items: cyclic queues in light traffic", *AIIE Transactions,* Vol. 10 (1978), pp. 307–314.

[89] Gross, D. and Ince, J.F., "Spares provisioning for a heterogeneous population", Technical Report T-376, Program in Logistics, The George Washington University, 1978.

[90] Gross, D., Kahn, H.D. and Marsh, J.D., "Queueing models for spares provisioning", *Naval Research Logistics Quarterly,* Vol. 24, No. 4 (1977), pp. 521–536.

[91] Gross, D. and Harris, C.M., "On one for one ordering inventory policies with state dependent leadtimes", *Operations Research,* Vol. 19, No. 3 (1971), pp. 735–760.

[92] Gross, D. and Harris, C.M., *Fundamentals of Queueing Theory,* John Wiley & Sons, Inc., New York, 1974.

[93] Gross, D. and Schrady, D.A., "A survey of inventory theory and practice", Chapter II in Marlow, W.H. (Ed.), *Modern Trends in Logistics Research,* MIT Press, 1974.

[94] Haber, S.E., and Sitgreaves, R., "Inventory model for intermediate echelon when repair is possible", *Management Science,* Vol. 21, No. 6 (1975), pp. 638–648.

[95] Hadley, G. and Whitin, T.M., *Analysis of Inventory Systems,* Prentice-Hall, Inc., Englewood Cliffs, New Jersey, 1963.

[96] Hannsman, F., "Optimal inventory location and control in production and distribution networks", *Operations Research,* Vol. 7 (1959), pp. 483–498.

[97] Hax, A.C. and Meal, H., "Hierarchical integration of production planning and scheduling", in Geisler, M. (Ed.), *Logistics,* North-Holland Publishing Company, Amsterdam, 1975.

[98] Heyman, D.P., "Return policies for an inventory system with positive and negative demands", *Naval Research Logistics Quarterly,* Vol. 25, No. 4 (1978), pp. 581–596.

[99] Higa, I., Feyerherm, A. and Machado, A., "Waiting time in an $(S-1, S)$ inventory system", *Operations Research,* Vol. 23, No. 4 (1975), pp. 674–680.

[100] Hillier, F.S. and Lieberman, G.J., *Operations Research,* Problems 25 and 29, Holden-Day, Inc., San Francisco, California, 1968, pp. 376–377.

[101] Hoekstra, D., Deemer, R.L. and Gajadlo, S., *Optimal Procurement Decisions for Spare Aircraft Components,* Frankfort Arsenal, Philadelphia, Pennsylvania, 1965.

[102] Iglehart, D., "Optimality of (s, S) policies in the infinite horizon dynamic inventory problem", *Management Science,* Vol. 9, No. 2 (1963), pp. 259–267.

[103] Iglehart, D., "Recent results in inventory theory", *Journal of Industrial Engineering,* Vol. 18 (1967), pp. 48–51.

[104] Iglehart, D., "Dynamic programming and stationary analysis of inventory problems", Chapter 1 in Scarf, H., Gilford, D. and Shelly, M. (Eds), *Multistage Inventory Models and Techniques,* Stanford University Press, Stanford, California, 1963.

[105] Iglehart, D. and Lalchandani, A., "An allocation model", *SIAM Journal of Applied Mathematics,* Vol. 15 (1967), pp. 303–323.

[106] Ignall, E. and Veinott, A.F., "Optimality of myopic inventory policies for several substitute products", *Management Science,* Vol. 15, No. 5 (1969), pp. 284–304.

[107] Kaplan, A.J., "Projection of aggregate statistics subject to random variation", Interim Report, Institute for Logistics Research, AD 717049, 1970.

[108] Kalymon, B.A., "A decomposition algorithm for arborescence inventory systems", *Operations Research,* Vol. 20, No. 4 (1972), pp. 860–874.

[109] Karlin, S., "Optimal inventory policy for the Arrow-Harris-Marschak dynamic model", Chapter 9 in Arrow, K.J., Karlin, S. and Scarf, H. (Eds), *Studies in the Mathematical Theory of Inventory and Production,* Stanford University Press, Stanford, California, 1958.

[110] Karlin, S. and Fabens, A., "A stationary inventory model with Markovian demand", Chapter 11 in Arrow, K.J., Karlin, S. and Suppes, P. (Eds), *Mathematical Methods in the Social Sciences,* Stanford University Press, Stanford, California, 1959.

[111] Karlin, S. and Scarf, H., "Inventory models of the Arrow-Harris-Marschak type with time lag", Chapter 10 in Arrow, K.J., Karlin, S. and Scarf, H. (Eds.), *Studies in the Mathematical Theory of Inventory and Production,* Stanford University Press, Stanford, California, 1958.

[112] Karmarkar, U.S., "Convex/stochastic programming and multilocation inventory problems", *Naval Research Logistics Quarterly,* Vol. 26, No. 1 (1979), pp. 1–19.

[113] Karmarkar, U.S., "Infinite horizon multilocation inventory problems", presented at ORSA/TIMS joint meeting, New Orleans, Louisiana, 1979.

[114] Karmarkar, U.S., "Multilocation, multiperiod inventory problems", presented at ORSA/TIMS joint meeting, Los Angeles, California, 1978 (to appear in *OR*).

[115] Karmarkar, U.S. and Patel, N., "The one-period, *N*-location distribution problem", *Naval Research Logistics Quarterly,* Vol. 24, No. 4 (1977), pp. 559–575.

[116] Kaufman, R., *Computer Programs for (s, S) Policies Under Independent or Filtered Demands,* ONR and ARO Technical Report No. 5, School of Organization and Management, Yale University, 1976.

[117] Kaufman, R., *(s, S) Inventory Policies in a Nonstationary Demand Environment,* ARO Technical Report No. 11, School of Business Administration and Curriculum in Operations Research and Systems Analysis, University of North Carolina at Chapel Hill, 1977.

[118] Kennington, J.F., "A survey of linear cost multicommodity network flows", *Operations Research,* Vol. 26, No. 2 (1978), pp. 209–236.

[119] Kettelle, J.D. Jr., "Least cost allocation of reliability investment", *Operations Research,* Vol. 10, No. 2 (1962), pp. 249–265.

[120] Klincewicz, J.G., *Inventory Control Using Statistical Estimates: The Power Approximation and Sporadic Demands (Variance/Mean = 9),* ONR and ARO Technical Report No. 9, School of Organization and Management, Yale University, 1976.

[121] Klingman, D.D., Ross, G.R. and Soland, R.M., "Optimal lot-sizing and machine loading for multiple products", *Proceedings of the Conference on Disaggregation,* The Ohio State University, Columbus, Ohio, March 1977.

[122] Kruse, W.K., Letter to the Editor, *Operations Research,* Vol. 27, No. 4 (1979), pp. 852–854.

[123] Kruse, W.K., "Waiting time in a continuous review (s, S) inventory system with constant lead times", Technical Report, U.S. Army Inventory Research Office, Philadelphia, Pennsylvania, 1978.

[124] Kruse, W.K., "Waiting time in an $(S-1, S)$ inventory system with arbitrarily distributed leadtimes", Technical Report, U.S. Army Inventory Research Office, 1977.

[125] Kruse, W.K. and Kaplan, A.J., "Comments on Simon's two echelon model", *Operations Research,* Vol. 21, No. 6 (1973), pp. 1318–1322.

[126] Kunreuther, H. and Morton, T., "Planning horizons for production smoothing with deterministic demands: I", *Management Science,* Vol. 20, No. 1 (1973), pp. 110–125.

[127] Kunreuther, H. and Morton, T., "Planning horizons for production smoothing with deterministic demands: II", *Management Science,* Vol. 20, No. 7 (1974), pp. 1037–1046.

[128] *LMI Availability System: Procurement Model,* Logistics Management Institute, 4701 Sangamore Road, Washington, D.C., 1978.

[129] *LMI Availability System: Levels of Indenture Model,* Logistics Management Institute, 4701 Sangamore Road, Washington, D.C., 1978.

[130] *LMI Task 72-3, Measurements of Military Essentiality,* Logistics Management Institute, 4701 Sangamore Road, Washington, D.C., AD 748–621.

[131] Lambrecht, M.R., "Capacity constrained multi-facility dynamic lot-size problem", unpublished doctoral dissertation, Katholieke Universiteit Leuven, 1976.

[132] Lambrecht, M.R. and Vander Eecken, J., "A facilities in series capacity constrained dynamic lot-size model", *European Journal of Operational Research,* Vol. 2 (1978).

[133] Lambrecht, M.R. and Vander Eecken, J., "A capacity constrained single-facility dynamic lot-size model", *European Journal of Operational Research,* Vol. 2 (1978).

[134] Lawrence, M.J., "An integrated inventory control system", *Interfaces,* Vol. 7, No. 2 (1977), pp. 55–62.

[135] Levine, D.B. and Hibbs, H., *Factors Underlying Recent Trends in the Operational Availability of Shipboard Equipment (Material Support Study)*, CNS 1080, Center for Naval Analysis, Arlington, Virginia, 1977.

[136] Lieberman, G.J., "LIFO vs. FIFO in inventory depletion management", *Management Science,* Vol. 5, No. 1 (1958), pp. 102–105.

[137] Little, J.D.C., "A proof for the queueing formula: $L = \lambda W$", *Operations Research,* Vol. 9, No. 3 (1961), pp. 383–387.

[138] Logistics Management Institute, *A Model to Allocate Repair Dollars and Facilities Optimally*, Task 74–9, Washington, D.C., 1974.

[139] Love, S.F., "A facilities in series inventory model with nested schedules", *Management Science,* Vol. 18. No. 5 (1972), pp. 327–338.

[140] Lundin, R. and Morton, T., "Planning horizons for the dynamic lot size model. Zabel vs protective procedures and computational results", *Operations Research,* Vol. 23, No. 4 (1975), pp. 711–734.

[141] Lureau, F., "A queueing theoretic analysis of logistics repair models with spare units", Technical Report No. 167, Department of Operations Research and Statistics, Stanford University, 1974.

[142] MacCormick, A., *Statistical Problems in Inventory Control,* ONR and ARO Technical Report No. 2, School of Organization and Management, Yale University, 1974.

[143] Manne, A.S., "Programming of economic lot sizes", *Management Science,* Vol. 4, No. 2 (1958), pp. 115–135.

[144] Marshall, K.T., "Linear bounds on the renewal function", *SIAM Journal of Applied Mathematics,* Vol. 24, No. 2 (1973), pp. 245–250.

[145] McLaren, B.J., "A study of multiple level lot sizing techniques for material requirements planning systems", unpublished Ph.D. dissertation, Purdue University, 1976.

[146] McLaren, B.J. and Whybark, D.C., "Multi-level lot sizing procedures in a material requirements planning environment", Discussion Paper No. 64, Indiana University, 1976.

[147] Miller, B.L., "Dispatching from depot repair in a recoverable item inventory system: on the optimality of a heuristic rule", *Management Science,* Vol. 21, No. 3 (1974), pp. 316–325.

[148] Miller, B.L. and Modarres-Yazdi, M., "The distribution of recoverable inventory items from a repair center when the number of consumption centers is large", *Naval Research Logistics Quarterly,* Vol. 25, No. 4 (1978), pp. 597–604.

[149] Miller, R.G., *Simultaneous Statistical Inferences,* McGraw-Hill, New York, N.Y., 1966.

[150] Mirasol, N.M., "A systems approach to logistics", *Operations Research,* Vol. 12, No. 5 (1964), pp. 707–724.

[151] Muckstadt, J.A., "A model for a multi-item, multi-echelon, multi-indenture inventory system", *Management Science,* Vol. 20, No. 4 (1973), pp. 472–481.

[152] Muckstadt, J.A., "A three echelon, multi-item model for recoverable items", *Naval Research Logistics Quarterly,* Vol. 26, No. 2 (1979), pp. 199–222.

[153] Muckstadt, J.A., "Analysis of a two-echelon inventory system in which all locations follow continuous review (s, S) policies", Technical Report No. 337, School of Operations Research and Industrial Engineering, Cornell University, 1977.

[154] Muckstadt, J.A., *Consolidated Support Model (CSM): A Three-Echelon, Multi-Item Model for Recoverable Items,* The Rand Corporation, R-1928-PR, 1976.

[155] Muckstadt, J.A., *NAVMET: A Four-Echelon Model for Determining the Optimal Quality and Distribution of Navy Spare Aircraft Engines,* TR No. 263, School of Operations Research and Industrial Engineering, College of Engineering, Cornell University, 1976.

[156] Muckstadt, J.A., "On the probability distribution for inventory position in two-echelon continuous review systems", Technical Report No. 336, School of Operations Research and Industrial Engineering, Cornell University, 1977.

[157] Muckstadt, J.A., "Some approximations in multi-level, multi-echelon inventory systems for recoverable items", *Naval Research Logistics Quarterly,* Vol. 25, No. 3 (1978), pp. 377–394.

[158] Muckstadt, J.A. and Isaac, M.H., "An analysis of a single item inventory system with returns: the single echelon case", Technical Report 431, School of Operations Research and Industrial Engineering, Cornell University, 1979.

[159] Muckstadt, J.A. and Isaac, M.H., "An analysis of a single item inventory system with returns: the multi-echelon case", Technical Report 432, School of Operations Research and Industrial Engineering, Cornell University, 1979.

[160] Muckstadt, J.A. and Thomas, L.J., "Are multi-echelon inventory methods worth implementing in systems with low-demand rates?", *Management Science,* Vol. 26, No. 5 (1980), pp. 483–494.

[161] Nahmias, S., "A comparison between two dynamic perishable inventory models", *Operations Research,* Vol. 25, No. 1 (1977), pp. 168–172.

[162] Nahmias, S., "Higher order approximations for the perishable inventory problem", *Operations Research,* Vol. 25, No. 4 (1977), pp. 630–640.

[163] Nahmias, S., "Myopic approximations for the perishable inventory problem", *Management Science,* Vol. 22, No. 9 (1976), pp. 1002–1008.

[164] Nahmias, S., "Optimal ordering policies for perishable inventory – II", *Operations Research*, Vol. 23, No. 4 (1975), pp. 735–749.

[165] Nahmias, S. and Pierskalla, W.P., "Optimal ordering policies for a product that perishes in two periods subject to stochastic demand", *Naval Research Logistics Quarterly,* Vol. 20, No. 2 (1973), pp. 207–229.

[166] Nahmias, S. and Pierskalla, W.P., "Optimal ordering policies for perishable inventory – I", *Proceedings of the XXth International Meeting, The Institute of Management Sciences,* Vol. II, Israel: Jerusalem Academic Press, 1975, pp. 485–493.

[167] Nahmias, S. and Pierskalla, W.P., "A two product perishable/nonperishable inventory problem", *SIAM Journal of Applied Mathematics,* Vol. 30 (1976), pp. 483–500.

[168] Nahmias, S. and Rivera, H., "A deterministic model for a reparable item inventory system with a finite repair rate", *International Journal of Production Research,* Vol. 17 (1979), pp. 215–221.

[169] O'Malley, T.S., "A method of treating common recoverable components in the LMI military essentiality model", *LMI Task 76-5,* Logistics Management Institute, 4701 Sangamore Road, Washington, D.C., 1976.

[170] Palm, C., "Analysis of the Erlang traffic formula for busy-signal arrangements", *Ericsson Technics,* No. 5 (1938), pp. 39–58.

[171] Paskowitz, S., "Fleet satellite communications system. Lessons learned", *Supply Corps Newsletter,* Department of the Navy, Washington, D.C., 1978.

[172] Phelps, E.S., "Optimal decision rules for the procurement, repair or disposal of spare parts", Rand Memorandum RS-2920PR, The Rand Corporation, Santa Monica, California, 1962.

[173] Pierskalla, W.P., "Optimal issuing policies in inventory management", *Management Science, Theory*, Vol. 13, No. 5 (1967), pp. 395–412.

[174] Pierskalla, W.P., "Inventory depletion management with stochastic field life functions", *Management Science, Theory,* Vol. 13, No. 11 (1967), pp. 877–886.

[175] Pierskalla, W.P. and Roach, C., "Optimal issuing policies for perishable inventories", *Management Science,* Vol. 18, No. 11 (1972), pp. 603–614.

[176] Pinkus, C.E., "The design of multi-product multi-echelon inventory systems using a branch-and-bound algorithm", Technical Paper Serial T-250, Program in Logistics, Institute for Management Science and Engineering, The George Washington University, 1971.

[177] Pinkus, C.E., "Optimal design of multi-product multi-echelon inventory systems", *Decisions Sciences,* Vol. 6 (1975), pp. 492–507.

[178] Pinkus, C.E., Gross, D. and Soland, R.M., "Optimal design of multi-activity, multi-facility systems by branch and bound", *Operations Research,* Vol. 21, No. 1 (1973), pp. 270–283.

[179] Porteus, E. and Lansdowne, Z., "Optimal design of a multi-item, multi-location, multi-repair type repair and supply system", *Naval Research Logistics Quarterly,* Vol. 21, No. 2 (1974) pp. 213–238.

[180] Prastacos, G.P., "Allocation of a perishable product in a region", *Operations Research* (to appear).

[181] Prastacos, G.P., "Allocation of a perishable product inventory", Working Paper 78-04-06, Department of Decision Sciences, University of Pennsylvania, 1979.

[182] Prastacos, G.P., "LIFO distribution systems", *Journal of Operational Research Society,* Vol. 30 (1979), pp. 539–546.

[183] Prastacos, G.P., "Optimal myopic allocation of a product with fixed lifetime", *Journal of Operational Research Society,* Vol. 29 (1978), pp. 905–913.

[184] Prawda, J. and Wright, G.P., "On a replacement problem", *Cahiers du Centre d'Etudes de Recherche Operationnelle,* Vol. 14 (1972), pp. 43–52.

[185] Raiffa, H. and Schlaifer, R., *Applied Statistical Decision Theory,* Cambridge: Harvard University Press, 1961.

[186] Richards, F.R., "A stochastic model of a repairable item inventory system with attrition and random lead times", *Operations Research,* Vol. 24, No. 1 (1976), pp. 118–130.

[187] Richards, F.R., "Comments on the distribution of inventory position in continuous review (s, S) inventory system", *Operations Research,* Vol. 23, No. 2 (1975), pp. 366–371.

[188] Rinnooy Kan, A.H.G., *Machine Scheduling Problems: Classification, Complexity, and Computations,* Martinus Nijhoff, 1976.

[189] Rockafellar, R.T., *Convex Analysis,* Princeton University Press, Princeton, New Jersey, 1970.

[190] Rose, M., "The $(S-1, S)$ inventory model with arbitrary backordered demand and constant delivery times", *Operations Research,* Vol. 20, No. 5 (1972), pp. 1020–1032.

[191] Rosenbaum, B.A., "Service level relationships and implications for safety stock placement in a multi-echelon inventory system", Technical Report, Eastman Kodak Co., Rochester, New York, 1977.

[192] Rosenbaum, B.A., "Service-level relationships in a multi-echelon inventory system", Eastman Kodak Co., Rochester, New York, 1979.

[193] Rosenman, B. and Hoekstra, D., *A Management System for High-Value Army Components,* U.S. Army, Advanced Logistics Research Office, Frankfort Arsenal, Report No. TR64-1, Philadelphia, Pennsylvania, 1964.

[194] Ross, G.T. and Soland, R.M., "A branch and bound algorithm for the generalized assignment problem", *Mathematical Programming,* Vol. 8, No. 1 (1975), pp. 91–103.

[195] Ross, G.T. and Soland, R.M., "Modeling facility location problems as generalized assignment problems", *Management Science,* Vol. 24, No. 3 (1977), pp. 345–357.

[196] Sahin, I., "On the stationary analysis of continuous review (s, S) inventory systems with constant lead times", *Operations Research,* Vol. 27, No. 4 (1979), pp. 717–729.

[197] Sand, G.M., "Predicting demand on the secondary echelon", Eastman Kodak TP&R Working Paper No. G-05-06, 1979.

[198] Scarf, H.E., "Stationary operating characteristics of an inventory model with time lag", Chapter 16 in Reference [10].

[199] Scarf, H.E., "The optimality of (s, S) policies in the dynamic inventory problem", Chapter 13 in Arrow, K.J., Karlin, S. and Suppes, P. (Eds), *Mathematical Methods in the Social Sciences,* Stanford University Press, Stanford, California, 1960.

[200] Scarf, H.E., Gilford, D.M. and Shelly, M.W., *Multistage Inventory Models and Techniques,* Stanford University Press, 1963.

[201] Schrady, D.A., "A deterministic inventory model for repairable items", *Naval Research Logistics Quarterly,* Vol. 14, No. 3 (1967), pp. 391–398.

[202] Schultz, C.R., "*(s, S)* inventory policies for a wholesale warehouse inventory system", Ph.D. Dissertation, Curriculum in Operations Research and Systems Analysis, The University of North Carolina at Chapel Hill, 1979.

[203] Schwarz, L.B., "An examination of the United States Air Force (Q, R) policies for managing depot-base inventories", Working Paper Series No. 7640, Graduate School of Management, The University of Rochester, 1976.

[204] Schwarz, L.B. and Schrage, L., "Optimal and system myopic policies for multi-echelon production/inventory assembly systems", *Management Science*, Vol. 21, No. 11 (1975), pp. 1285–1294.

[205] Shanker, K., "An analysis of a two echelon inventory system for recoverable items", Technical Report 341, School of Operations Research and Industrial Engineering, Cornell University, 1977.

[206] Shannon, R.E., *Systems Simulation of Art and Science,* Prentice-Hall, Inc., New Jersey, 1975.

[207] Sherbrooke, C.C., "Discrete compound Poisson processes and tables of the compound Poisson distribution", *Naval Research Logistics Quarterly,* Vol. 15, No. 2 (1968), pp. 189–204.

[208] Sherbrooke, C.C., *Discrete Compound Poisson Processes and Tables of the Geometric Poisson Distribution,* The Rand Corporation, RM-4831-PR, 1966.

[209] Sherbrooke, C.C., "An evaluator for the number of operationally ready aircraft in a multi-level supply system", *Operations Research,* Vol. 19, No. 3 (1971), pp. 618–635.

[210] Sherbrooke, C.C., "METRIC: a multi-echelon technique for recoverable item control", *Operations Research,* Vol. 16, No. 1 (1968), pp. 122–141.

[211] Sherbrooke, C.C., "Waiting time in an *(S−1, S)* inventory system-constant service time case", *Operations Research,* Vol. 23, No. 4 (1975), pp. 819–820.

[212] Ships Supply Support Study Group, *Ships Supply Support Study (S⁴),* Sponsor-Material Division (OP-41), Deputy Chief of Naval Operations for Logistics, Department of the Navy, Washington, D.C., 1973.

[213] Showers, J., "A multifacility inventory model with transshipments", presented at the ORSA/TIMS joint meeting, New Orleans (May 1979).

[214] Silver, E.A., "Inventory allocation among an assembly and its repairable subassemblies", *Naval Research Logistics Quarterly,* Vol. 19, No. 2 (1972), pp. 261–280.

[215] Silver, E.A. and Dixon, P., "A decision rule for establishing run quantities for the case of time-varying demand and production capacity constraints", Working Paper 124, Department of Management Sciences, University of Waterloo, 1978.

[216] Silver, E.A. and Meal, H.C., "A heuristic for selecting lot-size quantities for the case of a deterministic time-varying demand rate and discrete opportunities for replenishment", *Production and Inventory Management,* Vol. 14, No. 2 (1973), pp. 64–74.

[217] Simpson, V.P., "Optimum solution structure for a repairable inventory problem", *Operational Research,* Vol. 26, No. 2 (1978), pp. 270–281.

[218] Simpson, V.P., "An ordering model for recoverable stock items", *AIIE Transactions,* Vol. 2 (1970), pp. 315–320.

[219] Simpson, K.F., Jr., "A theory of allocations of stocks to warehouses", *Operations Research,* Vol. 7 (1960), pp. 797–805.

[220] Simon, R.M., "Stationary properties of a two echelon inventory model for low demand items", *Operations Research,* Vol. 19, No. 3 (1971), pp. 761–777.

[221] Simon, R.M., "The uniform distribution of inventory position for continuous review *(s, Q)* policies", The Rand Corporation Paper 3938, Santa Monica, California, 1968.

[222] Simon, R.M. and D'Esopo, D.A., "Comments on a paper by S.G. Allen and D.A.

D'Esopo: 'An ordering policy for reparable stock items' ", *Operations Research,* Vol. 19, No. 4 (1971), pp. 986–989.

[223] Singer, H., "An analysis of one warehous, N retailer production inventory systems", Technical Report No. 394, School of Operations Research and Industrial Engineering, Cornell University, 1978.

[224] Sivazlian, B.D., "A continuous review (s, S) inventory system with arbitrary interarrival distribution between unit demands", *Operations Research,* Vol. 22, No. 1 (1974), pp. 65–71.

[225] Slay, F.M., and O'Malley, T.J., *An Efficient Optimization Procedure for a Levels-of-Indenture Inventory Model,* AF-605 (draft), Logistics Management Institute, Washington, D.C., 1978.

[226] Smith, J.W. and Fisher, W.B., *A Model to Allocate Repair Dollars and Facilities Optimally,* Report 74-9, Logistics Management Institute, 4701 Sangamore Road, Washington, D.C. (1974).

[227] Sobel, M.J., "Production smoothing with stochastic demand I: finite horizon case", *Management Science,* Vol. 16, No. 3 (1969), pp. 195–207.

[228] Takacs, L., "On the generalization of Erlang's formula", *Acto Mathematico, Acedemial Scientiorum Hungerical,* Tomus VII (1956), pp. 419–432.

[229] Tan, F., "Optimal policies for multi-echelon inventory problem with periodic ordering", *Management Science,* Vol. 20, No. 7 (1974), pp. 1104–1111.

[230] Taylor, J. and Jackson, R.R.P., "Application of birth and death processes to the provision of spare machines", *Operational Research Quarterly,* Vol. 5 (1954), pp. 95–108.

[231] Tijms, H., *Analysis of (s, S) Inventory Models,* Mathematical Centre Tracts 40, Mathematisch Centrum, Amsterdam, 1972.

[232] Van Zyl, G., "Inventory control for perishable commodities", unpublished Ph.D. dissertation, University of North Carolina at Chapel Hill, 1964.

[233] Veinott, A.F., Jr., "Minimum concave cost solution of Leontief substitution models of multi-facility inventory systems", *Operations Research,* Vol. 17, No. 2 (1969), pp. 262–291.

[234] Veinott, A.F., Jr., "Optimal ordering, issuing and disposal of inventory with known demand", unpublished Ph.D. dissertation, Columbia University, 1960.

[235] Veinott, A.F., Jr., "Optimal policy for a multiproduct, dynamic, nonstationary inventory problem", *Management Science,* Vol. 12, No. 3 (1965), pp. 206–222.

[236] Veinott, A.F., Jr., "The status of mathematical inventory theory", *Management Science,* Vol. 12, No. 11 (1966), pp. 745–777.

[237] Veinott, A.F., Jr. and Wagner, H., "Computing optimal (s, S) policies", *Management Science,* Vol. 11, No. 5 (1965), pp. 525–552.

[238] Von Neumann, J., "Distribution of the ratio of the mean square successive difference to the variance", *Annals of Mathematics Statistics,* Vol. 12 (1941), pp. 367–395.

[239] Wagner, H.M., *Statistical Management of Inventory Systems,* John Wiley & Sons, Inc., New York, 1962.

[240] Wagner, H.M., "A postcript to 'Dynamic problems in the theory of the firm' ", *Naval Research Logistics Quarterly,* Vol. 7, No. 1 (1960), pp. 7–12.

[241] Wagner, H.M., *Principles of Operations Research,* Edition 1, Prentice-Hall, Englewood Cliffs, New Jersey, 1969, pp. A41–A43.

[242] Wagner, H.M., O'Hagan, M. and Lundh, B., "An empirical study of exact and approximately optimal inventory policies", *Management Science,* Vol. 11, No. 7 (1965), pp. 690–723.

[243] Wagner, H.M. and Whitin, T., "Dynamic version of the economic lot size model", *Management Science,* Vol. 5, No. 1 (1958), pp. 89–96.

[244] Weiss, H.J. and Pliska, S.R., "A Markov model with applications", unpublished manuscript, Department of Management Science, School of Business, Temple University, 1977.

[245] Yen, H., "Inventory management for a perishable product multi-echelon system", unpublished Ph.D. dissertation, Department of Industrial Engineering and Management Sciences, Northwestern University, 1975.

[246] Zabel, E., "Some generalizations of an inventory planning horizon theorem", *Management Science,* Vol. 10, No. 3 (1964), pp. 465–471.

[247] Zacks, S., "Bayes sequential design of stock levels", *Naval Research Logistics Quarterly,* Vol. 16, No. 2 (1969), pp. 143–155.

[248] Zacks, S., "On the optimality of the Bayes prediction policy in two-echelon multi-station inventory models", *Naval Research Logistics Quarterly,* Vol. 21, No. 4 (1974), pp. 569–574.

[249] Zacks, S., "Review of statistical problems and methods in logistics research", Chapter 10, *Modern Trends in Logistics Research,* Marlow, W.H. (Ed.), Cambridge: The MIT Press, 1976.

[250] Zacks, S., "A two-echelon multi-station inventory model for Navy applications", *Naval Research Logistics Quarterly,* Vol. 17, No. 1 (1970), pp. 79–85.

[251] Zacks, S. and Fennell, J., "Bayes adaptive control of two-echelon inventory systems, I: development for a special case of one-station lower echelon and Monte Carlo evaluation", *Naval Research Logistics Quarterly,* Vol. 19, No. 1 (1972), pp. 15–28.

[252] Zacks, S. and Fennell, J., "Bayes adaptive control of two-echelon inventory systems, II: the multi-station case", *Naval Research Logistics Quarterly,* Vol. 21, No. 4 (1974), pp. 575–593.

[253] Zacks, S. and Fennell, J. "Distribution of adjusted stock levels under statistical adaptive control procedures of inventory systems", *Journal of American Statistical Association,* Vol. 68 (1973), pp. 88–91.

[254] Zangwill, W., "A deterministic multi-product, multi-facility production and inventory model", *Operations Research,* Vol. 14, No. 3 (1966), pp. 486–509.

[255] Zangwill, W., "A backlogging model and a multi-echelon model of a dynamic lot size production system: a network approach", *Management Science,* Vol. 15, No. 9 (1969), pp. 506–527.

[256] Zangwill, W., "Minimum concave cost flows in certain networks", *Management Science,* Vol. 14, No. 7 (1968), pp. 429–450.

Tims Studies in the Management Sciences 16 (1981) 391–395
© North-Holland Publishing Company

NOTES ABOUT AUTHORS

James P. Caie, Jr. ("Hierarchical Machine Load Planning") is a Senior Project Engineer in the Planning and Operating Systems Department of General Motors Corporation, Manufacturing Development. He holds a B.S. and M.S. in Industrial Engineering from the University of Michigan. Mr. Caie has spent most of his time at General Motors developing production planning and distribution systems for various divisions within G.M. He has made extensive use of mixed integer and integer programming solution techniques in these systems.

Andrew J. Clark ("Experiences with a Multi-Indentured, Multi-Echelon Inventory Model") is a staff member at CACI, Inc. He received B.S. degrees from Colorado State University and University of California at Berkeley, with graduate work being performed at the University of California at Los Angeles. He was on the staff of the Logistics Department at the RAND Corporation for ten years and the Planning Research Corporation for five. He has authored papers in various books and professional journals, mostly on inventory theory.

Morris A. Cohen ("Analysis of Ordering and Allocation Policies for Multi-Echelon, Age-Differentiated Inventory Systems") is Associate Professor of Decision Sciences at the Wharton School, University of Pennsylvania, Philadelphia, Pennsylvania 19104. He received a B.A. Sc. in engineering science from the University of Toronto and a Ph.D in operations research from Northwestern University. Over the past few years he has been involved in research in areas which include perishable inventory and its application to blood bank management, multi-echelon storage and service systems, health systems regionalization, and stochastic patient flow models. His published work has appeared in *Operations Research, Management Science, Naval Research Logistics Quarterly, Health Service Research,* and *Transfusion.* He is a member of TIMS, ORSA, AAAS and Sigma Xi.

W. Steven Demmy ("Multi-Echelon Inventory Theory in the Air Force Logistics Command") is Associate Professor of Quantitative Business Analysis at Wright State University, Dayton, Ohio 45435. He holds B.S.I.E., M.Sc., and Ph.D. degrees in industrial engineering and operations research from the Ohio State University, and he is a Registered Professional Engineer and a Certified Public Accountant in the State of Ohio. Before joining Wright State, he served as a management consultant with Ernst and Ernst, and as an operations research analyst with Headquarters, Air Force Logistics Command. His current research interests include large scale mathematical programming, production and inventory control, and data processing applications in the decision sciences.

Bryan L. Deuermeyer ("A Model for the Analysis of System Service Level in Warehouse – Retailer Distribution Systems: The Identical Retailer Case") is currently Assistant Professor of Industrial Engineering at Texas A&M University, College Station, Texas 77843. He received a B.A. in chemistry from the University of Minnesota, an M.S. and a Ph.D. in industrial engineering from Northwestern University. He previously served on the faculty of the Krannert Graduate School of Management at Purdue University. His current research interests are in multi-level inventory systems, multi-product perishable inventory theory, polynomial approximations in dynamic programming, mathematical models of population dynamics, and maintenance scheduling problems. His publications have appeared in *Operations Research, Management Science, Naval Research Logistics Quarterly,* and in other journals. He is a member of ORSA, TIMS, AIIE, and Sigma XI.

Richard Ehrhardt ("*(s, S)* Policies for a Wholesale Inventory System") is an Assistant Professor in the Curriculum in Operations Research and Systems Analysis at the University of North Carolina at Chapel Hill. He received a B.S. in physics from The Cooper Union, an M.S. in physics from the University of Massachusetts, an M.S. in nuclear engineering from the University of California at Berkeley, and a Ph.D. in operations research from Yale University. His present fields of interest are inventory theory, computer simulation techniques, and stochastic models. He is a member of ORSA and the Institute of Management Science.

Gary D. Eppen ("Centralized Ordering Policies in a Multi-Warehouse System with Lead Times and Random Demand") is Professor of Industrial Administration and Associate Dean for Ph.D. studies in the Graduate School of Business, University of Chicago. He received a B.S. and M.S.I.E. from the University of Minnesota and a Ph.D. from Cornell University. His research interests lie primarily in the area of operations management.

Stephen C. Graves ("Multi-Stage Lot Sizing: An Iterative Procedure") is an Assistant Professor of Management at the Alfred P. Sloan School of Management, Massachusetts Institute of Technology. He received an A.B. and M.B.A. from Dartmouth College, and a Ph.D. in business administration from the University of Rochester. He has published several articles in the area of production and operations management. His current research interests include planning for logistics systems, production planning and scheduling, and the design of automated production systems.

Donald Gross ("Designing a Multi-Product, Multi-Echelon Inventory System") is Professor and Chairman of the Department of Operations Research at The George Washington University. He holds a B.S. in mechanical engineering from Carnegie-Mellon University and an M.S. and Ph.D. in operations research from Cornell University. His current research interests are approximations in queueing theory, queueing models for inventory provisioning, and multi-activity, multi-location inventory systems. Professor Gross has published articles in several journals and is coauthor of *Fundamentals of Queueing Theory* (with C.M. Harris), John Wiley and Sons, Inc., 1974. He is a member of ORSA, TIMS, AIIE, and a past president of WORMSC (Washington Operation Research/Management Science Council).

Uday S. Karmarkar ("Policy Structure in Multi-Stage Production/Inventory Problems: An Application of Convex Analysis") is an Assistant Professor of Operations Management at the Graduate School of Management of the University of Rochester, and has taught previously at the University of Chicago and at the Massachusetts Institute of Technology. He holds a Ph.D. in management science from the Sloan School, M.I.T. and a B. Tech. in chemical engineering from the Indian Institute of Technology, Bombay. Dr. Karmarkar has published papers on multi-location inventory theory, behavioral decision models and the investment-consumption problem. His current research interests also include production scheduling and design problems. Dr. Karmarkar is an Associate Editor of the Naval Research Logistics Quarterly and is affiliated with ORSA and TIMS.

Marc R. Lambrecht ("Review of Optimal and Heuristic Methods for a Class of Facilities in Series Dynamic Lot-Size Problems") is Assistant Professor at the Katholieke Universiteit Leuven. He holds a Managerial Engineering Degree from K.U. Leuven and is Doctor in Applied Economics from the same University. He has published several articles in the area of Operations Management. He is a member of TIMS.

William L. Maxwell ("Hierarchical Machine Load Planning" and "Coordination of Production Schedules with Shipping Schedules") is a Professor of Operations Research and Industrial Engineering at Cornell University. He is a member of AIIE, TIMS, ACM, and ORSA. He received a B.M.E. and a Ph.D. from Cornell University. He is an associate editor of *Management Science and Operations Research*. His research in the areas of scheduling, simulation, and materials handling are represented in many published articles. Professor Maxwell has been a consultant with numerous industrial organizations.

John A. Muckstadt ("Coordination of Production Schedules with Shipping Schedules") is an Associate Professor of Operations Research and Industrial Engineering at Cornell University. He is a member of ORSA, TIMS, and MAA. He received an A.B. in mathematics from the University of Rochester and an M.A., M.S., and Ph.D. from the University of Michigan. He was an officer in the U.S. Air Force for 12 years prior to joining the Cornell faculty. His current research interests are in production and inventory control and he has published many papers on these topics. Professor Muckstadt is currently a consultant to several industrial organizations and the RAND Corporation.

Steven Nahmias ("Managing Reparable Item Inventory Systems: A Review") is an Associate Professor of Quantitative Methods in the School of Business at the University of Santa Clara. He holds a B.A. in mathematics and physics from Queens College, a B.S. in industrial engineering from Columbia University, and M.S. and Ph.D. degrees in operations research from Northwestern University. Prior to joining the faculty at Santa Clara, he taught at the University of Pittsburgh and Stanford University. He has consulted for Litton Industries, Westinghouse Corporation, the Air Force, and the Xerox Research Center. Professor Nahmias has published approximately 35 articles in various professional journals including four in *Management Science*, primarily in the area of inventory control. He is a member of ORSA and TIMS and Omega Rho, Alpha Pi Mu and Sigma Xi honoraries.

William P. Pierskalla ("Analysis of Ordering and Allocation Policies for Multi-Echelon, Age-Differentiated Inventory Systems") is the Executive Director of the Leonard Davis Institute of Health Economics and the Director of the National Health Care Management Center, as well as Professor of Decision Sciences at the University of Pennsylvania. He holds B.S. and M.B.A. degrees from Harvard University, an M.S. from the University of Pittsburgh, and M.S. and Ph.D. degrees from Stanford University. His current research interests include regional and local models of health care delivery, health screening, and technology assessment. Dr. Pierskalla is the Secretary of the Operations Research Society of America, and Editor of the *Journal of Operations Research*.

Charles E. Pinkus ("Designing a Multi-Product, Multi-Echelon Inventory System") is Associate Professor, Management Sciences Department, School of Business Adminstration, California State Polytechnic University, Pomona. He received A.B. and B.S. degrees from Rutgers University, an M.S. from Cornell University, and a D.Sc. from The George Washington University. He is the author of several papers and articles on multi-echelon inventory theory.

Victor J. Presutti, Jr. ("Multi-Echelon Inventory Theory in the Air Force Logistics Command") is the Chief of the System Sciences Division in the Directorate of Management Sciences at Headquarters, Air Force Logistics Command (AFLC). He received a B.S. Degree in mathematics from Syracuse University (1961), a M.S. degree in mathematics from Syracuse University (1966), and has 45 quarter-hours towards a Ph.D. in operations research from Ohio State University. He was one of two Air Force representatives to the Department of Defense Advisory Group for Secondary Item Requirements. Most of his work has been in the inventory theory area. While on active duty with the USAF, he was awarded the Air Force Commendation Medal for Contributions in Consumable Item problem areas. He has authored numerous professional papers, earned six AFLC outstanding performance ratings and was runner-up for the 1978 Dayton Area Federal Employee of the Year Award. He is currently heading a study to determine what drives AFLC's requirements for spares.

Barbara Amdur Rosenbaum ("Inventory Placement in a Two-Echelon Inventory System: An Application") is an operations research analyst in the Distribution Division of the Eastman Kodak Company, Rochester, New York, 14650. She received a B.A. degree in mathematics from the University of Maryland and a M.B.A. degree in operations management from the University of Rochester. Her work involves the applications of operations research techniques to the areas of inventory control, forecasting, product handling, and transportation.

Gene Sand ("Predicting Demand on the Secondary Echelon: A Case Study") was an operations research analyst for the Distribution Division of Eastman Kodak Company in Rochester, New York. Her experience includes mathematical modeling of finished goods inventory, transportation, warehousing, and production requirements. She holds a B.S. in mathematics from the University of Delaware and is currently a Ph.D. student in operations research at Cornell University.

Linus Schrage ("Centralized Ordering Policies in a Multi-Warehouse System with Lead Times and Random Demand") is Professor of Applied Mathematics and Production Management at the Graduate School of Business, University of Chicago. He received his B.S. from St. Louis University and his M.S. and Ph.D. from Cornell University. He is the author of papers in scheduling, queueing theory, inventory control, linear and integer programming, court management, vehicle routing, and simulation.

Carl R. Schultz ("(s, S) Policies for a Wholesale Inventory System") is a lecturer at the Anderson School of Management of the University of New Mexico. He received a B.S. in mathematics from Central Michigan University, an M.S. in statistics from Michigan State University, and a Ph.D. in operations research and systems analysis from the University of North Carolina at Chapel Hill. He is a member of The Operations Research Society of America and The Institute of Management Science.

Leroy B. Schwarz ("A Model for the Analysis of System Service Level in Warehouse – Retailer Distribution Systems: The Identical Retailer Case") is an Associate Professor of Management at the Krannert Graduate School of Management, Purdue University. He received his M.B.A. and Ph.D. degrees from the Graduate School of Business, University of Chicago, where he was supported by an APICS Fellowship. After graduation he taught at the Amos Tuck School, Darthmouth College and, subsequently, at the Graduate School of Management, University of Rochester. His research interests are in the management of multi-level production/ inventory systems, facility location, and automatic warehousing systems. Professor Schwarz has published papers in the *AIIE Transactions, Socio-Economic Planning Sciences, Management Science,* and *Operations Research*. He has consulted for a wide range of organizations, including IBM, Aetna Life and Casualty, and Bausch and Lomb. He is a member of TIMS and ORSA; he serves as Associate Editor in Logistics for *Management Science.*

Richard M. Soland ("Designing a Multi-Product, Multi-Echelon Inventory System") is Research Professor of Operations Research at the School of Engineering and Applied Science of The George Washington University, Washington, D.C. 20052. Professor Soland was previously on university faculties in Austin, Texas and Montreal, Canada, and in addition has had visiting appointments in Finland, France, and Venezuela. His current research interests include multiple criteria decision making, locational decision problems and integer programming, and he has published 30 papers in these and other areas. He is a member of TIMS, ORSA, CORS, and IEEE.

Jacques Vander Eecken ("Review of Optimal and Heuristic Methods for a Class of Facilities in Series Dynamic Lot-Size Problems") is Professor of Operations Management at the Katholieke Universiteit Leuven. He is a member of ORSA, TIMS and AIDS. Professor Vander Eecken holds a Managerial Engineering Degree from K.U. Leuven, and an M. Phil and a Ph.D. in operations research from Yale University. He has published several articles in the general area of operations management.

Hugo Vanderveken ("Review of Optimal and Heuristic Methods for a Class of Facilities in Series Dynamic Lot-Size Problems") was Research Assistant at the Katholieke Universiteit Leuven. He holds a Commercial Engineering Degree from the same university and has co-authored a number of articles in the area of operations management.

Harvey M. Wagner ("(s, S) Policies for a Wholesale Inventory System") is Professor of Business Policy at the School of Business Administration at the University of North Carolina at Chapel Hill. He previously served for two years as Dean of the School. He also has taught business subjects at Yale, Stanford, M.I.T., and Harvard. He has been a consultant to McKinsey and Company since 1960 and has consulted with The Rand Corporation, the U.S. Department of Energy, and EPRL. He received a B.S. and M.S. in statistics from Stanford and a Ph.D. in economics from MIT. Professor Wagner has published more than 50 articles and has written or co-authored five books, one of which, *Principles of Operations Research,* won two national awards and has been reprinted in several foreign-language editions. He is a member of ASA and ORSA and is a member and past president of the Institute of Management Science. His current research area is decision control models.

H.-C. Yen ("Analysis of Ordering and Allocation Policies for Multi-Echelon, Age-Differentiated Inventory Systems") is a member of technical staff at Bell Telephone Laboratories, Piscatway, New Jersey 08854. He received a Ph.D. in industrial engineering and management science from Northwestern University. His current research interest is in the application of optimization and inventory theories to network planning.

Shelemyahu Zacks ("Statistical Problems in the Control of Multi-Echelon Inventory Systems") received his B.A. degree from The Hebrew University, Jerusalem, in 1956; his M.Sc. degree from the Technion, Israel Institute of Technology in 1960, and his Ph.D. degree from Columbia University, New York, in 1962. He served as Research Associate in the Department of Statistics, Stanford University, 1962–63; Senior Lecturer, Department of Industrial and Management Engineering, Technion, 1963–65; Professor of Statistics, Kansas State University, 1965–68; Professor of Mathematics and Statistics, University of New Mexico, 1968–1970; Professor of Mathematics and Statistics, Case Western Reserve University, 1970–73; Professor of Statistics, Tel Aviv University, 1973–74; Professor and Chairman of the Department of Mathematics and Statistics, Case Western Reserve University, 1974–79; Professor of Statistics, Virginia Polytechnic Institute and State University, 1979–. Professor Zacks has published over 80 articles on various topics in statistical inference, design of experiments, control of queueing and inventory systems, sampling from finite populations, etc. In addition, he has published a comprehensive book entitled *The Theory of Statistical Inference,* John Wiley, 1971. From 1967, Professor Zacks has been a consultant to the Program in Logistics, The George Washington University, and consultant also to the U.S. Army as well as to private industry. Professor Zacks was elected as Fellow of the Institute of Mathematical Statistics, Fellow of the American Statistical Association and a Regular Member of the International Statistical Institute.

TIMS Studies in the Management Sciences 16 (1981) 397–398
© North-Holland Publishing Company

AUTHORS' ADDRESSES

James P. Caie
General Motors Corporation

Andrew J. Clark
79023 Sears Road, Cottage Grove, Oregon 97424

Professor Morris A. Cohen
The Wharton School, University of Pennsylvania, Philadelphia, Pennsylvania 19104

Professor W. Steven Demmy
Wright State University, Dayton, Ohio 45435

Professor Bryan L. Deuermeyer
Department of Industrial Engineering, Texas A&M University, College Station, Texas 77843

Professor Richard A. Ehrhardt
Curriculum in Operations Research, University of North Carolina, Chapel Hill, North Carolina 27514

Professor Gary Eppen
Graduate School of Business, University of Chicago, Chicago, Illinois 60637

Professor Stephen C. Graves
MIT, Cambridge, Massachusetts 02139

Professor Donald Gross
Department of Operations Research, George Washington University, Washington, D.C. 20052

Professor Uday S. Karmarkar
Graduate School of Management, University of Rochester, Rochester, New York 14627

Dr. Marc R. Lambrecht

Department of Applied Economics, K.U. Leuven, B-300 Leuven, Belgium

Professor William L. Maxwell
School of Operations Research and Industrial Engineering, Cornell University, Ithaca, New York 14853

Professor John A. Muckstadt
School of Operations Research and Industrial Engineering, Cornell University, Ithaca, New York 14853

Professor Steven Nahmias
Department of Quantitative Methods, University of Santa Clara, Santa Clara, California 95053

Professor Charles E. Pinkus
Dept. of Operations Research, The George Washington University, Washington, D.C. 20052

Barbara A. Rosenbaum
Eastman Kodak Company, 2400 Mt. Read Boulevard, Rochester, New York 14650

Gene Sand
Operations Research Department, Cornell University, Ithaca, New York 14853

Professor Linus Schrage
Graduate School of Business, University of Chicago, Illinois 60637

Professor Carl. R. Schultz
University of New Mexico, Albuquerque, New Mexico 87140

Professor Leroy B. Schwarz
Krannert Graduate School of Management, Purdue University, West Lafayette, Indiana 47907

Professor Richard M. Soland
California State Polytechnic University,
Pomona, California 91768
Dr. Jacques Vander Eecken
K.U. Leuven, B-300 Leuven, Belgium
Dr. Hugo Vanderveken
K.U. Leuven, B-300 Leuven, Belgium

Professor Harvey M. Wagner
School of Business Administration, Uni-
versity of North Carolina, Chapel Hill,
North Carolina 27514

Professor Shelemyahu Zacks
Virginia Polytechnic Institute and State
University, Blacksburg, Virginia 24061